AF352508

Honorable and Brilliant Labors

Honorable AND *Brilliant Labors*

ORATIONS OF
WILLIAM GILMORE SIMMS

EDITED BY JOHN D. MILLER

Published by the University of South Carolina Press
Columbia, South Carolina 29208

uscpress.com

Printed in the United States of America

Library of Congress Cataloging-in-Publication Data
can be found at https://lccn.loc.gov/2024000526

ISBN: 978-1-64336-483-4 (hardcover)
ISBN: 978-1-64336-484-1 (ebook)
DOI: https://doi.org/10.61162/BZJM2617

Publication of this book is made possible in part by the generous support
of the Watson-Brown Foundation, together with the Caroline McKissick
Dial Publication Fund of the South Caroliniana Library and the
University Libraries of the University of South Carolina.

The inclusion of this book in the Open Carolina
collection is made possible by the generous funding
of the University of South Carolina Libraries.

To my parents.

Contents

William Gilmore Simms

A Biographical Overview

David Moltke-Hansen

Harper's Weekly put it succinctly in its July 2, 1870, issue: "In the death of Mr. Simms, on the 11th of June, at Charleston, the country has lost one more of its time-honored band of authors, and the South the most consistent and devoted of her literary sons" (qtd. in Butterworth and Kibler 125–26). Indeed, no mid-nineteenth-century writer and editor did more than William Gilmore Simms to frame white Southern self-identity and nationalism, shape Southern historical consciousness, or foster the South's participation and recognition in the broader American literary culture. No Southern writer enjoyed more contemporary esteem and attention, at least after Edgar Allan Poe moved north. Among American romancers (or writers of prose epics), only New Yorker James Fenimore Cooper was as successful by the 1840s. In those same years, Simms became the South's most influential editor of cultural journals. He also became the region's most prolific cultural journalist and poet, publishing an average of one book review and one poem per week for forty-five years.

Before his death Simms saw his national reputation fall along with the Confederacy he had vigorously supported and with the slave regime that many in the North had come to despise. Nevertheless, reprints of most of the twenty titles in the selected edition of his works, first published between 1853 and 1860, appeared up until World War I. Thereafter only *The Yemassee,* an early romance about an Indian war in colonial South Carolina, continued in print. The tide began to turn in the 1950s, when five volumes of Simms's letters appeared, and a growing number of his works came out in new editions. Publication in 1992 of the first literary biography by John C. Guilds and establishment of the William Gilmore Simms Society and the *Simms Review* the next year at once reflected and fostered this revived interest. Yet not until the 2011 launch of the digital Simms edition of the South Caroliniana Library of the University of South Carolina did scholars of Southern, American, and nineteenth-century culture begin to have digital access to all of Simms's separately published works. Through the University of South

Carolina Press, readers also may now obtain in book format more of Simms's works than the author ever saw in print at one time.

Clearly the decline in the critical standing of, and historical attention to, Simms and his oeuvre in the century after his death has reversed in the years since. The last three decades of the twentieth century saw more published on Simms than the previous hundred years (Butterworth and Kibler 126–200; MLA International). The last decade of the twentieth and two decades of the twenty-first centuries saw more dissertations and theses on him than had appeared in all the years before. This is not to say that Simms is yet given the attention directed to some of his contemporaries. The Modern Language Association International Bibliography lists roughly four times as many scholarly publications on James Fenimore Cooper, more than ten times as many on Nathaniel Hawthorne, and sixteen times as many on Edgar Allan Poe. Not surprisingly, therefore, Simms is not yet included in most anthologies of American literature, although he is a subject or a source in an expanding and ever more diverse body of scholarship.

To prepare to read Simms, it is important to see his writings in multiple contexts. He rarely wrote about himself outside of his more personal poems and his letters (some 1,500 of the many thousands of which survive). Yet he systematically drew on his background, personal experience, and relationships in his work. He also shaped that work through a progressively developed poetics and philosophy of life, history, and art. He did so in the context of his very broad reading of both contemporary and earlier Western literature and amid multiple professional engagements and responsibilities. The richness and variety of these writings and involvements make Simms a key figure for future understanding of the literary culture, issues, and networks in mid-nineteenth-century America.

Background

Simms's family history reflected the dynamics that fueled the southward and westward spread of the populations, plantation economy, and society of the South Atlantic states. Simms's ancestry also reflected the Scots-Irish and English roots of what became identified by the 1830s as Southern culture—this a generation after the end of most immigration to the region. Two of Simms's grandparents, William and Elisabeth Sims, were Scots-Irish and migrated to South Carolina from Ulster. One, John Singleton, was an American-born son of putatively English immigrants, who had come to South Carolina from Virginia. The fourth, Jane Miller, was daughter of two Scots-Irish and Irish-descended people—John Miller, of North and then South Carolina, and Jane Ross. Ross's family also migrated to South Carolina from western Virginia where members lived cheek by jowl with other Scots-Irish families, who migrated to the Carolinas (White). Simms's father (also William Gilmore) and Uncle James migrated in 1808 from Charleston to Tennessee, then to Mississippi. This was after the bankruptcy of the elder William's business and the deaths of his wife and their other two sons. Following the last of these losses, the elder Simms's hair turned white in a week. To his anguished eyes, Charleston appeared "a place of tombs" (qtd. in Guilds, *Literary Life* 6, 12).

For the son, however, Charleston was home—so much so that he refused to leave his maternal grandmother and move to Mississippi when his uncle came to get him at age ten in 1816. Then the fifth largest and by far the wealthiest city, as well as one of the greatest ports, in America, Charleston was at the peak of its influence (Moltke-Hansen, "Expansion" 25–31; G. Rogers, *Charleston*). Cotton culture on the Sea Islands to the south, begun in 1790, and rice culture in impounded Lowcountry tidal marshes meant that the port was filled not only with sailors of many lands and languages but also with enslaved people of many African and Creole cultures and speech ways (enslaved Africans continued to be imported legally in large numbers until 1808). This street life made vivid the transnational nature of plantation agriculture and the fact that the developing region's dramatically expanding borders "were not just geographic; they also were human, historical, and intellectual" (Moltke-Hansen, "Horizons" 19).

Even more important for the future author, the expanding region's borders and nature were taking imaginative shape. The West of the senior William Gilmore Simms and the first Creek War in which he fought, the Revolutionary War of the young Simms's maternal grandfather, the backcountry of many related Scots-Irish settlers, all became grist for a lonely, energetic boy born in 1806 who spent as much time with books as he could (Simms, *Letters* 1:161). The possibilities of such settings, incidents, and characters were not confined to history alone. Simms reported that he "used to glow and shiver in turn over 'The Pilgrim's Progress,'" while "Moses' adventures in 'The Vicar of Wakefield' threw [him] into paroxysms of laughter" (Hayne, "Ante-Bellum" 261–62). Sir Walter Scott's Border and medieval romances and James Fenimore Cooper's Leatherstocking tales also deeply colored his imagination (Simms, *Views* 1:248; and Moltke-Hansen, "Horizons" 6–15). Just as affecting were the ghost stories and Revolutionary War tales of his grandmother and the verses sent, and tales told, by his father.

These diverse tales became reasons to explore—in books, but also on the ground. As a boy, Simms ranged through the city and along the banks of the Ashley River, which fed into Charleston Harbor. He did so in search of scenes of colonial and Revolutionary battles and incidents (*Letters* 1:lxii). He first heard his uncle's and father's many Irish and frontier stories when they visited in Charleston in 1816 and 1818, respectively. He heard more on his trips to Mississippi during the winter of 1824 through the spring of 1825 and again in 1826. The first trip took him through Georgia and Alabama, where he saw elements of the Creek and Cherokee Nations. At the time, Simms later reported, he was a boy "cumbered with fragmentary materials of thought, . . . choked by the tangled vines of erroneous speculation, and haunted by passions, which, like so many wolves, lurked, in ready waiting, for their unsuspecting prey" ("Social" 75). When he first got to Mississippi, traveling partly by stage, partly by riverboat, and partly by horse, Simms learned that his father had just come back from "a trip of three hundred miles into the heart of the Indian country" (Trent 15). Later father and son "rode together on horseback to various settlements on the frontier of Alabama and Mississippi" (Guilds 10–11, 17–18). Simms recalled as well "having traveled 150 miles beyond the Mississippi" (Shillingsburg, "Literary" 120). The next year he returned to the Old Southwest by ship. "During this [second] trip he carried a 'note book.'" There he jotted episodes, encounters, stories heard, characters seen, and descriptions of the landscapes unfolding around him. He also wrote "at least sixteen poems" (Kibler, "First"; Shillingsburg, "Literary" 123).

Simms took a third western trip five years later, writing letters back to the newspaper that he was by then editing (*Letters* 1:10–38). Together these three trips provided materials for his writings over more than forty years. "The first . . . produced mainly short fiction; the second inspired much poetry; . . . the first and third . . . yielded three novels written in the 1830s" (Shillingsburg, "Literary" 119). This was, in part, because of the trips' timing. Sixteen years after the first trip, Simms told students at the University of Alabama that in the interval their world had changed from a howling wilderness into a place of growing civilization (Simms, "The Social Principle" 75–76). Had he not gone when he did, he would have been too late to see the frontier. Later travels took him many other places and also provided much grist for his writing. Never again, however, did he experience the frontier firsthand. Furthermore, on these later trips Simms was a practiced professional writer, no longer that boy haunted by passions.

Personal Life

After the ten-year-old boy's momentous refusal to leave Charleston, his grandmother sent Simms for two years to the grammar school taught on the campus and by the faculty of the nearly moribund College of Charleston. By then he already was "versifying the events of the war [of 1812]," just concluded, publishing "doggerel" in the local papers, and learning to read in several languages (*Letters* 1:285). His trip west a decade later helped him decide to pursue both literature and a career in law, albeit in Charleston—this despite his father's urging that he stay in Mississippi. Upon his return home, the younger Simms began to read law and also launched a literary weekly, the *Album,* which ran for a year. He became engaged as well to Anna Malcolm Giles, daughter of a grocer and former state coroner.

A year later the young couple married. This was six months before Simms was admitted to the South Carolina bar, on his twenty-first birthday, and not long before he was appointed as a city magistrate. Although living up the Ashley River in the more healthful, less expensive village of Summerville, Simms kept a law office in the city. Shortly after using his maternal inheritance to buy the *City Gazette* at the end of 1829 and moving down to Charleston Neck, just north of the city limits where he had lived as a boy, Simms lost both his father and his maternal grandmother. He also found himself attacked because of his Unionist stance in the Nullification crisis resulting from South Carolina's rejection of a federal tariff. Then, in early 1832, Simms's wife died. Soon after, he took his four-year-old daughter back to Summerville to live and determined to sell his newspaper and leave the state for a literary life in the North.

Fueling his ambition was the correspondence Simms had begun several years earlier with an accountant whom he had published in his *City Gazette* but had not yet met—Scots immigrant James Lawson. At the time, Lawson, seven years Simms's senior, edited a New York City newspaper and, in addition to writing plays and poetry, was a friend (and, later, informal literary agent) to a wide circle (McHaney). Simms's trip north in the summer of 1832 began a lifelong friendship between the two, cemented as they squired ladies about and interacted with Lawson's literary circle. In subsequent years Simms multiplied the number of his friendships in both the North and the South, making them in some measure a replacement for the family that he had lost. Lawson remained the closest of his Northern friends, while James Henry Hammond, a future governor and US senator, became his closest friend in South Carolina.

Late in 1833, after his Summerville house burned, Simms wrote Lawson to say that he was enamored of "a certain fair one" (*Letters* 1:73). Seventeen-year-old Chevillette Eliza Roach was the daughter of "a literary-minded aristocrat of English descent" with two plantations on the banks of the Edisto River in Barnwell District, later Bamberg County (Guilds 70). The courtship was protracted, as Simms felt it necessary first to clear debts that friends had bought up on his behalf. He also was determined "to marry no woman" before he was "perfectly independent of her resources, and her friends" (*Letters* 1:78). Therefore he did not propose until the spring of 1836. The nuptials took place seven months later, and as a result, Simms came to call the four thousand acres of Woodlands Plantation, with its seventy enslaved people, home. It was twenty years, however, before he took over management of the plantation and, then, only in the wake of his father-in-law's final sickness and death. Five years after that, he lost his wife, the mother of fourteen of his fifteen children. Nine of the children Chevillette bore him had already died, devastating Simms repeatedly. Five were still living (three sons and two daughters), as was Simms's daughter by his first marriage, who helped raise the youngest of her siblings. Those remaining children—even Gilly, who fought in the Confederate army—all outlived their father. Gilly and a brother-in-law ran Woodlands after the war, when Simms, though dying of cancer, was earning what he could by writing again for publications in the North and editing one or another South Carolina newspaper.

Career

The trip north in 1832 did not result in Simms moving there. Except during the Civil War, however, he returned to the North almost every year. This was because the contacts he made, and the exposure to literary culture that he enjoyed, helped him define his future as an author. Earlier he had written fiction and criticism as well as journalism, filling the pages of several short-lived cultural journals and his newspaper, but between the ages of nine and twenty-six, Simms focused his literary efforts primarily on poetry. Beginning with his first book of verse in 1825, he published five small volumes in Charleston. A couple had received positive notice in New York, and in the fall of 1832, J. & J. Harper issued the sixth anonymously from there, *Atalantis: A Story of the Sea.* Coming back the following summer, Simms had in hand for the Harpers a gothic novella, *Martin Faber,* and after his return south, he also would send the manuscript of his first two-volume Border romance, *Guy Rivers: A Tale of Georgia.*

The reception of these and the romances and short stories that followed quickly made Simms one of the nation's most successful fictionists. He continued as well to issue poetry—roughly a collection every three years over the thirty-seven years that he worked as a professional author. But this output was dwarfed by the fiction—on average a title every year (counting several serialized works but not counting the many revised editions). Then there were the two dozen separately published orations, histories, and biographies as well as edited collections of documents and dramas and a geography of South Carolina. Add to these the revised editions and the further printings of his own works and it appears that Simms saw a title coming off the presses at the rate of one every three months or so. Making that figure all the more astounding is the fact that, during more than a dozen of those years (the early to mid-1840s, the late 1840s to early 1850s, and the mid-to-late 1860s), he also was editing a cultural journal or newspaper. Furthermore, he contributed reams of reviews and poems, hundreds of op-ed pieces and columns, and dozens of short stories and public addresses, which were never collected and published in volume form in his lifetime.

His career mapped an arc. It ascended meteorically in the 1830s and peaked in the early to mid-1840s before beginning to descend. One reason was the popularity of the historical fiction that Simms began to write. When he left behind the law, his first newspaper, and the Nullification controversy, historical fiction was all the rage. Sir Walter Scott had fueled the craze, beginning with the publication of his first border romance in 1814. He died in September 1832. James Fenimore Cooper, the closest America had to a Scott at the time, was at the peak of his reputation and success, having started publishing his romances in 1820, being seventeen years Simms's senior. Thus, the way had been prepared for a writer of Simms's historical imagination and preoccupations. Within five years of his first trip north, moreover, Lawson's (and now his) circle became loosely affiliated with a nationalistic and Democratic group, self-styled Young America, named after Young Italy and similar ethnic, nationalist, European cultural and political movements (Moltke-Hansen, "Horizons"). Edgar Allan Poe and other members gave Simms's initial fiction positive, if not uncritical, attention.

By the end of the 1830s, paradoxically, Simms, like Cooper, found his success attracting unauthorized editions of his works because Britain and America did not have an international copyright agreement. Further, in the wake of the Panic of 1837, Americans bought fewer books. Simms's response was to diversify his portfolio. He turned to biography and history, including his hugely successful *Life of Francis Marion* (1844). He also returned to the editor's chair, overseeing one and then another cultural journal. These were unlike the ones he had edited in the 1820s: They included contributions by numerous authors, not just those from Charleston but also from the region and the North. The ambition motivating the journals was to connect and promote Charleston intellectually. Consequently, the journals more closely resembled metropolitan quarterly reviews in their offerings.

The mid-1840s saw Simms involved in politics, even serving a term in the South Carolina legislature. By the middle of the Mexican-American War in 1847, he had concluded that the South needed to become an independent nation. Thereafter, although he maintained ties with many in the Young America circle, he no longer promoted his writings as fostering Americanism in literature (*Views*). Instead, he increasingly emphasized the ways in which his three romance series—the colonial, the Revolutionary, and the Border—were making tangible and meaningful the origins and development of the future Southern nation and the sad but inevitable consequences for Native Americans (C. Watson, *Nationalism;* cf. Nakamura). Sectional politics colored more and more of Simms's perceptions, speeches, and private communications. The rising tide of abolitionism had him aghast. It also fed his growing sense that his position in American letters was slipping. He returned to editing, and his poetry, which was more often explicitly about the South, became increasingly patriotic in tone. Although his first biographer, William Peterfield Trent, insisted that Simms's declining standing reflected the change in literary fashion from historical romances to realistic novels, Simms in fact wrote more and more as a social realist in the 1850s (Wimsatt, "Realism").

The Civil War consumed Simms. As he wrote Lawson, "Literature, especially poetry, is effectually overwhelmed by the drums, & the cavalry, and the shouting" (*Letters* 4:369–70). He did manage to editorialize often and to rework and finish things long on his desk, including poems, a novel, and a dramatic treatment of Benedict Arnold, the Northern traitor in the Revolutionary War. Then, in the wake of the Confederacy's loss and the failure of his vision for the South, he found himself recording the loss in a new newspaper, dealing with the trauma in his poetry, and becoming more existential and psychological in his fictional treatments. Simms's old New York friends tried to help. He did edit and see through publication a volume of Confederate war poetry. Yet it is a measure of his reduced stature that the several new romances he published appeared only in serial form. In part this may have been because he was in a sense competing with himself. Publishers were beginning to reprint volumes out of the selected edition of his writings. Many of Simms's works were available in book form, just not new works.

Associations

As his correspondence testifies, Simms had complex, overlapping networks of friends and colleagues. When a boy and young man, he received the friendship, patronage, and commendation of a variety of well-placed people in Charleston, including Charles Rivers Carroll. It was Carroll with whom he read law, to whom he dedicated his first romance, and after whom he named a son. Both men were Unionists during the Nullification controversy. So were Hugh Swinton Legare (later US attorney general) and the considerably older William Drayton, as well as lawyer and editor Richard Yeadon and Greenville, South Carolina, newspaper editor Benjamin Franklin Perry. Also considerably older was James Wright Simmons, who joined with Simms to launch the *Southern Literary Gazette* in 1828, when Simms was twenty-two. Through him Simms had direct contact with such British literary figures as Leigh Hunt and Lord Byron (Kibler, *Poetry* 15).

The next group of influential friends and collaborators that Simms acquired were members of the Lawson circle and included such figures as Edwin Forrest, the Shakespearean actor, and Evert Duyckinck, who published several of Simms's volumes in the Wiley and Putnam's series he edited, Library of American Books. Among the many others were poets and editors William Cullen Bryant and Fitz-Greene Halleck. Simms also made non-literary friends in New York and Philadelphia, such as John Jacob Bockee and William Hawkins Ferris, the cashier at the US Treasury office in New York who, after the war, helped Simms, Henry Timrod (poet laureate of the Confederacy), and others.

As a Barnwell planter, Simms met a widening circle of South Carolina's leaders and literati. His acquaintance with James Henry Hammond began in the late 1830s and deepened into a friendship in the early 1840s. It was in the early 1840s, too, when he again was editing cultural journals, that Simms became friends with many Southern writers. He regarded several of them, including

Virginians George Frederick Holmes, Edmund Ruffin, and Nathaniel Beverley Tucker as members, together with Hammond and himself, of a "sacred circle." Uniting the circle were members' devotion to the South and a shared sense of the marginal status and critical importance of the life of the mind in a largely rural and unintellectual region (Faust, *Sacred*). Others of Simms's wide connections in the region did not interact as much with each other, but Simms long corresponded with Maryland novelist and lawyer John Pendleton Kennedy, Irish-born Georgia poet Richard Henry Wilde, Alabama lawyer and writer Alexander Beaufort Meek, and Louisiana historian and assistant attorney general Charles Gayarré, among others. By the 1850s, when Simms once more returned to editing a cultural journal, many of the writers whom he recruited were members of a younger generation. Poets Paul Hamilton Hayne and Henry Timrod were two. Often, they and a half-dozen others of Simms's and their generations met in John Russell's Charleston bookshop and adjourned to dinner at Simms's Smith Street home, "dubbed 'The Wigwam'" (*Letters* 1:cxxxvi). Shortly before his death fifteen or so years later, Simms wrote Hayne, "I am rapidly passing from the stage, where you young men are to succeed me" (*Letters* 5:287).

Thought

The welter of Simms's works disguises unities and dynamics of the thought underlying them. From early on Simms was convinced that art ennobles or transforms, as well as gives voice to individuals and societies; therefore, it must be cultivated assiduously. Without the potential for high artistic attainment, he insisted, societies are not ready for the independence and regard of free peoples. This is where Simms the historian joined Simms the poet. Societies develop, he argued (using the stadialism of the Scottish historical school), from imitation through self-assertion to achievement and also from savagery through strife to settled agricultural communities and, ultimately, to a hierarchical civilization supporting a rich artistic life. It was the job of the artist to help envision the goal, inspire the pursuit, and inform the process. That process was at once progressive and dialectical. Order, without dynamism, stifled development, as did the obverse—the dominance of ungoverned impulses or uncontrolled license. This was true in the individual but also in societies as a whole. War was necessary for civilization, but its success was measured in the securities of the home, which, for Simms, was the center of cultural production and reproduction.

Whether in the public or in the domestic arena, "the true governor, as [Thomas] Carlyle call[ed] him—the king man—" guided rather than impeded the forces of change and progress (Simms, "Guizot's" 122). There were few such men with the capacity to lead. The same was true of nations. Neither all people nor all peoples were equal in either capacity or attainment. That was why Native

Americans were overrun and Africans had been enslaved by European peoples in the New World. Indeed, Simms argued, "slavery in all ages has been found the greatest and most admirable agent of Civilization," giving education and examples to less evolved peoples (*Letters* 3:174). The degree to which a people had evolved mattered. That was why, he held, Americans had won independence from the most powerful empire in the world. They had done so through their Revolution, led by an elite that correctly felt its time had come (Simms, "Ellet's" 328). By mid-1847 that also was Simms's judgment for the South: the region had evolved enough to become independent (*Letters* 2:332). The hope inspired and then failed him and the people he sought to lead.

While not all men could rise to the highest rank, they all had the same responsibility at home. There the father was patriarch, protector, and head, while the mother was nurturer, moral instructor, and heart. There, too, children's characters and minds were formed by age twelve (Simms, "Ellet's"). Children's upbringing was critical to citizenship, and it was through her sons and through the support of her husband, father, and brothers that a woman shaped the public sphere. The culture and character instilled in the child expressed and informed not just the household, but the larger society—the people.

"The history of peoples and their embodiments in institutions, states, and artistic productions—these were the great subjects" in Simms's view (Moltke-Hansen, "Horizons" 120). Yet "poets were the only class of philosophers who had recognized" this until his own day, when at last "we now read human histories. We now ask after the affections as well as the ceremonies of society" (Simms, "Ellet's" 319–20). Peoples or races—that is, ethnic groups—were not unchanging any more than were their politics and their cultures. They either advanced or were overrun by history. Further, new peoples emerged, and old identities were submerged. The Spanish conquistadors were the creation of centuries of conflict with the Moors: Their motivation was the glory of conquest, not the routine of trade or the plow. On the other hand, the English settlements in North America reflected the impulse to transform the wilderness into verdant farms and to build society (Simms, *Views* 64, 178–85; Simms, "The Social Principle" 78). The same impulse drove Americans westward in Simms's own day and gave Americans their Manifest Destiny.

To explore these facts of the South's settlement and its place in international conflicts, Simms wrote all together, between 1833 and 1863, two romances set in eighth-century Spain, two set during the Spanish exploration and conquest of the Americas and two during the later English colonization of South Carolina, seven set during the American Revolution, and—depending on how one counts—perhaps eight set on the borders of the nineteenth-century South. After the war he published one more Revolutionary romance and two more that, like it, were set beyond the boundaries of civilization. He also left two unfinished romances, also set beyond society's normal reach. These late works, however, no longer had as their framing justification the cultivation of the South's future and civilization.

White Southerners had their independence foreclosed by the war. In his last works, therefore, Simms found himself exploring the psychological, philosophical, and historical impulses that led to the Confederacy's demise and what, in the aftermath, it meant to be a good man and to build for the future, however impoverished. On the first score, he argued that the impulse to idealism behind abolitionism ignored historical realities, becoming inhuman in its consequences. On the latter score, he affirmed responsibility for one's dependents and the virtues of stoicism, as well as a continued commitment to the beauty and truth of art and the impulses to the cultivated life and fields. Therefore, in the face of the burning of his Woodlands home and library in February 1865—during the march of General William Tecumseh Sherman's US Army through the Carolinas and in the midst of desperate circumstances—he insisted that home, or the ideals and past characterizing its potential, still was at the center of true civilization but only if elevated by art. It was wrong to measure civilization by the getting, spending, and mad dashing, or material progress and utilitarianism, characteristic of both a capitalistic North and many Southerners. These traits he often had attacked even before the war, insisting that "the work of the Imagination, which is the Genius of a race, is only begun when its material progress is supposed to be complete" (Simms, *Poetry* 12).

Writings

Simms expressed many of his ideas most personally in letters and most cogently in essays, speeches, and occasional introductions to his books. But he illustrated them most fully in his fiction and poetry. By the time he arrived in New York in 1832, he had formed many of the core ideals and beliefs that would shape his work. His application of them, however, modified his understanding over time. Growing as a writer and growing in knowledge and experience, he also grew as a thinker.

In his hierarchy of values, poetry came first. It was a prophetic calling as well as evocative of the deeply felt (or, sometimes, the fleeting) and thus testimony to the perdurance and transcendence of the beautiful and the human spirit. Yet, as Simms often ruefully reflected, prose spoke to many more people. That was a principal reason why he turned to writing prose epics or romances. He gave his most concerted consideration of poetry's value and roles in three lectures in Charleston in 1854. Over the prior three years he had given portions of them in Augusta, Georgia; Washington, DC; and Richmond and Petersburg, Virginia. Titled "Poetry and the Practical," they did not see print until 1996, as Simms never found the time to expand them as he wanted. On the other hand, his last address on the same themes, "The Sense of the Beautiful," was issued soon after he delivered it, also in Charleston.

Many of his important reviews have not yet been gathered. A recent collection of *William Gilmore Simms's Selected Reviews on Literature and Civilization* appeared in 2014, and Simms collected some of his *Views and Reviews in American Literature, History and Fiction,* which came out in 1846 and 1847 in two "series." Beginning with a consideration of "Americanism" in literature, the first series explored the themes and periods of American history for treatment by the novelist. Simms argued there and in forewords to several of his romances that fiction rendered the past more truthfully, interestingly, and tellingly than histories and biographies could because fiction—like poetry—required imagination to look beyond what is not known or expressed. The second series examined additional American writers and what distinguished them, for instance, in their humor.

Despite their early success, Simms's romances, novellas, and stories provoked mixed reviews. Poe eventually concluded that Simms had become "the best novelist which this country has, on the whole, produced" but also insisted that "he should never have written 'The Partisan,' nor 'The Yemassee.'" This was in a review of *Confession.* That novel, like the gothic *Martin Faber,* demonstrated, Poe contended, that Simms's "genius [did] not lie in the outward so much as in the inner world." Yet he nevertheless wrote of Simms's short story collection *The Wigwam and the Cabin* that "in invention, in vigor, in movement, in the power of exciting interest, and in the artistical management of his themes, he has surpassed, we think, any of his countrymen." Other critics, especially in the genteel and Whiggish Knickerbocker circle, joined Poe in condemning what they considered to be the excessively graphic and vulgar qualities of many characters and scenes as well as Simms's prolixity and sententiousness in his romances (Butterworth and Kibler 64, 50).

The violent realism and earthiness of the romances did not result in realistic novels. Although Simms received early praise for his characterizations (particularly of women), he used the romance formula, with its stereotypic heroes and heroines, predictable themes, and conventional polarities. People were on quests or had lost their way or were fighting long odds or were carrying forward the banner of (and modeling) civilization or were mired in the slough of despond or were resisting all the claims of civilized society and behavior or were pursuing love interests. Deceitfulness, selfishness, and greed opposed honor, high-mindedness, and honesty against the backdrop of the South's development from the earliest days of Spanish exploration to the westward movement in Simms's own youth.

It was only gradually that Simms married the psychological acuity of some of his portraits of the interior struggles of his gothic characters and fiction to the historical romance. Helping him think through how to do so were the bi-ographies he wrote in the mid-1840s and also the incidents on which he focused particular fictions, such as the murder in *Beauchampe; or, The Kentucky Tragedy* (1842). However incomplete the blending of realism and romanticism or of ste-reotypical and socially individuated renderings through the 1840s, by the 1850s Simms fundamentally had made the transition to social realism in such works as *Woodcraft* and *The Cassique of Kiawah.* Indeed, some scholars have considered *Woodcraft* the first realistic novel in America (Bakker, "Literary Frontier"; Wim-satt, "Realism").

In some sense disguising the transition is the fact that Simms also increasingly wrote as a humorist and, in so doing, often rendered his late narratives fabulisti-cally, when not writing social comedy or stories of manners. This dimension of Simms's work was largely hidden, however, until the 1974 publication of *Stories and Tales,* volume 5 in the Centennial Simms edition, edited by John C. Guilds. There, for the first time, readers had access in print to "Bald-Head Bill Bauldy." There, too, for the first time one could read together "Legend of the Hunter's Camp" and "How Sharp Snaffles Got His Capital and Wife," which was pub-lished posthumously in *Harper's Magazine* in October 1870. These and other stories and tales made it clear that Simms was a fecund contributor to Southern and American humor.

Humor let Simms take up issues that he could not otherwise address in print and still expect to be well received. He did so both during and after the war. The war also pushed Simms past the emerging fashion of social realism. Having de-stroyed the familiar, the preoccupation of much realistic fiction, the war made the liminal central (Shillingsburg, "Cub"). While his romances and tales had often explored life on the edge or in extreme circumstances, whether in war or on the frontier or on the verge of madness or in fanciful realms, they had done so against a backdrop of and with the goal of affirming social norms and development. In the war's wake, that goal seemed absurd. Mythologized memories of a healthy past might nurture a sense of the beautiful but could not help one deal with the present. Thus Simms's conclusion, in a March 1869 letter to Paul Hamilton Hayne: "Let us bury the Past lest it buries us!" (*Letters* 5:214). Fifteen months later he lay dead in the 13 Society Street, Charleston, home of his oldest daughter, with the shell holes in the walls of the bedroom he had shared with several children.

Posthumous Reputation

The twenty years after Simms's death saw him often respectfully treated, first in obituaries, later in memoirs and columns, and in literary dictionaries and encyclo-pedias. Yet Charles Richardson's 1887 *American Literature: 1607–1885* proved a har-binger of a shift: Simms, Richardson observed, was "more respected than read," having "won considerable note because he was so sectional" and then having "lost it because he was not sectional enough," although he showed "silly contempt for his Northern betters" (qtd. in Butterworth and Kibler 130). Five years later Trent's biography of Simms appeared. It was the first full-length, scholarly treatment. Its central thesis was that Simms's environment frustrated his abilities: The South was inimical to art and the life of the mind, and Charleston high society's hauteur marginalized Simms despite his talent and character. Trent's second thesis was that Simms's commitment to the romance and his romanticism meant that his works had become largely unreadable in an age of literary realism. Although Vernon Parrington and later scholars recognized Simms's impulses to realism, the two theses long shaped Simms criticism and, indeed, also helped frame study of antebellum Southern literature and intellectual life (Parrington 2:119–30).

A Virginian born in 1862, Trent was a progressive who wanted a New South radically different from the old. He saw his pioneering study of Simms as an opportunity to criticize what the Civil War had made untenable. From his perspective the Old South was not the expanding and rapidly developing environment with a deep history that Simms portrayed, but a place where enslavement stultified and stunted the growth and progress displayed by the North. Southern—especially South Carolinian—writers occasionally challenged Trent's agenda and conclusions, but those critiques had little impact. Not until after publication of the Simms letters in the 1950s did scholars begin to consider the author in the historical and contemporary contexts that he had rendered in his poetry and fiction. And not until after the centennial of his death did a growing number of scholars, having concluded that Southern intellectual history was not an oxymoron, begin to study in detail the culture in which Simms participated and to which he contributed so voluminously and variously.

Some of these scholars also have had agendas: They have wanted to see Simms included in the American literary canon, for instance, or they have wanted to defend the heritage that in their view Trent, and so many others, inappropriately belittled or ignorantly dismissed. More fruitfully, other scholars have begun to reframe the understanding of nineteenth-century American intellectual life by stripping away preconceptions that characterized earlier evaluations of Simms and his contemporaries. They are closely examining the historical record and transatlantic and other contemporary contexts and developments in the process. Although the pursuit of canonical status in a post-canonical age seems quixotic at this point, the explosion of the canon is leading to more varied fare being offered and may, therefore, mean that Simms, now that his work is widely available, will be more often anthologized as well as studied. Defensiveness about Simms and the antebellum South may warm the hearts of like-minded people, just as critics of the Old South have been encouraged by shared presuppositions and disdain. Yet dueling cultural ideologies do not advance comity and may only reinforce mutual incomprehensions. Continued, deep research in original sources and the theoretical reframing that Atlantic history, the history of the book, and other perspectives offer—these approaches promise most for further study of Simms, his works, and his world.

Acknowledgments

I cannot imagine a more collegial, supportive group of scholars than those whose interests include Simms. I am grateful for their mentorship and assistance over the years, particularly Nick Meriwether, David Moltke-Hansen, David Newton, Matt Brennan, and Katie Burnett. Special thanks go to Todd Hagstette, who provided this project and me with more "succour" than even Simms can allude to in a single oration. I am likewise appreciative of the patience and astuteness of Alex Moore and Ehren Foley of the University of South Carolina Press.

The institutional support, resources, and staff (past and present) of the South Caroliniana Library at the University of South Carolina made this project possible, particularly Graham Duncan, Brian Cuthrell, John Heiting, and Lorrey Stewart. No library anywhere is as helpful and hospitable. The generosity of the William Gilmore Simms Initiatives and the Watson-Brown Foundation also enabled this endeavor.

The encouragement of the leadership and my colleagues at Longwood University has been instrumental, especially when tracking down fugitive Greek, Medieval, and British allusions. Thank you to Jeff Everhart for his assistance with the Spartanburg address.

My family's confidence in this project sustained my own. Thank you to my parents, Catherine, Larissa, and Barbara for inspiring in and sharing with me a love of literature and history.

Introduction

William Gilmore Simms as Orator

The correspondence between lecture committees and orators in the antebellum South followed an effusive script. Reputations were flattered in invitations to speak, followed by fulsome replies acknowledging the honor of the request. The phrasing of an 1854 solicitation from a group of prominent Charleston, South Carolina, gentlemen to William Gilmore Simms to give his "Poetry and the Practical" address that summer is typical. The members of the city's intellectual and social elite wrote Simms that they "desire to profit by the opportunity . . . of listening to" his lecture addressing the significance of the arts that he had given elsewhere in the South to "marked praise." This appeal to the vanity of the speaker was pro forma. Equally rote was the invitation's reverential conclusion, though the connotations of its language likely resonated with the 48-year-old author, editor, historian, and lecturer in ways that the committee may not have imagined. The Charlestonians wrote Simms that they "beg, at the same time, to tender you our cordial wishes for the continued success of your honorable and brilliant labors" ("Mr. Simms' Lectures").

Simms's reply followed the formula of graciousness, acknowledging their "kind and complimentary application" and agreeing to speak, but the notion that his orations were considered "honorable and brilliant labors" likely struck him as factually correct but also as figuratively meaningful. On one hand, Simms's correspondence to friends that reference his work on his orations during his—by that time—fourteen-year career at the lectern reveal that composing a lecture lasting close to an hour was, indeed, laborious. Simms sandwiched his research and composition of orations amid an outpouring of poetry and prose, periodical editing, and correspondence, not to mention a busy homelife that included the management of a plantation and the birth of a child (and often its death) almost every two years. Simms was hectically multitasking as he worked on his orations, often finishing just before he traveled to deliver them. Yet on the other hand, these "labors" did yield dividends in the form of rare public recognition of Simms's "brilliance." Over the years, reviewers praised his "fine voice and agreeable manner," his "masterly and impressive" command of topics, and the "rapturous enthrallment" in which he held audiences as a public speaker, acknowledgments of his talent that he elsewhere complained were far too infrequent ("Editor's Table" 79; "Mr. Simms' Lecture" 1; "Opening of the Female College" 2).

Yet the notion that these labors were also considered "honorable" may have been even more significant to Simms than the positive reviews from critics. A son of Charleston from a modest social background who pursued a career outside of the customary masculine occupations of the American South, Simms consistently felt himself to be on the periphery of traditional centers of authority and prestige in the state and the region. He felt this way despite publishing close to fifty novels and collections of tales, hundreds of poems, over a half-dozen book-length histories and essay collections, plus his work writing for and editing periodicals, much of it ideological labor in service to his native state and region. To have his orations characterized as "honorable" by men of Charleston's privileged class, given all that term's regional connotations respecting public image and reputation, would have seemed an even more significant legitimization of his career, one conferring respect on his standing in the community.

That Simms is today less well known as an orator than as a poet, novelist, historian, and editor is partly due to his more prolific output in the latter genres but is also a consequence of his laboring at a time when many public speakers were brilliant. Simms's public speaking career coincided with what historians call the "Golden Age of American Oratory." Barnet Baskerville explains that in the decades before the Civil War "oratory, even when directed at the most practical ends, was regarded by both speaker and audience as an art form, to be cultivated and admired for its own sake" (33). Figures such as Henry Clay, Daniel Webster, John C. Calhoun, Frederick Douglass, and Charles Sumner remain as well known today as in their lifetimes for the eloquence of their expression and for the substance of their ideas. Simms was working on smaller stages. His emergence as a speaker in the early 1840s coincided with and was enabled by the flourishing of "popular" lectures. Open to the public for modest admission charges, these talks were arranged in cities, towns, and hamlets by lyceums, literary and historical societies, young men's groups, and trade associations. A response to antebellum Americans' appetite for advancement and self-improvement, popular lectures aspired "to satisfy their seemingly insatiable craving for 'useful knowledge,'" explains Donald M. Scott, especially the kind that "would give them the hold on life that their aspirations seemed to require" (791, 801). The lectures typically eschewed politics but otherwise "included all the basic categories of knowledge and an almost limitless range of topics" (Scott 802). Filling this need were professors, clergymen, physicians, lawyers, and reformers but also authors and public intellectuals, including Ralph Waldo Emerson, Henry David Thoreau, Oliver Wendell Holmes, William Ellery Channing, and Horace Greeley, who, like Simms, supplemented their incomes by lecturing (Scott 794).

Historians have acknowledged that oratory was especially significant in the Old South, where, with only a couple of notable exceptions, Simms's speaking career was centered.[1] Simms himself noted the sectional significance of public speaking in an 1851 review of recently published speeches, observing "[l]ectures, orations and addresses, in the South, are required to assert a higher rank than they are apt to do in other regions" ("Popular Discourses and Orations" 319). More was expected of them, Simms explains, because the dearth of Southern cities and attendant intellectual coteries and markets of readers hampered traditional belles lettres (320). Orations filled the cerebral and cultural voids in an agricultural society. "In these performances," says Simms, "lie the most ample proofs . . . of our intellectual activity" (319). Moreover, given the physical dispersion of Southerners and their inability to support (or their indifference to) traditional channels of thought like books and periodicals, orations were the "only open medium by which the leading minds of the South may approach their people" (319). Public speaking was the preeminent means for aspiring public intellectuals and not just politicians to influence the "people"—an audience, but also the character and the spirit of the society to which listeners belonged (Faust, *Sacred Circle* 88). As Simms's own orations in this volume make apparent, he was among these ambitious "leading minds" of the South. He earnestly believed in the power of articulate and insightful thinkers and speakers to inform, elevate, and shape the consciousness of a region. Simms believed "all his efforts—in politics, in editing, in public lecturing, in literature per se—were directed to the intellectual betterment of the region and his nation," observes biographer John C. Guilds (112).

The orations in this volume reflect this aspiration of Simms. They address a wide variety of topics, but what they share is a desire to guide fellow Southerners and Americans through the manifold societal changes they were then experiencing. Like other writers and public intellectuals, North and South, conservative and progressive, Simms harbored mixed feelings about the pace and symptoms of progress during the antebellum era. The rapid commercialization of the economy, innovations in transportation and communication technology, the acceleration of westward national expansion, and the democratization of politics resulted in sustained financial prosperity (with notable exceptions during the Panics of 1819 and 1837), mobility, and personal freedom for white men. These trends were collectively characterized as material progress by Simms and like-minded American thinkers and writers. And although they embraced the improved quality of life that accompanied these changes and cheered the spirit of initiative that seemed inherent to the character of the United States, Simms and others simultaneously professed concern that moral progress did not seem to be keeping pace with change. In fact, progress often seemed to come at the cost of virtue and tradition. Affluence, for instance, also appeared to encourage self-interestedness and materialism. Declining respect for religion's authority allowed spiritual indifference and utilitarianism to flourish. Access to affordable lands in the West undermined ties to communities. And in the South, enslavement further complicated intellectuals' relationship to progress. As Eugene Genovese observes, progress was customarily imagined to result from the extension of personal and economic freedom to the broadest number of people. Southerners were thus obliged to reconcile progress with its ostensible antithesis (14).

As Genovese, Michael O'Brien, Drew Gilpin Faust, David Moltke-Hansen, and Adam L. Tate have documented, Simms was among an intellectual class of slaveholders who aspired to be stewards of progress by bettering the minds and elevating the character of their fellow white Southerners, including through orations. If they could foster an appreciation for a balance of material and moral progress by inculcating the values inherent to regional traditions and hereditary institutions, the disruptive tendencies of change might be minimized and the beneficial qualities of the past preserved. The popular touchstones for these conservative Southern intellectuals, Simms included, included religion, the family, the experience of history, and agriculture. Foremost among these, though, was the institution of slavery and the ostensible social influence conveyed by its alleged paternalistic character.

It would be reasonable to ask whether, following the removal of so many memorials to slaveholders, the orations of one of slavery's defenders still merit attention. Particularly from a writer and thinker whose contributions were not always original, as some of the most astute students of Simms have observed (Kibler, *The Poetry of William Gilmore Simms,* 12; Moltke-Hansen, "Ordered" 139; O'Brien 1:451, 452). But what is singular about Simms's treatment of progress in his orations and thus why they continue to demand study is the attempt to navigate the contradictions of progress by synthesizing the different responses of his era to it, including seemingly incongruous perspectives. Simms uses typical patterns of Southern conservative thinking, its reprehensible defense of enslavement included, with approaches typically considered more characteristic of Northern progressivism, particularly its leading Romantic authors. Simms may have spoken most often to Southerners, but he drew from a much larger intellectual and cultural context, one whose currents he adapted to or integrated with his topics and purposes. Moreover, the expansive, diverse scope of Southern life that Simms believed his syntheses relevant to was likewise unusual among his peers. His orations sought to integrate its different dimensions. To the modern mind, for example, public support for the humanities and secession may seem incongruous, as would manuring and Transcendentalism. The orations in this volume offer insight into the ways Simms created meaning out of unexpectedly complementary topics to inform the culture of "the people" in an era of dizzying change.

These patterns of thought can be found elsewhere in Simms's novels, tales, biographies, histories, essays, and poems. His "thinking was remarkably of a piece," James Everett Kibler Jr. observes (*The Poetry of William Gilmore Simms* 35). But in contrast to the volume of—and, frequently, the verboseness of—other texts in his oeuvre, Simms's orations are a more concise, accessible index of the relationships he established among his topics and how he articulated them in his role as a public artist and intellectual. The orations chosen for inclusion in this volume thus reflect the circumstances of progress that were as much the exigences of his orations as the invitations that solicited them. They also represent Simms's syntheses of conservative and progressive responses. Finally, they reflect the influence of national and transatlantic patterns of thinking upon Simms, which link him, despite his growing sectionalism beginning in the late 1840s, to a community of thinkers and writers outside of the South. To a lesser degree, these selections also reflect the range of genres of orations that Simms gave over the course of his public speaking career.

Special consideration was given to orations that served earlier generations of scholars well as primary documents, but which exist only in manuscript form at the University of South Carolina's South Caroliniana Library and thus are not readily accessible to all students of nineteenth-century literature, oratory, and intellectual history. Hence the inclusion of "Choice of a Profession," the Social Moral series, and "Antagonism of the Social Moral." However, these criteria also informed the decision not to include Simms's most "inspired" lecture, "Poetry and the Practical," since a modern edition has been published and edited by Kibler ("Introduction," xii). Similarly, Simms revised some of his favorite orations into essays, including *The Epochs and Events of American History*, which appeared in *Views and Reviews in American Literature, History, and Fiction* and is readily available in both digital and print form thanks to the Simms Initiatives. The Initiatives has likewise digitized copies of published pamphlets of some of Simms's orations, including the Barnwell Agricultural Society address, "The Social Principle," "Sources of American Independence," "Inauguration of the Spartanburg Female College," "South Carolina in the Revolution" (a version of which is reprinted in volume three of Simms's *Letters*), and "The Sense of the Beautiful," all of which are included in this volume for their representatives of the aforementioned motifs. However, if a manuscript existed for these orations, it was used as the source text, given that Simms revised his orations after their delivery if they were intended for publication. A complete list of Simms's known orations and their probable dates of composition can be found in the appendix at the end of this volume.

The orations are organized by themes that are a part of the nexus of aforementioned ideas and by chronology to reflect different periods and rhetorical contexts in Simms's three decades-long speaking career. Part I is the exception. Simms's lifelong faith in the spiritual dimensions of Nature, especially as an alternative to institutional religion and to ameliorate materialism and pragmatism, is best exemplified by his first major speech in 1840 and by his last one in 1870. His advocacy of Nature's divine, elevating influence coincided with two watershed moments for South Carolina, one a crisis of outmigration and the other the aftermath of military defeat. In part II the orations are interpretations of national and regional history Simms offered in the mid-1840s amid growing sectional tensions between North and South and the Eastern Seaboard and the Old Southwest. Simms's narratives accentuate the social virtues inherent to the experiences of the past that he argues are still relevant to social stability and posterity. Part III represents Simms's perspectives on gender, education, and the private and public sphere in the mid-1850s. Simms celebrates women's education but is more restrained on where and how young women ought to use that knowledge, echoing broader antebellum debates on women's opportunities and responsibilities. Similarly, Simms embraces the emergence of a professional class in the South but advises the young men aspiring to its ranks that duty and self-discipline must temper professional ambition. Part IV includes Simms's addresses from the late 1850s, including his disastrous attempt at a lecture tour in the North following a period of heightened regional animosity. His failure leads him to make a vehement case for Southern independence based on distinctive regional characteristics, including those stemming from the institution of slavery. Yet the same series of orations reflects Simms's most urgent demand for recognition of the artist as a public servant, as the figure most responsible for articulating a region's culture to establish its permanence. As is typical with Simms, though, all these topics engage one another, and it will not be unusual to find throughlines in thought, albeit adapted to changing circumstances over the course of his career.

The introductions to each part provide context and relevance for reading the addresses. Each introduction offers the circumstances for the orations' occasions and their reception. Each also includes synopses of the address, given Simms's propensity to use one topic as a metaphor for, or to signify the consequence of, another sometimes-seemingly anomalous, subject. The introductions also offer background on Simms's treatment of the subjects, with an emphasis on connecting him not only to Southern patterns of thought, particularly on progress and the role of the intellectual in shaping society's response to it, but also to other influences. The introductions do not address the oratorical features of the text, but notes are included to suggest relevant scholarship that discusses the rhetorical conventions of an oration's genre.[2]

In transcribing the orations, deviations from modern-day usage of spelling, grammar, syntax, and punctuation in the original documents were preserved. Simms's idiosyncrasies were systematic, suggesting they reflect not so much carelessness as much as his personal style (or perhaps the absence of consistent standards during his childhood and early education). Where the addition of punctuation or a missing letter seemed necessary to clarify the meaning of the text, or if there was an apparent typesetting error in the orations copied from pamphlets, it has been corrected silently. Keeping the long dashes, underlining, and exclamations suggests the performative nature of his public orations—the pauses for dramatic effect, the rising emotion, and points of emphases. Simms's handwriting becomes less legible the faster he was apparently writing (ostensibly to meet his deadline), and when words are illegible, either a best guess has been substituted in brackets or is signaled by a question mark.

Hindsight demonstrates that in only a few cases was Simms ultimately able to influence the minds of the people. When he was most persuasive, as in the case of his advocacy for secession to defend the rights of white Southerners to enslave African Americans, his logic was abhorrent. Furthermore, given the subsequent mortality of the Civil War, the consequences of his success were appalling (emancipation notwithstanding). In other words, many of Simms's oratorical labors do not incline us to consider him especially honorable or particularly brilliant. Nevertheless, because Simms's orations demanded that their listeners reflect on the progress of their nation and be mindful of its direction, these calls to action still merit heeding. In looking back on what Simms sought to do in the cause of honor and brilliance, the orations lead us to question our own assumptions about what constitutes progress, and they challenge us to envision more just ways to advance society.

NOTES

1. For information on the history and distinguishing characteristics of Southern oratory, see Waldo W. Braden, ed., *Oratory in the Old South*, and W. Stuart Towns, *Oratory and Rhetoric in the Nineteenth-Century South*.

2. For the broad patterns of oratorical traditions and conventions on which Simms drew, see Winifred Bryan Horner, *Rhetoric in the Classical Tradition*; Robert T. Oliver, *History of Public Speaking in America*; and James Perrin Warren, *Culture of Eloquence: Oratory and Reform in Antebellum America*.

PART I

Nature and Its Social Uses

Introduction

William Gilmore Simms's 1840 address to a South Carolina agricultural society and his 1870 lecture before a Charleston horticultural association were congruent bookends to his long public speaking career. Simms, a planter and avid gardener, thought often and deeply about the land, what grew on it, and man's relationship to it.[1] Simms's first oration and his final oration offered occasions for sharing these perspectives. Both speeches also address a broader array of topics that seem nominally less germane to agriculture and horticulture. The reason for this is because the orations were as much responses to moments of seismic social change as they were to invitations from the respective organizations. The year 1840 represented an ostensible environmental, demographic, and political crisis, precipitated by the diminished fertility of cropland. In 1870, challenges to the South's traditional gender and racial hierarchies in the wake of the Confederacy's defeat were on Simms's mind. Simms's assumption of the roles of interpreter and guide for the public during critical moments like these would also be characteristic of the rest of his public speaking career.

Simms, like other public intellectuals in the South, realistically expected change to occur. He was amenable to it so long as it did not threaten the social institutions responsible for the moral character of the region's white population, the culture derived from that temperament, and the societal permanence for which culture was a precondition. Christianity, family, agriculture, and enslavement were among the South's traditional moral foundations, important sources of individual virtue and thus social order. Agriculture encouraged diligence, for instance, the home promoted ties to place, the institution of slavery ostensibly cultivated duty and responsibility, and faith diminished materialism. But in 1840 and 1870—and at many points in between—undesirable symptoms of progress threatened the institutions responsible for fostering these values: rootlessness in pursuit of "the main chance," radical reform movements aspiring to alter social relationships, empiricism's ascendency, utilitarianism becoming a measure for behavior, and new claims to rights made in the name of democracy. Simms and other members of the South's intellectual class knew they could neither entirely stop progress nor "return to the past," observes Adam L. Tate (189). However, through their intellectual and artistic work, including public speaking, the region's thought leaders "could construct, at least partially, a culture devoted to conservative principles" to provide some continuity of tradition to resist or mitigate what they believed was reckless progress (189). Simms's discussion of not just crops and flowers but also topics such as enslavement and separate gendered spheres are representative of these patterns of conservative thought.

However, the Barnwell Agricultural Society Oration and "The Sense of the Beautiful" are singular in their prescription for a Romantic engagement with the natural world. The orations' emphasis on a spiritual relationship with Nature is an uncommon complement to Southern conservative touchstones such as enslavement and True Womanhood. Simms's 1840 oration, for instance, celebrates the individual's ability to apprehend the divine qualities represented by and shared with Nature. 1870's "The Sense of the Beautiful" elaborates on how this elevates an individual's consciousness, ennobling and redeeming their character and, by extension, the society to which they belong. It was more typical among Southern intellectuals to emphasize Christianity as a means of furthering moral progress (Genovese 27, 29). Instead, Simms substitutes claims more commonly associated with Northern, progressive peers such as Ralph Waldo Emerson and Henry David Thoreau or with British and German Romanticism, influences that Simms shared with these writers.[2]

Simms imagined this synthesis of conservative values and less orthodox spiritualism in the Barnwell Agricultural Society Oration and "The Sense of the Beautiful" as part of his blueprint for ensuring stability in a world threatened by change, or, in the case of Charleston in 1870, a semblance of stability approximating the order overturned by the Confederacy's loss and by Emancipation. Simultaneously, the cultural work done by the orations aspired to confirm and to sustain Simms's position among the intellectual and cultural vanguard of white Southerners. "By rehabilitating thought and then demonstrating its value to society at large," explains Drew Gilpin Faust, Simms, along with his peers, "believed they would contribute to the solution of the social dislocations of the day, as well as to the improvement of their own status" (*Sacred Circle* 70). Such were the impetuses that led Simms to launch his public speaking career in 1840 and agree to speak in the throes of late-stage terminal cancer in 1870.

The first major oration of Simms's career had its origins in a January 1840 meeting of planters in South Carolina's Barnwell District (today known as Barnwell County), a cotton-growing locality bordered to its south by the Savannah River. The planters gathered "for the purpose of forming a District Agricultural Society" and voted to hold two seasonal meetings, the winter gathering featuring an oration ("From the Carolina Planter"). Former congressman and future governor and senator James Henry Hammond, one of South Carolina's more conscientious planters, was among the Society's organizers. It was probably Hammond who proposed that Simms—his new friend, another Barnwell planter, and a recently famous novelist—give the inaugural address in November.

Simms first references the oration in a July 27, 1840, letter to his New York friend James Lawson, sharing that his "hands will soon be filled with . . . various labors," including "my agricultural oration" (*Letters* 1:180). Simms's "various labors," which included finishing his novel *The Kinsmen,* were apparently demanding. On September 28 Simms sounded exasperated, writing Lawson that he is still working on "an agricultural oration which I am to deliver in Barnwell on the 2nd of November—a task, which will somewhat interfere with other tasks, to me of far greater importance" (*Letters* 1:191). Simms's prioritization of the lecture over work allegedly "of far greater importance" suggests that he attached a special significance to addressing the new agricultural society. On one hand the novelist shared the interests of the group. In February 1840, for example, Simms wrote Hammond to thank him for some seeds, expressing that "sober attention to the soil, is worth all the commercial Bank & Rail Road conventions in the world" (*Letters* 1:168). On the other hand, there were personal and professional reasons for Simms launching his public speaking career in 1840 at this small rural agricultural society meeting.

Faust observes that Southern agricultural societies like Barnwell's were "almost exclusively the preserve of the planter class" ("Rhetoric and Ritual" 47). Simms was a relative newcomer to both Barnwell and this social stratum. He moved to Woodlands plantation in 1836 after marrying his second wife, Chevillette. Simms himself did not own the plantation—his father-in-law Nash Roach owned and largely managed the property until his health failed in 1855 (Guilds 225). Simms was the author of five novels and four books of poetry at the time of his marriage, but he did not bring much economic or social capital to the union. Despite his burgeoning body of work and favorable notices in Northern periodicals, Simms felt that popular acclaim remained elusive, especially close to home, says biographer John C. Guilds. The novelist and poet believed "his literary efforts had gone largely unappreciated, particularly by fellow Southerners" (103). Simms's ambitions for recognition and the desire to establish himself as a member of the planter class may explain why he was willing to pause work on a novel for a national audience to try his hand at a new genre for a more provincial one. Speaking on issues of economic and social importance to the district's agricultural society would be an opportunity to establish credibility among local social and political elites.[3]

The only existing assessment of the speech is Simms's own. He reported to Lawson on January 8, 1841, that "[m]y agricultural oration seems to have pleased the audience" and that the society had requested the manuscript for publication. Simms was vacillating, saying, "[I] know not that I shall consent" (*Letters* 1:212). By February Simms decided to put the address to a more lucrative use, revising it for publication in the New York-based periodical *The Ladies' Companion* (*Letters* 1:233). The *Companion* was "one of the leading women's magazines in the nation during this period," according to Kathleen L. Endres and Therese L. Lueck, and its editor, William W. Snowden, had a "reputation for paying contributors well and promptly." This meant the magazine attracted the "leading popular writers of the day" (166). A byline among well-known authors, a national audience, and reliable renumeration were likely more appealing to Simms than a pamphlet with limited circulation published by the society once the immediate occasion of—and social benefits accruing from—the oration were past. Thus, two extracts from the Barnwell oration appeared in the *Companion* in 1841 under the titles "The Ages of Gold and Iron" (in May) and "The Good Farmer" (in August), for which Simms received $50 (*Letters* 1:276).

The manuscript of the original oration is missing. Simms apparently sent it to Hammond, perhaps as a reference for the latter's own address before the State Agricultural Society of South Carolina on November 25, 1841 (*Letters* 1:276). However, comparing "The Ages of Gold and Iron" and "The Good Farmer" to Faust's analysis of the conventions of Southern agricultural orations reveals that the two excerpts generally correlate to patterns of the genre. It thus seems plausible to assume "The Ages of Gold and Iron" and "The Good Farmer" represent the substance of Simms's text for November 2, allowing, of course, for edits apropos to publication in a national women's periodical.

The first published excerpt, and likely the Barnwell oration itself, begins by focusing its audience's attention on the history of agriculture, a trope of the genre that Faust explains was intended to testify to farming's timeless nobility ("Rhetoric and Ritual" 39). Simms invites his listeners to reflect on the Ages of Gold and Iron, an adaptation of the Ages of Man, the classical myth of early human history. First appearing in Hesiod's *Works and Days* (ca. 700 BCE) and retold in Virgil's *Eclogues* (37 BCE) and Ovid's *Metamorphoses* (8 CE), the Ages are an account of the decline of man from an idyllic existence to a state of depravity and warfare. In classical iterations of the myth, the Golden Age follows the creation of man by the Gods of Olympus. It is an era of happiness and harmony; there is no labor or illness because the fertility of the land provides for men, and their innate virtue means that peace reigns. The subsequent Ages of Silver and Bronze are less prosperous and harmonious, characterized by men's indifference to the Gods and a growing contentiousness. Declension reaches its nadir in the Age of Iron, an era of labor, amoral wickedness, and rampant warfare.

The Ages of Man is a flexible myth that was frequently adapted by later Christian and Renaissance authors. Simms's 1840 Barnwell Agricultural Society Oration likewise takes creative liberties, condensing the timeline to just the Ages of Gold and Iron and positing agriculture as essential to the harmony of the first epoch. Contrary to the typical claim that the land provided for early man without the need for tillage, Simms says the Age of Gold was the "period when the great majority of mankind was engaged in agriculture" (31). He explains that farming was bestowed to man by God, "the great first planter" (31). Capitalizing on the resources God created, "kings and princes drove the harrow, and dropped the grain . . . and, for ages, the destinies of the world were happily committed to the hands of man, whose chief distinction lay in their superior use of the sickle and the ploughshare" (32). Also contrary to the conventional belief that labor was a punishment for or was associated with a state of degeneracy, Simms claims working the land was instead responsible for the virtue of men and the amity of human society. He explains that agriculture "had the natural effect of subduing the passions of men, of regulating their appetites, promoting gentleness, harmony, and universal peace among them" (31). Simms concludes the image of an agricultural Age of Gold by imagining its poets singing its "praises, without qualification, that it gave health to the body, strength to the frame, energy to the will, and nobleness to the purpose—that it conduced temperance, pure desires, devout thought, and becoming patriotism . . ." (32).

To Faust's point that Southern agricultural society orations referenced history to honor the institution of farming, Simms's revision of the Ages of Man myth dignifies the avocation of Barnwell's planters as "a divine institution" (31). They are ostensibly participating in a sacred tradition that is a cornerstone of civilization and is elemental to human happiness and prosperity. Simms's anomalous inclusion of labor in the Age of Gold also aspires to flatter and inspire his listeners by drawing on another equally long tradition equating agriculture with character. Farming's industry, simplicity of life, and insulating distance from urban depravity allegedly fostered behaviors associated with personal and civic integrity. "The republican virtues, including modesty, self-discipline, sobriety, and frugality, grew most readily, according to common belief, among farmers," observe Edwin C. Hagenstein, Sara M. Gregg, and Brian Donahue (14). In espousing these connections, Simms's Barnwell address is also part of a Georgic tradition that included early American participants Hector St. Jean de Crèvecoeur, Thomas Jefferson, and John Taylor of Caroline.[4]

If Simms's Age of Gold was an appeal to the self-regard of his audience, the liberties he subsequently takes with the mythic Age of Iron may have been to encourage his listeners to reflect on their potential moral complacency. In Simms's version of the narrative, indifference to labor and a diminished investment in the soil trigger a decline in prosperity, moral dissoluteness, and social volatility. It begins, incongruously enough, with shepherds. Once herding became plausible, the men who attended flocks "were required to contend with the yet unsubdued monsters of the wilderness" to protect their animals (33). This led to hunting, and "the use of arms brought with it a passion for their exercise" (33). Soon hunters of animals transitioned "to hunting MAN! and WAR" followed (33). Warriors "knew the weakness of the peaceful and unsuspecting farmer" and "gathered their harvests with the sword," leading to the suffering that characterized the Age of Iron: "the desertion of fields, the depopulation of countries, the desecration of altars, the famine, the slaughter and undiminished misery every where!" (34).

Simms emphasizes it was the dereliction of man's duty to labor—in this instance, hunting for sport rather than defending livestock—that precipitated the end of the Age of Gold. "These crimes . . . were the inevitable result, accruing from the adoption . . . as a trade and occupation, of one of the incidental necessities of his [man's] condition. The first ordinances of the Deity were forgotten. The decree of labor . . ." (34). Simms also suggests that an ambivalence to work, especially agricultural, was the root cause of the vulnerability of the victims of the Age of Iron. Similar to how harmony and fortitude are byproducts of farmers' diligence, antipathy to labor led to a moral rot manifested by self-interestedness and factionalism. It undermined communities' ability to unite and effectively resist external threats. "Toil had given place to cunning," observes Simms, "and the barriers of moral and physical defence were all swept away" (35).

The long literary history of the appropriation and the revision of the Ages of Man, Simms's version included, validates rather than distorts the purpose of this myth, explains Harry Levin. Broadly speaking, the narrative accounts for "how men came to be alienated from nature and why they have lived too seldom in peace and plenty, justice and freedom, leisure and love" (4). The durability of this theme despite its many versions speaks to the sustained resonance of these discrepancies to subsequent generations as well as to the relevance of their underlying causes. Each reiteration of the myth invites its audience to consider not only the original reasons for a mythic fall from grace but also to reflect on analogies in their own era. It also invites consideration of what is necessary to reapproximate the prelapsarian ideal (Levin 4). The conclusion of "The Ages of Gold and Iron" (and probably the first half of the oration) signals the gravity Simms attaches to the former proposition. He ends on an ominous note, warning that "The story is every where the same. It admits of no variation. . . . The nation whose sons shrink from the culture of its fields, will wither for long ages, under the imperial sway of Iron" (35).

Simms's grim admonishment was typical of antebellum agricultural society addresses, and, in general, the agricultural reform literature of the era. According to orators and writers for periodicals such as *The Cultivator, The Farmer's Register, The American Farmer,* and *The Southern Agriculturalist,* America was on the threshold of—or was already in the throes of—an analogous Age of Iron. The mythic motifs in the first half of Simms's Barnwell oration symbolize these antebellum anxieties. At the root of them was the concern that a century or more of traditional farming practices in Eastern Seaboard states had depleted the soil. New York's Jesse Buel, for instance, was candid with the readers of his *Farmer's Companion* in 1839: "Generally speaking, our practice is bad. Its tendency is to exhaust the soil of its natural fertility—to render the products of our farms less and less annually—until they become too poor to support our families, or pay us for our labor" (qtd. in Carman 4). The decline of nutrients in the soil had various causes, but the most commonly cited ones included a failure to rotate crops, a reluctance to let fields lie fallow, and an indifference to amending the soil.

As Buel observed, the immediate impacts of the decline in soil fertility were smaller crop yields and diminished earnings. The reformers, including Simms, also feared there were or would be long-term demographic and political implications. The availability of affordable, fertile acreage in western territories meant it was cheaper to move to and clear new lands rather than invest the time, labor, and capital in regenerating existing fields. Agricultural reformers believed this "heedless expansion represented a threat to the economy and society of the old states," explains Steven Stoll (24). Emigration by farmers from the seaboard states did, in fact, soar, especially following the compelled cessations of lands and removal of Indigenous peoples. Once-thriving communities declined as land values and populations did.

South Carolina was especially susceptible to outmigration. James David Miller estimates that "free South Carolinians were almost 80 percent more likely than other Americans to have left their state in the first half of the century" (19). A decline in population also reduced a state's political representation in Congress. For example, the South's percentage of seats in the US House of Representatives declined from 43% in 1810 to 39% in 1840, the year of Simms's Barnwell oration (McCardell 339). For Southerners like the planters of the Barnwell District, this decline in economic vitality and of legislative clout had portentous implications for the institution of slavery. Not only were they reliant on their political representatives to thwart growing abolitionist demands to end enslavement but also they relied on a robust economy to demonstrate the value of enslaved labor. Consequently, poor soil management and outmigration seemed analogous to the causes of the Age of Iron. Émigrés' antipathy to diligently improving their hereditary acreage was linked to the specter of barren fields and empty homes in South Carolina and the threat of lost autonomy. "No figure proved more incomprehensible . . . than the planter emigrant: a man who not only abused his land but then deserted it," explains Miller (48). In Simms's mythic context, this phenomenon was a rejection of the sacred "decree of labor" to pursue easier profits elsewhere.

To reverse these trends, agricultural reformers enthusiastically encouraged strategies to replenish the soil and make older fields profitable again. Buel, for instance, promoted new methods of plowing, and he supported curricula for teaching scientific agriculture (Carman 5, 6). Manuring and soil amendments were popular proposals, too, with Virginian Edmund Ruffin among their leading advocates. Solutions like these were often expensive, labor-intensive, and contrary to local tradition, but their adoption was justified as "improvement."

In this context, explains Stoll, "improvement" meant "a link between an endur-ing agriculture and an enduring society in the long-settled places"; it connoted "the changes that enabled land to be cultivated in the most prosperous possible way over the longest possible time" (Stoll 20, 21). Such intentional investments in the soil, argued reformers like Buel, Ruffin, and Simms, would thus return economic, social, and political stability to the seaboard states.

In addition to inspiring periodicals, the spirit of soil improvement fueled "the formation of hundreds of state and local agricultural societies," observes Albert Lowther Demaree (201). South Carolina was typical of this pattern. "Between 1826 and 1847 the number of these [agricultural societies] nearly tripled, from eleven to thirty-two" (Faust, "Rhetoric and Ritual" 46). Barnwell District's new organization was one of them. The societies' objectives were in keeping with the mission of improvement: identify local examples of successful cultivation and animal husbandry, share those methods and other research at society meetings, and encourage and reward the breeding of superior examples of livestock. The annual orations like Simms's Barnwell address were also important rhetorical tools to raise awareness of the need for and to advocate methods of improvement. "So important were the annual addresses that prominent men were, without dif-ficulty, prevailed upon to deliver them," notes Demaree, including Martin Van Buren, Daniel Webster, and Henry Clay (210).

In keeping with these conventions of its genre, the second half of Simms's Barnwell oration pivots from ancient myth to focus on present-day circum-stances to urge the improvement of the soil, and by extension, the vitality of the district, state, and region. Simms's estimation of South Carolina's planters in the second half of the Barnwell address, excerpted as "The Good Farmer" in *The Ladies' Companion,* echoes Buel's assessment of contemporary husbandry, for ex-ample. Simms observes that "[i]n the cultivation of his fields, the Good Farmer, in our country, is not often to be found" (40). The typical planter has carelessly exploited the natural fecundity of the soil and "has grown heedless," leading to "the wasteful manner of our cultivation" (40). Simms demands a new approach. He advises Barnwell's planters that "[i]t is becoming more and more necessary, with the progress of each day's experience, to make our toils more general, to make our tillage more thorough, more analytical, and, in consequence, more in-tellectual" (40). The specific measures Simms advocates are similar to those pro-moted in other agricultural society orations and publications: planting crops best suited to local conditions, manuring fields, embracing agricultural education, and conserving woodlands rather than clearing them. Complementing these is a commitment to the soil of the "paternal acres which bound his [the farmer's] fortunes" (36). New practices and attitudes can restore the profitability of inher-ited land, preventing emigration and its consequences and thus "bring back the golden ages of the world!" (35).

The good farmer is also a judicious enslaver, according to the Barnwell oration. Simms first emphasizes the authority of the planter, who "insists on obedience" which "he promptly enforces, without faltering and without delay" (38). He explains that the resulting respect for enslavers' authority ultimately mitigates the need for violence, for "in this way, and by this only, can he ['the good farmer'] avoid the humiliating necessity and pain of punishment" (38). Simms then expounds on the ostensibly mutual benefits of bondage. Invoking the customary paternalistic metaphor of a family, Simms imagines the good farmer as a firm but beneficent father figure who perceives "his servants as so many children, entrusted to his guardian management, whom he is to subdue to obedience, and instruct in the regular toils of industry" (38). The language echoes imagery elsewhere in the address. As a child, "the good farmer" himself was likewise "subject to the daily duties which belong to his lot in life" (36). Simms here is naturalizing enslavement as part of the obligation to labor that all men are allegedly providentially destined to perform. The planter, though, has an alleged moral responsibility to compel enslaved people to do so. This authority and its ostensible counterpart, compassion, are joined in the oration's subsequent observation that the good farmer only "compels their [the enslaved workforce's] labor in moderation" (38). Simms elaborates on this putative humaneness of enslavement, claiming a good farmer "rejoices to increase their [enslaved people's] comforts, and to behold their growing improvement. Upon this depends equally their happiness and his own" (38). This, too, echoes Southerners' stock arguments of paternalism, namely that involuntary servitude allegedly improved the moral and intellectual condition of Africans and African Americans.[5] As benevolent guardians, enslavers were as invested in this development as were their alleged wards.

The oration's characterization of the good farmer as a good enslaver served dual purposes. Pragmatically, Simms's argument reflected the link that planters imagined between the administration of an enslaved workforce and agricultural output. They believed "management practices . . . underpinned increased productivity," explains Caitlin Rosenthal (102). More broadly, though, Simms's emphasis on the character of the enslaver was part of the oration's response to the self-interestedness that Simms saw as endemic to material progress and that underlay the neglect of older farmlands and westward migration. Paternalistic slavery ostensibly contributed to the good farmer's morality and, collectively, that of the society to which he belonged. The practice of self-control, generosity, and responsibility to others was an antidote to the vices characteristic of reckless progress, including the impulse to make money at the expense of ties to hereditary communities.

Simms segues from the discussion of enslavement to other virtues of the good farmer that simultaneously encourage soil improvement and resistance to the sins of the age. "He is, himself, industrious, methodical in all his proceedings, and inflexibly temperate" (39). Like the diligent citizens of the Age of Gold, the good farmer "knows nothing of that cowardly temper which skulks from the sight of the industrious, and shrinks from the manly toils which the moral citizen delights to grapple" (39). Simms may also be responding to the popular abolitionist image of the indolent planter. (Ironically, Southern agricultural orations' denunciations of planters' indifferent management of the soil suggested there may have been some credibility to such a caricature.) Claiming the good farmer "rises among the first at morning and lies down among the last at night . . . [and] finds sufficient employment for all the intervening hours" effaces the incongruity between the customary belief that husbandry fostered integrity and the fact that enslaved people were actually cultivating the land, not planters (39). Aside from imagining planters as more rustic "farmers," visualizing their "manly toils" provides the link between tilling the soil and the virtue that purportedly accrues from it.

Slavery and agriculture were among the institutions that Southern conservatives often argued were responsible for the region's character and subsequent balance of moral and material progress. The Barnwell oration makes its case for soil improvement by echoing this traditional causal relationship. However, Simms relies on Romanticism, and not Christianity as so many of his fellow Southern conservatives did, to conceptualize the spiritual life of the good farmer. Simms likewise positions it as simultaneously relevant to improvement and as a corrective to the pragmatism and materialism of the modern age. To wit, he argues that the land possesses more than just commodity value; the planter's relationship to it enables him to capitalize on the land's spiritual capacity as well.

Like other Romantics, Simms believed that the tangible properties of Nature represented underlying principles and truths imbued by its creator. By virtue of man sharing these divine origins, there was a correspondence between natural phenomena and human consciousness. When man contemplates the landscape, the intuitive recognition of its latent divinity elevates his mind, soul, and taste beyond worldly and prosaic desires and anxieties. Simms explains that "all men, turn, at length, for relief and restoration, to the unsophisticated face of nature, and find solace and refreshment" there (37). The farmer's intimacy with his land facilitates his apprehension of what its physical dimensions symbolize. Walking his property and observing the appearance of a young plant "awakens him to thoughts and fancies . . . true to the cravings of his immortal spirit" (37). Simms posits that physical beauty is symptomatic of virtue, and the good farmer experiences "a moral grace which the mind . . . decidedly derives from the contemplation of innocent and lovely objects . . ." (42). Consequently, the good farmer derives not just his livelihood but also moral character from a commitment to his land. If he nourishes its soil, it will nourish his soul.

The oration's argument that Nature elevates the soul and is a mitigating influence on the corrosive effect of material progress is more akin to New England Transcendentalism than Southern conservatism. Simms tended to sneer at Transcendentalism, dismissing it in 1852, for instance, as "simply balderdash, and very bald balderdash too . . . neither more nor less than a laborious mystifying of the common-place" ("Critical Notices" 544). However, as Matthew Guinn observes in his analysis of Southern critical responses to Emerson, such deprecations were often informed by perspectives of style (damning the propensity of Transcendentalists to "mystify [. . .] the common-place") and resentment of New England's literary pretentiousness (181–82). There were also substantive differences between Simms and the Transcendentalists relating to conceptions of freedom as well as the relationship of the artist and intellectual to society. Simms did not believe in the primacy of the individual and their conscience, nor did he share the Transcendentalists' humanism, especially their faith in the perfectibility of man or that all men were inherently created equal. Moreover, in contrast to the New England inclination that the intellectual ought to remain independent from society to honestly critique its traditions, Simms believed the public intellectual and artist was a part of the community, molding public opinion with the help of its hereditary institutions, slavery included (Moltke-Hansen, "The Critical Revolution" 202; Kibler, "Introduction" xx). The latter issue was itself an important difference in opinion contributing to Simms's public ambivalence toward his peers in Concord.

These important distinctions, though, should not obscure the significant congruencies between Simms's and the Transcendentalists' faith in the underlying moral properties of the natural world and their ability to elevate minds and redeem souls imperiled by skepticism, pragmatism, and capitalism. At a minimum, the similarities reveal the influences of European Romantic philosophers and authors that Simms shared with Emerson and Thoreau, among others. For example, in his *Aids to Reflection* (1825) Samuel Taylor Coleridge, influenced by Immanuel Kant, appropriated Reason from its customary empirical connotations to instead refer to humans' supersensual faculty for intuiting the divinity inherent within the environment (Hochfield 40). This concept is at the heart of Emerson's *Nature* (1836). Four years later, Simms's Agricultural Society oration likewise claims that the contemplative farmer's "soul feels the force of that Divine benediction . . . written on the wide face of universal nature," that his "mind wanders among mysterious apprehensions" after reflection upon young plants, and that moral "truth lies within our hearts and beneath our feet . . ." (37, 42). As for the environment's ameliorating effect on a humanity that was spiritually impoverished by the demands of modern life, Matthew Brennan notes that Simms shared William Wordsworth's faith in "the power of nature . . . to teach and nurture the soul" ("Simms" 37). The Barnwell oration's claims that the good farmer's relationship with the environment "fill[s] his mind with religious musings" and leads to "[w]orlds of moral discovery . . ." echoes themes in *Lyrical Ballads* (1798), not to mention *Nature* (38, 42).[6]

Cumulatively, the oration's claims about the spiritual yield of the environment and the harvests of its manured land sought to encourage Barnwell's planters to confirm their commitment to their native soil and resist the temptations of easier profits elsewhere. The good farmer "seldom departs from his estate, and only in compliance with the requisitions of society and the laws," though Simms did not specify what these were (37). Simms uncharacteristically took his own advice, experimenting with manures and guano, aggressively rotating crops, and judiciously clearing land to allow for their rotation (Ensley 7, 8). Eric William Ensley observes that Simms's management practices at Woodlands following the illness of his father-in-law "demonstrate a sensibility that, while reverent towards nature's beauties, he possessed no qualms about further developing its resources in order to increase his crop yields . . ." (9). Capitalizing on the moral and material qualities of the earth were not mutually exclusive, as long as both were done concurrently.[7] However, Simms was an anomaly. Stoll observes that South Carolina's planters typically disregarded the guidance of agricultural orators and editors. Even when experiments demonstrated improvements in yields (or when rhetoric made the spiritual benefits of farmland seem plausible), as long as planters had more wooded acreage they could transform into fields or as long as fertile western lands remained affordable, there was little incentive for collecting and applying manure and waiting for its effects (Stoll 34, 35). Despite fears of outmigration or, less often, Romantic handwringing about ignoring the moral dimensions of the environment, in reality there was little incentive for an individual planter to change his traditional habits. Simms acknowledged this inertia in 1841 to Hammond, ruefully observing "[t]he accursed routine character of all our performances is perhaps the most invincible barrier in the way of our success or even improvement" (*Letters* 5:350).

In the three decades that separated Simms's "Barnwell Agricultural Society Oration" from his "The Sense of the Beautiful," circumstances other than indifferent management of the soil led to the disastrous economic and political instability that Simms was trying to avoid in 1840. Four years of total warfare from 1861 to 1865 left South Carolina in ruins. The state bore a heavy cost for the conflict that its leading men, Simms included, precipitated. Walter Edgar notes that over 30 percent of South Carolina's white male population of military age died during the war. The economic toll, especially relating to agriculture, was likewise devastating. Land values diminished by 60 percent, and South Carolina lost more livestock than any other former Confederate state (374, 375). "The fields are shriveled up in their dimensions, and the general aspect of houses, fences, and settlements—all declare for the terrible impoverishment of a region," Simms reported in an 1867 dispatch for the Charleston *Daily Courier* (qtd. in Rogers 191). Households, towns, and even the capital city of Columbia were destroyed (Edgar 374).

Simms shared in this post-War suffering. His son survived the conflict, albeit wounded in battle. When William T. Sherman's Union army neared Woodlands, Simms fled to Columbia, only to become an eyewitness to its burning (Guilds 294, 297). When his son returned to their plantation in the summer 1865, he found it had been declared abandoned by the Freedmen's Bureau. It was being farmed by its formerly enslaved workers who resisted attempts to direct their labor (Foley, "Nimmons" 98). The house itself was no longer there, having burned twice during the war, the second time ostensibly by men from Sherman's army. If "the reduction of his family to almost abject poverty" was not disorienting enough for the once-proud planter, allegations that one of Simms's enslaved workers was responsible for the second fire deeply unsettled an orator whose antebellum work predicated white male identity on paternalistic enslavement (Guilds 300; Foley, "Nimmons" 102).

Simms was not unique in feeling that the principles that ordered life in the antebellum South—those that he himself had articulated in orations like the Barnwell address—no longer offered direction after Appomattox and during Reconstruction. "In a world turned upside down," observes Dan T. Carter, "white Southerners had lost their bearings" (149). Yet 1870's "The Sense of the Beautiful" sought to orient its listeners via a much-diminished assemblage of values that Simms maintained faith in despite his losses, his frustration, and, by then, his painful suffering from cancer. Nature was still central to them. His belief in human receptiveness to Nature's beauty, the universal, immutable truths represented by it, and their uplifting influence on the character of mankind could not be shaken (Moltke-Hansen, "When History Failed" 4). Within the "sense of the beautiful lie all the best securities of the race," Simms explains. "It is this sense which develops all the soul's activity. It endows the soul with the eyes to see, the heart to feel, and all the subordinate senses to enjoy the marvellous beauty in this beautiful world which comes to us . . . directly from the hands of God" (XXX).[8] The oration also attempts to argue that this ennobling influence can collectively inspire a resumption of the domestic-based order and hierarchies of the antebellum era. For a white population nostalgic for their former hegemonic authority, "The Sense of the Beautiful" aspires to reconstitute its patriarchal foundations using Romantic paradigms. However, mindful of the disruptions of the Civil War, Emancipation, and Radical Reconstruction, Simms accommodates and attempts to leverage the recent experiences of women in assigning them the responsibility for doing so. Even though "feeling badly," as Simms wrote his son the week before he was scheduled to deliver "The Sense of the Beautiful," he felt "it is incumbent upon me to prepare my address" and its message for the sake of a demoralized public (*Letters* 5:310).

The occasion for "The Sense of the Beautiful" was the opening of the first floral fair held by the Charleston County Agriculture and Horticultural Association. On the evening of May 3rd, the city's Academy of Music was "beautifully decorated with wreaths and festoons of evergreens and flowers" as Simms took the stage to address participants, visitors, and local dignitaries ("Floral Exhibition" 2). The arrangements from Charleston's gardens provided the putative inspiration as well as a complement to Simms's paean to Nature's effect on the human soul and society.

Simms begins "The Sense of the Beautiful" by reminding his listeners that Nature and Beauty exist for them but also exist within them. By "Beauty" Simms again meant not only the pleasing physical attributes of an object but also the underlying divine qualities responsible for that attractiveness. "Beauty . . . becomes the visible representative of a principle and a virtue" (54). These truths and morals are interpreted as beautiful by individuals whose capacity to recognize them as such is developed "involving models which govern our inventions, even as they refine our tastes; which elevate our genius even as they conciliate our affection" (54). The capacity for reflection on and the interpretation of flowers and other aspects of Nature animates the soul. Again, this conceptualization is not unlike what Emerson outlines in *Nature* and what Simms himself argued thirty years before in his Barnwell oration and in dozens of poems in the intervening decades. Like Emerson, Simms explains to his gathered listeners that every person possesses the capacity to apprehend Beauty and the virtues and wisdom represented by it. However, very few have cultivated this intuitive faculty.

Simms characterizes the reasons for this underdeveloped ability as the powerful inclinations of "the animal": "eager appetites, fiery passions, lowly instincts" of basic, worldly needs and instinctual desires (44). Simms calls the opposing force in humanity the "angel." "The Sense of the Beautiful" locates this innate spiritual inclination in each individual's "head and heart" but emphasizes it must be carefully cultivated (44). The responsibility for doing so follows traditional divisions of gendered labor, ostensibly because the qualities of the angel manifest themselves "in the development of a beautiful femininity, which involves fidelity, gentleness, tenderness and love, the grand necessities as they are the grand virtues of humanity" (45). These sensibilities make women the logical candidates for fostering these virtues in children. Fittingly for an audience of gardeners, Simms advises them to train children as vining plants themselves are trained: "You twine about the delicate tendrils of his mind and heart, about his sensibilities and susceptibilities of taste and fancy, a little thread of blended love and authority" (45). First by walks in nature, where the child learns not only the names and properties of its surroundings but also by a cultivated appreciation for "their wondrous beauty of form and color, and delicious sweetness of scent" (45). This introduction to the physical representations of wisdom and virtue is perpetuated by carefully monitoring the child's activities and influences so the child can "take light, color, form, sweetness and sentiment into his soul" instead of succumbing to the temptations of "the animal" (45).

Simms begins expanding the scope of virtues Beauty can connote by associating it with other responsibilities historically under women's purview. For instance, Beauty also signifies the sanctity of a domesticity that women were responsible for according to the tenets of True Womanhood (Welter 162–65). Simms includes a lengthy imagined scene of rustic domestic tranquility in which the husband plants, the wife maintains the household, and a young daughter earnestly tends the family garden and livestock. Beauty attaches itself to every member laboring according to their ostensible Providential roles, and thus this microcosm of society "may realize this exquisite ideal of a Golden Age" (52). Juxtaposed to this ideal are the consequences if the Sense of the Beautiful is "left untrained . . . and die[s] out like so much unexercised muscle" (48). What atrophies are the virtues that the Beautiful represents and encourages in mankind. Simms imagines "the father an idler at the tavern—the mother a slattern" (49). The son of such a couple is "[a]t home a scullion; abroad, . . . an incipient ruffian" (49). The daughters of such parents, untrained to recognize the supernal qualities of Nature's beauty, become insipidly ostentatious: "Vanity, will prompt them thus to decorate their persons, as for a market, while their habitations are as foul and barren as their souls" (50).

Simms's emphasis on the responsibility of women for the moral education of their children and their husbands, not to mention their duty to supervise a wholesome, well-ordered household, echo motifs of gender in his antebellum orations, including "The Social Principle" (1843) and "Inauguration of the Spartanburg Female College" (1855), both of which are included in this volume. At the same time, though, Simms subtly acknowledges that the Civil War, Emancipation, and Radical Reconstruction occasioned changes to traditional spheres of influence and hierarchies of social order. For instance, amid his prescription for the training of children, Simms directly address the "women of Carolina," asking them, "do you not see, in the performance of this precious duty of training your young, the noblest as it is the fittest employment of the noble woman[?] You are the only trainers and teachers for the infantile mind, and when you know that the whole moral of the future life is shaped and moulded by the first twelve years, you will feel the solemn responsibility which rests upon you" (45–46). The rhetorical question "do you not see" begs the question of what other "employment" women may have been imagining or remembering in a post-War environment. The conflict itself had offered women opportunities to take an expanded role in their households, and, in more limited ways, in the public sphere.[9] Some of the latter was voluntary and reflected women's prescribed domestic roles, such as participation in Soldiers' Aid societies or nursing. Oftentimes, though, women involuntarily participated in the public sphere by assuming the responsibilities of farm manager or bill payer and collector while male relatives were at the front or after they were killed or returned home maimed. This fostered a sense of independence from men for the first time in many of these Southern women's lives. LeeAnn Whites observes that after the war, some women may have been reluctant to renounce that autonomy when male relatives returned: "The war had made some women less dependent and less willing to defer to the wishes of men" (233).

The emphasis in "The Sense of the Beautiful" on the congruency of Nature with femininity, and its association of Beauty's virtues with conventional domesticity, is a subtle attempt to deter women's interest in preserving or expanding that independence, albeit cloaked in the respect typical of the praise showered upon the True Woman (Welter 152). For example, Simms praises the aesthetic spirit that inspired the Floral Fair, which its female planners ostensibly organized for the sake of Beauty itself, "not merely the market garden, the money consideration" (46). This assumed renunciation of economic interests follows a loaded question of whether the women present would want to extend their authority in the public sphere in other ways associated with male, historically white, privilege. Simms asks whether the women present would "prefer the hustle at the polls with Clym Chowder, for the great privilege of casting your vote for George Washington Bangs, who is opposed, for the Senate, by Napoleon Bonaparte Brick" (46). Simms questions the femininity of any woman inclined to neglect their alleged domestic obligations to participate in the democratic process by reminding them that "[w]hile thus engaged abroad in loathsome associations, the beast is making fearful havoc with all your little angels at home" (46).

In contrast, Simms encourages his female listeners to imagine "[h]ow beautiful the spectacle of the young mother training her offspring, on her porch, under mantling vines, under God's grand school house of azure arch, surrounded by his great colonnades of trees, and freshened by the pure breezes bringing perfumes from those gardens which have yielded you all these Floral Beauties that begird us now" (46). It is a pastoral image also made "beautiful" by the domestic virtues it portrays. Simms's emphasis on the woman's position in the home, dutifully raising her children to become spiritually enlightened citizens who can make a better world, echoes conservative models of femininity, including Republican Motherhood, wherein women were encouraged to make their contributions to public life through dedication to their families (Kerber 202). Additionally, it replicates the template for gender conventions among the white Southern planting class before the Civil War. Elizabeth Fox-Genovese observes that although the productive capacity of the antebellum household discouraged strict separation of spheres, the gendered nature of domestic responsibilities persisted (80). Southerners, she explains, "shared an ideal of the universal division between women and men. They agreed that defined male and female spheres constituted the bedrock of society and community" (195). Simms championed these gender paradigms before the Civil War, including in his 1850 review of Elizabeth Ellet's *The Women of the American Revolution* (1850), wherein he lauded how women fostered the patriotism, valor, and resilience that led to victory in the War for Independence. From the home, explained Simms, "spring all the virtues and securities of a nation. . . . The household, in fact, is not only the source but the true guardian of the nation" (320). Simms's enthusiastic declaration in "The Sense of the Beautiful" that "the *pater familias* must be a man! His help-meet, a woman," the latter ennobled by her "grace, domestic duty, motherly watch over dutiful children, and that cheery and elastic spirit which ever welcomes with smiles, conciliation and tenderness" echoes that patriarchal order of the antebellum world of planters (51).

Simms's encouragement in "The Sense of the Beautiful" for a return to the gender status quo represents a desire for, or at the very least, a nostalgia for, a return to a broader hierarchy of authority founded on white supremacy that was upended by the end of enslavement and Reconstruction. References to race in "The Sense of the Beautiful" are infrequent and veiled, allusions to "brute and baboon and barbarous days" (52). They reflect an anxiety, if not anger, at being required to share political power with African Americans.[10] Since his 1837 defense of enslavement, Simms, like other apologists, had denounced literal interpretations of the founding documents' claims respecting natural rights. Following the thirteenth, fourteenth, and fifteenth amendments, such complaints had new salience. "We are told by wretched traders in politics, and the stupidest of all philosophies, that all men are born equal. Even if this were true, it is not possible, as the world's experience has shown, to keep them so" (48). Simms continues by arguing that "[s]o far from men being equal, it is the absolute necessity of society that men should be unequal, unlike, different in tone, temper, attribute and faculty, so that each shall act an individual part, playing into the hands of one another, in various occupations, for the common good" (48). Emancipation's upsetting of white hegemony as well as white Carolinians' (and Simms's own) struggles to remain solvent following African American emancipation and resistance to exploitative labor arrangements add a new subtext to familiar demands that Carolinians—including female and African American—abide by their allegedly destined role in a supposedly natural hierarchy. As Ehren Foley explains, "Simms's view of African American character had not changed; what had changed was the context" ("Nimmons" 102). Thus when Simms wistfully imagines a scenario "were each to find out the use for which he was designed, and pursue it, the reign of Astræa would prevail again on earth, and the golden age be no longer a fiction of the poets," he may not be thinking of the era imagined by Hesiod, Virgil, and Ovid, but of the pastoral image of a well-cultivated, highly cultured antebellum South led politically and socially by white men (49). Ironically, one that, white men aside, never materialized before the war, no matter how eloquently and earnestly he advocated for it.

Sick with the cancer that would kill him on June 11th, Simms was as proud of his stamina on May 3rd as he was of his text. He sent his faithful friend Lawson a copy of the address the next day, explaining that he "delivered [it] last night at the Academy of Music to a large & brilliant audience . . . I was quite feeble, & exhausted from delivery, but contrived, by sheer will, to hold out & hold forth to the last" (*Letters* 5:313). Simms's performance was well received according to the *Charleston News,* who ended a lengthy summary of the oration by noting that Simms "received round after round of applause" ("Floral Exhibition" 2). The Charleston *Courier* also did Simms the honor of publishing the address in its May 4th edition (*Letters* 5:313n68). Though Simms did not allude to any requests for its publication in his correspondence, that may have been a consequence of his ill health. It may have been after his death that the oration was published in Charleston by the Agricultural Society of South Carolina, which had merged with the Horticultural Society. If so, it was Simms's elegy to himself, one testifying to the transformative power of Romanticism that neither war nor cancer could kill.

If the "Golden Age" in "The Sense of the Beautiful" refers to reapproximating an imagined social order of a pastoral prewar South rather than the mythic origins of man, history suggests Simms's socially relevant Romanticism may have appealed to women in 1870 more than it did male planters thirty years earlier. Sara Georgini observes that "white women came to the fore of Simms's postwar program" for rehabilitating the South, and that the oration was part of a broader trend of texts that encouraged women to channel the vestiges of their wartime authority into becoming "savvy caretakers of home, hearth, and culture" (221). Culture, especially public memory, may be the most visible evidence of how women responded to calls to action like Simms's in "The Sense of the Beautiful." If nurturing the sense of the Beautiful also meant figuratively fostering a usable memory of a past social order, thereby providing some imagined continuity despite all the social change, then the promotion of the myth of the Lost Cause— the noble culture whose virtues were ostensibly destroyed by the war—allowed white Southern women to serve a public purpose in helping chart a new South based on the old. "In acting as guardians for the sacred past, Southern women joined in restoring the old domestic order," but in ways that seemed analogous to their former roles in the domestic sphere, observes George Rable (228).

The final oration of Simms's life may have been his most prescient regarding the direction of his region's culture. As a harbinger of postwar Southern orations advocating the Lost Cause and women's stewardship of its putative virtues, "The Sense of the Beautiful" anticipated a sequence of events whose culmination Americans are only now witnessing. "The orators of the Lost Cause," explains W. Stuart Towns, "reinvented the past and their vision of what they recalled and how they wanted to remember it," and in doing so shaped the narrative of antebellum Southern history for subsequent generations (*Enduring Legacy* xii). The school textbooks white Southern women authored, the pageantry their descendent groups hosted, and most tangibly, the statuary for which they raised money, shaped not only the narrative of history of Southern combatants but also the cause they defended. But as the twenty-first century has revealed, even stone monuments, like the spoken word, can be ephemeral.

NOTES

1. On the subject of Simms and agriculture and gardening, see James Everett Kibler Jr., "Simms the Gardener: Reconstructing the Gardens at Woodlands," and Eric William Ensley, "Farmer Simms and his Agricultural Critique of Nash Roach."

2. In these two orations and elsewhere, Simms acknowledged man's duty to God and the need for faith as a means to regulate individual behavior and the moral direction of society. However, espousing a spiritual tradition with an aesthetic dimension that positioned authors as ministers to society may have been more appealing to Simms than conventional Christianity. Simms's idiosyncratic personal religious views may also have made standard religious arguments seem less persuasive. See Tate, 204–9, and Faust, *Sacred Circle*, 66–67.

3. Simms was not alone among aspirational Southern public intellectuals in imagining a link between their peers' indifference to agriculture and their own talents, says Faust. "For the men of mind, imagery of degeneration came to represent what they viewed as the decline of Southern civilization on every level, from the erosion of its physical resources to the decay of its moral and intellectual endowment. . . . Just as society had to nurture the land and produce food to survive physically, so, too, . . . it must cultivate the thinker; his contributions were as indispensable as the fruits of the earth" (*Sacred Circle* 13).

4. Kibler makes the claim that the two excerpts from Simms's Barnwell address "are extraordinary Jeffersonian statements proving that Simms had become a true agrarian" ("Simms's 'Barnwell Agricultural Society Oration'" 2). Thomas S. Govan cautions against such anachronistic connotations that Kibler and other scholars associate with "agrarianism," noting they originate in early twentieth-century usage of the term, including by the Twelve Southerners in their 1930 *I'll Take My Stand* (43–44). In the early republic, "agrarianism" was associated with radical schemes of land redistribution, and by Simms's era, it became "a rubbery epithet, a loose, ambiguous term of denunciation and abuse" (38).

5. Simms had already vigorously defended slavery as a paternalistic institution in 1837 in a review of Harriet Martineau's *Society in America* (1837) for the *Southern Literary Messenger*, which was republished as an 1838 pamphlet titled *Slavery in America.*

6. For the relationship between Simms's Romanticism and that of his influences and peers, see also James Everett Kibler Jr.'s Introduction to *The Poetry of William Gilmore Simms*; Kibler, "Perceiver and Perceived: External Landscape as Mirror and Metaphor in Simms's Poetry"; Matthew C. Brennan, *The Poet's Holy Craft: William Gilmore Simms and Romantic Verse Traditions*; and David W. Newton, "Voices from the Enchanted Circle: Simms and the Poetics of the American Renaissance."

7. Agriculture was a topic Simms would address as a periodical editor as well. See, for instance, "Southern Agriculture," *Magnolia* 4, no. 3 (March 1842): 129–42; "Editorial Bureau—Agriculture in South Carolina," *Magnolia* n.s., no. 2 (March 1843): 200–203; and "Our Agricultural Tradition," *Southern and Western Monthly Magazine* 1 (1845): 73–84.

8. Similar themes are the substance of "Poetry and the Practical" (1854). In fact, Kibler notes that the phrase "sense of the beautiful" appears three times in the final version of the orations in this series. Kibler speculates that Simms may have borrowed this phrase from Edgar Allan Poe's 1849 lecture "The Poetic Principle" (xxix).

9. The following discussion on femininity during and after the Civil War is adapted from John D. Miller, "A Sense of Things to Come: Redefining Gender and Promoting the Lost Cause in *The Sense of the Beautiful*" in *William Gilmore Simms's Unfinished Civil War.*

10. Simms would tell Virginia novelist John Esten Cooke in 1868 that "Any effort to resist its [Radical Reconstruction's] headlong tendencies now only adds fuel to the flame," but Simms hedged resignation with advice to prepare for a race war, advising him to "organize promptly in every precinct; get good weapons, establish places of rendezvous, provide signal & pass words . . . & keep your powder dry" (*Letters* 5:131). For an overview of former enslavers' political and violent extrajudicial strategies to reclaim power in Reconstruction South Carolina during this period, see Richard Zuczek, *State of Rebellion*, especially chapters 1–4.

"Barnwell Agricultural Society Oration" (1840)

The period, fancifully denominated the age of gold, was not one of simple fiction. It had its date and existence, without a doubt, in the progress of every primitive nation. It was, unquestionably, that period when the great majority of mankind was engaged in agriculture—when there were no strifes of commercial enterprize—when the jealousies of trade provoked not to war, and its attractions seduced none from the paths of industry—before cunning had sapped the strength from manhood, and baseness had corrupted the soul of magnanimity! Agriculture, being expressly a divine institution, had the natural effect of subduing the passions of men, of regulating their appetites, promoting gentleness, harmony, and universal peace among them. The earth was enriched by judicious cultivation, and the population of the world was necessarily and proportionately increased:

> "Their harvests ever swell
> The sower's hopes: their trees o'er laden, scarce
> Their fruit sustain; no sickness thins the folds:
> The finny swarms of ocean crowd the shores,
> And all are rich and happy."[1]

The principles of agriculture were simple, exceedingly. That they might be made so, God, himself, was the great first planter.[2] He wrote its laws, visibly, in the brightest, and loveliest, and most intelligible characters, every where, upon the broad bosom of the liberal earth; in greenest flowers, in delicate fruits, in beguiling and balmy flowers! But he does not content himself with this alone. He bestows the heritage along with the example. He prepares the garden and the home, before he creates the being who is to possess them. He fills them with all these objects of sense and sentiment which are to supply his moral and physical necessities. Birds sing in the boughs above him, odors blossom in the air, and fruits and flowers cover the earth with a glory, to which that of Solomon, in all his magnificence, was vain and valueless. To his Hand we owe these fair groves, these tall ranks of majestic trees, these deep forests, these broad plains covered with verdure, and these mighty arteries of flood and rivers, which wind among them, beautifying them with the loveliest inequalities, and irrigating them with seasonable fertilization. Thus did the Almighty Planter dedicate the great plantation to the uses of that various and wondrous family which was to follow. His home prepared—supplied with all resources, adorned with every variety of fruit and flower, and chequered with abundance, man is conducted within its pleasant limits, and ordained its cultivator under the very eye and sanction of Heaven. The angels of Heaven descend upon its hills, God, himself, appears within its vallies at noonday—its groves are instinct with life and purity, and the blessed stars rise at night above the celestial mountains, to keep watch over its consecrated interests. Its gorgeous forests, its broad savannahs, its levels of flood and prairie, are surrendered into the hands of the wondrously favored, the new-created heir of Heaven! The bird and the beast are made his tributaries, and taught to obey him. The fowl summons him at morning to his labors, and the evening chaunt of the night-bird warns him to repose. The ox submits his neck to the yoke—the horse moves at his bidding in the plough, and the toils of all are rendered sacred and successful by the gentle showers and the genial sunshine which descend from heaven, to ripen the grain in its season, and to make earth pleasant with its fruits.

The origin of agriculture being thus dignified, the art was pursued by the Grey Fathers of the infant earth! Its kings and princes drove the harrow, and dropped the grain, and danced, with songs of thanksgiving, around the harvest. Their exercises continued to ennoble it; and, for ages, the destinies of the world were happily committed to the hands of men, whose chief distinction lay in their superior use of the sickle and the ploughshare. These were the patriarchal ages. Toil, then, if a duty, was no less an unadulterated blessing. Nothing can exceed the sweetness and felicity with which the poets expatiate upon this happy period. They sang, in its praises, without qualification, that it gave health to the body, strength to the frame, energy to the will, and nobleness to the purpose—that it conduced temperance, pure desires, devout thought, and becoming patriotism— that it inspired happy feelings among the people, brought the young together in fruitful marriage, and blessed the eyes of the patriarchal fathers with glimpses of a third and fourth generation. These were the very days of Astraea—the days of peace, and sunshine, and innocent mirth—of a long life of youth, unembittered by disease—health to the last—and when Death drew nigh, his approach was gentle and kind, like that of some friendly attendant, who lets down the curtains around us, and soothes us to repose. The toils of the day, in this happy period, were begun and closed in music. The shepherds led their flocks over the mountains, to the delicious strains of flute and flagelot—drew them together by the same process when they wandered, and, with a like summons, compelled them to follow homeward at the approach of evening. But the Golden Age was of short duration only. The same sweet instrument, in course of time, became the agent of a sterner influence. That which had been the chosen voice of love, now spoke in louder language at the requisitions of hate! The herdsmen and shepherds, when they became warriors, went into battle,

> "In perfect phalanx to the Dorian mood,
> Of flutes and soft recorders."

Hence the origin of martial music. The plaintive notes which had led the shepherds and their kine, and responded to their doubts and hopes, in melodious murmurs which betokened gentleness and peace, were now exchanged for those of angry warfare, wild passions, and insatiate ambition.

> "So violence
> Proceeded, and oppression, and sword law,
> Through all the plain."

The application of an agent, once so innocent, whose only language, hitherto, had been that of love, to the purposes of strife and aggression, betrays, of itself, how large and how sudden was the change which had taken place in the minds and condition of the people. But this belongs, seemingly, to the usual, if not the natural order of events. The age of Iron had succeeded to that of Gold. Sterner feelings and passions overthrew the simplicities which had hitherto characterized the primitive races of the earth; even as the stronger appetites and desires of the man overgrow and absorb those, more gentle and limited, which prevail in the bosom of the child. Change naturally follows in the paths of prosperity, and the very accumulation of wealth occasions new desires, and suggests new necessities. When men had so far advanced in art as to be enabled to tame and gather within their folds the wild herds of the plain and prairie, a portion of their numbers was necessarily withdrawn from the cultivation of the earth, and assigned the duties of herdsmen. These were required to contend with the yet unsubdued monsters of the wilderness—to grapple with the Asiatic tiger, the swarthy and fierce lion of the Numidian deserts, and to level their sharp arrows at the breast of the Caucasian vulture. The herdsman consequently became the hunter, and the use of arms brought with it a passion for their exercise. The world soon became filled with a class, of whom Nimrod, that mighty hunter before the Lord, is a sufficient sample. The transition was not difficult, from hunting the wild beast of the forest, to hunting MAN! and WAR became the next and natural employment of the hunter. It was not easy for men, who had been accustomed, for years, to rove at will, in pursuit of their prey, to fall back, after their final conquest of the common enemy, upon the peaceful and regular employments of agricultural life. The occupation was too tame, too wanting in those excitements, the desire for which had become habitual, in consequence of their employments; and they yearned for the licentious pleasures of their wild and warlike pastimes. They had tasted the sweets of power—they had acquired the appetite for blood—they felt their strength—knew the weakness of the peaceful and unsuspecting farmer, and they selected him as their victim. He was more profitable as a victim, and far less to be feared as an enemy, than the lion of Numidia. The grain was no sooner ripened, than the warlike tribes descended from the mountains to the plains, and gathered their harvests with the sword. Vainly did the farmer strive to defend his possessions. The savage, inured to arms, and delighting in his exercise, was necessarily triumphant. Butchery followed, and the devastated fields grew fat in the blood of those who could till them no longer. Who shall predict—or limit the penalties which flow from every departure from the impervious line of duty? These crimes—this fatality, were the inevitable result, accruing from the adoption, by the herdsman, as a trade and occupation, of one of the incidental necessities of his condition. The first ordinances of the Deity were forgotten. The decree of labor, pronounced by the Creator as a judgment, has ever been borne, except for the brief and blessed period described in the age of Gold, with discontent, by the creature. The herdsman gladly becomes the hunter—the hunter, the warrior—the warrior, the robber; and the peaceful farmer is sure to be the victim. Hence, the desertion of fields, the depopulation of countries, the desecration of altars, the famine, the slaughter and undiminished misery every where! In proportion as the pursuits of agriculture became insecure, the races of men decline! This is the unerring law of God's providence, and the unerring consequence of man's disobedience. It cannot well be otherwise; and with the decline of population, will be the equally certain decline of prosperity and happiness. Such has been the history of all the nations. With the lapse of the patriarchal ages, Asia, the first and loveliest garden of the earth, became a desert, or something worse—Africa, a land of howling cannibals, which it must long continue; and when, in the progress of pursuing centuries, Europe grew maddened with the perpetual and exhausting strifes between the despoiled and the spoiler, the providence of God vouchsafed America as a new Land of Promise, and of refuge to the fugitive. But in that new land—that seemingly virgin empire—what was the melancholy history? The colonists found a wilderness, but there was no peace. Even here the same bitter seed had been sown, and the same bitter fruits were gathered. The same inevitable fate had followed the same wilful disobedience of mankind. The departure from those holy laws which enjoined industry, and blessed with abundance, had produced, among the red men of the new world, the same profitless scenes of strife and carnage which had distinguished the career of the ancestral nations. It was the wretched boast of the American savage, that he was the conqueror of the country! That he had invaded a numerous and highly civilized people—that he had ravaged their fields—sacked and destroyed their walled places—and having consumed the common enemy, had, at length, in the absence of all other victims, turned the barbed edges of his thirsty tomahawk upon his own brother. But what was the history of the people thus destroyed? Were they wise—were they virtuous? For what unhappy sins had the Deity delivered them into the power of their wild invaders? Had they become inert in the accumulation of superfluous wealth? Did they disregard the wholesome laws of their creation? Did famine enfeeble their energies; or, in the sweet peacefulness of a golden age, that disarmed every domestic enemy, did they become heedless of those dangers which might follow the sudden presence of a foreign one? Perhaps, if we might trace the tale of their fortunes to its source, it would not be unlike that of all the rest! There was strife among themselves, which facilitated the progress of the invader, and sharpened his arrows. Faction strove with faction for the treasures of the commonwealth, or—which is the same—for its control. Then perished the public liberties. Then labor became a mercenary, and changed his ploughshare for the deadly brand of battle. Then industry and art were dispossessed of their fruits, and so, dishonored; and the city grew rank and ready for any pollution. When its suburban fields flourished no longer in smiling yellow beneath the mellowing signs of the autumnal heavens, its golden age was gone—gone for ever! Then was it only fitting that the mountain robber should descend to the harvest that was ready to his hands. So long as he heard from its busy streets the clink of the morning hammer, and beheld the keen scythe throughout the long hours of the autumnal day, so long did he tremble to encounter the muscular hands which grasped them. But when these tokens of sure strength and manly virtue were withdrawn, then did he know that the Age of Iron was begun. Toil had given place to cunning and the barriers of moral and physical defence were all swept away.

The story is every where the same. It admits of no variation. The golden age is the age of agricultural preeminence. The nation whose sons shrink from the culture of its fields, will wither for long ages, under the imperial sway of Iron. It may put on a face of brass, but its legs will be made of clay. It may hide its lean cheeks, and all external signs of its misery, under the harlotry of art, but the rottenness of death will be all the while revelling upon its vitals, and a poisonous breath will go forth from its decay which will spread its loathsome taint along the shores of other and happier and unsuspecting nations![3]

The Earth is ours as a sacred trust, and we must put it to good interest. It is to go through the hands of our sons, and our sons' sons—it is to be their patrimony, and is to provide the portions of our daughters. Originally yielded to man as a garden, shall we return it to the Giver as a wilderness? Not if we feel the solemnity of our trusts—not if we are true to ourselves and faithful to our children. The Good Farmer will shrink from none of his obligations, but, in their cheerful acknowledgment, he will bring back the golden ages of the world! He will address himself to his labors with a zeal which will prove him equally sensible to his duties and his fortunes. He, above all men, will be soonest likely to learn obedience to that stern religious truth, which teaches, that it is only by treading always in the path of duty, that we can promote our substantial interests. I have depicted, in my mind's eye, the noble character of a perfect agriculturist—perfect, I mean, within the limits of our human capacity for perfection. I assume him to be taught in his art from the earliest moment of his boyish performances. His eyes have first opened upon the fields of green in Summer, and have seen their maturing progress to the golden fruition of the Harvest. His earliest tasks have been to follow the husbandman, and to imitate, within his strength, the toils that he beholds. The exactions of a judicious parent subject him to the daily duties which belong to his lot in life, and to the profession which he is required to pursue. Taught thus, by early habit and education, to subdue his duties to the narrow limits in which his lot has been cast, the approach of manhood is marked by no violent transitions of his moral nature. The appetite which craves for change and various excitement, has no longer a power over his performances; and he passes into his new condition of superior trust and duty, with no other feeling than one of an increased human responsibility. The course of tuition to which he has been subjected, admirably subdues the presumption which is but too much the characteristic of all inexperienced intellect. He has learned to obey, as the grand initial lesson in the task of governing. He beholds around him the few paternal acres which bound his fortunes, and which, he wisely resolves, shall bound his appetites also. Commanded to toil, by the direct decree of God, and equally by the obvious moral and physical advantages which result from daily labor, he addressees himself to this necessity with a smiling countenance, a manly energy, a cheerful heart, and a steady resolution. His neighbor salutes him with tidings of great gain in the cities by trade and speculation—of fortunes made in the twinkling of an eye, and by the mere motion of lips or finger—but he remains unseduced. The sun, which contributes so greatly to perfect his toils, is not more regular in his rising and his setting. He knows no fluctuations of resolve—his duties are designated from week to week, and month to month, and season to season; full of variety, but always the same, and going on as certainly as any one of the thousand operations in the natural world, of which he hourly avails himself. By this stability he establishes the first just proof of his superior moral strength. The caprices of intellect are always to be regarded as conclusive proofs of an inferior moral nature. For, in the language of Samson, the wrestler,

> "What is strength without a double share
> of wisdom—vast, unwieldy, burdensome;
> Proudly secure, yet liable to fail,
> By weakest subtleties?"

The Good Farmer knows that he can only be successful by a constant, patient, undeviating adherence to his daily duties. Nor, pursuing them with patience, will he ever find them wearisome. There is nothing in nature less monotonous than the aspect of the progressing seasons, and the changing, and all lovely, aspects which they, in turn, effect upon the earth. From the world of forensic strife—from the cup of social scandal—from the loud laugh of the lively coterie—from the toils of the city and the camp—all men, turn, at length, for relief and restoration, to the unsophisticated face of nature, and find solace and refreshment; and he who contemplates her daily, discovers even in her seeming uniformities, and pure and placid transitions, the progress of a change, as constant as that of the magician's glass, and far more wonderful than any in Arabian story.

The Good Farmer stands in the sight of God, in a three-fold aspect. As a subject of his power and his bounty—dependent upon his indulgence, and commanded by his laws—as the citizens of a community, variously composed, but of creatures having alike nature with himself, governed by like necessities and supplied by like weaknesses—and as an individual man, having a duty to himself not inferior to any of the rest, and, under the guidance of just laws of reflection, happily harmonizing with all their requisitions. In his first relation, the Good Farmer will seek to know, and endeavor to perform, all the obligations of religion. The first of these is labor, that being the first law ever delivered by the Deity to expatriated man. He will know, that, without industry, all his prayers and painstaking, all his gifts to the church, and all his forbearances to his fellow, will still leave incomplete those performances which the Divine decree has pronounced to be essential. He will avoid all immoral contact and drive evil passions from his thoughts. For these, indeed, there will be little or no room in the heart of one who prosecutes his daily duties with energy and zeal. Such a man seldom departs from his estate, and only in compliance with the requisitions of society and the laws. No foreign attractions can beguile him from those fields, which, through long cultivation, he at length learns to regard with something of the same affection which he feels for the children of his loins. In truth, the children of his thoughts, and hopes, and labors, are every where around him. The old walks grow natural to his footsteps—the old trees wear the faces of familiar friends. He loves to linger as he traverses the daily paths; to rest beside the fountain, or beneath the tree, and surrender himself to peaceful meditations. It is in this way that the choice humanities grow up and gather about his heart. It is by this sort of contemplation that his soul feels the force of that Divine benediction which is written on the wide face of universal nature; "peace on earth, and good will to all men!" and higher musings than these arouse him to loftier if not to lovelier desires. The growth of the tender plant, the tiny shaft of grass, or the pale blue flower of the spring time, awakens him to thoughts and fancies, which, if they were less vague and mysterious, would be less true to the cravings of his immortal spirit. The progress of the infant plant and flower carries him away from themselves to their mighty original, and his mind wanders among mysterious apprehensions of those yet more wondrous mysteries, the Future and the

Eternal! These musings naturally arise to the thoughts of one who contemplates, long and earnestly, the fluctuations of the seasons—the beautiful forms of birth, and the scarcely less beautiful aspect of decay, in the vegetable nature. It is surely no less wonderful than beautiful to behold the first shoot, the small green spear of the infant plant, as it pierces, in April, the cold and heavy clod, which vainly strives to bar its progress into life and light. The Good Farmer is, in some sort, the creator of that plant; and this conviction is well calculated to fill his mind with religious musings. To be a Good Farmer, he must, indeed, be something of a religious man. If he has properly attended to his daily concerns, he must have acquired a habit of contemplation which suffers nothing in the visible world to escape his sight, and subjects all that he sees to the action of an equally vigilant thought. The most silent and unobtrusive changes of the season, command his attention and awaken his solicitude. He beholds, with serious eye, when the forest, casting its green mantle, wraps itself in robes of the still gorgeous but melancholy autumn. The sombre tone of the wintry heavens deepen the shadow upon his countenance, as, in the progress of the year to its close, he is reminded of the shortness of life and its melancholy termination: nor is the change in his reflections unnatural and unbecoming, when, with the opening of another spring, he glows in sympathetic rejoicing with that sun, whom he now beholds, caparisoned like a bridegroom, and preparing to run his fresh career of strength and youth and loveliness.[4] The slightest changes in the woods, or upon the fields, awaken his intelligence and invigorate his industry; and like the sailor, to whom loneliness of life teaches a habit of contemplating the minutest aspect of the uncertain world in which he wanders, he learns to study the face of the heavens, and the language of the winds, and to trace, in the motion of clouds, and the pale but lovely light of different and distant stars, that knowledge, imperfect but still of use, which warns him of the approach of foul, and counsels him to take advantage of favorable weather. The representative of God on earth—the especial agent of his will—selected from all other animals to receive his laws, and carry out to their fit completion, his divine purposes on earth—can it be doubted that the elements are commissioned in his service, even as the beast whom he subjects by his arts, and the savage whom he overcomes by his valor?

In the economy of his plantation the Good Farmer insists upon obedience. The responsibility is his, and the authority is necessarily his also. This, he promptly enforces, without faltering and without delay; and in this way, and by this only, can he avoid the humiliating necessity and pain of punishment. He regards his servants as so many children, entrusted to his guardian management, whom he is to subdue to obedience, and instruct in the regular toils of industry. He compels their labor in moderation, and rejoices to increase their comforts, and to behold their growing improvement. Upon this depends equally their happiness and his own. His example is such as must contribute daily to raise their respect for his authority, and increase their attachment to his person. He is, himself, industrious, methodical in all his proceedings, and inflexibly temperate. Just in his dealings with all men, he exhibits to all an example of justice which must be felt, and will inevitably be followed in time by all in his neighborhood. The seeds of good are never entirely lost—the germ is indestructible—though they ripen slowly, and perhaps only in the shade. He incurs no debt which may be avoided, and is thus secure from those harassing cares, and wretched annoyances, which so certainly pursue the debtor—drive him from his labors, subject him to all sorts of shifts and subterfuges, and, finally, hunt him down to infamy and ruin. He rises among the first at morning and lies down among the last at night. He finds sufficient employment for all the intervening hours. Time never hangs wearily upon his hands. He has no yawning exercises. He knows nothing of that cowardly temper which skulks from the sight of the industrious, and shrinks from the manly toils which the moral citizen delights to grapple. He suffers none of those gnawing miseries which dog the steps of the profligate and idle. His slumbers are instantaneous and refreshing. He springs from his couch with the cheerfulness of the bird, that darts upward to Heaven with the first blush of sunlight, and bathes its enthusiastic wings in the soft blaze of its dawning splendor. His habits of dress and diet are uniformly simple. His carriage and manners are direct but gentle, frank but unobtrusive. His mind is prompt and lively, while the regularity of his exercise renders his body healthful and his spirits elastic. He loves amusements for their own sake, and for the vast moral good which their employment engenders—but his amusements, like those of the ancient Greeks, are such as interfere with no duties, produce no physical evils, and tend either to the exercise of manliness, skill, or ingenuity. He does not, because he is a laboring man, fancy that books are no part of his business. He knows better. He knows that they are essential to his duties. He knows that knowledge is virtue and power—that ignorance is beastliness and shame, and that books contain these lessons of wisdom and experience—scarcely desirable from any other source within the seventy years of human struggle on earth—which, if rightly studied, will enable him to increase, equally, his virtues, his worth, his knowledge and his interests. He knows, besides, that, in our country, and in the recent state of the world, there is no excuse for ignorance. The means of knowledge are comparatively easy of attainment, and if there be difficulties, the love of knowledge will find it easy to overcome them all, even were they twice as great, as numerous and strong. Ignorance is, *prima facie,* evidence, of a slothful temper, a mind disposed to low indulgences, and a moral sense that will not often scruple, if temptation be obvious and the prospect of impunity strong. For his children, in particular, the Good Farmer will carefully provide all the means of education. Not those vicious helps in the shape of juvenile keys, guide books, vocabularies, etc., intended to make the road to knowledge a royal one, which is the pernicious sin of book-making in the present age—but those humble and much neglected books of the olden time, which first showed the way to the beginner, furnished him with a helping hand 'till he could step fairly, and then left him to rough out the rest, by dint of his own diligence and unremitting perseverance. The Good Farmer feels the importance of knowledge for his children, to be far greater now than it was in his boyhood, for the world every where around him is growing wiser and stronger, and the child who grows up in ignorance to day, will fall an easy prey to the sharper, whose activity necessarily keeps pace in every country with the activity of the national mind. Besides, there are among us, more honorable reasons for his education. It is the virtue of democratic institutions to lift the humble into hope—to elevate the worthy—to subdue the arrogant—to stimulate and force modest merit into performance and noble purpose. The honors of the country are free to the poorest son of the soil. The only distinctions which they require are those of virtue and intelligence. Such, at least, is the theory, and such will be the working of that theory, whenever education shall so far lift the laboring and the poor, as to make them superior to the glazing artifices of smooth demagogues and lying prophets. Shall he, who has the largest interest in the soil, its honors and responsibilities—shall he be the last to bring forward his sons in their contemplation? Shall they alone be excluded, by his indifference, from the high dignities and proud trusts to which the institutions of their country invite? Will he, who has so large an interest in their pride, their glory and their future happiness—cut them off from the honorable toils of that competition, which may confer upon the family name a lasting reputation, transmitting it to future generations in fortunate connection with that of the Franklins, the Pinckneys, the Hamiltons, and the many illustrious beside of that glorious catalogue, whose titles to immortality, are contained in the same charter which established the liberties of the country? He would be a most unnatural father who could consider this misfortune, and recognize it as the sure result of his own wilfulness or indifference.

In the cultivation of his fields, the Good Farmer, in our country, is not often to be found. The providence of God has been so heedful of the wants of man, that the creature has grown heedless and improvident for himself. We have very few really good farmers. Nature, the universal and blessing mother, has heretofore left us little to prepare. But we have tasked her indulgence too far, and the necessities of our condition, under the wasteful manner of our cultivation, and the increasing numbers of our population, are forcing upon us, providently, the tastes of superior labor, industry, and ingenuity. It is becoming more and more necessary, with the progress of each day's experience, to make our toils more general, to make our tillage more thorough, more analytical, and, in consequence, more intellectual. The business of a Good Farmer is not that of the hod-man.

He must think as well as plow. He must carry into the cultivation of his fields a spirit of inquiry and a habit of research, such as necessity has already forced into nearly every other department of human occupation. The topic of inquiry and discovery are not less numerous in Agriculture than in Commerce, Mechanics, Manufactures, and those nobler arts, which refine the manners, elevate the mind, and subdue the heart to love, forbearance, and that rational temper, which makes us delight in seeking, and rejoice in finding, all the thousand concealed forms of beauty which God has every where scattered around us, in waiting for our search. The Good Farmer will seek for these. He will cultivate with care the lovely objects of his own land—he will require from the hands of Commerce the gifts, the fruits, the flowers of other countries. He is, however, first supposed to inquire what the genius of the place in which he lives demands. What will best grow under the climate and in the soil which he designs for tillage. He clears the sufficient quantity of land, estimated with due reference to the labor he resolves to bestow upon it—and, at the outset, as he designs to preserve his woods from waste, he proceeds, by the only agent through which he can hope to accomplish this object, to make manure as an essential part of his annual crop. This is the grand essential which, until lately, has been grossly disregarded in our country.[5] For this object, he preserves the brush, the stubble, the leaves, and all that easily destructible matter which his more profligate neighbor consumes. There is very little mystery in the preparation of manure. An observing mind will soon adopt the best method. All matter which goes rapidly to decay, is proper for this purpose. How beautifully does nature, herself, suggest the adoption of this economy, when she every where provides, contiguous to the soil, the substance, whether of marle, clay, lime, or leaves, which is to maintain its fecundity and preserve it from decay. There is not an element of prosperity, in the whole history of the earth's cultivation, which he may not gather from a close analysis of the land which he tills—and labor, regular but in moderation, will produce the necessary exercise of thought and scrutiny, which leads inevitably and equally to his own, and the improvement of his soil. He very soon perceives and venerates that provision of maternal nature that causes the tree to cast its leaf on the approach of winter, that the earth may be warmly clad and protected from its biting frosts, while its saps descend for shelter, at the same period, into the same venerable sanctuary. As the leaf rots, the soil receives the benefit of this primitive manure, and is thus prepared for the stimulating influence of that warmer season when its duties of regeneration are required to begin. With this certain and regular provision before his eyes, the Good Farmer readily sees where he may find the substance which will always resuscitate his fields. Once in possession of the allotted number of open acres, he preserves his forest from those two merciless assailants, so commonly and improvidently employed among us, the axe and the torch. He lays bare no new fields but renovates the old by a resort to the natural comfort of those woods which he thus protects. The mighty trees which, with ignorant and savage profligacy, we daily overthrow, he regards as sacred objects. It is with something of a pang that he sometimes feels the necessity of laying the axe to their roots. In preserving them, he does more than simply acknowledge a reverence for majesty, and years, and beauty. Their preservation involves a great physical good. They are so many natural barriers against *mal'aria,* and stand between his children and that host of diseases, various and fatal, which are almost certain to follow all new clearings. Nay, more, he selects the forest trees and transfers them at convenient periods of leisure to his open grounds, increasing the beauty of the one, and securing the posterity of the other. To promote the loveliness and grace of all objects which meet his eye, is—if he be a father, and would desire that his children should grow up in a proper taste for the harmonious, the beautiful and the gentle, as much the duty of the Farmer, as it is of the Poet and the Painter. There is a moral grace which the mind as decidedly derives from the contemplation of innocent and lovely objects, as in the daily study of abstractions which have this purpose for their end. Then, as his taste ripens and his judgment expands, smooth green lawns appear upon his landscape; the trees are grouped in patriarchal families about his habitation; his avenues conduct the eye through lovely vistas, into favorite haunts of solitude and beauty, while his fields, green and golden, lift their clusters and sheaves of promise, in profuse tribute to the indulgent Heavens which have smiled upon their increase. The Good Farmer may easily realize all these blessings and create all these beauties. These make the Golden Age—these restore the prosperity of his race. Worlds of moral discovery, volumes of latent good, benefits that bless equally the one explorer who seeks, and the fortunate many who find, lie beneath the surface, to be secured only by a fervent adoption, and the patient practice, of the few natural laws which I have here laid down. The picture might be enlarged; the canvas might receive a thousand new tints and aspects, all tributary to the prevailing sentiment which makes it beautiful, and leaves it pure. But the imagination of each must fill up the outlines for himself, and if thought co-operate with the desire, and the love of truth be a consideration, then will the performance be easy. Truth lies within our hearts and beneath our feet, even as the forms of beauty lie couched among the stationary rocks, and simply waiting for the ethereal fingers of the creative artist. If we seek we shall find. This is true of all the forms of human labor; but, that which is devoted to the cultivation of the earth, into which we must all be resolved, is sure, if properly pursued, of greater discoveries. Love, Charity, Peace, Religion, and numberless saints beside, work with the Good Farmer, and lovely beyond compare is the sweet progeny which spring from their co-operation.

Only suffer them to see that you desire their help, and oh! how happy will they be to descend at your bidding.

NOTES

1. Cowper [Simms's Note].

2. Jo. Milton,—the Jovran planter [Simms's Note].

3. The section of the address published as "The Ages of Gold and Iron" in the May 1841 issue of the *Ladies' Companion* ended here.

4. I am indebted to James Everett Kibler Jr. for recognizing that Simms meant to use "caparisoned" in this sentence.

5. It must be remembered by the reader, that this address, though applicable to the general history of agriculture in our country, was yet particularly intended for a Southern audience [Simms's note].

"The Sense of the Beautiful" (1870)

The uses and the beauties of all things in Nature exist chiefly in our susceptibilities. It is in the degree in which we can find the use and appreciate the beauty,
that the one is valued as of profit, the other as of pleasure. There shall be two
persons walking together through the avenues of a glorious garden. To the eyes
of one of these all the lovely and fragrant creations which surround his footsteps,
shall be instantly apparent, pregnant each with the charms of scent, form and
color; and he will absorb, even as he walks, the flower, in all its sweetness, into his
very self. The other will see nothing but himself, and will turn with ill-concealed
impatience from the rapturous emotions which his companion will express. He
would discourse only of himself, his petty schemes of policy; his petty policies of
gain; and no divine intimations of beauty will enter his narrow brain and mercenary soul. He has only sought the garden walks for security—that no third party
shall penetrate his secrets.

This little word in itself, which we call "man," is possessed from his very birth
by two powers which seem to contend for his possession. The one is immortal,
an angel; the other wholly mortal, an animal. The antagonism between them
never ceases till the mortal shall put on immortality. The animal is one to make
fierce battle. He possesses very terrible powers; eager appetites, fiery passions,
lowly instincts. Like all other animals his paramount craving is for food, drink,
sleep; ample pastures, comfortable beds. These are his most evident necessities.
Cherished by habit, they will rage at seasons, the animal asserting itself in every
aspect of savage terror. He will take on him, in turn, every characteristic of the
wild beast; he will be wolf or fox, tiger, serpent, or cur.

These, in their blind rages, will rend themselves or one another. They will
shed and lap human blood; lie in cover to sting the wayfarer, or bark spitefully at
his heels, where they lack courage to bite. These are very terrible attributes. How
shall the angel subdue this animal? What are his attributes of power designed for
the subjugation of these terrible passions?

These are many; very powerful also, and quite adequate to their duty, if the
guardian angel does not slumber on his post. They occupy what we call the soul.
They abide in head and heart, and in the daily growth, in the individual, of the

sensibilities and susceptibilities; showing themselves in the development of a beautiful femininity, which involves fidelity, gentleness, tenderness and love, the grand necessities as they are the grand virtues of humanity. With these, at once of intellect and sentiment, the angel watches the growth of the instincts and passions in the child animal. He curbs the appetites in season; checks every tendency to excess; to presumption; to usurpation; keeps the boy, by loving restraints, from all evil associations. He confers upon him at the earliest moment, two of the gifts most precious to the young, innocent amusements and good society. In brief, "trains" the child in the way he should go. Train, you will remember is the word. The Bible does not say teach. There is the greatest difference between the two. We have quite too much teaching in the world—vulgarly misnamed education—and too little training, and this is one of the greatest sources of the sorrows and miseries of humanity!

And how very simple and how very grateful, once understood, is this task to train. You take the child as you take the vine or flower. You twine about the delicate tendrils of his mind and heart, about his sensibilities and susceptibilities of taste and fancy, a little thread of blended love and authority, just as you would the vine which you thus train to dart up from earth, to share in those bursts of sunlight which are gushing through your lattice. You take him with you through walks that are calm, sweet, lovely to the eye, and gently stimulating to the innocent curiosity which is growing in his spirit. You teach him to rank and name the flowers as you go. You have a little history for each and. you take care to tell him that not one of these innocent beauties but has been made to symbolize a virtue and a blessing during six thousand years of time. You are heedful to show what is peculiar in vine, and tree, and shrub and flower. You describe their properties, whether found in mere common, medical or domestic use, or in their wondrous beauty of form and color, and delicious sweetness of scent.

Losing no opportunity of bringing to his knowledge whatever shall awaken proper tastes, proper affections, and becoming fancies, you are even more careful to bring him into no contact which is not healthful to his undeveloped nature. You will not take him into the promiscuous crowd, in which Evil, almost of necessity, makes herself a dangerously conspicuous attraction. So shall he take light, color, form, sweetness and sentiment into his soul; for it is with man as with the chameleon, which takes the color of the leaf on which it runs. The hearts, minds, thoughts, fancies and desires of men are even thus impressed by the associations of their youthful days. Thus are the habits established, and as habit is perhaps the most imperious of all despots, so it becomes the guardian angel to see that the habits of the child shall all be good. And oh! women of Carolina, mothers and daughters in our Israel, from which so much of the glory has departed, do you not see, in the performance of this precious duty of training your young, the noblest as it is the fittest employment of the noble woman. You are the only trainers and teachers for the infantile mind, and when you know that the whole moral of the future life is shaped and moulded by the first twelve years, you will feel the solemn responsibility which rests upon you.

How beautiful the spectacle of the young mother training her offspring, on her porch, under mantling vines, under God's grand school house of azure arch, surrounded by his great colonnades of trees, and freshened by the pure breezes bringing perfumes from those gardens which have yielded you all these Floral Beauties that begird us now. Or would you prefer the hustle at the polls with Clym Chowder, for the great privilege of casting your vote for George Washington Bangs, who is opposed, for the Senate, by Napoleon Bonaparte Brick. While thus engaged abroad in loathsome associations, the beast is making fearful havoc with all your little angels at home.

You little know, mothers and daughters of Carolina, what large succor you can bring to the angel in his conflict with the animal. It is possible that your society here conceives it and hence the new institution, and this grand display to-night. It is not merely the market garden, the money consideration, with you. You aim at something more. You have felt the volume of meaning in the line—

"A thing of beauty is a joy forever."

Aye, and a study forever for the eyes that can see. Alas! for the myriads who have never seen, who never can see the beautiful. They have not been taught and trained in that profounder truth—"The *Sense* of Beauty is a SOUL forever!" For it is only when you can receive and cherish this sense of the beautiful in your bosom that you can subdue the animal. It is then that he crouches at the feet of the angel, and submits to the chain, woven wholly of flowers, which is wound about his neck!

Yes, in this sense of the beautiful lie all the best securities of the race. It is this sense which develops all the soul's activity. It endows the soul with the eyes to see, the heart to feel, and all the subordinate senses to enjoy the marvellous beauty in this beautiful world which comes to us freshly, with every dawning, directly from the hands of God.

It is through this divine sense only that we are first taught to behold the latent beauties in the things we see, and to discover and to love the beautiful in the things we do not see. It is not the mere capacity to recognize the gorgeous glory in the sun, or the external charm in moon and star and system; the grandeur in the blue vaults above us, or the wooing softness in the verdure of the green lawns which spread below. True, we may exult in the grand tracts of forest, prairie, rock and cataract; rejoice in their attractions, and find a certain degree of pleasure in wandering among their shades or solitudes. But, to feel them, we must first effect that couching of the eyes of the soul, which shall develop the beautiful within ourselves;—the grand, the beautiful, the sweet, the pure, set to grow within our bosoms, in Imagination, fancy, sentiment, warm sympathies with all that humanity should love, without which love there is no humanity.

Under the guidance of this sense of the beautiful, the soul itself becomes the explorer, and finds a new world of beauty springing about her with every progress which she makes. She sees the statue in the stone, and summons art to cut it out; sees the temple in the rock, and calls Michael Angelo to hang its mighty dome in air! What to-day was the shapeless mass, tomorrow develops into the shrine, the grotto, or the temple; what was a worm yesterday, becomes, to her great surprise to-day, a winged and beautiful creature, rich in all colors of the rainbow, a very flower of the air, in whose apotheosis the soul discerns its own—its own immortality and capacity for flight.

This Sense of the Beautiful once actively developed in the man, and he loses nothing in nature which his senses should absor[b] within themselves as so much aliment. He perceives, with each day's consciousness, new and increasing powers of perception in himself. The sounds issuing from the great forests, or the mountain gorges, are no longer mere gusts and murmurs of a senseless force in Nature, but they resolve themselves into a song of the winds, telling the story of their capricious wanderings over land and sea. The solitude is no longer companionless. There are those who walk beside him, who speak with numerous voices to his newly developed faculties. He finds the Beautiful in all her retreats; his ear opens with a new capacity for music, which enables him to hear the Spring-time chant from earth, in the murmur of the infinite tribes that toil below for extrication from the seed and the bondage of the soil. All the senses grow in turn, and triumph in the fresh delight of that wondrous fountain, newly welling in the soul, now first made capable to feel all the glory that harbors in the grass, all the splendor that blushes and bourgeons in the flower. We become sensible of the majesty, the dignity and the frankness, as well as the magnificent beauty in the rose, and it glows before us with the charm of an exquisite and perfect woman. We linger with delight to survey the fearless, yet pleading innocence which looks to us from the virgin lily. The delicate appeal which is made to us in the equal beauty and odor of the pink, moves us to place it in our bosoms; and, briefly, we discover, with our own developed sense of the beautiful, that, in the cultivation of the flower of the valley, we have cultivated a very rose of Sharon, blossoming for immortality in each loving heart and soul. It is not a mere shrub or flower which we nurture with so much care; it is a sentiment, a song, a virtue. It is our own best nature which we thus train to beauty, through every agency of sense, sentiment and sensibility, to the full development of that greatest of all human virtues—a perfect manhood. It is not merely eye and ear and nose which are the satisfied feeders among these flowers. But here thought broods with new discoveries, which bring new hopes; fancies spring with fresh desires, that take all their aspects from innocence; love glows with generous and sweet emotions, and the man becomes complete in the exercise of all his fulness of quality, in beauty, majesty and strength. Studying well the arts of the cultivator, he has read from those books of Nature which practice no frauds upon the intellect, assail no moral in his soul; teach no errors; beguile to no crimes or vices; and sensibilities, thus tutored, minister lovingly to all his moods, whether in joy or sorrow, whether it be care or triumph, pain or pleasure, that is looking, meanwhile, over his shoulder.

> "And this, our life, exempt from public haunt,
> Finds tongues in trees, books in the running brooks,
> Sermons in stones, and good in everything."

The thousand exquisite media which have been employed in developing the sense of the beautiful, enable the seeker to advance pace by pace, with all sensibilities quickened to all electrical affinities, until he ascends to the sublimest source of the beautiful, made sensible in some degree of the great original, with whom perfection and the beautiful are one, the incomprehensible but ever paternal God. The sense of the beautiful, my friends, is one of the first essentials of religion.

Now, whatever the thousand inequalities among men, there is a latent germ of this sense lodged for growth in the soul of every human creature. It is, as we have sought to show, the great business of education, so to train this germ, as to bring out its full development and perfect uses. It is a great life-long labor that this germ should be made to sprout and grow, 'till it flowers in a beautiful maturity. However small the gift in the individual, it will flourish under the parental culture. However large, if left untrained, it will perish, wither in the ungenial soil, and die out like so much unexercised muscle. Man, if he develops into manhood at all, is always an individual. He is himself and can be no other—as individual as pine, oak, cypress, cedar, or any other individual and well defined tree, shrub or flower. The modes of training must vary with the characteristics of the individual, and we must need study these characteristics, in order to [tend to] their proper and profitable cultivation. We are told by wretched traders in politics, and the stupidest of all philosophies, that all men are born equal. Even if this were true, it is not possible, as the world's experience has shown, to keep them so. The doctrine is simply a miserable *ad captandum,* designed to flatter vulgar vanity in defiance of common sense; and but for the vanities of men, the assurance would be received on all sides with a howl of scorn. The notion is in ludicrous antagonism with all human experience. So far from men being equal, it is the absolute necessity of society that men should be unequal, unlike, different in tone, temper, attribute and faculty, so that each shall act an individual part, playing into the hands of one another, in various occupations, for the common good. There will then be no malignant rivalry—no ruinous competition, while there will be employment for all in the thousand avocations of life. Were it not for the vanities, cowardice, and indolence of men, seeking ease and affluence from the toils of others, and were each to find out the use for which he was designed, and pursue it, the reign of Astræa would prevail again on earth, and the golden age be no longer a fiction of the poets. Every vocation essential to man and society, no matter how humble, is honorable, and I would as soon make my fortunes out of' turnips and cabbages, tulips and roses, as from the fields of rice and cotton. And there is no reason why farmer, blacksmith, mechanic, laborer, should not all be trained as gentlemen, though they be trained to toil; the quality of the gentleman depending upon the honorable purposes, the good conduct, the considerate sensibilities, and, in no degree upon the occupation which is pursued. The development of this Sense of the Beautiful in their souls, will suffice to make them so.

But, left untrained, undeveloped—the angel left unsuccoured to do battle alone—the boy without home culture—the father an idler at the tavern—the mother a slattern—having no uplooking eyes—no ideas beyond the bacon and collards which constitute her abdominal moral—the sole one which she possesses—what can be hoped for in the case of that poor boy for whom the angel and the beast contend. At home a scullion; abroad, even accompanying his father, an incipient ruffian. See the pair as they attend at the village, at the courthouse, sale, muster and election days. The father sprawls at full length on the village counter, half besotted and half asleep. The boy follows the paternal example. The father will rise only to new potations of fiery whiskey. The boy more stealthily follows in his footsteps 'till he becomes old enough and bold enough to take the old man by the throat. Already he carries in his pocket a huge plug of tobacco, which he does not seek to chew in secret. He is striding rapidly forward to that shamelessness which makes vice a brawler and impudence a criminal. Father and son lose the day whenever they go forth to the village, even on pretexts of duty. The voter, having given his vote, does not return to his home and farmstead. His disease is empty-mindedness. He has no one faculty of soul developed; no appetite for anything which is not specially demanded by the beast; no love for trees or flowers—no feeling for the sweets in Nature or Art. No love for music, books or pictures—never reads a book—will not look at a picture, though the divine Raphael appealed to him from a canvas all streaming with the beautiful. Yet the miserable creature sickens of his own society, incapable of higher associations, and only finds repose in that stupor, which is rather inanity than sleep. What of that father? What of the poor boy, who follows in his footsteps? You see that the angel is beaten from the ground. The beast cannot but triumph. And you see in these portraits a true history of all that pestilent curse, which has left glorious fields of God to barrenness, souls of noblest susceptibilities to blight, and the whole moral atmosphere, for thousands of miles, tainted with leprosy, and sin and shame.

What of the wretched woman, the slattern whom we left over her pot of bacon and greens? And what of her two slatternly daughters, exactly after her pattern? Show me how the woman keeps her house, and I will tell you what she is. Here all is wretched. The floors filthy, unwashed, unswept. All is miserable. No signs of the woman hand, the woman nurture, the woman heart or womanly sensibilities. Yet see this wretched mother and her daughters at the village church next Sunday. Behold them in their motley of gaudy calicoes and faded ribbons— the miserable gewgaws of shining copper in their ears, around their necks, and on arms and fingers. That miserable sneaking, but most inveterate passion, Vanity, will prompt them thus to decorate their persons, as for a market, while their habitations are as foul and barren as their souls. What the husband and father will consume in whiskey and tobacco, they waste on these monkey trappings. Each after some fashion, thus proclaims the ascendancy of the beast. Are such people human? Is there a soul among them? Alas! My friends, the germ of soul is of very little account, among men or women, unless trained and developed into the Sense of the Beautiful, which is ever a sense bringing us nearer to God. He teaches this to all our senses;—since, nowhere, in all His creation, has he failed to blend the types of beauty with every work of his hands.

Yes, my friends, you will travel a thousand miles through whole districts of our country as I have done, and never once behold the most solitary proof of the woman's hand or her sensibilities. Naked fields, naked farm-houses, wretched culture, without head or heart suggesting the slightest thought or care for improvement. There shall be no shrub, no flower, set to grow; no vine trained to rise about the porches. But, according to my experience, at the Sunday gathering you see her bedecked in all the poor vanities with which she keeps hope in exercise with vague anticipations of some rustic Darby. Nor, my friends, was this barrenness of prospect confined to the poor cotter's homestead. The more stately abode of the man of wealth was almost equally lacking in the signs of culture. It was a rare thing to see rose, or geranium, or japonica, embellishing lattice or veranda. But you meet the ladies at the dinner-table usually in silks and satins, and plentifully decked with jewels, which, for aught I know, might be as precious as the pebbles of California.

Yet, with the Sense of the Beautiful, developed in moderate degree, and the poorest cotter, wife and daughters would command better food—and the taste for good food is a moral sense—and would greet the eyes of the traveller, with a pictured homestead of refreshing sweetness. It is only to begin with work. Work keeps down the animal. Work is healthful; prompts observation; observation compels thought; thought makes discovery, and discovery, once begun, provokes desire, curiosity, inquiry and search; thus opening up, step by step, all the avenues, even to the highest civilization. Work, reflection, self-study, all implied in the desire to know, these, with the proper economy of time, provide the best education known to man. But this very economy of time, the most precious of all mortal gifts of God to humanity, is that duty to which our people have always shown themselves most indifferent.

Let us turn from these melancholy specimens to nobler types. It is grateful to know that all is not barren of culture, whether of home or self, among us. We possess many model cottages and farmsteads, though they occupy few acres. Ten acres of land in our country, with one good mule, one honest ploughboy, and judicious cultivation, are quite enough for the ample support of a thrifty family of ten persons. But here, the *pater familias* must be a man! His help-meet, a woman.

These are noble titles. Man and woman—none nobler in the world; nothing more noble, in all God's creation, than a perfect man and woman, working together, lovingly, harmoniously. He in his walks of courage, energy, industry and intelligence. She in hers, of grace, domestic duty, motherly watch over dutiful children, and that cheery and elastic spirit which ever welcomes with smiles, conciliation and tenderness. They may be poor together in worldly goods; but rich in all the essentials which make life a permanent pleasure while it lasts. Look at their homestead. See how the cottage gleams through the green woods, white and glossy. It is whitewash, not paint, and put on by the good man himself. The garden blooms beside it. There are flowers, there are fruits; and the little fields thicken with luxuriance. His horn is sounded with the dawn, when he drives afield his mule or oxen. He will waste no hours abroad or in idleness, and the honest sweat of his industry will be as so much dew in nurturing his humble fortunes. Healthy with toil, and cheerful with hope, the cottage receives him at night, unexhausted and ready for romp or lesson with the happy children. While he drives afield at dawn, you see the cottage windows open. There is a tall damsel hanging out her bird-cages. She has mocking-bird and canary. She sings, and they sing together, the song of the happy roof-tree. You see her as she comes forth into the little veranda. There she waters her geraniums, her shrubs and flowers. What a collection that young girl has made. What a property in beauty and use, simply from having forgotten herself. She hath had no vanities to afflict and make her worthless. Tier upon tier of common shelves of pine, not a foot of which is vacant, support her numerous boxes of shrub and flower. The little piazza gleams with them; the air is saturated with their sweetness. These are all acquisitions of love and maiden taste, under that Sense of the Beautiful, which glows within her, but which she herself could never define. Anon, that girl of sixteen has the breakfast table ready; when she goes forth—for what?—to milk Brindle. Jackey, her brother, brings up the cow! The chickens next are seen to, the poultry let forth, and while Chanticleer is straining his throat proclaiming the sunrise, she finds her way to the garden. There are strawberries and radishes to be gathered for breakfast, and she must look around the garden to see that the rabbits have not broken somewhere through the pale, to the great danger of her young green peas.

And so, passing from one little office to another, singing as she goes some cheerful ditty, that one young girl, with only one little brother for her ally, will pass through all the morning duties of garden, house, pantry, poultry and dairy with ease, without any real effort, having learned to rise early, being economical of time, having a mind trained to method, happy that she is doing and capable to do. There may be an hour's hoeing daily to be done in the garden, quite enough for a single acre, and she and Jackey will do it ere the sun grows hot. The dinner table that day will give you the earliest varieties of the season. The head of the family will have done his work ere the day closes, and has no doubt that Sally has done hers. How cheery is the supper table that night. All is neat and clean; all is abundant. The invalid mother smiles languidly, but happily upon the scene, and thanks God that she is in such loving keeping. Then there will be music—why not? The farmer takes down his violin, and Sally has her accordion. Nay, she has her guitar also, and with no master, has taught herself the use of both. The scene varies according to the humors of the household. Perhaps Sally will read to her mother. Perhaps the father takes down his Shakespeare (why not?) and gives a scene, well read, from "As you Like it," [sic] possibly rising to sublimer aims, will, from "Comus," give to the dawning spirituelle in the girl's mind, her loveliest conception of the Sense of the Beautiful. This portrait is no fancy sketch. Our model farmer is the son of a Scotchman, and from Burns he has passed to the grand domains of Shakespeare and Milton. "The Cotter's Saturday Night" is always read, as a sort of closing service of the week. No matter how small the cottage, how limited the resources, how humble the aims in life, the absolute necessities of life being once made sure, the good farmer, here and everywhere, may realize this exquisite ideal of a Golden Age. You shall even, in our own abased country, in these brute and baboon and barbarous days, find a few such good farmers, and model homesteads. Nay, more,—you shall also be able to find a Sally, who will rise with the dawn, sing like the skylark, rear flowers of loveliness around your walks, decorate your dwelling—yet never think to decorate herself; never once repining that she has no copper ornaments or California pebbles upon her person, to make terrible sensation on street or alameda. With her simple white dress, easily fitting, no bends from Greece, no bandages, no elaborate flouncings, no gaudy ribands streaming wide in air; and, instead of jewels, one white rose just stuck within her hair, there will be some sensible Darby who shall seek Sally Ashley out in her cottage, while the fashionable damsel vainly looks for him along the highways.

Yes, the humble cottage may be an empire within itself, when once its tenants are possessed of this Sense of the Beautiful; it may teem with poesy, glow with song, sparkle with sentiment, and all will begin to exist in the simple study of Nature through her flowers. With its thousand antennae this sense of the beautiful will develop all latent powers of the soul, the fancies that enliven, and the thoughts which elevate. They will tutor the affections to warmth and activity, rouse proper sentiments and sensibilities, purify the taste, teach consideration and gentleness of manner, all of which are virtues needed to render human nature desirable. Thus love becomes a first necessity and sweetens all the tasks of duty, while home becomes a very temple of the heart. How lovely such a home, where the Sense of the Beautiful takes all the sting from the necessity of toil. Trained in such a home your children grow up in a daily consciousness of what is innocent and lovely, a knowledge of which the world rarely has the power to strip them when they emerge into the great arena of life. Alas! my friends, for the miserable millions in whom this Sense of the Beautiful never develops. The man is a living care and sorrow to himself—and passes into the beast,—the fox, the wolf, the serpent or the cur. What of the woman, similarly untrained? We dare not paint the picture. Enough, there are no loving influences to cheer their firesides. And, still worse, their miseries are entailed upon the future to the third and fourth generation. Their boys, unless saved by special interposition of Providence, or by the power of an innate gift which is too strong for corruption, grow into sturdy ruffians; their girls into simpering idiots of vanity—sworn slaves of one or other of those terrible passions which we have personified as beasts.

You cannot too soon familiarize your young with the ideas and images of' beauty. A few even ordinary pictures on your walls, on which their eyes open every morning, will become their teachers. The Greeks understood this secret. They placed grand and beautiful ideals, perfect models, whether in painting or statuary, in the pathways of their children, well knowing that, by a natural law, in degree as we admire or love an object, we grow to resemble it; even as the cattle of Laban took their streaks and stripes from the peeled wands of Jacob, in the waters where they went to drink. Familiarize your young with flowers, trees, shrubs, the beauties of the landscape, the rosy tints of dawn, and the warm blushes of the evening sky. I take for granted, ladies, that to your culture, in a measure, and largely to your taste, we owe the beautiful display of floral loveliness with which you have inaugurated this Society. I assume that there is hardly one among you, but rears her own roses and lilies, her geraniums, and other favorites of the garden and conservatory. Think how meanly all ornaments show, the mere work of art, with such as your hands can rear in the walks of Nature. "Consider the lilies of the field; how they grow. They toil not, neither do they spin; and yet I say unto you that even Solomon, in all his glory, was not arrayed like one of these!"

And yet, unless this Sense of the Beautiful be awakened in your souls, the lilies of the field shall show to your eyes no such charm as they possessed in the eyes of that Divine Master to whom we owe this exquisite floral illustration.

Happy was Eve as a floriculturist—happy in her innocent flowers—till beguiled from their saving sweetness by the subtle persuasions of the beast. Bitter the repentance and terrible the doom that followed. She must have loved her flowers. Milton thought so. Very touching is the farewell speech of her anguish, at parting with them forever:

> "Must I thus leave thee Paradise"? Thus leave
> Thee, native soil—these happy walks and shades.
> Oh! Flowers,
> That never will in other climate grow,
> My earliest visitation—and my last,
> At even! which I bred up with tender hands,
> From the first opening buds, and gave ye names;
> Who now shall rear ye to the sun, or rank
> Your tribes, and water from the ambrosial fount."

Alas for us! Alas for her! The world's first woman sacrificing beauty to the beast.

To conclude. Beauty, my friends, implies the most exquisite symmetry and the most perfect organization. It thus represents the highest law—the perfection of moral in the being who creates, and thus establishes an absolute law for the nature of him who beholds. That we should learn this lesson and duly esteem this law, it was made to appeal, through every possible variety of form, color and aspect, to our tastes and senses. Beauty thus becomes the visible representative of a principle and a virtue, involving models which govern our inventions, even as they refine our tastes; which elevate our genius even as they conciliate our affection. There is not a bud that blows, not a bird that flies, not an insect that chirrups beside our walls, not a cloud that drifts along the skies, but fully displays its uses to the soul whose eyes have been fully opened to the sense of the beautiful—in the fancies they inspire, the tastes they awaken, and the morals which they teach.

With a single illustration—one of the humblest which occurs to me—I shall leave you to your individual studies of the beautiful. Look now—there is a flower at your feet, such as the Spring flings everywhere along our common highways—one of those insignificant forms—not finger high from earth—with four little leaves of violet—possibly five—and a tiny bright eye in the centre. It is in your pathway. You would tread upon it, but for the sense of beauty in your soul. You pause. Something arrests your footstep—some little nimble fancy, which whispers your thought, and checks your movement. Meanwhile, other fancies glide into activity, and what a crowd of human associations suddenly possess the mind! You are under the dominion of a spell of reverie. You dream—and your thought wanders back over long tracts of time. You recall sacred memories which have all been awakened by the eye of that simple little flower, looking upward and pleading to your own. You recall your own innocent childhood, when you had no fear of being trodden upon—when your only craving was to be loved—your only care how to consume the sunshine and be happy along the highways. With this memory, human forms and faces gather beside you. There are all your young playmates. They seem to occupy the places of all the little violets about you; and, as your reveries grow, you suddenly behold, rising in the midst of them, one pale, sweet, sad looking damsel—your LILY once—so real, so near that you feel that you can take her to your bosom by simply stretching forth your arms. You know her, perhaps, as the one dear sister, who helped rear with you the garden flowers; shared in your boyish sports, and soothed all your childish sorrows. You have seen these little violets strewing her grave with beauty, and the vivid fancy is due to this simple association; and when the vision disappears, you turn heedfully aside from the innocent daisy you were about to bruise—you walk away with slow and careful footsteps, so that you shall not graze a single leaflet. The flower and the fancy together, have done their work! The loving and the loftier moods are active within you. Your soul becomes lifted—your heart softened, and you feel—God grant that you do feel—that you are a better man that day!

PART II

Progress and Its Fragility

Introduction

Following his major debut as an orator in 1840 in front of his local agricultural society, Simms received requests to speak before different audiences in South Carolina and beyond. The invitations to address lyceums, historical societies, undergraduate organizations, and municipal celebrations in the first half of the 1840s reflect Simms's growing prominence as an author and public intellectual.

Extant manuscripts and correspondence suggest that American history tended to be the focus of the orations Simms wrote and gave in the early 1840s, including "The Social Principle" (1842), "The Epochs and Events of American History, as Suited to the Purposes of Art in Fiction" (1842), and "The Sources of American Independence" (1844). The two addresses chosen for this section, "The Social Principle" and "The Sources of American Independence," reflect Simms's understanding of historical processes and their relevance to contemporary public affairs. Both orations interpret the stimuli for the "progress of society" ("The Social Principle" 76). In "The Social Principle," Simms alleges that it was the domesticity of British colonists that was responsible for their successful settlement of North America. Subsequent generations of Anglo-American colonists inherited this disposition, and their regard for their homes led to their unexpected success during the War of Independence. In "Sources," Simms traces Americans' love of freedom back to Great Britain's early medieval period, arguing that the American Revolution was the legacy of a hereditary Anglo-Saxon spirit of liberty.[1]

"The Social Principle" and "The Sources of American Independence" also address the modern threats to the continuation of this national progress. In short, the moral character responsible for America's settlement and independence is waning. "The Social Principle" argues that Americans' allegiance to their homes and their communities is being eroded by a spirit of materialism. Similar to the claims of the "Barnwell Agricultural Society Oration" two years earlier, Simms claims the lucrative lands and opportunities in the west are a temptation, facilitating migration. The second threat was more sectional in nature: "Sources" claims aggressive Northern abolitionism endangers the autonomy of Southerners. Simms believed both were existential perils. First, mobility diminished the value historically attached to the home, which Simms believed was the repository of society's cultural virtues, as David Moltke-Hansen explains in his biographical introduction. An itinerant people thus imperil one of the sources of their moral character (others being agriculture, the institution of slavery, faith, and gendered spheres, as the previous two orations argued).[2] Second, the longevity of a society is endangered if its people do not assertively defend their prerogatives. The past demonstrated that complacency and deference were dangerous: "People . . . were not unchanging. . . . They either advanced or were overrun by history" (Moltke-Hansen, "Biographical Overview" xviii).[3] "The Social Principle" and "The Sources of American Independence" seek to inspire the attitudes necessary to reverse these trends, avoid those consequences, and sustain the Nation's and region's progress. "The Social Principle" encourages loyalty to hereditary homes and communities, also making the case that domesticity's relationship to the arts can influence the moral character of society. "Sources" encourages its listeners' vigilance against infringements on Southerners' Anglo-Saxon birthright of self-determination.

The occasion for 1842's "The Social Principle" was the anniversary of the establishment of the Erosophic Society at the University of Alabama, founded in 1831. The Erosophic (roughly translated, the love of wisdom) Society was the oldest of the two undergraduate literary organizations at the university located in Tuscaloosa, then the state capital. Extracurricular societies ostensibly existed for the purpose of cultivating their members' knowledge of literary, historical, and cultural topics, which probably accounts for the invitation to Simms to speak. However, the societies were also opportunities for undergraduates to learn about and practice debating other topics, observes James B. Sellers (176, 178). Michael O'Brien notes that such societies offered "a training for oligarchy," the members imagining themselves in courtrooms and statehouses after graduation (1:422). The lectures the societies heard from guest speakers synthesized the humanities with these ambitions. Alfred L. Brophy's survey of antebellum orations at the University of Alabama, for instance, reveals an emphasis on the relevance of education to national progress, social stability, and civic leadership (379).

The themes of Simms's address on December 13, 1842, likewise "celebrated the role that education might serve in leading progress" (Brophy 380). In "The Social Principle," Simms argues that antebellum Americans, Southerners in particular, are not perpetuating the characteristics of their British colonial forebearers that led to the successful settlement of North America and, later, Americans' eventual independence from the mother country. The oration's assessment of the nature of progress begins with a comparison of the motivations and the experiences of the continent's European explorers and colonizers. Simms attributes the Spanish and French failures to establish permanent communities in North America to the fact that the disposition of their colonists was soldierly. Simms imagines that the Spanish and French were brave and earnest but "lacked the only one [quality] which makes conquest permanent. . . . That domestic feeling" (80). In contrast, British colonists were ostensibly less martial in their colonization, were from allegedly less prestigious backgrounds, and were comparatively under resourced. But because "[t]hey came to colonize and not to conquer," they were successful in spite of these handicaps (77).

Simms explains that the British were inspired to recreate "the sacred character of home" that colonists had either left behind or that was taken from them due to conflict or persecution (78). This devotion to the "social virtues" that home and family life encourage were also what ultimately inspired English-speaking colonists to revolt against Great Britain. Simms claims that by the eighteenth century, Americans allegedly felt the crown and its colonial representatives were committing "abuses and usurpations" against colonists' sacred hearths (79). American patriots rebelled to preserve their homes, "the repose and security of society," not to resist unreasonable taxation, says Simms (79). This willingness to defend their homes and the values they nurture revealed American colonists had assumed "custody of the social principle" from their British ancestors (80).

However, Americans' esteem for their homes and communities had waned during the post-Revolutionary period of nation-building, according to Simms. "The Social Principle" theorizes that "[t]he latent enthusiasm of the English character, grew into flame, in that progress from enterprize to enterprize, from danger to danger, which distinguished the career of the Anglo-American . . . [and] English imperiousness became American impetuosity" (95). Confidence born from Revolutionary successes and postwar growth led to a modern-day reckless impulsivity. This tended to be gratified in wasteful, materialistic pursuits. Simms alleges it "stimulates largely, and equally, our thirst for acquisition and the profligacy with which we waste our gains" (95). The ancestral communities that British colonists so carefully established were among the victims. An "insatiate rage for gain" and affordable, fertile western lands diminish the traditional "veneration for the soil" of one's ancestors, says Simms, leading to the "desertion" of old homesteads, including the graves of elders (96, 85). Rather than imagining the frontier as the site of new communities and networks of kinship, though, Simms perceives its absence of domestic institutions and traditions that provide order and discipline as an invitation for Americans to further neglect their hereditary moral character. "In degree, all wanderers cease to be laborers," Simms claims. "Their habits become desultory and unsettled. They obey impulses rather than laws, and toil in obedience to their humours rather than their necessities" (93). Simms imagines the consequences for his listeners. "The Social Principle" invites the audience to consider "the change produced in the case of an individual family, emigrating to a wild from a long settled region of country. The restraining presence of society once withdrawn—the provocation to civilization which the ancient customs of a settled neighborhood once inspired,—at an end,—and how indifferent do the wanderers become to all appearances.—Into what a miserable hovel does the father and the husband crowd his little family, once so accustomed to all the luxuries and charms of civilization" (93).

This interpretation of America's colonial and early 19th-century history as an evolutionary—and perhaps devolutionary—process is characteristic of Simms's stadialism. Rooted in Scottish historical philosophy from the previous century, stadialism posits four phases that societies universally pass through: hunting/ gathering, herding, agricultural-based sedentary societies, and, ultimately, more commercially focused communities (Dekker 76). George Dekker observes that Scottish historians such as Adam Ferguson, William Robertson, and Dugald Stewart "believed that society was stepping forward further than it was falling backward" (76). However, the realization of this final stage did not necessarily entail the permanence of civilization. Progress became a liability if it was measured solely in terms of economics, technology, individualism, or by other pragmatic criteria. Dekker says the Scottish historians "feared the withering effects on essential human charities and relations of a society divided, for the sake of material progress, into wholly separate and self-interested callings" (83). Lacking equivalent moral development, such societies—Rome was looked at as an example— were liable to be victims of their own material success; it would become a cancer that would prove fatal to the permanence of a society.

The universality of the historical experience that stadialism imagined, and the susceptibility of progress to stagnate or even reverse itself that it posited, created the need for intellectuals to interpret the trajectory of history for the benefit of their society. Simms and his intellectual peers in the South believed that "in the records of past events lay the empirical data for the derivation of social laws," says Drew Gilpin Faust, and students of history were necessary to extrapolate them (*Sacred Circle* 73). Simms, along with George Frederick Holmes, Nathaniel Beverley Tucker, James Henry Hammond, and, to a lesser degree, Edmund Ruffin, capitalized on this opportunity to leverage historical enquiry into public awareness of what constituted desirable progress. In "The Social Principle" Simms characterizes this kind of work as a "duty," and he invites the University of Alabama's young scholars "to inquire . . . by what agency we have triumphed,—what means have effected our successes" (76). What is apparent about the past respecting domesticity is still relevant to today: "The more we examine this proposition, by a reference to British and other histories, the more certain, we imagine, will appear its truth. Having security in the homestead . . . and a farther appreciation of the vast importance to civilization of a community, at once stationary, yet susceptible of progress . . . how naturally does the man improve his condition" (82).

Simms is carefully emphasizing here the connection between man, homestead, community, and civilization. What was historically true for the moral character of the man would be historically true for the moral character of his society given their contingent relationship. Sean Busick explains that Simms believed "history was intimately linked with ideas of nationalism and progress. In order to be truly great, a nation needs to progress morally" (7–8). For example, Simms reminds his listeners that "[w]e obey the laws of progress as promptly as any other nation—perhaps much more so" (101). As post-Revolutionary events revealed, moral progress would not keep pace with its material equivalent on its own accord. Without some governing consciousness or established institutions to guide progress, Simms and his intellectual peers imagined that it would, at best, be defined by material and utilitarian benchmarks and, at worst, lead to anarchy that would foreshadow the end of the new nation (Busick 8). Already, Simms warns in "The Social Principle," the rampant pragmatism and avarice of American society has twisted notions of what its citizens imagine to be improvement. "We hear *ad nauseam,* the applause of those toils or inventions which may be applied to the acquisition or the preservation of property, and this seems to be the whole amount of our national idea of progress" (98). The desertion of old homes and communities to migrate west and make a quick fortune epitomized this: It ostensibly marked material progress in terms of the expansion of American borders and economic output, but "The Social Principle" argues that it ignored the precedent of early Anglo-American colonial history.

To avoid the examples of Rome's fall and Great Britain's later colonial failures, progress had to follow the lessons of history. James Everett Kibler Jr. and David Moltke-Hansen explain that Simms believed progress "had to be carefully considered and carefully, intelligently, and vigorously managed" ("Man of Letters" 10). Simms's and others' historical analysis showed that the "restraining presence of society" and the "ancient customs of a settled neighborhood" reliably controlled growth and change and led to sustained national prominence. At the heart of both was the home, hence its centrality to "The Social Principle." Simms believed it to be "the center of cultural production and reproduction," Moltke-Hansen explains in his biographical overview.[4] The oration argues that the values necessary for the orderly operation of society are here first taught and nurtured. Simms argues "[o]ur reform must begin . . . at home—in each home—in all homes—by the hearths we are too prone to abandon" (100). They prepare citizens to exercise their rights and fulfill their responsibilities outside the home, especially to each other and their community rather than in the pursuit of self-interest.[5]

"The Social Principle" helps the student members of the Erosophic Society, who, qualified by their learning to be the vanguard of reform, make these connections. The value of domesticity, says Simms, "provides always against the future,—makes home comfortable,—cares for the feeble,—exalts the woman,—protects her with no common courage, and hedges her in with a pains-taking solicitude that suffers not the winds of heaven to blow too rudely upon her cheeks. She, in turn, thus guarded,—thus elevated and endowed,—becomes a creature of superior sentiments,—refines the worship which she receives, and softens the stern bosom which she charms" (80). Home life fosters the human relationships that provide social security, not to mention the complementary values of patriarchal strength and feminine moral suasion—all virtues needed for moral progress. "The Social Principle" likewise illustrates how domesticity cultivates authority, deference, and duty. Simms asks his listeners to visualize a "snug mansion always distinguished by plenty,—the cheerful fireside, equally clean and unpretending, enlivened by the happiest faces, and the sweetest evening recreations,—the curtained chamber,—the decorated walls,—the order which regulates without being seen,—the authority which is felt without being heard. The prompt, unpresuming attendance of servants,—the reverential bearing of children,—and that warm but subdued current of domestic love" (82). Even the fastidiousness and orderliness of the decor reflect and inspire respect for order and authority, which itself is an exercise learned and practiced in walls of the home.

In addition to the home's ability to foster the virtues that guide (and sustain) healthy progress, "The Social Principle" posits that the home encourages the sensibilities that appreciate art, especially literature. This would seem to be a curious digression were it not for Simms's own esteem of art and literature, which he likely assumed his student audience shared. Simms boldly claims that "next to religion, the business of Literature, is the noblest concern of human society" (86). Its analogous ability to develop moral character, encouraging the individual to higher and better aspirations, testifies to its ability to manage progress as well. Simms's hypothetical household, for instance, posits:

> [i]f gentle spirits make it desirable within, the busy fingers of an equally gentle fancy render it attractive without. Vines and flowers encircle the habitation, birds . . . fill the atmosphere with song,—whilst art, with a rival melody, astonishes and provokes the imitative ability of the natural musician. With the progress of one taste to perfection, is the birth of another. With newer desires of sentiment, industry is impelled to exertion, that the demands of sentiment shall be satisfied; and thus it is that men advance, by the natural and moral process of accumulation, step by step, to the possession, not only of superior fortune, but of superior refinement. (80)

Art ostensibly contributes three things to moral progress. First, it elevates taste and imagination to a state "of superior refinement" than transcends the utilitarian values of modernity. Second, similar to other social touchstones like slavery, agriculture, and domesticity, art cultivates the intellectual sensibilities and virtues of people, offering a counterweight to self-interestedness. Finally, the existence of an artistic canon demonstrates that a society had reached a stage of civilization ripe for its culture's expression. "Literature . . . and the sister arts were the crowning glory" of a civilization, explains Moltke-Hansen, a validation of its place on the world stage and in the pages of history ("Ordered Progress" 130). Society needed to be sedentary enough, though, to foster the necessary preconditions. Hence Simms's demands in the final minutes of "The Social Principle" that we "abridge our propensity to wander," "concentrate our energies upon the little spot in which we take up our abodes," and practice "a more devout adherence to the laws of domestic comfort," eschewing the material forms of progress that falsely promised happiness (100, 101). In an evocative conclusion, Simms tells his young listeners, "I do not believe that all the steam power in the world can bring happiness to one poor human heart. Still less can I believe that all the rail-roads in the world can carry one poor soul to heaven" (102).

Though Simms was not alone among his intellectual peers in imagining that emigration posed a threat to the home, art, and, consequently, moral character, James David Miller observes that "[f]or most planters, emigrant or otherwise, their society was not dying; it was in the process of changing into something else" (58). Consequently, admonishments like "The Social Principle" "left most slaveholders cold" (Miller 58). The undergraduate lovers of wisdom at the University of Alabama apparently felt otherwise. In their letter soliciting the manuscript of the oration for publication, members of the Erosophic Society expressed their appreciation for the "highly interesting and deeply instructive manner" of "The Social Principle."[6] The reviewer for Tuscaloosa's *Independent Mirror* echoed their estimation, describing it as "one of the most eloquent and polished Discourses ever listened to in the South-West" (qtd. in *Letters* 6:59n5). It may have been false modesty, but Simms's own assessment of "The Social Principle" was more restrained. He told fellow novelist John Pendleton Kennedy that the oration was "a performance to which I attach no great value myself" (*Letters* 5:382). The pamphlet version of the speech was reviewed by Thomas Caute Reynolds in a July 1843 notice in the *Southern Quarterly Review*. Reynolds characterizes Simms as "a vigorous writer and a patriot" and claims the oration "contains more matters worthy of note, remembrance and commendation, than most of the productions ordinarily elicited by such occasions" (247). Elsewhere in the review, though, Reynolds does suggest that Simms overstates his argument. He suspects Simms "carried his theory of home rather too far" in claiming that it was one of the impetuses for British emigration and American independence (242). He also disputes Simms's claim that the abundance of western lands contributes to the desertion of "paternal estates" (244). Thus in spite of his appreciation for the oration's style, Reynolds was, like Southern planters, cool to the argument.

Simms's next major oration, "The Sources of American Independence," an Independence Day address in Aiken, South Carolina, in 1844, also addresses

American history. Not unexpectedly, this was typically the focus of a genre of oration dedicated to a national holiday. Fourth of July speakers were invited by communities or patriotic organizations "to recall the historical significance of the anniversary of the Declaration of Independence or to use the occasion to interpret contemporary life for their neighbors," says Howard Hastings Martin (1). However, by the 1840s, Southern iterations of Independence Day addresses were more circumspect about celebrating the birth of a Union that seemed increasingly indifferent or hostile to sectional interests.[7] Southerners interpreted the increasingly vocal antislavery activism of Northerners as violating the respect ostensibly owed to Southern states and their institutions. As a consequence, Southern Independence Day addresses began offering interpretations that "praised the states as the guardians of individual liberties," observes Martin (157). By the end of the decade, says Paul Quigley, "[m]any celebrations of the Fourth . . . were marked by an emphatically conditional unionism" predicated on whether Southern autonomy would be respected (95).

This political valence characterizes the historical subjects of "The Sources of American Independence." Politics may have also contributed to Simms giving the address in the first place. He was running for the state legislature in 1844, and the invitation to speak may have been arranged by his political supporters.[8] Just a little over two weeks from the occasion he wrote to his friend James Lawson in New York to share that "I am appointed, only think at this time of day, to deliver the fourth of July oration at the town of Aiken in the interior." The parenthetical comment suggests his "appointment" may have been a last-minute opportunity for additional public exposure. He had recently been speaking on the campaign trail, for in the same letter he tells Lawson that "[m]y neighbors have put me in nomination for the Legislature. They have had me making stump speeches" (*Letters* 1:419). Despite the quick turnaround, though, Simms completed "The Sources of American Independence" by the end of the month (*Letters* 1:421).

James Perrin Warren describes "Sources" as "an abstract narrative of spiritual and ethnological development," beginning with British history, then American Revolutionary history, then culminating in contemporary events (145). Simms promises his listeners that an exploration of the ancient transatlantic roots of Americans' freedom is necessary to understand the national holiday and the spirit it celebrates. "What a sufficient subject in itself," he enthuses, "to trace the gradual progress of English liberty, from the days of Hereward the Saxon, to the period made famous in the usurpation of Cromwell!" (106). It is in "the study of that long conflict of the Saxon with his Norman conqueror . . . [that] we trace the first dawnings of our own emancipation" as an independent people (107). Simms does not actually devote much time to British precedents for American freedom other than to reference leaders and conflicts traditionally associated with self-determination. Instead, he is more interested in the teleology that leads to America. Here, the "sovereign principles" associated with the Anglo-Saxons' struggles in Britain "accompanied our grandsires into the wilderness," and the "American Revolution, was but a closing act of the great drama begun on the fatal field of Hastings" (107). In fact, English-speaking America "was the appointed battlefield for European liberty" between the freedom-loving Anglo-Saxon and the inflexible Norman (108). However, now the former was assumed to be the American colonists, and the latter, the British themselves.

Simms explains that North America was the providential site for the flourishing of liberty because of the absence of institutions and orders invested in maintaining a status quo of hereditary deference, including the monarchy, the aristocracy, and an established church. In addition, the scale of the land itself ennobled the character of Americans and prepared them for the responsibilities of freedom: "The broad wildernesses of our forest land . . . were as necessary to the development of the natural man for the unsealing of his mental vision—for his extrication from that social training, which, in highly sophisticated communities, is apt to emasculate the simplicity of a great soul" (114). Consequently, "[s]eventy years of self-training, in the new world, added to the glorious inheritance of thought, and character, and ancient experience, which had come from their European ancestry, had brought out all the vigor of the Anglo-Saxon race;—had opened to their eyes the most startling visions of a great truth,—visions full of the most glorious promise,—by which they were lifted, in moral respects, very far above the great body of the people they had left" (111).

Similar to "The Social Principle" two years earlier, Simms denies that unfair taxation precipitated the Revolution. "It was not because of any miserable tax on stamped paper, or any half-penny duty upon teas. It is high time that these absurdities should be blotted from our books," he grumbles (112). The real reason for the Revolution, Simms repeats, was that a cadre of American leadership was intellectually mature enough by 1776 to lead their people themselves. "It was a revolt of the native mind of the country, confident of its strength, assured of its resources, and resolving, with equal patriotism and courage, that no nation can be permanently safe which is not under the direction of the native intellect" (112). Local leadership had emerged—"Sources" cites "the Henries, the Franklins, the Gadsdens, the Adamses, the Marions, and the Washingtons"—to assume responsibility for American affairs, but it was prevented from doing so by Great Britain (112). This was a "wrong done to the native genius," says Simms. He is careful here to emphasize that it is in "the advent of the superior intellect that we are to behold the first proofs of a people's capacity for freedom" and that "self government does not imply, as is sometimes erroneously imagined, the universal diffusion of a capacity for rule among the great body of a people" (111). Similar to the "Barnwell Agricultural Society Oration" and "The Sense of the Beautiful," Simms argues that abstract ideas about innate equality are an "absurdity" (111). Not every member of a community has to be—or even can be—suited for freedom, claims "Sources"; the best minds of a people can govern the progress of the rest in their appropriate capacity.

After a brief survey of South Carolina's valor in the Revolutionary War to demonstrate its people's devotion to liberty, "Sources" pivots to more recent history. Simms interprets patterns of events in the 1840s as posing new threats to the self-governance of South Carolinians, the inheritors of the independence-loving Anglo-Saxons, in ways that seem analogous to pre-Revolutionary circumstances. There is a new adversary that allegedly presumes to impose an inimicable authority on Carolinians and their rights. In the years since the end of the Revolution, Simms says South Carolina has "firmly and honorably held to all the conditions of our compact" of the Union. "We never penetrate the borders of a sister State to interfere with its laws, to denounce its customs, to disturb the harmony of its society. We pry not into their concerns, vex not their abodes with our surveillance,—disturb none of their securities," Simms assures his audience. "We conceive the duties of forbearance, to be quite as imperative as those of performance" within the Union, but, he claims, the same respect and deference deference has not been extended to Carolina (117).

The perpetrator of these improprieties is "the people of Massachusetts Bay" (117). Perhaps Bostonians themselves, but more likely Northern abolitionist groups and politicians in general for whom Massachusetts and the Puritans had become metaphors. In a series of rhetorical questions, Simms demands answers he already knew regarding their alleged lack of respect for South Carolina, a putative obligation due to a state on equal footing in the Union. Simms asks whether Northern abolitionists have "yielded the same deference to our intellect, the same heed to our securities," if they do "not hourly encroach upon our rights, insult our pride and denounce our institutions," and if they have "not converted the halls of our common council . . . into an arena for most fearful conflict, and the least justifiable passions" (117–18). These affronts to intellectual freedom, physical security, sovereignty, honor, and political decorum all have to deal with, of course, enslavement. The "war upon our domestic institutions must have an end," Simms demands, includes attempts to limit the westward expansion of enslavement by preventing the annexation of Texas (118). "Sources" reminds its audience that the same Anglo-Saxon spirit of freedom that motivated American patriots still lingers in the character of Carolinians today, and that encroachments on South Carolina's autonomy will enflame it. "The same sense of mental independence which prompted our ancestors to enter the field in 1776, with the British oppressor, will make us warm now, and watchful, to resent every assault upon the province of our local government, from whatever quarter it may come," warns Simms (118).

Simms leaves the door open to the possibility that the South ultimately may have to leave the Union to preserve its sovereignty, its honor, and the moral character its white residents derived from the allegedly paternalistic practice of enslavement. This may have been paradoxical in an address on the anniversary of American independence if Simms had not already established that a spirit of liberty predated the Union and that abolitionists were in violation of the national compact that followed the war. For the moment, though, Simms advises his listeners to be patient but watchful. Texas will likely join the Union as a slave state, and Northern aggressions are a test of the national compact. Simms explains, "[w]e are now only engaged in the trial of our institutions. Let us give them a fair trial. Our experiment was one of equal difficulty and novelty. We must not despair of its final success, because of the vicissitudes which attend its progress" (122). If secession should occur at some future date, "Sources" claims that Northerners' rashness will be responsible, and the potential consequences "shall mock and mortify the whole world's hope of Liberty" (122–23).

Simms thus imagines an ancient racial conflict possibly playing out along sectional lines in the near future. He was not alone among Southerners in associating national and, increasingly, regional identities with early medieval identities, nor was he unique among Independence Day speakers in associating Anglo-Saxonism with liberty (O'Brien 1:321; Martin 180). References to "race," as O'Brien observes, were "used by Southerners with marked eclecticism, though most often as a synonym for a 'people,'" differentiated by characteristics other than skin color (1:233). Thus "the Anglo-Saxon race" could be characterized broadly as "a stubborn, an invincible people—not easily deceived—not easily driven from their purpose, and never to be mocked in their hope," and "Normans" could be identified by their "despotism," explains "Sources" (110, 107) This criteria of race and people worked to the benefit of Southern commentators like Simms, who, while compiling a selective historical tradition to interpret present circumstances, could swap in protagonists and antagonists as part of an ongoing struggle to achieve the final imagined outcome of freedom. "Sources" also uses these white racial categories to legitimize speculative regional differences between North and South based on labor. As will also be apparent in Simms's orations in the late 1850s, free labor and enslaved labor were imagined as the basis of the collective character of the (white) inhabitants of their respective regions. Different categories of white "race" like the Normans and the Anglo-Saxons neatly accommodated and helped naturalize the emergent conflict between abolitionists and enslavers.

Moreover, a racial taxonomy founded on assumed shared characteristics and values eventually provides a rationale for disunion, which "Sources" tentatively broaches. Quigley observes that there was "a generally accepted differentiation between a government—the institutional apparatus of a nation-state—and a nation—a group of people who shared common interests, mutual affection, and a national identity" (65). In other words, the people could justifiably leave the government if it impinged on their essential character. Hence the validity of America's revolution from Great Britain when its leading minds had sufficiently matured to assume responsibility for their people, as well as Simms's claims that the Union in 1844 is contingent. "The common cause did not make us a common family," he is careful to point out to Carolinians, "and the government which grew out of common concessions, can only be maintained by a continuance of such concessions. The ligaments which now chiefly bind us together, are those of our political union,—a tie, the value of which, as it was originally the fruit of compromise, can never be beyond calculation" (122). In other words, it is not a covenant to be assumed to be permanent if "concessions" to South Carolina and its institutions are not made by the people and elected representatives of the North. It would not be disloyalty to the Union if South Carolina left. The federal government ceased to fit the character of South Carolina's people, and their freedom within it was being curtailed by Northern encroachments. As long as Southerners, as a people, had progressed sufficiently, and as long as they had mature leaders ready to assume responsibility for independence, history would ostensibly justify secession.

As Quigley, Michael Woods, and Robert T. Oliver have all observed, Southerners imagined themselves as being victimized in what was supposed to be an association of equals within the Union, which "must not be made the instrument for the annoyance or the destruction of its individual members" (118). Simms is like other speakers of the time period in portraying political debates on enslavement as an insult to the honor of enslavers and as potentially inciting violence among enslaved people themselves. "Our pride, not less than our securities, requires that the discussion of this matter shall not be suffered to invade the halls of our National Council," he asserts (118). But Simms, again similar to other Southern speakers and politicians, also perceived that Southerners were being forced into "a minority status in the Union" on several fronts (Quigley 58). The battle over the annexation of Texas, for instance, was a proxy fight in the conflict over enslavement. If the newly independent Republic joined the Union, enslavement not only had room to expand, but the balance in legislative power in Washington, DC, would be preserved.[9] "Without this balance of power, we have no securities. . . . A vast domain, essential to our safety, and, with time, to the natural expansion of the race, is not to be flung from our grasp to satisfy a sectional prejudice, and secure votes for hungry candidates . . . indifferent to the great destinies and the superior prospects of the nation" (121). Likewise, the Tariff of 1842 appeared to protect the interests of Northern manufacturers at the expense of Southern planters, who depended on international markets to sell cotton and consumed British imports, which were now more expensive. Simms decries these alleged "miserable abuses of the tariff,—the creation of unnecessary treasures, unequally gathered for still more unequal distribution" (119).

Simms was not quite ready to propose that South Carolina was safer out of the Union than within it—that would come in 1847.[10] In addition to giving the Union time to demonstrate its promise, he knew it would take time for Southerners to progress to the point that that they were prepared for independence. "Sources" suggests that one of the delaying factors was leadership. As Moltke-Hansen observes in his biographical overview, citing Simms's review of Francois Guizot's *Democracy in France* (1849), the orator believed that individuals of special character were necessary to assume responsibility for managing the destiny of a society. "'[T]he true governor, as [Thomas] Carlyle call[ed] him—the king man—' guided rather than impeded the forces of change and progress" (xvii). However, these figures in the South were lacking, especially compared to their Revolutionary predecessors. Simms believed that "most politicians failed as representatives because they were too careerist and not sufficiently visionary and decisive," explain Kibler and Moltke-Hansen ("Man of Letters" 3). Simms imagines someone who will serve the interests of the South alone, and like Patrick Henry and his generation, rally Southerners to a common understanding of their shared interests and mobilize their strength in the spirit of Anglo-Saxon struggle. Simms imagines a "statesman, who, armed only with the sufficient spear of truth, shall make a political progress among us—who shall devote his genius and his life to this consummation,—whose eloquence shall bind conflicting parties,—who shall compel the deference of sordid politicians,—and teach, with the eloquence of a perfect faith, the single principle, 'the South, and the South all together,'— and shall succeed in rallying our united powers in the great domestic issues which are before us . . ." (120). Noteworthy here is the distinction Simms draws between the "sordid" politician and a statesman characterized by his "genius."

Simms might have had in mind his friend James Henry Hammond, then governor of South Carolina, as such a leader. It is also possible that Simms was branding himself as a statesman that would represent the interests and the character of his potential constituents (and like-minded people elsewhere) rather than those of South Carolina's political factions. However, it is equally plausible Simms was imagining public intellectuals like himself and his "sacred circle" (including Tucker, Holmes, and Ruffin as well as Hammond) as encouraging a regional consciousness among Southerners as well as their awareness of their rights and the threat posed to them. Simms wonders aloud whether there exists "some one great patriarchal mind among us . . . with the view to this glorious consummation!" (119). He reflects on the possibilities of the present situation: "why should there not be gatherings of the people,—and great orators—in this[?]" (119). Like the statesman's "eloquence [that] shall bind conflicting parties," similar to his ability to "teach, with the eloquence of a perfect faith," and akin to his "deep thought and searching eloquence," public intellectuals possess the vision, articulateness, and persuasiveness that are the requisite qualities for leadership (120, 112). Simms may be trying to demonstrate, as Warren observes was typical of public intellectuals and public speakers of this time period, that "through eloquence, the prophetic genius exercises a quasi-sacred form of stewardship on the audience" (143).

Campaigning for office or his desire to influence audiences beyond Aiken may have informed Simms's agreement to have the oration published by Aiken's town council. The pamphlet was in proofs by the end of July and was printed by August 12 (*Letters* 1:428, 430). Simms apparently sent a copy to *The Charleston Mercury,* if not other newspapers, whose August 19, 1844, review observed that "[t]he sketch of the progress of Anglo-Saxon liberty . . . is full of animation and freshness." In what Simms may have imagined was an endorsement of his ideas, if not his eloquence, the paper quoted at length the end of the oration, given its relevance to "subjects of present interest . . . which will be found worthy of study" (2).

Simms's orations of the early 1840s reflect his abiding interest in history, but also the purposes for which he used it. The cycle of history and the character of people were means of understanding the laws that governed present-day circumstances: They revealed warning signs, and they suggested opportunities for moral progress. Public speaking was certainly not the only way by which Simms aspired to share these messages directly with the public whose minds he sought to shape.[11] But due to the prestige conferred upon oratory, especially in the antebellum South, his addresses assumed a cachet not associated with even the cultural periodicals he edited. But as Miller recognizes, Southerners seemed less inclined to heed admonitions about moral progress or the circumstances affecting it. The opportunities afforded by migration to the Old Southwest, especially relating to the sustained profitability of enslavement, not to mention the racial privilege founded on it, mitigated receptiveness to the problems that history suggested accompanied geographic mobility. Simms found more ready listeners in his interpretation of the Nation's revolutionary past as a justification for Southern independence. On this topic, Simms's message dovetailed with the interests of enslavers. Later in the 1840s and into the 1850s, Southern radicals would assert that "slavery and the civilization that had developed around it provided the South with a distinctive national identity," one that "warranted—even demanded— political independence" (Quigley 50). Simms would continue to advocate for this distinctive identity for the rest of his career.

NOTES

1. As David Moltke-Hansen has carefully documented in "Southern Literary Horizons in Young America," Simms was indebted to Sir Walter Scott's Border Romances

for his historical models of ethnicity, if not his stadialist vision of history itself. For more information on antebellum uses of medieval ethnicity in general, see Ritchie Devon Watson, *Normans and Saxons*, and Michael O'Brien, *Conjectures of Order*, especially chapter five.

2. The social costs of emigration to the Old Southwest were a persistent theme of Simms's work, especially in the 1830s and '40s. In addition to Simms's address to the Barnwell District Agricultural Society in part I of this volume, see also Simms's 1831 series of travel essays, *Notes of a Small Tourist* in *The Charleston City Gazette*, especially "No. 3" and "No. 9," collected in *Letters* 1:10–38; his poem "The Western Immigrants" in the June 1836 *Southern Literary Journal*; his essay, "The Spirit of Emigration," also in the June 1836 *Southern Literary Journal*; and chapter IX, "The Emigrants," of his 1838 novel, *Richard Hurdis: A Tale of Alabama*.

3. Moltke-Hansen's essay "Ordered Progress: The Historical Philosophy of William Gilmore Simms" remains the most comprehensive and succinct overview of Simms's understanding of progress. Chapters Four through Six of Adam Tate's *Conservatism and Southern Intellectuals* is a broader comparative overview.

4. Simms's 1850 review of Elizabeth Fries Ellet's *The Women of the Revolution* (1850) offers the most thorough discussion of his perspectives on the social and cultural relevance of the household that he maintained throughout his life.

5. For Simms, freedom did not exist outside of a network of social relationships and was only granted in the degree to which it could be assumed and exercised responsibly. See Moltke-Hansen, "Ordered Progress," 126; Tate, *Conservatism and Southern Intellectuals*, especially 196–97; and Faust, *Sacred Circle*, 84.

6. Michael O'Brien cautions against assuming that the publication of an oration as a pamphlet is suggestive of its quality, wryly noting that "ubiquity had a way of disguising significance" (1:527). James Perrin Warren suggests more personal and pragmatic criteria for Simms's choices whether to allow his orations to be published by the sponsoring organizations. If Simms did not plan to use the oration again in front of an audience or if it was written for a specific occasion, he tended to agree to its publication. If he imagined using it again or adapting for another genre, he would decline (153). This explains the contrast between "The Social Principle" and "The Epochs and Events of American History, as Suited to the Purposes of Art in Fiction," the orations he presented to the Tuscaloosa Lyceum on December 15 and 16, the latter manuscripts of which he retained. They were the basis for the essays that appeared in seven issues of *The Southern and Western Monthly Magazine and Review* in 1845 and *Views and Reviews in American Literature, History and Fiction, First Series* in the same year (*Letters* 1:287n117).

7. James Perrin Warren's *Culture of Eloquence* outlines the structural conventions of the genre of Independence Day orations, and Howard Hastings Martin's *Orations on the Anniversary of American Independence* is a thorough analysis of the genre's customary themes.

8. Jon L. Wakelyn interprets *Sources* as a political speech, albeit one in support of Robert Barnwell Rhett's growing radicalism and as an "opportunity to wrest political power from [John C.] Calhoun," whom Simms perceived to be a threat to the career of his friend Hammond (92). In contrast to Wakelyn's interpretation of Simms's association with a "new radical sentiment," John W. Higham argues Simms "stood squarely against

state resistance" proposed by Rhett, instead positioning Simms as a cooperationist seeking to build regional unity, which the oration bears out (Wakelyn 94; Higham 215). Simms seems to have been invited to speak at Aiken's Independence Day celebration in 1842, but apparently deferred—and postponed his run for state legislature that year—due to a bout of depression following the death of a daughter in April (*Letters* 1:304; Guilds 234–35).

9. For Simms's evolving views on Texas, see Wakelyn, *The Politics of a Literary Man*, 95, 98.

10. John W. Higham offers that it was not until 1847 that Simms "had come to regard it [disunion] as ultimately inevitable, although not immediately desirable" (220). By 1850, Higham observes, Simms "repudiated all further compromise" and lost patience with political parties "as obstacles in the way of southern unification and independence" (220).

11. Orations were certainly not the only means by which Simms aspired to be an intellectual steward of the American South and sought to steer the progress of the region. He was editor of *The Magnolia* when he gave "The Social Principle" and, according to William Stanley Hoole, was guest editing *The Orion* when he gave "The Sources of Independence" (50, 51). For an excellent analysis of Simms's career as an intellectual steward in periodicals, see Kibler and Moltke-Hansen, "Introduction: The Man of Letters as Critic" in *William Gilmore Simms's Selected Reviews on Literature and Civilization*.

"The Social Principle" (1842)

It is now nearly twenty years, my friends, since the individual who addresses you, first made his acquaintance with your city; and that glance at our mutual past, which the present visit has occasioned, discovers a strange similitude in our common fortunes. What I am in the regards of my friends and countrymen,—whether well or ill-deserved,—is sufficiently attested by my presence here, in the midst of such an assembly,—engaged in the honorable duty which your gracious opinion has confided to my hands. But, in the proud fortunes of the community by which I am surrounded,—remembering what she was in that day of my obscurity,—I am forcibly impressed with those wondrous effects of time, which we never so clearly understand as when they are somewhat associated with our individual experience. Little did I imagine that the rude and scattered hamlet which I then surveyed,—a fragmentary form, not half made up,—was, in so short a space of time, to become so eminent a city;—her dwellings informed by intellect and enlivened by society;   her sons refined by education,—her daughters ennobled by sentiment;—Learning at home, with an allotted and noble mansion in her high places, and Taste secure in her dominions of equal peace and prosperity. Still less was it in my thought, that, in that same little space of time, the unknown and obscure boy who then beheld her in that unimproved condition, was to be summoned from his distant home in Carolina, to minister at her most sacred anniversary,—to prepare the altar for the offerings of her infant literature,—and to join with her sons in the holy sacrifice to that Genius, equally proud and pure, in whose honor the song of the bard, and the voice of the orator, "never should be mute."

Then—a decapitated Colossus—the forest tree lay prostrate before her threshold,—the wild vine swung luxuriantly across her pathway,—and, at the close of evening, the long howl of the wolf might be heard, as he hungered upon the edges of the forest for the prey that lay within her tents. Scarcely less wild, in its unpruned, uncultivated condition, was the mind of that youthful spectator,—cumbered by fragmentary materials of thought,—choked by the tangled vines of erroneous speculation, and haunted by passions, which, like so many wolves, lurked, in ready waiting, for their unsuspecting prey.

The egotism of this comparison will be forgiven for its truth. We are now, both of us, to a certain extent, free from these incumbrances and enemies. The danger is withdrawn from our immediate neighborhood,—the pathway is open for our present footsteps. The security which waits on social order, has rendered your avenues peaceful; and the passions in my bosom, if not entirely overcome, are, I trust, kept in subjection to those ordinances of God and society, which alone preserve in freedom the community and the man. We have both succeeded to that condition of prosperity, which enables us sometimes to rise from the immediate struggle, and to look around us with the eye of a well-satisfied contemplation; and it becomes us to inquire, as a matter of equal duty and acknowledgment, by what agency we have triumphed,—what means have effected our successes,—and why, indeed, we are now assembled here. The inquiry is not one of very serious difficulty. The answer in one case will naturally be suggestive of the other. To account for the successes of individual mind, will go far to account for those of the community; and the history of a community, will, in turn, measurably illustrate the progress of its individual minds. Your prosperity is the due result of whatsoever degree of thought has been expended upon your progress, and whatever measure of energy has been concentrated upon the plans and purposes of your intellect. The same causes which lead to prosperity will secure permanence. Unhappily, for great cities and great nations, they do not always perceive, or do not always regard, with sufficient respect, a truth so equally valuable and obvious. It is only by venerating the mind which has made, that the works of mind may be preserved, unimpaired, for posterity.

This glance at our mutual past awakens many reflections, the principal of which, as it relates to that strange philosophical romance, the progress of society, may well enchain our attention, and constitute the legitimate topic of our present essay. Traversing the then dreary wastes of this south-western region,—contemplating with a superior sense of awe the numerous cities of her solitude,—the recollections of her European history rushed through my thoughts, and in recalling the course of French, Spanish and British invasion, through the then spacious empire called Florida, I was struck with the remarkable fact, that, of the efforts of these three powerful nations, to establish the banner of Civilization within this wondrous province, two of them should so utterly have failed. That a nation, in that day of such gigantic powers,—endued with such superhuman energies, as Spain,—grasping at the acquisition of territory, with a tenacity which looked less like policy than passion;—that a people of such constitutional ardor as the French,—so capable of endurance in the prosecution of a favorite purpose,—so full of resource in finding means of progress, and in providing against defeat—that neither of these should have been able to secure themselves in the homes which they overran,—and that it should be left to a race of traders—fewer in number—poorer in purse and spirit—less practised in war—less fervent in zeal—to achieve the conquest in which they found nothing but defeat,—would seem a difficult problem for the solution of the philosopher. And yet, I fancy, that a just survey of the true objects of these several nations, and of the usual progress of society among them, will lessen, if not entirely remove, this difficulty. The solution may be found in a single sentence. While the Spaniards and the French, in the new world, sought either for gold, for slaves, or for conquest, the English sought for nothing but a home. While Ponce de Leon, in the decline of life, when the place of his abode should have been already endeared to him, close almost as the human affections which Time had consecrated to his need,—abandons all in a wild and visionary search after delusive waters, which are to reverse the usual destiny of man, and lift him to the condition of immortality;—while De Soto,—blest with those ties which love should have rivetted to his soul, dear as its own vital springs,—abandons wife, family, friends and security,—those very things for which man is alone justified in departing from his birth-place;—while similar purposes, in like manner, invite to the new world the arms of thousands more, French and Spanish,—we are constrained to perceive, in the aims and objects of the British colonists, nothing wild, nothing irrational—no purposes not plausible, no plans not feasible—no design not comprehended within the well-recognized wants of a free and wholesome state of society. They came to colonize and not to conquer, though, in effecting the one object, they necessarily secured the other. In this simple fact consists the great secret of their success. The purposes of society are the most rational, perhaps the only rational, in which man can ever engage. His nature constitutes him for these purposes, and their very prosecution, without any other object, includes a virtual promise of security for his possessions and his life. His instincts acknowledge these truths even where his mind fails to examine them, and he tacitly yields himself to the sway of a government, in which these objects seem to be the most thoroughly guarantied, as well by the common sympathies as by the common law.

And yet, if we compare the people of these three countries, according to their own standards, so far as relates to their usual moral and education, we shall find the superiority to rest, almost entirely, with the unsuccessful adventurers. With De Soto came the nobility of Spain—her cavaliers and courtiers—prime warriors and distinguished gentlemen. The French adventurers were, in like manner, accomplished in arts and arms—noble in birth and bearing—graceful and courteous—and with an ambition sufficiently lofty, to give a seeming elevation to their most inferior pursuits. Both nations professed a religion, which, mingling with the enterprise in hand, imparts, more than any other influence, zeal and confidence to the soul of the individual. Nor did their superiority rest here. The sanction of their respective sovereigns—their friendly countenance, and, frequently, fostering provision,—added an importance and dignity to their commissions, which alone might have afforded them the happiest auguries of success. Very different, indeed, was it with the English colonists. These were generally a destitute, if not a dissolute people. They did not by any means represent the learning, the tastes, or the accomplishments of the mother country. Roundheads or Cavaliers, they came still as mere private adventurers—few in number, homeless and houseless,—sometimes the rebel fugitives of a lost battle, sometimes the profligates of a prison,—men seeking safety, peace, home, liberty,—not plunder, not conquest, not the vain honors of a mistaken and misnamed renown. As in the instance of the Puritans, so far from receiving government assistance, they were rather in danger of her chains. This was a fierce, intractable sect,—restive under any rule,—sullen and dogged,—rude and stubborn,—but having that hearty English sense of the social virtues, which is the true bond of union by which a nation is strengthened for gigantic purposes. The Cavaliers, whether of Virginia or Carolina—thoroughly different in their general characteristics— more lavish—given to more license of morals and manners—practised more in the vices as well as in the graces of Courts—and with a less rigid adherence to the Dii Penates, than distinguished the eastern colonies,—were yet not without their sense of what is due to the sacred character of home. After long, feverish and fearful strifes, they sought equally its security and repose. They had been tainted by a pernicious familiarity with the French and Italian customs of the sixteenth and seventeenth centuries,—they had drunk deeply of the excesses of a monarch, whom they had served with a too unscrupulous and unmerited devotion,—but they had never entirely surrendered that wholesome English feeling, which, in the word "Home," finds only another meaning for the word "Comfort." They bore with them the household gods of their fathers,—they set them up with observant rites in the wilderness, and dignified the forests of America with altars, in scrupulous imitation of those which they had left forever. Their ambition was to found a *New*-England,—new homes, worthy of those which they had abandoned, and in whose sweet similitude the whole aspect of their future world was drawn. They had succeeded. They had endowed these homes with the whole treasure of their sympathies,—those English sympathies which embody a whole world of treasure in the little world of home. Hence, it was no difficult matter, when, in '76, the mother country prepared to violate their social securities, to awaken the whole people, from Maine to Georgia, to the necessity of making common cause in a quarrel, which was yet, strictly speaking, the quarrel of a single section only. What mattered it to the Cavaliers of Carolina, that the English government trampled upon the privileges of Massachusetts Bay,—and why should the Puritans of New-England care whether the Cavaliers of Carolina were or were not permitted the right of choosing their own civil and military officers?[1] There was no love lost between these separate communities. They had few affinities of taste or temper. Foes in the old country, they were not likely, very soon, to overcome their antipathies in the new. Yet they did overcome them, and, with the sagacious instincts of the Anglo-Saxon nature, in the maintenance of those social securities, which, whatever might have been the difference of treatment to which they were severally subjected, had been, in respect to both, almost equally out-raged. It is well to remark, in support of this opinion, that, in our Declaration of Independence, the wrongs done, the provocations suffered, are spoken of only as so many aggressions upon society; and the understanding is never for a moment outraged or offended, by a single abstraction about that Liberty, which, save in name, is nothing more than a spirit of refined society. They shook themselves free from the King of Great Britain, for the same reason which first prompted them to seek refuge in the wilderness,—the comfort and the security of home. Not so much with the view to the assertion of an abstract principle, the neglect of which might, at some future day, have involved them in probable loss of right or privi-lege, but because of absolute present abuses and usurpations. It is a rhetorical exaggeration which may lead to evil, to speak of British taxation only, as the cause of our Revolutionary war. I do not doubt that we should, in process of time, have dissolved our connection with the mother country, under any circumstances, and any sort of treatment. It was not in the nature of things that the two countries should very long remain under the same authority. But we are to look for the true causes of the Revolution, as enumerated in the Declaration, to the most atrocious offences against society,—the violation of life and liberty, and other crimes of like character, which, to have submitted to, would have been fatal to all its securities. There was nothing speculative in the causes of complaint, and taxation was not the sort of tyranny which led to war. These causes consisted in the denial of laws which were essential to the peace of society,—in the presence of a military which was insubordinate to society,—in the imprisonment of the citizen in regions away from the society to which he belonged,—in the murder of the citizen in the ordinary walks of society,—and in rescuing his murderer from justice. To have taken up arms for other than these offences—to have invoked a seven years' war of the most brutal nature, for less provocation—would have been equally against the spirit of society and religion,—would have incurred a guilt, which the calm, conscientious, moral nature of the fathers of the Revolution would have prayed in sackcloth and ashes, for a far longer period of years, to avert. We have but to read the famous instrument to which we have given a passing reference, to see that the wrongs done by Great Britain are dwelt upon as wrongs to people, rather than to principles,—to the repose and security of society, rather than to that elementary principle of human equality, which the same instrument begins with declaring. *That,* indeed, was the principle made apparent by the wrong, yet, but for the wrong, the principle might have slept for ages in the dormant bosom of the savage or the slave.

There is a deep significance in these facts, which we are not often brought to see. A people thus moved only by proper provocation,—thus studious to justify themselves before the world,—thus solicitous of those concerns only which seem counselled by human reason, and enforced by natural justice,—is a people, above all others, to have the custody of the social principle. They will not sleep above their trust. Such a people are not prone to change—are slow to excess—slow to revolution—considerate of life—reserved, cautious—fond of acquisition—apt to be moral, proud, prudent and persevering. If they are selfish, they exhibit this selfishness in a becoming attitude. They are selfish in regard to superior objects. They are distinguished by the primary qualities of social permanence, method and consideration. Their consideration provides always against the future,—makes home comfortable,—cares for the feeble,—exalts the woman,—protects her with no common courage, and hedges her in with a pains-taking solicitude that suffers not the winds of heaven to blow too rudely upon her cheeks. She, in turn, thus guarded,—thus elevated and endowed,—becomes a creature of superior sentiments,—refines the worship which she receives, and softens the stern bosom which she charms. The home thus rendered sweet to the affections, becomes necessary to the tastes. If gentle spirits make it desirable within, the busy fingers of an equally gentle fancy render it attractive without. Vines and flowers encircle the habitation, birds whose strains attest that they do not repine for an unnecessary liberty, fill the atmosphere with song,—whilst art, with a rival melody, astonishes and provokes the imitative ability of the natural musician. With the progress of one taste to perfection, is the birth of another. With newer desires of sentiment, industry is impelled to exertion, that the demands of sentiment shall be satisfied; and thus it is that men advance, by the natural and moral process of accumulation, step by step, to the possession, not only of superior fortune, but of superior refinement. The progress of one man, thus endowing his little cottage with love and comfort, provokes the emulation of his neighbor, and thus hamlets rise, and great cities, even in the bosom of a wilderness like this! Why are not the Spanish and French adventurers who traversed these regions three hundred years ago, marching with armies and banners,—a noble and a bright array,—in all the pomp of fame and chivalry,—why are they not now in possession of these dominions,—the masters of this city,—speaking the sonorous language of the one nation, or the courtly dialect of the other,—and engaging, this hour, in the gorgeous and imposing rites of their peculiar religion? Why is it that the French and Spaniards are in possession of so few of their colonies and conquests,—driven, either wholly or in great part, from the West-India Islands,—from Mexico, from Central, and from South-America,—odious in all, with so few memorials of their power, unassociated with its crimes? I answer, because they pursued not these humble processes of comfort,—because, with all their qualities of conquest, they lacked the only one which makes conquest permanent! That domestic feeling, which is equally a sentiment and passion with the Englishman,—the appreciation of a social impulse which no fashion can easily subvert,—a sort of household religion, from whose sweet and simple altars no accursed love of lucre can ever thoroughly beguile. Imbued with this religion of the house and heart, the Englishman makes a castle wherever he plants a footstep. It is his law and fortress, and raising this moral superstructure wherever he lays his hearth-stone, he has founded his lordly dwelling in the four quarters of the earth. His drum—such is his haughty boast—still keeps sonorous sounding time, responding, like ancient Memnon, to the progress of the sun, in every known region which he honors with his beams. In each of these,—such has been his devotion to the substantial objects of his nature,—his treasure is too great to suffer him to forego his possession. He is rooted there like some natural growth of the forest,—he takes root,—readily maintains his foothold with his life,—and you can only dispossess him by a recognition of those social laws by which he is governed, and by a stern patriotism, which, in the assertion of a natural right, finds a superior impulse to his own. In no other way can we account for the fact, that these haughty islanders, of all living conquerors, have alone maintained their conquests,—seldom baffled,—and never, but in a single instance, driven from the ground where they had found foothold, and then only by the arms of a people sprung from the same ancestral loins with themselves. Nay, even this exception must have its qualification. They were not expelled from America,—they maintained themselves in America. The invader was a foreign despot—hostile to British liberty—and the expulsion of British arms from our soil, was one of the noblest efforts of British freedom. It was the struggle of the Briton's fireside, against Britannia's avarice,—the social man against those usurping passions of a government, which too frequently war upon the sacred hearth, in the name of church and sceptre.

Yet the original conquest and retention of America by the British people, was a matter of no easy performance. We see in it a conclusive proof of the superior means of conquest, which is possessed by the social principle, in spite of all disadvantages. The colonists, few in number, were wanting in resource; and though brave in spirit, and of powerful frame and muscle, not ordinarily accustomed to arms. A rude militia, they could endure, and they could strike; but their military skill—their acquaintance with the arts of national murder—was limited in the extreme. To these were opposed the veterans of France and Spain, men already in possession of the soil,—brought up to arms,—having no other business,— superior in number,—superior in all the extrinsic aids and appliances of a military and mighty nation. To reconcile this disparity, and overcome these deficiencies, the British had nothing to oppose, but a patient habit of mind and body,—a well-ordered and compact social system, which had trained them to a feeling of the vast importance, in all enterprises, of mutual obligation and support,—and a religious regard to those duties, which, as they were single, and circumscribed within natural boundaries, seemed reasonable, and justified in their prosecution the fiercest valor and the firmest resolution, that ever rendered inflexible the will of man. Whatever may be the temptations of gold or conquest, be sure that no man fights so stubbornly, as he who, knowing the value of his home, fights upon its threshold; and the very humbleness of the British homestead in America, increased the indignation with which he strove against his foreign invader. The very moderation of his aims, was a virtual assurance of their justice, and made him as stubborn in their assertion, as if the home for which he struggled had been endeared to him by the domestic associations of a thousand years. It is not the value of the thing for which he combats. It is because that thing is *his own;* and it is partly to the veneration shown by British law to the British land-holder, that this lesson, teaching the profound value of the homestead to the meanest of Britain's sons, has served to make compact her social institutions, while the world around her was threatened with social overthrow. To this same valuable lesson, we ascribe the passion of the Englishman and American to be the owner of land,—each to have his little *peculium,*—his home,—in the language of the domestic proverb, "however homely."

The more we examine this proposition, by a reference to British and other histories, the more certain, we imagine, will appear its truth. Having security in the homestead, with that feeling of dignity which a conscious permanence of position inspires,—and a farther appreciation of the vast importance to civilization of a community, at once stationary, yet susceptible of progress,—and how naturally does the man improve his condition. Compare, with this idea in mind, the comfort of an English home with that of any other people. Nay, it is the boast of the Englishman, that this very word, with the host of dear associations which belong to it, is peculiar to his own language. Nor is it the word only. The thing, itself, is almost peculiar to the English. Even we, their descendants in America, are scarcely in possession of it. We have a thousand luxuries, but few comforts. I have often imagined, or striven to imagine, the comforts of an English home, as known to our ancestors some two hundred years ago;—its placid sweets,— its unaffected grace,—its hearty cheerfulness,—the sweetness of its repose—the polish of its simplicity—the frankness of its hospitality—its buoyant sensibility, and quiet raptures. The snug mansion always distinguished by plenty,—the cheerful fireside, equally clean and unpretending, enlivened by the happiest faces, and the sweetest evening recreations,—the curtained chamber,—the decorated walls,—the order which regulates without being seen,—the authority which is felt without being heard. The prompt, unpresuming attendance of servants,—the reverential bearing of children,—and that warm but subdued current of domestic love, which, passing from grandsire to grandson, seems to transmit itself, with an annually increasing tide, along with the family possessions, through the hearts of successive generations,—fertilizing in some degree the partially foreign bosoms of the venerable nurse and butler. Here I see youth brought up with the modest bearing and docile habits of the damsel,—manly without presumption, curious without obtrusiveness, and studious without being dull. The maiden, pleasing without pertness,—grateful for, without soliciting regard,—anxious to gratify, yet without yielding any thing of that pride which becomes *her* sex, and makes it becoming in the sight of ours. Then, for the more external picture,—the vigorous sports of the field, the necessary employments of the farm,—the chase, the merriment, the rustic revel,—the manly trial of strength or skill,—the hearty buffet with ball or cudgel,—strifes of buoyancy and blood, but not of hate,—and the cheerful uproar which terminates the simple and wholesome festivity, such as once conferred upon the country, in the language of other nations, the name of "Merrie Englande." I confess, the hearty and generous nature which spoke out in those days, dashed, it might be, by a little excess of that rustic simplicity which became rudeness, has a charm for contemplation, which makes it half doubtful whether civilization, in refining too much upon this character, has not impaired some of its most valuable virtues. But the horse play which, in the rustic *charivari,* should sometimes show too many of its heels, did not then seem to impair the becoming veneration of the people, for the sacred sweets and patriarchal authority of home. The sport itself was licensed by religion, and did not often exceed its allotted boundaries. Nay, so long as it was a licensed sport, it was satisfied with its limits; and the son did not the less honor his father, nor the village lads their pastor, nor the whole people the presiding Druid, the venerable Genius of the Homestead, because they were occasionally suffered to forget themselves in a homely saturnalia. You are all reminded of the sweet picture in Goldsmith's "Deserted Village."

> "Dear, lovely bowers of innocence and ease,
> Seats of my youth, when every sport could please;
> How often have I loiter'd o'er thy green,
> Where humble happiness endear'd each scene,—
> How often have I paused on every charm,
> The shelter'd cot, the cultivated farm;
> The never-failing brook, the busy mill,
> The decent church that tops the neighb'ring hill;
> The hawthorn bush, with seats beneath the shade,
> For talking age and whispering lovers made;—
> How often have I bless'd the coming day,
> When toil remitting, lent its turn to play,
> And all the village train, from labor free,
> Led up their sports beneath the spreading tree!
> While many a pastime circled in the shade,
> The young contending, as the old surveyed;
> And many a gambol frolick'd o'er the ground,
> And sleights of art, and feats of strength went round;

And still, as each repeated pleasure tired,
Succeeding sports the mirthful band inspired.
The dancing pair that simply sought renown,
By holding out to tire each other down;
The swain mistrustless of his smutted face,
While secret laughter titter'd round the place;
The bashful virgin's side-long looks of love,
The matron's glance that would those looks reprove;
These were thy charms, sweet village,—sports like these,
With sweet succession taught e'en toil to please;
These round thy bowers their cheerful influence shed,—
These were thy charms—but all these charms are fled."

If Goldsmith, even in his day,—the day distinguished by the American Revolution,—pronounced the domestic charms of England to have fled,—what has been the loss since? But Goldsmith spoke with the usual warmth, and consequently, with the usual exaggerations, of the Poet. The household virtues may have been on the decline,—nay, we know that they were,—but they were very far from having fled entirely. England is even now, over all countries, that in which the domestic tie is strongest,—in which the charm of home is sweetest,—where the patriarchal and social virtues are yet most fondly cherished. We do not now speak for the great body of her people, and we are by no means forgetful of the condition of the miserable operatives, who depend upon the employments afforded by machinery: but our reference is to that body of her citizens which have charge of the social principle,—that sacred fire which, like that of the Persian, is never suffered to go out, in any nation, unless its destruction has been first resolved upon. There is, no doubt, a community in every land, to whom its virtues are particularly confided,—to whom the great body of the people turn instinctively, in the moment of distress and danger;—a class which are thus tacitly distinguished as the permanent—the principled—those who obey neither the caprices of fashion, nor the impulses of speculation,—who pray for neither poverty nor riches,—whose hearths are always smiling in plenty, and whose industry never clamors for more. It is in the possession of a community like this, more than any other nation, that the great superiority of Great Britain, in all respects, is to be found. It is in consequence of this unquestionable social superiority, that the Englishman, let him go where he will from home, is always a discontent. His most ordinary and indispensable requisites are denied him in other lands, and the substitutes which are offered, only remind him, as if in mockery, of the superior value and attractions of those which he has abandoned. Doubtless, in the clamor which he makes, he not only betrays some feeblenesses of character, but is unjust to other people. But that he attaches too high a value to those things which make his home more dear to him than any other,—which make him love his country with an individual passion that seems to swallow up all others,—cannot well be said by those who behold, in this very attachment, the true secret of his own and country's eminence.

We might trace, did it need, and did our leisure and limits permit, to his peculiar mental constitution, to his religion, and general earnestness of temperament, a great portion of this tenacious and profound devotion to the spirit of the place. Something of it is due to his good common sense, which prompts him to address his thoughts and efforts to objects which are certainly attainable, and the uses of which are beyond all question. Something, unquestionably, to the fact, that his geographical boundaries at home are so much circumscribed,—a fact which necessarily impresses him with a just sense of the paramount value of land to him who was ordained a planter. It is because of the difference of circumstances in this respect, that we, in America, have lost, in a great degree, the benefits of this lesson. The quantity of land before us, deprives us of that veneration for the soil, to which the Englishman owes so many of his proudest virtues. The intrinsic value of his paternal estate, great in itself, is heightened by the recollection, that it has constituted the inheritance of his fathers, and is endowed with the numerous improvements of successive generations. Every race has striven in the same grateful employment of adding to its beauties. No spot is left unhallowed by the all-endowing hands of love and veneration. Every tree has its appropriate name and history; and if affection has not been able to keep from decay, these memorable fathers of the forest, she has, at least, decorated their hoary brows with the ivied green which mantles their desolation. It may seem something of an absurdity, in the eyes of a freeman, to assume as important, even to Liberty itself, these little concerns of life, these domestic additaments,—the small interests which make physical comfort, and address themselves somewhat to the sensuous nature. Doubtlessly, Liberty is the greatest social good—nay, without such liberty as becomes one's moral condition, there is no social good. But that sort of liberty which is entertained without human comforts,—which neither knows nor desires them,—is the liberty of the savage, which, insisting upon its freedom, returns only to its wallow. Now, the Englishman, with liberty, possesses a thousand other social goods, and those of the domestic hearth, of which we have spoken, are the greatest. They make his comforts,—they endear his home,—they couple his freehold with his freedom, and making his very self-ishness a patriotism, the love which he maintains for both, secures him in their mutual possession.

How much of this passion for the family homestead—how much of this social principle did the Briton bring with him to America? How much of it, when his authority over the soil was broken, did he transmit to his successors? Have we preserved the household virtues of the Englishman? Do we maintain his tastes in this particular;—do we honor those humanities which every lesson of our common ancestry should teach us to revere? Do we sustain the gentle—do we venerate the old? Are we, like them, solicitous always of the decencies of life and society? Do we bow to intellect? Seek we to promote, by letters, religion and the arts, the altars of a high civilization? Are our freeholds so identified, in our regards, with our freedom, that the abandonment or decay of the one, makes us tremble for the safety of the other? Where are we in the social world? What is our rank, compared with other nations, in the estimates of the civilized? Where are the proofs that we are nobler, gentler, purer, wiser than our ancestors,—for, let me remark,—no civilized people can continue stationary! The law of civilization is a law of progress; to fail in reporting which is a sure sign of retrograde, fatal to all our pretensions, and terrible in its consequences to posterity! These are questions to be answered,—not easy of answer. Oh! that in answering them, my friends, we too, like the noble mother of the Gracchi, could point to our children! I have but feebly and indifferently pursued this train of reflection, unless these questions have already suggested themselves, more or less directly, to every thinking mind in this assembly. This is a place, and the present an occasion, where and when, if ever, the thoughts should be lifted to the contemplation of the highest good. Our business here is mutual encouragement, in a common toil, for the attainment of this good; and, next to religion, the business of Literature, is the noblest concern of human society. Nay, Literature is the religion of society; the handmaid of that spiritual nature, whose constant yearnings are for excellence,—ideal conquests over a sublimated perfection, to which all other objects, of the social or individual man, are base and unworthy,—of his earth, earthy, and to be cast aside, and trampled out of sight, when he stands before altars such as these! With a trust, then, that what has been said, has not been wholly purposeless—has not fallen upon unheeding senses,—I renew these questions. Are you prepared to answer them?—Would I, too, could remain silent ! I should be spared a pang, my countrymen! could they be left unanswered;—for where is the son of the soil, who is pleased to answer to her shame—to point to her rags—to place the prying finger on her moral sores, and tent her to the quick with an examination of those mortifying places in her body, which still retain—fortunate that they do so—a morbid sensibility! But, though he feels no delight at the duty, it is still a duty. It is impossible that he should escape it. The orator is base, and unworthy of his vocation, who, speaking to his time, speaks only to flatter it—avoids the wholesome truth for the glozing compliment, and, with a selfish fear that regards his own, rather than his country's glory, disguises from his hearers that unbiased judgment of the future, which, as it will have no motive to conciliate favor, will have no reason to forbear condemnation. Happy, indeed, shall I be, if, in laying bare the defects of our people, I provoke any, the meanest among them, to strenuous performance—if, in the exhibition of those truths which may bring a common blush into our cheeks, I shall awaken the young hearts of my auditory to their solemn consideration. To the young I address myself, rather than the old. It is they who are in danger—theirs is the struggle, the long trial and the toilsome march. To them the strength for the conflict—the praise of deliverance as for a battle won—the triumph of well deserved and virtuous victory!

The revolution of '76 neither found nor left the American people in that condition, which was favorable to a very rapid improvement or a very high degree of social refinement. We have seen what was the character and condition of the early colonists—how generally poor in fortune—how commonly wanting in the higher education. To this period, though, in a comparative sense, successful,—they still continued to struggle against numerous necessities. They were hardy in *morale* and *physique,*—but mere hardihood, however favorable to virtue, health and ultimate prosperity,—is yet only to be regarded as a sort of moral groundwork, upon which the prouder virtues of civilization are yet to grow. The Anglo-Americans brought with them a taste of English life, but it was a taste only, and embittered by numerous recollections of strife and denial. England, to them, had been, in the words of one of their own simple ballads, "a garden," but they could add, from the same ditty,

"Many a bitter weed grew there."

They had been of that class, in the mother country, to whom a knowledge of the *dulce domum* came associated with the conviction that such sweets were denied to them. This conviction was, indeed, the true reason of their self-expatriation. They were resolved to seek in a foreign country what they beheld, but could not acquire, in their own. The painful toils and wanderings which followed—the conflicts with the wilderness and with its wild possessors—were not calculated to promote these tastes, or to ripen them into very prompt perfection; and we find, accordingly, that agriculture, the progress of which, in every country, must precede the superior arts, was, at the dawn of our resolution, in a very humble condition. Our people had learned to labor, but little more. Staple culture, may be regarded as generally unfavorable to agriculture—as tending to the improvement of one commodity at the expense of all the rest,—and the agriculture of the South, was then, as now, (though in a less criminal degree) confined almost entirely to staples which were ultimately destructive to the soil. Grazing, which is a kindred occupation with that of the Hunter, and almost equally unfavorable to civilization, was the employment of a large portion of our people; and the whole were wanting in those means of education for the young, which should be among the first objects of any people who duly appreciate the importance of social life;—for education, which refines the inferior nature, and lifts it to its proper uses, can, alone, make the passions subordinate to the wholesome dominion of a common law. In Puritan New-England, where the population was less scattered, and where the means of centralization, in groups and families, were most easily found, this deficiency was soonest overcome. In Virginia and South-Carolina, the wealthier families sent their sons to Europe for education—thus still farther lessening their ability to secure this precious boon at home—while the poorer sort were almost wholly abandoned, in mental destitution, to the soil. No combination of circumstances could be well conceived, more unfavorable to civilization; and it was due entirely to the inherent virtues of the Anglo-Saxon stock, by which a stern love of home was engendered as a duty, that the rich youth sent abroad for knowledge, and the poor youth abandoned to the soil without it, were yet ready to unite,—the one flying from his foreign *alma mater,* the other rising from the maternal furrows which he ignorantly dressed—in the common cause of a country which they seemed mutually to love by instinct. To tend the soil, indeed, is to make one love it, and this was the first office by which the British Colonist prepared to constitute of the forests of America, an English home—an office which the Spaniard in his pride, and the Frenchman in his levity, equally disdained to perform. To possess himself of a chosen spot to make of it a garden —to multiply its fruits around him; to live well and hospitably,—decently and reverently,—were his leading objects. Security and plenty were his first considerations—his children soon thickened about him, and though as yet the Parish School failed to salute his ears with the busy hum of juvenile study, the Parish Church, with its simple but imposing tower, denoted equally his recollections of the country from which he came, and the God who had thus far smiled upon his adventure. He had reached this stage of social progress in America—his dwelling and his Church were built—how well built may still be seen in many of the antique and solid structures of Ashley river—his graves lay in sight of his evening walks—and improving resources had added to his pride by enabling him to add to the simple virtues of the patriarch, the graces, comparatively speaking, of an English hospitality. It needed but repose from external pressure—time for contemplation—a respite, in which to grow the nobler plants of social culture,— taste and education, the arts and graces of civilization. But, at this very period —this nice moment so important to the nation's future—his increasing prosperity awakened in his foreign brother, that greedy appetite which led to the Revolution. The seven years of social war which followed was sadly detrimental to the social progress. In that time, employing every art and agent to prosecute his purpose,—reckless of all laws however sacred—all obligations of nature and humanity,—the German monarch of Great Britain at once deluged the land with savages and blood. Never, indeed, was such a war against the social virtues by a people professing to be civilized. *Væ victis,* was the cry with louder emphasis from the throats of British war, than ever saluted the ears of the conquered from the ranks of Gothic or Roman carnage. Domestic strifes were fomented—families divided—communities and cities; and a foreign people, not speaking our language, and having accordingly no sympathy with our condition,—were employed, in apt alliance with the Indians of our frontier, to make complete the work of devastation. Homes were abandoned in terror, and destroyed by hate. Hamlets perished by fire, and the domestic affections were extinguished in the blaze; while the disruption of all those ties which bound together, as one, the members of a family, effectually dissipated the *prestige* of domestic authority. It would not be difficult to say how much of the lawlessness and violence which now disgrace our country, and with which we are reproached by the modern British, is due to the reckless and detestable ambition of their ancestors—their greedy avarice—their insatiate thirst of power, and their total disregard, in that prolonged warfare, of all those redeeming usages of war, which sometimes entitle it even to the applause of humanity.—How well they paid for the service of the brutal Hessians—with what toilsome sagacity they stimulated the phrenzy of the native savage, and, with what cunning and cruel policy, they fomented the social differences among our people, until the world beheld with a horror, in which Britain did not share, the awful spectacle of father, brother and son, mangling the mutual throat before the family altar. Could these strifes be healed in a moment—could the feuds of a people be subdued—pangs and passions of the heart,—merely at the withdrawal of the foreign knife? Would the baffling of the foreign ally, soothe the excited nature of the native savage? If it be the work of ages to lift a people from the condition of the barbarian, to that of the civilized,—it is, perhaps, a work of almost equal time and difficulty to recover and regenerate a civilized people whom circumstances have hurried into the barbarism of Civil War. Homes, indeed, may be rebuilt.—Time may heal the ravages of sword and flame.—Even pecuniary prosperity, in a progress of years, may be restored to a nation;—but what can re-unite affections which have been sundered by the sword—bring back the sweet peace which made the homestead lovely—re-awaken the often-banished confidence in man—rekindle the fires of mutual zeal in the common cause of society—subdue those wild spirits whom a seven years war, suddenly ended, had cast loose, without employment, upon the country—of habits, reckless and dissolute, formed to idleness, incapable of a patient and slow-advancing industry? It need not be said that the return of peace was followed by little social improvement. The *lares familiares,* overthrown by hands of violence, were not soon reinstated by hands of peace. We do not find the American citizen pursuing the spoiler into the wilderness, as in the case of the Pagan father, of whom we read in Scripture, for the recovery of his teraphim. On the contrary, we are constrained to see in the history of our social progress, for the last fifty years, but few signs of that sober-thoughted love of home, the absence of which we regard as among the most alarming evils of our present social condition. Undoubtedly, as we have endeavoured to show, the Revolutionary struggle threw us back in this respect—how much we need not say, but to this cause we attribute the first impelling direction in this downward progress,—covered as was the face of the land with an impoverished soldiery—impatient of control, ready for strife, and reckless, under the pressure of necessity, of all human consequences.—For, it will be remembered, that, in the South at least, the whole body of the people had been in arms on one side or the other:—the citizen was the soldier, and nowhere was there a community, preserved from overthrow, sufficiently large and imposing to overawe the insubordinate, or subdue the brutal nature. What this domestic calamity may have spared to society, was more than usurped by the prevalent warfares of the frontier—the desperate assaults of outlawed men, leagued with the savage, who, once stimulated to phrenzy by British arts, could not be quieted by British exhortation—if, indeed, such exhortation was ever attempted among them. The interregnum of peace which followed, was simply a rest from war. But thirty years had elapsed from the peace of '83, when the doors of Janus were again thrown violently open, and we were again summoned to contend, for the liberties of society, in another bloody passage with our foreign brother. Old feuds were to be revived—old war-cries of the savage to be re-sounded, and the maternal love which now insists so much upon our inferior civilization, was once-more busy in the endeavour to help it forward by shot and sabre. Now,—the blessings of a superior civilization, are blessings which flow almost entirely from the reign of peace. A nation kept constantly at war, within its own borders, is necessarily demoralized. With but few intervals, and those of short duration, the people of America, from the first Colonial settlements, whether at Jamestown, Massachusetts Bay or Ashley River, were in continual conflict—now with the French and Spaniards, now with the savages, and finally, and worst of all,—a conflict not yet ended—with the mother country. It would be something wonderful, indeed, judging by the histories of other nations, if there should be a perfect state of civilization among us—if there should be no violence,—no strife,—no absence, in frequent regions, of just principles,—no social disquiets, discomforts, wild dwellings and wilder men. Immunity from such evils, under such circumstances, would be miraculous. There are no such immunities for mortals in the stores of providence, and with the help of our mother country, the curse is at our doors!

But I should regard it as a mistaken patriotism, however legitimate the plea, to endeavor to extenuate the faults, the follies or ferocities of our people, by showing how much they were occasioned by the ambition of Great Britain. We claim to be a sensible and Christian people—and the plea will not avail us any farther than to show the difficulties in the way of our virtue. It will not excuse us for having fallen in the struggle, for we need not to have fallen. It is enough to render sure our responsibility to show that we are not now ignorant of the claims of society—of what is due to ourselves, our children and our ancestors. It is not for us, speaking the language of Milton and Shakespeare, and claiming their writings as in part our heritage, to plead ignorance of what we owe to the humanities, to the arts, to the pure, the true, the beautiful and intellectual. Our responsibility is strictly proportioned to our knowledge. What *we know,* pronounces the judgment upon what *we are.* Nay, even evasion will not serve us, else how easy to show, from our British censors themselves, that they too have fallen—that they share in our shame—that they no longer maintain the virtues of their ancestors, and that the same vices which are conspicuous in ourselves, are of no mean prominence in them. Hear one of their own great minds—one of the greatest living minds among them. He invokes the genius of a greater.

> "Milton, thou should'st be living at this hour;—
> England hath need of thee—she is a fen
> Of stagnant waters! Altar, sword and pen,
> Fireside, the heroic wealth of hall and bower,
> Have forfeited their ancient English dower,
> Of inward happiness. We are selfish men;—
> Oh, raise us up, return to us again,
> And give us manners, virtue, freedom, power!"

Surely, such should be our prayer—but such we see is also hers—and if such be her deficiencies, what wonder that we, who,—shame upon us!—copy her failings with such religious strictness, should deserve a like and greater reproach. We have, indeed, what she has not,—pleas in extenuation, and we may plead them with tenfold utterance against herself—but she has none! Her soil has never known invasion, since the day that her civilization begun. Her Christian neighbors have never conducted the savage to her dwelling, armed with scalping knife and spear,—and given her villages to the midnight flame. If she has grown base, it is because of her own inward tendencies.

> "Hoc fonte derivata clades
> In patriam, populumque fluxit."

The same great poet in another noble sonnet thus more particularly dwells upon the vices of the modern English—vices, we may remark, which are quite as notorious to their neighbours, as ours are to them. Mark, as I repeat them, how sadly they apply to our social history.

> — — — — — — "I am opprest
> To think that now, our life is only drest,
> For show:—mean handy work of Craftsman, cook,
> Or groom! we must run glittering, like a brook,
> In the open sunshine, or we are unblest;—
> The wealthiest man among us is the best:

> No grandeur now in nature or in book,
> Delights us. Rapine, avarice, expense,—
> This is idolatry—and these we adore.
> Plain living and high thinking are no more;
> The homely beauty of the good old cause,
> Is gone—our peace, our fearful innocence,
> And pure religion breathing household Laws."

Certainly, it is a curious coincidence, that, just now, the very evils which the British find in us, they should denounce among themselves; vanity, ostentation, the worship of wealth, selfishness and want of manners. It would be a becoming study with the philosophical mind to trace the source of this coincidence. Doubtless, it is a result due to some defect in the character of both—something in the common customs or principles—some lamentable want in the popular education—the domestic policy,—all to be found, embodied among the constituents of the social principle. But our aim is less discursive—our limits too confined for such an examination. That we owe, however, many of our social vices to a miserable and servile imitation of the English, in their vain displays and boyish affectations, is beyond all question. It is this wretched love of show, this absence of plain living and high thinking, which is making us all bankrupt; hurrying us on, with gamester phrenzy, in change and speculation; and, placing before us ever the dazzling forms of unsubstantial and fraudulent desires, is momently beguiling us from that

> — — — — — — "Good old cause,
> And pure religion breathing household Laws."

But I note other causes among us, superior to these, for promoting this deteriorating social tendency. The first and most important is the wandering habit of our people. Now, the first requisite to the civilization of any people, is to make them stationary. To become stationary implies the necessity of labor, and this necessity is the origin of agriculture. With the increase of the community, a farther necessity arises for diversifying the objects of labor, and with this necessity spring the arts, mechanical and fine. I need not pursue this suggestion. A wandering people is more or less a barbarous one. We see in the fate of the North American savage, that of every nomadic nation. What is true of them, is true in degree of every civilized people that adopts, in whatever degree, their habits. Every remove, of whatever kind, is injurious to social progress; and every remove into the wilderness, lessens the hold which refinement and society have hitherto held upon the individual man. One of the securities of the Englishman, from a danger of this sort, was his moral and social inflexibility. It was his boast that he maintained his authority over the savage—that he made no concessions to the inferior nature; but, as we have already said, set up his household Gods, in whatever wilderness he sought abode. In this he differed from the Frenchman, who, when he built his lodge among the Hurons, with the levity of his character, surrendered in part his own, while adopting the habits of the Indians. He was won by the novelty, which the intense self-esteem of the Englishman made him treat with loathing. The latter surrendered nothing,—lost nothing of his original claim to moral authority,—preserved the superior organization of the society in which he had been taught, and, by this alone, maintained his foothold in the forest. There is no doubt that, had the British Colonists been sufficiently numerous for conquest, they would have saved the American Aborigenes—they would have subjected them to bondage, preserved them by the tasks of labor, and finally lifted them to a cognate condition with their own. In degree, all wanderers cease to be laborers. Their habits become desultory and unsettled. They obey impulses rather than laws, and toil in obedience to their humours rather than their necessities. With desultory habits, the moods of men become capricious, their resources uncertain and their principles unfixed. Let me illustrate the effect of these habits, upon the features and fortunes of our people, by a single example. You all have witnessed the change produced in the case of an individual family, emigrating to a wild from a long settled region of country. The restraining presence of society once withdrawn—the provocation to civilization which the ancient customs of a settled neighborhood once inspired,—at an end,—and how indifferent do the wanderers become to all appearances.—Into what a miserable hovel does the father and the husband crowd his little family, once so accustomed to all the luxuries and charms of civilization. How careless of decency become the master and the matron. How slovenly are the dress and the dwelling—how squalid the children—how ignorant,—how seldom clean, and how soon, as substitutes for the more delicate tastes of the abandoned home, do we find father and son engaged in the free use of whiskey and tobacco,—those two gross, brutal and terrible tyrannies of our nation. Society,—the presence and the restraints of neighbours, gentle, loving, and considerate—the cheerful home—the certain school house—the "decent Church that tops the neighbouring hill"—these had saved them from this miserable descent! And why have they wandered from these privileges and blessings? Why, O! why?—For gain! for the small increase—the miserable pittance—the little more to the Cotton heap,—and for this, the man is willing to convert the wife into the wench, and the dear children, who might be made the noblest pillars of the noblest republic, into horse-boys, or ruffians, or something worse!

And how was it that this love of gain became so completely the passion of the American people, as to make them lose that care for home, which was the superior passion with their ancestors. Not that we hoard money. Far from it. Our profligacy, on the contrary, keeps equal and active pace with our avarice. We are as active in squandering as in getting, and this is also a peculiar characteristic. Let us look a little into this matter, by briefly analyzing the constituents of character which distinguished our people from the beginning.

Whether, then, we consider the people of New-England, Virginia or Carolina, we find them all, at the outset, to have been a very poor people. It was their poverty, in truth,—the discontent with their present condition, and a desire to improve it, which first brought them to America. Their ground once chosen, the great struggle was for the means which should enable them to emulate the homes of the more fortunate whom they had left. Their toil was to establish homes like theirs—a social world which should realize that comfort which had been the ideal in their minds before. But, it must be remembered, that, with this desire, they lacked, in a great degree, the resources of taste and education which were possessed at that time by the mind of the British people. A colonizing expedition may represent the energies, the character, nay, even the genius of a nation, but seldom its highest absolute existing elevation. The Puritans were a coarse, uneducated people,—sensible of the value of learning as an agent of social prosperity, but totally regardless of its uses, as a minister to the tastes and sensibilities of a highly endowed intellectual nature. What they knew of Milton, was of Milton the politician, not the poet. The first settlers of Virginia could claim no decided advantages of education, and fresh from battle-field, and desperate in fortune, they were perhaps not equally virtuous—certainly, not equally methodical, persevering and industrious; while the Cavaliers of Carolina, though crowned with the more certain favour of the great, and possessed of more decided social tendencies, in consequence of the milder and calmer periods of their emigration,—were yet equally fierce in temper and rash in experiment. If they could boast of the manners of a court, they were yet cursed with such vices as gave a character of its own, in English history, to that of Charles the Second. The difference in moral respects, was, perhaps, not very substantial or great between these three maternal sections of our country.

The Puritans then, as their descendants now, were more studious of appearances—more rigid in forms—more bigoted in their prejudices and more presumptuous in their opinions. Their Southern neighbours preserve, in like manner, to this day, many of their original characteristics. They were more frank in manners, more considerate of the graces of society, more flexible in opinion, less heedful of religion, less methodical, and, with equal and even greater earnestness, less firm and consistent in the prosecution of their objects. In one respect they were all the same people. They were all creatures of a vexing discontent, which left them unsatisfied with any present condition. They had industry and skill enough to secure themselves in it, but, for such a people—pressed by necessities that grew in due proportion with their powers,—this was not enough. To perpetuate a conquest was to provoke the desire for newer enterprizes, and the fortification rendered secure behind them, they steadily pushed forward in search of newer conquests. The poverty in which they lived, with the desires which they felt, necessarily taught them to attach to wealth an undue importance; and the love of gain soon becomes a passion—soon takes the place, in every human bosom, of those, more legitimate, by which it is occasioned. This passion was farther heightened in the case of the American, by a radical change which his character underwent in his new condition. It is but a partial view of the subject, to speak of our love of money as our passion.—It would be more correct to say that all our objects become passions for the time. The latent enthusiasm of the English character, grew into flame, in that progress from enterprize to enterprize, from danger to danger, which distinguished the career of the Anglo-American. That deliberate, almost phlegmatic reserve, which, in the case of the Englishman, covers the earnest bosom of a giant in repose, driven from its barriers of convention, forced to throw aside its artifices of carriage and philosophy, became, with the American, a thirst, a fever, restive in restraint and sleepless in performance. English imperiousness became American impetuosity. Hence our earnestness in all our objects, the rapidity of our action, and—which is our failing—our caprice of purpose, which makes us abandon in hot haste, what in hot haste we have begun—our fretful dislike to the staid, the deliberate, the regularly progressive. This characteristic stimulates largely, and equally, our thirst for acquisition and the profligacy with which we waste our gains. It is at the bottom of most of our actions, whether for good or evil—and hurries the same mob which has just risked its hundred thousand lives in rescuing the city from conflagration, to the violation of the Laws,—equally, of society and man.

The genius of the American, sprung thus from the most noble and prolific source, and stimulated by a career and circumstances the most extraordinary, is naturally a genius of large expectations, as it is certainly one of mighty endowments. It grasps at wealth as one of the most obvious agents of the power which it seeks, and it employs this wealth in the most lavish manner, as an exercise of that power. Its chief misfortune is that it has so suddenly and unexpectedly come into such large possessions. With what levity does it sport with its attributes. What extravagance distinguishes its plans and purposes. How stupendous are its schemes, how wild, if not wonderful, its aims, and how full of hyperbole its most ordinary forms of utterance. Its proceedings remind one of a child spoiled by fortune—in the possession of toys the most costly, which it flings about with a recklessness and levity, that provokes in the spectator equal wonder and regret. Thus, we see, that, with all our toil for gain, there is a recklessness—a seeming scorn of the object of our toil, which sets ordinary speculation at defiance. This very recklessness is one of the most prominent of our national traits, the equal progeny of that self-esteem of the Englishman and that impulse of the American, which are never half so well content as when they can awaken the amazement of mankind.

Poor Richard addressed himself to the profligacy of our character, at a time when its exhibitions were very far inferior to what they have since become. One, indeed, being less of the seer than Franklin, might have supposed, that, in his day, lessons of thrift were unnecessary in New-England. An ordinary mind, not regarding the emulative nature of the American, in all parts of the country, would have assumed that, in his neighbourhood, similar necessities to those which had tutored him, would have forced like maxims of economy on every citizen. But, even then, they might have been properly addressed to the South, where a more genial climate and a more productive industry, had already sown, broad cast, the seeds of a lavish and profligate expenditure. But the passion for gain grew with the expenditure. It was necessary to it. Hence, in great part, the devotion of our people to staple culture, or to the production of that one commodity only which could find a market. The whole labor of the Planter was expended,—not in the cultivation of the soil,—for the proper cultivation of a soil improves it,—but in extorting by violence from its bosom, seed and stalk, alike, of the wealth which it contained. He slew the goose that he might grasp, at one moment, its whole golden treasure. A cultivation like this, by exhausting his land, left it valueless, and led to its abandonment;—and, unhappily, there was nothing in the circumstances of his progress, to make him reluctant to do so, and studious, by every means, to avert this necessity. His insatiate rage for gain had rendered him regardless of all other considerations. In few instances had he built the stately mansion, the solid walls and sweet manifold comforts of which would have prompted him to repeated toils and experiments, ere he had been persuaded to abandon it. He laid out no gardens, the gravelled walks and tropical beauties of which would have fastened, as with the spells of an Armida, his reluctant footsteps—planted no favorite trees, whose mellowing shade, covering the graves of father, mother or favorite child—would have seemed too sacred for desertion—would have seemed like venerated relatives whom it would be cruel to abandon in their declining years. These, are the substantial marks of civilization, by which we distinguish an improving people. Regardless of these, we find him regardless of still more sacred obligations. What is the condition of the homestead in moral respects? Do we find his daughters nourished with the food of thought, lofty sentiment, and the graces of such an education as becomes the position of their sex? How worthless is their education,—limited to what servile objects, and how commonly meant only for the purposes of a vain and selfish display of superficial accomplishments;—"plain living and high thinking"—those noblest of all the essentials of social life, being utterly set at naught! And, for the sons! In the prosecution of that same feverish, phrenzied passion for gain,—he has sent them forth, while their sinews were yet unhardened—their minds yet untaught—their tempers untuned—at the very time when, in their mental gristle, none other than the parental dwelling should be entrusted with their care—he has sent them forth in the same mad, pitiful thirst for gold—for the sordid traffic—the petty salary—the cogging, cunning world of speculation. The poor boy, thoughtless, but hopeful of the world—simple and confident, but oh! how vain, how rash, how impatient of the time and the truth—ere he has yet gone through his accidence—ere he has learned the lesson, most sacred and necessary of all, to honor his father and mother in the day of his youth;—is dispatched in the morning of that day from their controlling presence,—thrust among strangers, who care not for father or mother—care not for the boy,—care not that he has learned any but the one commandment—'thou shalt not steal!' This is the custom, worse than death, in the history of our American career— the most misery-bringing custom that prevails among us. Nothing can be so fatal to discipline—and without discipline all is lost—there is nothing worth remaining—power, wealth, talent, all are worse than useless, without this most necessary, soul-bracing, body-strengthening ordeal, which we call discipline.— Nothing is so fatal to this discipline as the emancipation of the boy, in his tender years, from the restraints of the maternal household—from the guidance of the parental hand and eye—from the pure and sobering influences—the regular habits and the cheering smiles of the domestic hearth and habitation. Nothing so soon prompts the boy to throw off his allegiance to years, to station, to worth and virtue, as the capacity of earning money for himself. Money is the sign, among us, unhappily, of the highest social power,—and the possessor of it soon learns to exercise it as a means of authority. It is new doctrine, certainly, in our country—but not the less true for that—to teach that the longer a boy is kept from earning money for himself—the better for himself—for his real manhood—for his morals—his own, and the happiness of those who love him. Unhappily, the infatuated parent beholds with delight the exercise of this capacity, though it might not be difficult, at the same time, to show, that, with this exercise comes presumption, insubordination and insolence—looseness of principle—recklessness of conduct—levity of manners, excess in indulgence, brutality in habit, drunkenness and debauchery, beastliness the most loathsome, and, frequently, crimes the most atrocious. What dreadful penalties are paid, by child and parent, for this premature exposure of the infant mind to the rank resort of the stranger, to the enslaving tyrannies of trade, to the crude admixtures of a heartless foreign society, and the absence of all those holy, love-compelling influences which are seldom or never to be found out of the sacred circle of family and home.

I have said nothing here of the effect upon the social world of this mal-appropriation of the mind by which it is to be governed. Yet of this appropriation you may predicate all the pernicious effects which are to follow. The domestic hearth will be without its attractions,—the domestic altar without its worshipper. Fireside and altar will be equally outraged by the narrowing concerns of trade. There will be but one topic, and that will be the how, the when and where of the successful speculation. There will be but one chaunt, and the chorus of that will be the eternal dollar.—There will be but one care wrinkling our souls as it wrinkles prematurely our cheeks, and that will be for the miserable secret, which shall turn our baser metals into gold, or at least, into a currency, which shall serve a present purpose. This is the only concern of newspaper and statesman. The schemes of the politician and the philosopher, are equally addressed to this one necessity. Even the government it is now assumed, must be made subservient to trade; and to hearken to the universal language of orator and press, it would seem as if the popular enterprise were the only consideration which deserved our esteem.—An improvement in Rail-roads or Steam Engines, is spoken of as a great moral improvement—a discovery in physical science, which may increase the powers of machinery, wins all the palinodes of the press, and we constantly deceive ourselves in this way by confounding the idea of a cunning or an ingenious with a great people. We hear *ad nauseam,* the applause of those toils or inventions which may be applied to the acquisition or the preservation of property, and this seems to be the whole amount of our national idea of progress. To morals, letters and the fine arts,—to the pure, reserved and delicate forms of taste and fancy—which to be won are to be worshipped, we are as profoundly indifferent as if we were no longer human, or as if there was no world beside to reproach us with our shame. How should such things deserve our regard? They can only minister to the affections—they can only elevate the soul—they can only tame the savage—they can only give birth to such stale virtues as veneration, filial love, meekness, charity, gentle moods and hallowing household graces. And what are these to him who wants money only—who knows no other want—whose heart seeks no other affections—whose taste demands no other objects of delight— whose soul is perfectly satisfied having no other God!

With impatient spirit, a heart swelling with diseased desires, a hope that knows no measure in modesty or reason—our country, at this moment, through its inappreciation of the social virtues, presents a deplorable picture to the eye and mind. It is a nation free from beggary. Never was nation so free at all times from this saddest of all conditions. No man lacks in food or clothing. Never was nation, in the whole broad eye of the sun, so well fed and habited,—with such various food—with such fine raiment. Plenty covers the land, and the God who has been thus bountiful in blessings, has withheld the arm of punishment. There is no pestilence in our cities—there is no savage at riot along our borders. Yet we clamor—we complain! Never was mouth so loud as the American in the language of complaint! Of what do we complain? That the Arts avoid our shores—that the Graces fly from our habitations—that we have lost

"Our peace, our fearful innocence,"

that we are selfish men—that we have no Literature worthy of the name—that our desires are base—that brutality stalks among us with a rare impudence—that crime is rising with hideous dimensions throughout the land? Is it of these things we clamour? No! No! These are matters of small significance—these call for no complaints—offend no feelings—alarm no virtues—occasion no lamentations. Our clamor is for something better, sweeter, dearer,—more necessary to our souls—for gold, for silver, or, more specious delusion still, though more harmless, for good current paper of banks not yet absolutely broken. The national appetite rages—is still unsatisfied—will never be satisfied. We are torn with the greed that works within us—our want, not our need,—raving that "promises to pay," will no longer enable us to fleece the poor of our own, and defraud the rich of a foreign nation!

This is a terrible picture! Is it not a true one? Where are we as a people? What is our moral rank among the nations? We cannot shut our eyes to the melancholy truth. We cannot close our ears to the accents of scornful denunciation. We are sunk, lamentably sunk in character—not our Government—do not delude yourselves,—but our people,—you, and I, and all of us. The Government of State and Nation is a name—the mere creature of the people, drawing breath at our will, dependent wholly upon our decree, and moving this way or that, at our ordinance. The sin is ours, and the shame, and we must face its consequences, with what courage is left us.—And yet, hear our orators—read our newspapers! Unless when dealing in the grateful toil of defaming a rival party, their language is that of the happiest self-complacency.—Their skirts, they fancy,—at least they allege,—are clear of the dishonor, and, if they allow themselves to speak at all of our foreign discredit, it is only to lament that the loss of fame will be a loss of money—will prevent us from getting new loans. I, for one, rejoice that the nation can procure no new loans. It is necessary for the national virtue that we should be humbled. We have run a long career of profligacy, and the humiliation which is due to our vices is necessary to our regeneration. We must be made to feel the want and the shame together. We must be made to see that while the foreign creditor points one finger at our violated obligations, he keeps the other tenaciously upon his money-bags.

GENTLEMEN OF THE EROSOPHIC SOCIETY:

The vices which have degraded the nation first had their beginning in the household. The character of a popular Government is that of its society;—and this consideration brings us back to our starting place.—Our reform must begin where our virtues faltered—at home—in each home—in all homes—by the hearths which we are too prone to abandon,—and prostrate before those family altars which we do not sufficiently venerate. We must endeavor, as rapidly as we can, to recall the domestic virtues of our ancestors—those which made them triumph over French and Spaniard—which enabled them to give you permanent seisin of this noble State and City—that profound reverence for the social tie, which is at the very root of all our human obligations, and, without which, no nation ever perpetuates its conquests. In this maternal virtue, (for such I consider it,) I have endeavored to show the good old English excellence. To the decline of this virtue among us, I ascribe our present feebleness, distress and discontent. There is distress among us, because there is discontent, and this distress and discontent are the more dangerous because they are without cause. They show that something is wrong in our morals, in our affections, in our hopes, in our economy. But it is our religion, not our fortune, which is at fault. We have need to pray rather than complain—to toil, rather than contend—to implore wisdom from heaven to our aid, rather than audaciously challenge the sympathies of heaven and earth, for a condition, which, but for our vices, would be the most enviable of that of any nation upon earth. We have much to attain, and much to overcome. We must moderate our desires—restrain our impatience,—learn to respect labor—abridge our propensity to wander, and narrow our ambition as much as possible to the sphere in which our affections should move. We must give up our vague and morbid cravings after a condition which few persons can, at any time, attain. We must put on a more subdued demeanour. We must acquire a temper of more content and cheerfulness. We must concentrate our energies upon the little spot in which we take up our abodes, and, in making that lovely to the mind, we shall discover in it abundant resources to satisfy all the mind's desires. These duties, Gentlemen, are particularly yours. To you are entrusted the large and teeming interests of the future. The happiness of our society, the destinies of our nation, depend upon those who now stand, half conscious only of their solemn position, upon the threshold of social and political existence. You have been selected from a large body of your fellow-citizens, to receive the advantages of superior culture. You have not been forced, by selfish parents, or ungenial necessities, to yield up your youthful souls to Mammon. Yours should be a nature, equally refined and unselfish. Your boyhood has been shielded from petty and pressing cares. These academic walks should have tempered your passions, while the study of the great masters of antiquity should have lifted your thoughts to the contemplation of the superior virtues and the highest excellencies of human nature. The education which you have received, has been calculated only to force upon each of you the exercise of his own intellectual individuality. To bring out that native mind and character which is the peculiar allotment of man over all other beings. Armed with this individuality, the discretion of an individual will is accorded you. You are to compare and to choose. You are to go forth in the exercise of that vocation for which God has designed you, to strive in its labors and to gather its rewards. To you over all, how important that the truth should be known. The adoption of an error, as a truth, at the beginning of manhood, is the adoption of a bondage which few men, though living out the seventy years of their allotted span, ever succeed in casting off. How necessary to think deliberately—to choose with as little impulse or passion as may be. I have already said that one of the great dangers of the American mind is its impatience—its impetuosity—its keen anxiety to take the field.—A generous quality if rightly governed; but which is too pleasing to the ambitious parent to be schooled, and too grateful to the ardent boy, to be voluntarily subdued. Happy if it takes up the right cause—fortunate if it finds the proper ally—but worse than wretched, and liable to utter defeat, in hope, heart and fortune, if the side chosen be wrong, and the alliance be with some natural enemy of virtue. After what has been already said, I need scarcely repeat, Gentlemen, how very wretched and dangerous I think our whole social system. We are all wrong, even as regards the search after fortune—for where are the fortunes of those who have been most searching, and, as they fancied, most successful? We are still more in error, as regards our pursuit of happiness. We lack too many qualities of training and education, to succeed well in either of these objects. We lack fortitude as well as patience—modesty and veneration—gentleness of behaviour and industry of habit. We neither know how to toil nor how to endure. We regard labor as slavish, and endurance as a sort of baseness. We indulge in the most confident assertion, at one moment, and, in the next, repine in the most dastardly complaint;—and in all our promises and performances, prove ourselves singularly insensible to the true objects of delight or happiness. These, I have shown, are to be found in a more devout adherence to the laws of domestic comfort. But these laws we do not admire and do not obey. We have no faith in one another. Our tastes are purely animal. Our appetites master us. We lack the simplicity of a truthful, earnest nature. We substitute rudeness for frankness. We look upon a gentle deportment as a proof of imbecility, and we are more pleased with the swagger of the ruffian, who yields nothing, to the courtly grace of the gentleman, who knows what a noble thing it is to yield gracefully. These, it will not be denied, are too much the characteristics of our social life. It is in this respect that we find all our deficiencies.—Viewed, externally, as a mere nation, we are a surprising people, and our vanity is sufficiently delighted in being called so. We obey the laws of progress as promptly as any other nation—perhaps much more so—in all those concerns which regard man as a machine, capable of certain physical performances, or those only beside, which, if not absolutely physical, concern nothing so much as physics. But these, believe me, are small triumphs—not to be counted in the history of progress in a great Christian nation. The powers of steam—the facilities of railroads—the capacity to overcome time and space, are wonderful things,—but they are not virtues, nor duties, nor laws, nor affections. I do not believe that all the steam power in the world can bring happiness to one poor human heart. Still less can I believe that all the rail-roads in the world can carry one poor soul to heaven. And these are the real objects of life—to live well, and do well, in preparation for the future. By keeping these objects in mind, you will patiently submit to the conviction that labor is the law of life, and that labor is not only honorable in itself, but ennobling to him who adopts it as his law. You will discard all thoughts of fortune-making. This is not the business of man,—nay, its pursuit is usually fatal to all his proper performances. On this subject we have a conclusive authority. What is it that we are authorized to ask for, in our morning prayer to God? "Give us this day our daily bread." No more,—Yet this is much—much more than any of us deserve. Millions rise every morning in Europe, with an overpowering apprehension, that day, that they shall get no bread,—neither for themselves nor for their little ones. Nobody contents himself, in America, with so humble a desire,—and were we to form any idea of our prayers, in this country, from our complaints, we should be seen, morning and night, before the throne of God, supplicating, not for bread, but fortune. The mere bread of life seems but a sorry object of prayer; and yet, without this prayer, no better future awaits us. Certainly, peace, security, happiness, are not ours, with all our toils, and with all our prayers to fortune. Gentlemen, we must pray to God, and not to fortune!

NOTE

1. This passage may seem to require explanation. We are all so accustomed in this country—influenced less by the authorities of history than by the generalizing declamation of popular orators—to ascribe to a common cause and common provocations, the grand movements, in all the colonies, of the American Revolution, that, with many persons, not well read in these matters, it may occasion great surprise to be told, that there were any wrongs, proposed to be redressed by that event, other than those which grew out of the Stamp duties and the tax on Teas. In this revolution, as in every other, there were latent causes of complaint, less said than felt, better understood than spoken,—which, perhaps, had a more active agency in bringing about the great result, than any of the more readily avowed provocations. There were social evils, every where, springing out of the ill-defined relation between the colonies and the parent country, to which our text could only suggestively advert, yet which, just as imperatively as any other, demanded the application of the most prompt and patriotic remedies. Thus, for example, though South-Carolina had always been one of the most favored of the British provinces—not conflicting, in any way, with the course of British trade—not threatening the wondrous progress of her manufacturing and her commercial powers—and liberally furnished, when needing

them, (and even when not needing them) with British arms and British money—yet she had her own grievances of which to complain, and those of a kind equally to endanger her liberties, and to mortify the honorable ambition of her sons. One of these,—and a sufficient cause of quarrel—consisted in the virtual denial, by the mother country, of her capacity,—and in the absolute denial of her right,—to officer herself from among her own people—a base and miserable policy, such as Great Britain still pursues towards her colonies, by which she lost the affections of the South, and by which, sooner or later, she will lose her Canadian possessions, as she has already lost the only guaranty which might secure them,—the loves, the hearts, of their people. The creatures of the court— creatures basely incompetent to their duties—were provided for by placing them in power over a people, to whose leading minds they were inferior, and for whose interests and in whose society, they had no sympathy. Not only were the civil offices filled in this manner, by their creatures, but the military also; and a studied disparagement of the native intellect, seemed to form a part of the government policy, as it were, to perpetuate more completely the dependence of the one, and the authority of the other people. Under the slavish results which followed, we suffer, to some extent, to this very moment; but of the direct evils which flowed from such a system, our entire colonial history is full of pregnant examples—a reference to one of which—that of Braddock—will suffice to illustrate the whole. It so happened that, in South-Carolina, the carrying out of this system, led to the absolute expulsion from the seats of civil authority of certain of the most influential natives, just about the time when the discontents were most active—without actually being war—in Massachusetts Bay. One of these gentlemen, was the celebrated William Henry Drayton, a statesman who in Carolina, contributed quite as much as any other one person to prepare the public mind for the final issue. He was driven from the seat of Chief Justice, and a creature of the court put in his place. But we have no space for examples, and our purpose is nothing more than to indicate the clue by which the student may pursue a train of inquiry not often suggested. In the memoirs and correspondence of Josiah Quincy, Jr., we find a few passages which will illustrate, in some degree, what we have been saying. This gentleman's share in the ante-revolutionary proceedings, is well known. He visited South-Carolina in 1773. His observations generally are those of an honest man and man of sense. In the extracts which follow, the reader will note the passages which I have italicized.

"In company were two of the late appointed assistant justices from Great Britain. Their behaviour by no means abated my zeal against British appointments. In company dined Thomas Bee, Esq., a planter of considerable opulence, a gentleman of good sense, improvement, and politeness. From Mr. ——— I received assurance of the truth of what I had before heard, that a few years ago, the assistant judges of the Supreme Court of the province, being natives, men of abilities, fortune, and good fame, an act of assembly passed, to settle £300 sterling a year upon them, whenever the king should grant them commissions, *quam diu se bene gesserint*. The act being sent home for concurrence, was disallowed, and the reason assigned was the above clause. I am promised by Mr. ——— a transcript of the reasons of disallowance, with the Attorney and Solicitor General's opinions relative to the act. Upon this, the assembly passed an act, to establish the like salary, *payable out of any monies that shall be in the treasury:*—not restricting it to any alteration in the tenure of their commission.

"Mark the sequel. No assistant judges had ever before been nominated in England. Immediately upon the king's approving this last act, Lord Hillsborough, in his zeal for American good, forthwith sends over one chief justice, an Irishman, and two assistant justices; the one a Scotchman, and the other a Welshman."
****

"The Constitution of South-Carolina is in very many respects defective, and in an equal number extremely bad. The whole body of this people seem averse to the claims and assumptions of the British legislature over the colonies; but you will seldom hear, even in political conversation, any warm or animated expressions against the measures of administration. A general doubt of the firmness and integrity of the Northern colonies is prevalent; they say 'the Massachusetts Bay can talk, vote, and resolve, but their doings are not correspondent.' Sentiments and expressions of this kind are common and fashionable. They arise from various causes, from envy and jealousy in some, and from artifice in others. The very remarkable difference in their manners, religious tenets, and principles, contributes to the same effect. It may well be questioned whether there is, in reality, any third branch in the constitution of this government. It is true they have a House of Assembly, but whom do they represent? The laborer, the mechanic, the tradesman, the farmer or yeoman? No,—the representatives are almost wholly rich planters. The planting interest is therefore represented, but I conceive nothing else, as it ought to be. Non-residents may be chosen to represent any town, if they have lands in the county, and hence a great majority of the House live in Charleston, where the body of the planters reside during the sickly months. A fatal kind of policy!—*At present the House of Assembly are staunch colonists. The council, judges, and other great officers are all appointed by mandamus from Great Britain. Nay, even the clerk of the board and assembly!—Who are, and have been thus appointed? Persons disconnected with the people and obnoxious to them. I heard several planters say, 'We none of us can expect the honors of the State; they are all given away, to worthless, poor sycophants.'"*
[Simms's "Note to Page 12." of the Erosophic Society's 1843 publication of the address.]

"The Sources of American Independence" (1844)

The advocate has great reason to rejoice, my friends, who, in addition to the merits of a noble cause, can lay claim to a perfectly sympathizing audience—who feels that he has only to unfold his own sentiments to embody theirs, and who, in the utterance of his own emotions possesses himself of all the avenues to their confidence. It is this fact, in some degree, that renders it, ordinarily, so easy a matter to play the orator on the great day of our nation. Hence, the many eloquent voices that fill the land at this period,—court and camp, city and country,—each, rejoicing in its peculiar organ of pride and patriotism—each strong and striving in the necessity of speech; old and young assembling with equal interest—the venerable and the beautiful,—the one to glory in the achievements of the past, the other to delight in the golden promise of the future, all exulting in that universal sentiment of country, which at once inspires the ear of faith and the tongue of eloquence. Soothed and enlivened equally by the common theme, the people grow indulgent to the speaker. Their sympathies lend him courage—their emotions excite his fancy and provoke his imagination; and sorry, indeed, must be the orator who shall utterly fail in kindling that enthusiasm which needs nothing but a spark; who, when his subject is already in their hearts—held there, and gloriously enshrined by the very proudest of memories—shall make no impression upon their senses—shall bring no freshening light into their eyes, and, from the consciousness which is so active in the souls that feel, shall gather no happy stimulus to inform the spirit of him who speaks!

But the subject so grateful, and the audience so indulgent, have their difficulties also; and these arise, strange to say, from their very accessibleness. Were the theme less familiar, were the hearer less friendly, there would be, for the speaker, a twofold motive to exertion; in the freshness of his materials, and in the necessity of proving and establishing their value. As it is, the subject,—hacknied by constant iteration,—may well be assumed to be almost, if not wholly stripped of novelty; while the audience, versed in the discussion which has so often filled their ears, are likely to yield but a listless attention to each new speaker who ascends the tribune. What can they hope to hear which they have not heard already? To how many orators, nobler and better graced, have they not listened on this day and subject? The fiery accents of Patrick Henry,—the energetic volume of John Rutledge,—the copious thought and stern propriety of Daniel Webster,—the classic freedom and Ciceronian fulness of Hugh Legare; and legions beside—great minds, majestic speakers,—have challenged their regards in turn, while dilating on the bounteous excellence of the occasion! The orator who follows such as these, may well shrink in his apprehension—overwhelmed with equal doubts of himself and of his subject,—may well, in anticipation of the probable question of his hearers, demand of himself, in secret misgiving,— "wherefore am I here?" How shall he hope to be heard after such wondrous excellence!—following in the wake of speakers, not less endowed by nature, than trained by art, to the business of lifting an audience from its feet, and hurrying away the unresisting soul into the most delicious imprisonment! How shall he hope to find freshness in the subject which has been winnowed by their thunders—how impart attraction to the argument which has been already adjusted by that Ithuriel spear which the heaven-gifted orator still carries in his grasp! Happy, indeed, is the speaker, who shall so far overcome these difficulties as to persuade his hearers into even momentary forgetfulness of those who have gone before him; who shall compel the attention which he seeks to inform, and, in imparting to his subject, the graces and the charm of novelty, who shall avail himself, not only of all the original freshness of the theme, but of all the first patriotic gushes of emotion in the bosoms of his audience.

I need not tell you that I despair of this,—and yet,—I do not despair of the subject. I am not among those who imagine that its freshness is exhausted, and that the soil, which has been so frequently and deeply furrowed, no longer possesses fertility. I am very sure, indeed, that such is not the case—very sure that there are tracts yet uncleared—virgin recesses, in which new paths may be explored, and new prospects unveiled to the eager eyes of patriotic inquiry. The true difficulty in the way of our orator seems rather in the variety than in the exhaustion of his material. It covers so vast a region, absorbs such numerous interests, contemplates so many principles, and unfolds so many performances, that the mind naturally becomes distracted in the survey, and it is in the difficulty of choosing his themes and concentrating his thoughts, rather than their poverty, that the orator is willing to abandon his subject in despair. He feels it less easy to write an oration than a history—less difficult to proceed in regular narration through the seven years war, and the long ill-concealed hostility by which it was preceded, than to embody, by a rapid and comprehensive generalization, the numerous interests from which it derives its character. If he were permitted only to detach its favorite parts,—but one or more of its numerous dependencies,—the task were equally easy and delightful. What a sufficient subject in itself, to trace the gradual progress of English liberty, from the days of Hereward the Saxon, to the period made famous in the usurpation of Cromwell!—to follow that small and subtle flame, from the moment of its first kindling in the sacred swamps of Ely[1]—a dawn rather than a light—to its successive sunbursts in the gloomiest days of Norman despotism,—defying the tyrannies of the Johns, the Stephens, the Edwards and the Henries, of that iron-handed race; and shining out at last, in a certain and confirmed refulgence, in the final expulsion of the Stuarts,—an event designated by the historians as the last grand era in the history of British liberty! Deeply interesting, indeed, to the American, should be the study of that long conflict of the Saxon with his Norman conqueror,—since, in that struggle, we trace the first dawnings of our own emancipation. We follow, with a painful sense of pleasure, the fortunes of the conquered people. We find them unsubdued by bonds, by exaction, by cruelty, and the most degrading privations. We note, with a keen sense of sympathy, their frequent spasmodic attempts to throw off the heavy shackles of their tyrants,—their hope exulting now in the elevation of a Saxon woman to the throne;[2]—struggling now with a bitter earnestness under the cowl of Thomas à Becket, and only stifled and silenced for a moment while the daggers of the assassin are clashing together in his consecrated person.[3]— Anon, making wondrous progress towards foothold and a certain strength, when summoned, by the necessities of the Barons, into importance and a new position at Runnymede, where the first great Charter of English liberty was extorted from the common tyrant by a Saxon people not less than a Norman Baronage;[4]— showing itself again successful, when compelling the ratification of this charter, at the reluctant hands of the Third Edward,—and, finally, extricating itself from the despotism of the Norman race, in the total exclusion of the Stuart dynasty from the throne! The study of these periods, alone, would amply compensate the orator who seeks to enlighten an American audience in the true sources of their own freedom;—for that history is ours;—the memory of that long conflict, and of the sovereign principles which it taught—was almost the only inheritance—an inheritance of equal pride and bitterness—which accompanied our grandsires into the wilderness. The American Revolution, was but a closing act of the great drama begun on the fatal field of Hastings, followed up at Runnymede by the successful union of the people with the Barons, and made terribly triumphant, at Marston Moor and Naseby, in the blood of Norman aristocracy. These battles secured the victory to the people against their oppressors. But they did not conclude the struggle. The political results were not commensurate with those of the conflict. The temporary ascendancy of the Puritans, abused by the superior will of Cromwell, was lost by his death; and the great object for which the people of England had striven, was only in part recovered, in the new line of succession, established by the Revolution of 1688.

The battle was thenceforth to be fought anew. The friends of popular liberty, were taught to see, in the caprices of their political fortunes, that something more than mere patriotism and numbers, was necessary to the success of the good old cause. In what did this deficiency consist? In the acquisition, simply, of a new field for the old conflict! A breathing spell, a breathing space,—a temporary repose—a fair field!—and the protracted struggle must be renewed. Neither the people nor the cause was wanting—it was the battle field alone. England offered none. No space in Europe was sufficiently large or unincumbered for the working out, by the masses, of that great problem, on the solution of which depended the divine right of kings or people! The existing despotisms—the established church,—the feudal nobility—these were the powers, armed to the teeth,—fenced in by the completest panoply of art and artifice—which were leagued in deadly hostility against the cause of man. Banded by common lusts and common dangers, the wealthier and more intellectual castes,—doubly strong because of their union with the wild and mercenary,—were in possession of all the strong-holds of Europe. The nations,—fettered by convention, every where coerced and kept in subjection by the linked hands and iron influences of a potent aristocracy, inflexible in it prejudices and watchful to strangle the man-child, Liberty, the very moment he should give sign of breath or being—left the old world without a single spot upon which the oppressed multitudes could rally and unite while erecting the banner of civil freedom. But Providence was not unmindful of the necessities of the race! The required field was furnished for the mighty conflict as soon as men were ready for the strife! It was at a moment most fortunate for human freedom that the new world was yielded to the knowledge of the old. America was the appointed battlefield for European liberty. Here was the old fight of the Saxon with his Norman tyrant, to be renewed, and set at rest forever! Here, with no walled fortresses to quell insurrection—with no legions of hireling soldiery to arrest the incipient efforts of freedom;—the spirit of mankind, collecting all its vigor from a thousand lands, was enabled to throw off the weight of that intolerable despotism which had cramped its mighty energies so long. Here, and here alone, could the scattered and suspected worshippers of liberty unite in safety for the erection of her altars. Here were no artificial bonds of society or law, subduing the free spirit of man to the condition of the brute,—till he himself, familiar with his shame, becomes wholly insensible to what might be his pride. Here were no inflexible fetters of routine, perhaps the worst, to baffle and to blind the intellect—to mock the hope—to arrest the uplooking desire of humanity—to restrain the yearnings of that noble spirit, bent on progress, which, once upon the track, with a firm grasp upon the clues leading to the undiscovered truth, can never be kept from its acquisition, unless by the arbitrary hands of power! The broad wildernesses of America yielded to Europe the field, which was alike necessary to its denied intellect and its down-trodden multitudes. Ignorant themselves of the destiny before them, of the great work for which they were chosen, we see them traversing the mighty deep, in their frail and cumbered vessels. Faint and few at first, in scattered groups, the hopeless outcasts of fortune, gathering from all parts of Europe, are taking their mournful way to the unknown realms of the Atlantic. Great hearts, yearning impulses of thought, spirits impatient of injustice,—a pride that will not bend to man,—a faith that strives in its own way to bend before God,—and that humble virtue, which is simply dissatisfied to dwell where wrong is every where triumphant,—these were the sources of that social strength which was to do battle, on the plains of America, for the nations of the earth.

We hear a great deal said, in these days, of what is due by this country to the gallant foreigner,—to the generous Irishman, the buoyant Frenchman, the fearless and much-enduring Pole. I shall not underrate their services. I shall not deny their valor. I thank them, and God! for the noble blood which they poured forth so freely in the cause of America. But that cause was their own! It was for this very conflict that America was yielded to Europe, and they were summoned to her fields of battle. The broad plains of America, undefaced by the gloomy towers of baronial strength and vassalage, afforded them severally what their own countries had denied—a fair field and fair play, for the struggle with their hereditary foes. Could Pole, or Irishman, or Frenchman, have been permitted to assert his freedom, successfully, in arms at home, we had never seen them here. They came here with the same motive that brought our sires! *They are our sires.* It is our pride that we spring from the united vigor of the noblest races of mankind,—that no exhausted stocks—no puny aristocracy, degraded and made diminutive as well in mental as in physical stature,—gave us the proud birth-right of free souls, and fearless hearts, and firm thews and sinews, which are the beginnings of our greatness. Let the weak and impotent boast of homogeneousness. The amalgam, which is our pride, is secure of a progeny, quite as noble and much more enduring. It is no shame to exult in the prowess of the foreigner, leagued with the native, in the glorious work of the Revolution. It was not simply the cause of the colonists for which they fought, but the cause of man; and what more natural than that man, from every quarter of the globe, should unite against an enemy which, in all other quarters of the globe, had shown itself too powerful for all his opposition! America was, by Providence, the appointed place of refuge, from the tyranny of the ancient world. The providential hand grows conspicuous in every stage of her progress! It was natural enough that the Spaniard, the most adventurous of European nations, should make the discovery of the country,—but how should the Spaniard, the most bigoted of all European people, be entrusted with the safety of a principle, so necessary to the growth and progress of the whole human family. The Frenchman, who had never yet been taught to resist the march of tyranny at home, was as little prepared for the responsibilities of such a trust. It was for the Anglo-Saxon race—a people early united against the oppressor—struggling for their rights from the beginning—struggling ever for the right—and losing no chance, whether by the exercise of their own strength, or by playing off their tyrants against one another, to increase their securities;—a stubborn, an invincible people—not easily deceived—not easily driven from their purpose, and never to be mocked in their hope;—it was for these, alone, to seize upon the sacred inheritance, and, training themselves quietly for the great conflict, to take secure foot-hold, and gain firm possession of the field, before unfurling that banner of stars which was to become the sun-burst of the world! It was in their very feebleness that the American colonists were enabled to lay the foundations of their own and the world's liberties! How should the great empires of Europe feel apprehensive from the infant labors of the scattered groups of settlers, who had wandered across the ocean into forests three thousand miles away? How should the regal tyrannies of Spain and England, ever dream to hear the trumpet-note of defiance sounded in their ears, from the rude hamlets that dotted the banks of Indian waters in America? Could human foresight have conjectured a danger such as this, how easy to have crushed them in the cradle!—to have extinguished, by a breath, the first faint glimmerings of that glorious flame; which now, lofty and radiant as the sun, looms out, from tower and temple of our vast republic, a wondrous beacon of hope and promise, for the still groping nations of the European world!

Here, then, alone, may be found a sufficient and splendid subject for the orator, who would dilate on the sources of American liberty. He has but to follow the stream of English history,—for it was really the old spirit of the Anglo-Saxon, warring with his Norman tyrant, that informed the revolution of America! Let this train of inquiry be pursued,—analyze our colonial history,—distinguish its frequent epochs,—and we find constant proofs of the stubborn spirit of the same race, struggling for the blessing which it did not dare to name, long before the triumphant issue which we this day meet to celebrate! Confine this examination to our own State, and we get a tolerably fair idea of the events in all the colonies. The career of Carolina, from the very first settlements on Ashley River, was a series of impatient strivings against a dominion, which, in one form or another, was always held in detestation. We find the people, from the earliest periods, torn with discontents and strife,—struggling with their domestic rulers, and throwing them off in banishment,—rebelling against their proprietary lords, and flinging them off in like manner,—and, finally, with arms in their hands, defying the authority of the sovereign. With what coolness, what caution, what gradual but certain steps, did they approach this conclusion,—after how many years of endurance and preparation! But the advantages of a new field, for the old fight, were felt as thoroughly by the great men of America, in 1670, as, one hundred years later, in 1776. The very possession of the new field, taught its own advantages; while the conditions of trial which it imposed, equally, upon mind and muscle, wonderfully developed their own strength and the resources of the country, to the hardy children of the soil. Great spirits, meanwhile, were ripening for the exigency. Seventy years of self-training, in the new world, added to the glorious inheritance of thought, and character, and ancient experience, which had come from their European ancestry, had brought out all the vigor of the Anglo-Saxon race;—had opened to their eyes the most startling visions of a great truth,—visions full of the most glorious promise,—by which they were lifted, in moral respects, very far above the great body of the people they had left. Prophets, too, had arisen among them,—men, like Moses among the Israelites, capable, not only of showing, but of conducting them in safety to the Land of Promise;—building for them, out of the indestructible materials of their own character and virtue, the glorious ark of their political covenant. It is in the possession of such master spirits that we are to recognize the first true sources of hope for a people in bondage. No nation, let me say, ever succeeds in throwing off its manacles,—nay, no nation has a right to succeed,—until, from its own ranks, it can raise up individuals who shall prove themselves able to grapple, on equal terms, with the highest intellectual strength of the oppressor. A race, inferior in mind and moral to that which subdues it, can never relieve itself from subjection; and no conquering nation, degenerating to the condition of the inferior, can ever maintain its authority over the conquered people. It was only when the Jews could produce a Moses—a man capable of contending with the ablest of the Egyptian priesthood,—that God ever sanctioned their prayer for deliverance. It was only when they could produce from among themselves, men capable of taking charge of them, and bound to their service by all the ties of blood and a common necessity, that they were suffered to go free. So, it was only in the miserable degeneracy of the modern Spaniard, that the Mexican could assert his independence. Nobody can suppose that the soldiers of Santa Anna, a slavish and timorous race, herds of whom would be annihilated by a single troop of Anglo-Saxon cavalry, could have stood, for a moment, the charge of veterans like those of Hernan Cortés! But, when Spain was begging help from Britain to maintain her position at home, it was absurd to suppose that she could keep her dependencies in America. The troops of Santa Anna, wretched as they are, were quite as good as those of the European sovereign; and the Mexican chief, inferior as we may think him, was no doubt quite worthy to oppose the best general in the Spanish service.

It is in the advent of the superior intellect that we are to behold the first proofs of a people's capacity for freedom. It is then, and then only, that they may be assumed to be equal to the perilous duties of self government;—and here, let me remark, that self government does not imply, as is sometimes erroneously imagined, the universal diffusion of a capacity for rule among the great body of a people,—for this would be an absurdity refutable with the experience of each returning day—but simply such a concentration of endowment among individuals rising from their masses, as will enable them to carry out the great popular trusts which are to secure the birthright of the race. And, long before the final struggle of the American colonist, with the British crown, such individuals were living in our forests; men, capable of counselling British statesmen,—of informing British philosophy,—of leading British armies to victory;—men, whose voices, strong in the virtues of genius and patriotism, could lead, at will, the delighted and reverential multitude,—philosophers, who could conduct to earth and disarm of its terrors, the wildest lightnings of heaven,—statesmen, who could pursue to triumphant issue the most complicated policies of empire,—and warriors, who could even extricate British valor from the slaughter to which it had been hurried by the blind wilfulness of British presumption. Such were the Henries, the Franklins, the Gadsdens, the Adamses, the Marions, and the Washingtons of infant America. These men were not only equal, but, in some important respects, very far superior to their European contemporaries. Men they were, of deep thought and searching eloquence; of equal nerve and purity; of great powers of endurance; unflinching in resolution, and of the most exquisite capacities for conduct. Compare the leaders of the Revolutionary movement in America, with the influential ministers of Great Britain during the same period—compare them with the public mind of that country,—and you will see, at a glance, why it was that our ancestors revolted from British dominion, and succeeded in shaking it off. It was not because of any miserable tax on stamped paper, or any half-penny duty upon teas. It is high time that these absurdities should be blotted from our books. These were pretexts only—the mere showing of persons who had resolved on the independence of the country, and were destined for its achievement, even though the British ministry had left the people entirely untaxed. These duties were usurpations doubtless, but they were not the adequate provocations to the bloody war that followed: nor would they have been followed by that war, but that the convictions of the British monarch led him at once to the true source of the discontents in America. The better reasons for the revolt are to be found in the fact that the time for our emancipation had arrived—because we could go alone, and needed British leading strings no longer. We had worked long enough for the Egyptians, and felt that it was high time to set up for ourselves. We had proved our independence long before we asserted it, and felt the shame and the dishonor,—having such mighty men in our own land,—of being governed by a people, in no respect superior, three thousand miles away! The injustice from which we suffered did not consist in the loss of the sixpences for which we were assessed by the foreign governor, but that we should have a foreign governor at all! It was a revolt of the native mind of the country, confident of its strength, assured of its resources, and resolving, with equal patriotism and courage, that no nation can be permanently safe which is not under the direction of the native intellect. For what else was this intellect assigned a people? What Deity confers the gifts of genius upon a slave,—endows, with the aspirations of soul, a creature destined only for the exactions of time,—lights a fire within the yearning heart of the freeman, only that it may be extinguished beneath the brutal heels of oppression,—or plants the seed of a heavenly virtue in the breast, while ordaining that it shall never grow? The possession of the endowment is the best authority for its use. The gifts of intellect to the people of America, were not decreed to rust in abeyance,—to grow worthless from inaction,—and mock with the reproach of the most wretched prostitution, the possessor, who, thus efficiently endowed, is yet content to crouch under the incubus of foreign dominion! Why, with Jefferson and Patrick Henry for our councils, should we prefer the rule of North and Bute, in London,—with Washington and Marion for our armies, should it be necessary to import Braddock and Sir Henry Clinton? The great struggle of American independence, was to prove that we could do without such assistance. Until that period, it had been the policy of Europe to assert that man degenerated in America,—that he could neither direct in council nor lead in battle. The Briton not only scorned to be tutored by the "buckskin," but arrogated the merit of his achievements.[5] Monsieur Buffon, and other philosophers, arguing from pre-conceived opinions, stoutly asserted the inferiority of all moral and even physical humanity in this country. Our men were to be puny of form, and base of understanding, and were to sink, dwarfed by successive generations, into marvels of curiosity for European speculation. It was in vain that we dwelt upon the stupendous and magnificent scale by which nature had wrought, in almost every part of her American domain. It was in vain that we pointed to our mighty rivers,—our towering mountains,—wide-spread continents, and wondrous oceans,—our gigantic trees,—our colossal remains,—our seas of forest, dense, tangled and venerable,—inhabited by beast and reptile, all of marvellous size and peculiar attributes,—and birds, of wing so capacious, as to hold dominion, almost at a single flight, from the Pacific to the Atlantic sea! Arguing from all analogies, there was good reason to suppose that man was not to be denied a corresponding development, by that liberal mother who had so fruitfully endowed his home. Our European sages were unwilling to discover this. They reasoned no less against facts than against analogies. It was their policy not to see, and not to believe. There was a something unfriendly to European nature in our soil,—

> "our skies,
> Where genius sickens and where fancy dies,"—

and, to such an extent was this absurd philosophy carried, that, when our great men began to show themselves, and to achieve their victories, they were believed in Europe to be neither more nor less than Englishmen in disguise. Washington himself, was, for a long time, asserted to be an European,—an error somewhat perpetuated to this day among our enemies, since we find a recent writer of Great Britain, claiming, for that country, all the substantial merits of his fame. "It is the highest glory of England," says Mr. Alison, in his eloquent but jaundiced history, "to have given birth, even amid trans-Atlantic wilds, to such a man!" If England did give birth to such a man in America, it is only wonderful that she did not equally succeed with her less questionable offspring at home. Something is undoubtedly due to the Anglo-Saxon origin of Washington. It is our pride to have descended from that tenacious and liberty-loving people. It is our glory to insist that the American Revolution was nothing less than the old conflict, the principles of which were partially declared at Runnymede. But the American patriots, with Washington at their head, were possessed of resources, in morals and in intellect, which were peculiarly American. The broad wildernesses of our forest land, which yielded a fair field for the contending races, were as necessary to the development of the natural man for the unscaling of his mental vision—for his extrication from that social training, which, in highly sophisticated communities, is apt to emasculate the simplicity of a great soul, and to subdue, in the patriot, those earnest essentials of independent character, without which the work of national deliverance can never be achieved, and would never be undertaken.

It was in the wrong done to the native genius,—in its denial of trust,—its exclusion from honorable consideration,—that made common cause, throughout all Saxon America, of the revolutionary struggle. How else should colonies, so little assimilated by constitution, by manners, or by occupation, have been brought together in this struggle? Here, at the very outset, in the seemingly simple act of union, lay the most remarkable circumstance in the history of the Revolution. It was only by a combination of their separate strength, that they could possibly hope to be successful; and yet, how few were the influences by which that union was likely to be brought about. The great work, therefore, was in the alliance, offensive and defensive, between colonies remote from each other, of rare correspondence, of infrequent communion, and strikingly dissimilar in tastes, habits and pursuits. They were not a people calculated to assimilate for any object, not, of itself, the most absorbing and imperious. What unity of feeling was there between the Bay of Massachusetts and the settlements on Ashley River? As little then as now! Nay, there was positive diversity, if not dislike, between them. Trained in differing and conflicting schools, hostile in opinion, doubtful of one another,—mutually distasteful and distrustful,—how were they to be reconciled,—moved to obey the joint necessity, and to march, shoulder to shoulder, against the foreign oppressor? Had Carolina been governed by no other considerations of anger, than such as arose from the expensiveness of British protection, she would, in all probability, have remained to this day under the rule of King, Lords and Commons! She had few or no causes of quarrel, of a pecuniary nature, with the mother country. She had no manufactures, requiring the forcing process of protection,—no shipping to crave the monopoly of the carrying trade,—was aiming at no rivalry with the commercial genius of Great

Britain. She was rather the pet and the favorite of that ambitious empire. Her raw productions, carried from our ports in British bottoms, were returned to us in British manufactures. The business of the two countries harmonized happily,—in no ways came into conflict,—and, had the British Parliament taken its cue from the British merchant, New-England might have been left to herself—even to this day—to carry out, her numerous schemes, whether of commerce, manufactures, or—philanthropy. In money, in means, in military help,—in various social affinities,—Carolina received from the maternal nation quite as much, in all probability, as she ever yielded to the British revenues. Why, then, should she go into the conflict? Why form an alliance, with this object, with communities which had so few claims upon her sympathies,—for which neither mutual interest, nor mutual esteem, furnished any sufficient motives? It was the difficulty of answering this question, which rendered one-half of her people, not merely reluctant, but hostile to the Revolution. Very far superior, indeed, to these, were the true motives for the struggle,—which brought together, to equal sacrifice, in the same bloody fields of danger, colonies that otherwise had scarcely one sentiment in common. We must not, at this day, suffer ourselves to be deceived by the suggestions which were relied on then, to influence the decisions of the people. It was not then considered politic to utter aloud the true reasons for the strife, or its superior incentives. The better argument was latent, and never declared to the multitude. Hence, indeed, the terrible civil war which followed, by which the plains of Carolina were drenched in fraternal blood. Hence it was, that one half of our people, unsatisfied of the alleged necessity, and remembering only the benefactions of Great Britain,—when the ultimate issue became inevitable,—arrayed themselves under the banner of the sovereign. If, in that day, it had been said that the war contemplated the emancipation of the national mind, and this had been urged as the sufficient motive for the struggle, in all probability our grandsires would have bared the sword in vain. The national mind would have been discredited, and the noblest yearnings of the national soul would have been trampled ignominiously out of sight by provincial subserviency. The movement would have been ascribed to the ambition, and not to the patriotism, of the popular leaders; and that same colonial servility, which, even to this day, turns ever with sycophantic devotion to the intellect and authority of Europe, as to a something, which, by nature, must be very far superior to our own, would have arrayed itself in venomous opposition to the holy cause of national individuality. We should have had thousands to say, as, indeed, they did say, and do say now, "the wisdom of England is quite good enough for us." To spirits such as these, it was deemed a much more imposing argument to show them the purse of the country in peril. They could better comprehend the necessity of national money than national brains,—would sooner fight for cash than character,—and willing, all the while, to recognize a divine right in a foreign despot to sway, with his own creatures, the destinies of a distant country,—to repudiate its mind, and dishonor its greatness,—were yet easily persuaded to perceive the monstrous absurdity and danger of suffering their money-bags in the same divine clutches. To the honorable—to the thoughtful and the noble—to those whom instinct and education taught to snuff tyranny in every foreign breeze,—the true motives for the Revolution were freely spoken, and never more proudly than by Carolina eloquence. They could understand that the cost was nothing, the tribute every thing,—that the foreign domination, when a nation is equal to its own rule, is the most degrading form of human vassalage.

Thus, then, superior to all sordid considerations, did South Carolina enter the confederacy. We need not ask how she bore herself in the conflict which followed. Happily for us, my countrymen, her history needs not to be written. It is already deeply engraven on the everlasting monuments of the nation. It is around us, a living trophy upon all our hills. It is within us, an undying memory in all our hearts. It is a record which no fortune can obliterate—inseparable from all that is great and glorious in the work of the Revolution. Take the name of Carolina from that volume which contains the history of our national existence, and you tear from it some of the brightest jewels in its collection. You take from it the fields of Eutaw and of Cowpens,—of King's Mountain and Fort Sullivan. You take from it the venerated names of Rutledge and of Gadsden, of Marion and Moultrie, of Sumter and of Pickens. You pluck from it some of the noblest cariatides by which its colossal triumphs are upborne. The battle fields which have been distinguished by Carolina valor, and rendered sacred by her blood, are among the most holy memorials of the republic. They stretch themselves in our sight, in unfading verdure, upon every hand. The humblest district in our country, the smallest river, gliding through our territories to the sea, bears some sufficient memorial, of the glory and the suffering of her sons in that bloody strife for independence. Crowned with no monuments, it is certain that they call for none more durable than those which speak through undying memories. The shepherd who conducts you to the plain of blood, who traces out for your survey, the faint outline of the ruined fortress, or the more distinct elevations of the mound of death, is himself a better memorial than any we can raise of marble. So long as he feels it well, on this returning day, to revive, at the altars of his country, the recollections which it brings, we shall need no better monument than himself. When he shall forget the field, the warriors who strove together, and the glorious occasion for the strife, it would be in vain that we would speak to him in brass or marble. Our monuments then would be as unmeaning and inexpressive as those which invite the steps and mock the curiosity of the stranger in the crumbling teocallis of Yucatan. God forbid that the day shall ever arrive, when the "Quien Sabe?" of our peasantry, as they contemplate the memorials of the past glory of their race, shall declare the degradation of the great Anglo-Saxon stock.

And what, since the victory is won,—since that common cause of native Independence for which we made common fight, has been rendered secure against the foreign enemy,—since the Briton no longer threatens our borders, and assumes the dominion in our land—since we have made ourselves one great community, and rejoice in the strength and virtues of a united people—what has been the deportment of Carolina—how has she borne herself as one of this confederacy of States? What have been her contributions of mind and patriotism to the national character? And how has the genius which made itself so gloriously conspicuous in the annals of '76, been honored and maintained by the name, which preserves for us, to this day, that individuality of which we were then so reasonably proud? Let the records show. The war of 1812, so honorable to the country, was a Southern measure, detrimental to the pecuniary interests of Carolina, in which she had conspicuous share. She has not scrupled to yield her interests when the honor of the country was at peril. Certainly, my friends, we have nothing with which to reproach ourselves in our relations to our sister communities. We have been true to them in peace and war,—shrinking from no danger, withholding no sacrifice, which the common interests might require at our hands. We have not faltered in our faith. We have not shrunk from any of our obligations. Our blood and treasure have been freely expended in the common cause of country. Envy and injustice have never dared to accuse us of any deficiency of trust or resolution. We have firmly and honorably held to all the conditions of our compact. We have maintained our relations, with a lofty sense of what is due to ourselves and country. We never penetrate the borders of a sister State to interfere with its laws, to denounce its customs, to disturb the harmony of its society. We pry not into their concerns, vex not their abodes with our surveillance,—disturb none of their securities. There are many things in their domestic economy which we could wish to see altered—some, we are very sure, that might very much be amended. But this is a business peculiarly their own. We should be guilty of presumption were we to trespass upon them with our notions of reform, and doubly criminal to attempt such reform in defiance of their wishes and opinions. We conceive the duties of forbearance, to be quite as imperative as those of performance; and, recognizing still, the great object of our revolution, to be the exercise and assertion of the native intellect, in all native concerns, we freely accord to the people of Massachusetts Bay, the exclusive duties of their own government!

Have they been equally forbearing—have they recognized this principle in regard to us? Have they yielded the same deference to our intellect, the same heed to our securities—to the rights which we possess, as well against themselves, as against the whole European world? What is the history? Is it not one equally offensive to our sensibilities and our Independence? Are they not daily trespassing, more and more, upon our securities. Do they not hourly encroach upon our rights, insult our pride and denounce our institutions? Have they not converted the halls of our common council,—where we are required to meet on equal terms, for the common benefit,—in pacific consultation, and mutually indulgent intercourse,—into an arena for most fearful conflict, and the least justifiable passions; and, in their insane fury, have they not flung from our possession a vast and noble territory, acquired by our kindred, and essential to the natural expansion of our race, simply because its acquisition might afford additional strength and new securities to the people of the South?

There must be an end to this, my countrymen! This bitter warfare will bring its issues, whether the fruits be good or evil. No people not utterly shorn of pride, of manhood, of all the most ordinary sensibilities of human nature; but must finally revolt, at all hazards, against the constant warfare, the prolonged annoyance, the denunciation and the indignity, and take measures of safety and precaution against the dangers which these necessarily imply. We cannot always be patient—we may not always submit with equanimity. The cup of wrath will one day fill to overflowing, and run over, it may be, in measureless retribution. The same sense of mental independence which prompted our ancestors to enter the field in 1776, with the British oppressor, will make us warm now, and watchful, to resent every assault upon the province of our local government, from whatever quarter it may come. The stipulations of our Constitution must be observed—the conditions of the compact, by which we entered the confederacy, must be held in spirit and in letter. The war upon our domestic institutions must have an end. It may be that we err in maintaining them. It may be that we lack some of those philanthropic lights, by which the buyer of the stolen property is the only criminal, and he who steals and sells it is the only saint. We shall not gainsay this morality, which seems to be so perfect a faith in the sons of the slave dealers of Old and New England. We simply deny any accountability to the modern Puritans of these regions. The subject is exclusively our own. Our pride, not less than our securities, requires that the discussion of this matter shall not be suffered to invade the halls of our National Council. The common government must not be made the instrument for the annoyance or the destruction of its individual members. I do not think that the danger is immediate, but the indignity to which a people submits becomes a danger, and every party which is in movement, is a growing party. We must check its growth. We care not for the abstract opinions of any set of men. We leave to the people of the North to think after their own fashions, but they must not put their opinions into action for our detriment. In this cause, against this danger, the people of the South must unite in season. Setting aside the consideration of all ordinary topics, they must address their unanimous will to the arrest of this imposing faction. Strong, equally, in the intellect as in the courage and integrity of her sons, she must compel that deference to her mind, which is, after all, the true security for her rights. It needs but this for our safety.

Let the South but show itself, moving together, in solid phalanx, as one man, and there will be no conflict worthy of the name. Without this union, we can do nothing. This secured, and the strife ceases—the storm cloud disappears, and the bright sun of peace and harmony, moves once more in our political firmament with the serene dignity of our own upsoaring eagle. It is only in our divisions that the enemy succeeds. It is in our very individuality of character—the source of so many of our proudest virtues, magnanimity, hospitality and courage—in the possession of so many proud and independent intellects,—that the common cause of our section is endangered. Our great men of the South are too much given to assert themselves rather than their country—are too easily persuaded to see a rival, rather than an ally, in each Southern brother. Thus it is, that Virginia and the Carolinas, Georgia and Alabama, and Mississippi, are to be found divided among themselves—warring with each other,—seeking to make Presidents, while the North, moving in solid body, is seeking only to make subjects. We must persuade our patriots to believe that the sources of a permanent distinction are to be found always in the assertion of popular, rather than individual claims. He who at heart strives for his people will never be abandoned by them. They cannot abandon him—if they would. They become dependent upon his virtues and his strength, and acknowledge, in his integrity and intellect, his right to rule. Persuade our statesmen to believe this, and our people will be as closely united in feeling as they are in fortune. That we are not so, is due to the selfish infirmities of those to whom we give our trust. Overcome this difficulty—array your Virginians, your Carolinians, your Tennesseans and Alabamians, your Georgians, and Mississippians, in one column, under one great leader, and we sweep away, as with a will, the whole vast meshes of Eastern cunning—their thousand threads and fibres, sufficient to bind us singly, would break like flax smitten by the fire, under the instant pressure of our united strength. The miserable abuses of the tariff,—the creation of unnecessary treasures, unequally gathered for still more unequal distribution,—the brutal fanaticism of abolition,—the thousand schemes of fraud which may be practised and perpetrated under the seemingly innocent sanction of a "general welfare" doctrine—all the myriad arts by which cunning toils ever to wind her web about the limbs of the unsuspecting,—would be dissipated, by the single act of union among ourselves, as easily as the strong man at morning dashes the seal of slumber from his eyelids. Could we engage Southern statesmen in this great object! Could some one great patriarchal mind among us, set forth with the patriotic single-heartedness of Father Mathew, with the view to this glorious consummation! And why should there not be gatherings of the people,—and great orators—in this, as in the temporary cause of local parties, and presidential elections? How unworthy are such inferior objects when the glorious rights which have rendered past struggles sacred, are escaping from our grasp. Let us labor to instil this lesson—to inculcate this duty—to bring our kindred States together in the common cause. To the statesman who, armed only with the sufficient spear of truth, shall make a political progress among us—who shall devote his genius and his life to this consummation,—whose eloquence shall bind conflicting parties,—who shall compel the deference of sordid politicians,—and teach, with the eloquence of a perfect faith, the single principle, "the South, and the South all together,"—and shall succeed in rallying our united powers in the great domestic issues which are before us,—there shall be an eminence of fame superior to that of President or Sovereign—a fame worthy of that of Washington, as proud, as peaceful, as enduring. We can reduce the tariff—we can recover Texas—we can bring statesmen once more back to the Constitution, without strife, without violence or bloodshed,—we can strengthen the old, and acquire new securities for our sectional rights, and all by the simple act of union among ourselves. There is a virtue in such an act, the magic of which would disperse all the sophisms of candidates, and cast down all the cunningly-devised schemes of cliques and classes—silence the hundred clamors of abolitionist and spinning-jenny, and purge the floor of our Council House of the rankness which offends it.

Nor, need we doubt, in the meantime, that Texas shall become ours. Of its loss there is little danger. Armed, as we are, with a jealous watchfulness of Great Britain, she dare not make any movement upon our borders, which shall ally this nation against her. She dare not accept of that cession which we refuse. She is sagacious enough to know certain things, of which our own politicians seem to be ignorant. She knows that nothing would so soon unite the American people as external pressure;—and she as well knows that a republic, the weakest of all nations in time of peace, is the strongest of all nations, engaged in foreign war. It is only in seasons of conflict, that popular governments, like ours, exhibit any of the forces of centralism. It is then, and only then, that heart speaks to heart, in the far-spread regions of our country,—pulse responds to pulse, mind to mind, and the whole kindred nature of the vast republic, efficiently aroused, supplies, with the necessary aliment of blood and spirit, the thousand arteries which feed our energy and strength. Let the provocation ever again occur,—let our country a third time be called to arm against its hereditary enemy,—and, I believe, as I trust, that we shall not forego that warfare, until we banish the British ensign forever from our skies. Cuba, Canada, the West-Indian Islands, are all, no less than Texas, the natural dependencies of our hemisphere, and must, in the inevitable progress of events, become portions of our national domain, and integrals of our spreading empire. It will be for Britain and Mexico to say, whether these shall fall, sooner or later, into our possession. With the increase of our strength, a national and manly foreign policy must make them ours, without the necessity of dissipating the cobweb sophistries of week-day politicians. The absurd pretences by which the acquisition of Texas has been deferred for the present, will not long impose upon the people of America. They are quite too shrewd for that herd of slender statesmen, who, in measuring their own stature by their own standards, are very apt to dwarf their constituencies. Blinded by their besotted selfishness, they seem to have never had any idea of country, separate from the dugs of office. The South demands the annexation of Texas, avowedly, as necessary to the proper balance of power. Without this balance of power, we have no securities. But the great interests of the nation demand it, not less than ourselves. A vast domain, essential to our safety, and, with time, to the natural expansion of the race, is not to be flung from our grasp to satisfy a sectional prejudice, and secure votes for hungry candidates,—creatures, scarcely less blind to their own fortunes—in their excess of selfishness,—than they are indifferent to the great destinies and the superior prospects of the nation. As for faith with Mexico, we have none to break, and our politicians know it. But for their home interests, they had never thought of Mexico. We have recognized Texas as an independent power, and have done business with her as such,—such business,—indeed, the establishment of a definitive boundary,—as could not be transacted with any but a thoroughly independent nation. It was, then, in the power of Texas,—recognized by us,—to say where her boundaries should be. It was just as easy, then, to have said, that the United States territory should reach to the Rio Bravo, as to the Rio Roja. The violation of faith with Mexico, was just as complete in the one as in the other instance. We are not to look behind the curtain to the domestic relations of foreign States. We recognize that government as independent which maintains its independence. The principle is a simple one, which saves a world of trouble. If Texas rebels against Mexican authorities, let the latter compel the contumacious member to obedience. We have made no treaty with her to abstain from treating with any other nation. Her clamors and threats are equally impertinent and ridiculous, and of a piece with the arguments of our domestic statesmen, from whom, indeed, she gathers most of her audacity. These arguments come with monstrous bad grace from those who have been for hurrying us into war with England, because of territory in Oregon, and a strip of land necessary to the profits of the Maine lumber cutters. The indignation of Mexico, no doubt, will be a very fearful thing, but with a good conscience, and a few good frigates, we must endeavor to meet it with what philosophy we may. But the annexation of Texas will give us no war with Mexico, or, if it should, Texas will be perfectly able to do all our fighting. Mexico will be pleased, in reality, to extricate herself from the prosecution of a conflict, in which she has hitherto met nothing but disgrace; and her honor will be spared the humiliation of treating for boundary with a rebellious subject. Her policy is doubly urgent with her to sanction this cession,—allowing her the moderate privilege of a few wry faces,—since, in no other way, can she be secure against the continued encroachments of a people, constantly acquiring new strength, and unfettered by any of those obligations of international law, which alone could keep them from daily aggression upon an enemy, at once feeble and insulting.

There are many topics, brethren of the South, upon which we might discourse. Enough for us now, that we are in a transition state, and must prepare for changes. We should be blind beyond recovery, if we did not behold the signs of their approach. We are not, as I have said already, in a condition of security,—nor has the nation at large attained that stability of position, when we might look with composure on all political fluctuations. It is our common error to regard the close of our revolutionary contest, as settling permanently our institutions. This is a very great mistake. That struggle determined nothing but our independence. Our policy is a more subtle and difficult necessity, which we must elaborate with patience, forbearance, great caution, and with the best wisdom that we can command. We are now only engaged in the trial of our institutions. Let us give them a fair trial. Our experiment was one of equal difficulty and novelty. We must not despair of its final success, because of the vicissitudes which attend its progress. How far it will stand the pressure of the unfriendly influences warring upon it, from without and from within, is a question somewhat depending upon our own philosophy and patriotism. We cannot disguise from ourselves, that the moral and social ties which have bound us to the North, are greatly weakened,—I had almost said sundered. These, as I have shown, were never very strong at the beginning. The common cause did not make us a common family, and the government which grew out of common concessions, can only be maintained by a continuance of such concessions. The ligaments which now chiefly bind us together, are those of our political union,—a tie, the value of which, as it was originally the fruit of compromise, can never be beyond calculation. A conviction of the necessity of such a bond, is almost the only additional security for its permanence. The latter may be easily overborne and forgotten in the excitements of domestic strife,—reckless fanaticism on the one hand, and blind fury and desperate defiance on the other. The other is a form and a shadow, rather than a substance. These ligaments need but little for their rupture. They are too slight to resist the insolence of despotism, and the unreckoning violence of a minority, conscious only of injustice. A few more shocks—one ruder blow—the phrenzy of an audacious, or the malignity of a hostile spirit,—and the noble temple of our confederacy, built by the mighty Architects of the Revolution, is thrown down in irretrievable ruin. When that time shall arrive, my countrymen,—when the sound shall go forth, of fate, and a bitter lamenting through the land,—let it be our boast that our hands have not prepared this overthrow,—that we are not guilty of this ruin. The guilt and the shame of a catastrophe, which shall mock and mortify the whole world's hope of Liberty, must not rest on the fair fame and the conscience of the South.

NOTES

1. For the interesting narrative of Saxon struggle against Norman oppression, see the modern history, by M. Thierry, of the Conquest of England—a history, which, written by a Frenchman, gives us the first and best notions of the protracted conflict of the conquered people for the retention and recovery of their liberties. The fortunes of Hereward the Saxon, are in themselves a romance, and would furnish admirable material for such a master as Walter Scott. The swamps of Ely, were places of refuge and retreat for this brave patriot. Like our own famous partisan, Marion, he made his home in their morasses; in which, for a long time, he baffled the whole force of the conqueror, and was only driven out at last by the treachery of the priesthood [Simms's Note].

2. Editha, afterwards Matilda, an orphan daughter of Malcolm, King of Scotland, and of Margaret, sister to the Saxon King, Edgar. She was married to Henry I. Her name was changed, to flatter the Norman Nobles, into that of Matilda. The unhappy Saxons entertained large hopes from this event, but they were fruitless. The Norman nature was not of that flexible sort, which the influences of love, or of woman, might subdue to gentleness, or beguile into the indulgence of the restive race over which it swayed. It does not appear that Matilda, herself, took any pains to serve her people. She was scarcely so true—perhaps not so influential—as the noble woman, from among the Hebrews, whom Ahasuerus took to wife [Simms's Note].

3. The history of M. Thierry places the career of the Saint, in a light much more favorable to his patriotism than is the case with other historians. According to his narrative, Thomas à Becket was a true lover of his country—a Saxon rather than a priest,—and it is to his patriotism rather than to his tenacious pride, or passion for his order, that we are to ascribe his fierce and unbending opposition to Henry II. It is certainly placing the character of this martyr in a light more grateful to the lover of liberty, when it is understood that he perished because of his devotion to his people, and not in consequence of that stiffnecked arrogance of the churchman,—mingled with the vain and unbecoming desire for temporal authority—which it has been customary to regard as the sources of his contumacy [Simms's Note].

4. De Lolme [Simms's Note].

5. Hence the defeat of Braddock at Duquesne, who refused to take counsel from Washington. It is not so generally known that Col. Middleton, who led the provincial regiment of Carolina, against the Cherokees, in co-operation with Col. Grant, in 1761, subjected the latter gentleman to personal chastisement in the streets of Charleston, because of his arrogating for the foreign troops all the merits of victory. Yet, in the great battle of Etchoee, which decided the war, the forlorn hope was led by Marion at the head of a small corps of natives, and it was by the native rangers that the gloomy defiles were first penetrated, which the Cherokees had crowded with their warriors. Indeed, in all conflicts with the French and Indians in America, the provincials always constituted the advanced bodies of the English armies [Simms's Note].

PART III

Class, Gender, and the Purpose of an Education

Introduction

When William Gilmore Simms talked about students, his orations focused on their lives after graduation, only occasionally touching on their experiences in the classroom. This may be a consequence of Simms's own modest education as a child, "the want of which I often feel & shall continue to feel while I live," he told James Henry Hammond in 1839 (*Letters* 1:161). A couple of indifferent years in Charleston's "common schools" and two more at a grammar school operated by the College of Charleston were the extent of his education before ultimately being apprenticed to a pharmacist around age thirteen (Guilds 8, 15). Simms lacked a point of reference to discuss college life. He was largely an autodidact, his curiosity and voracious reading substituting for a standard curriculum.

As the orations of the preceding sections indicate, Simms's self-taught knowledge of ancient and American history, not to mention his careful study of current events and trends, provided an education on the progress of civilizations, including his own. Societies rose and fell, and the United States and the American South were no different, though he thought he could steer the evolution of these, especially the latter, with his insights. So he resumed this purpose, albeit more indirectly, when he took as his subjects the postgraduate lives of South Carolina's college students for two 1855 orations. "Choice of a Profession" and "Inauguration of the Spartanburg Female College" discuss the responsibilities of men and women, not only for the well-being and prosperity of the individual but also for the society to which they belong. Simms elaborates on the principle that individuals have a responsibility to their homes and communities, the particulars of which are based on their innate talents. These unique endowments determine how a person should contribute to society, and in turn, it determines their place in society's hierarchy and the privileges that accompany that position. "*The capacity to be useful in one's proper sphere* is that alone which affords the only real right which we possess . . .," Simms explains in "Inauguration" (175). Other than what is due because of one's ability, "[w]e have no rights inconsistent with our endowments" (175). This may not have been what ambitious, optimistic undergraduates wanted or expected to hear. But if they aspired beyond their means to positions of professional or political authority, it invited an apocalyptical reckoning that his self-taught course in history repeatedly revealed. As he argued in "Choice": "all the mischiefs done by licensed Ignorance . . . [and] hence most of the corruption, growing, and festering as they grow . . . precipitate [. . .] the fate of Empires & the destruction of a race. Reading the histories of men . . . the most direct & destructive agency of Evil, has been invariably the incompetence of men in power" (143). In matters of education and the professions as well as in agriculture and community, freedom is best managed within the parameters of what is owed to home and society, not to one's personal interests.

"Choice of a Profession" was the first of Simms's two speeches on these topics in 1855. It was initially written for the College of Charleston's Chrestomathic ("useful learning") Society, and Simms read it on the literary society's anniversary on February 23, 1855. It is not clear when the undergraduates invited Simms to speak, but as was becoming his habit, Simms worked on the address almost until he left Woodlands to give it, juggling writing the draft with other major projects. He wrote John Esten Cooke on February 20 to say that "[a] confounded college oration is now taxing my brains, and I have a novel [*The Forayers*] in preparation." He confessed to his fellow author that "I am thoroughly sickened with sight of pen & paper" (*Letters* 3:364).

What Simms ultimately collected from his harried brain was an oration that addresses the familiar topic of individual rights and societal responsibilities, but through the lens of gender and, more obliquely, class. Simms discusses the occupation of planting, including the importance of incorporating science into agriculture like he did in his Barnwell address in 1840. However, *Choice* focuses more on the "professions"—medicine, law, the clergy, and education. Contrary to stereotypes that antebellum Southerners were rigidly class-conscious (likely due to the retrospective fiction of later Southern authors like Thomas Nelson Page and Margaret Mitchell), Michael O'Brien observes that antebellum Southerners did not have a consistent understanding of class or class criteria other than to acknowledge that different economic categories of people existed, albeit fluidly and contingently. Southerners inherited from the previous century an understanding of what some class positions or labels meant, but these seemed increasingly less relevant to their society. Southerners were also informed by emergent paradigms, and "professional and commercial people . . . were in the middle of an evolving social order," as Jonathan Daniel Wells explains (10). Furthermore, says O'Brien, "[b]y the late 1840s . . . there is some evidence that a quasi-Victorian idea of a middle class was beginning to develop, such a class being defined as urban, respectable, and the chief guarantor of social order and progress" (1:375). The class of "the professions" dovetailed with the latter two concepts. They were on one hand a category of occupations, but, on the other hand, they had a nascent class sensibility and social significance that seemed more relevant than anachronistic notions of social "aristocracy." That respectability implied responsibility, as O'Brien notes, to be stewards of society's development. "Choice" advises students on how to make sure a young man is not only suited for a profession, but also for the contribution he will make within it to the order and progress of his people.

"Choice" begins with a long anecdote about John Abernethy, the turn-of-the-century British surgeon and teacher who allegedly looked at a lecture room of five hundred medical students and asks, "Good Heavens! young Gentlemen,—what is to become of you all!" (137). Simms wonders the same thing in 1855. He was concerned about the literal overcrowding of and competition within professional fields and especially about the experiences of recent graduates whose aspirations led to misguided choices. Imagining the medical field of Abernethy, for example, Simms offers that many physicians "have abandoned the profession in disgust. Many more but indifferently pursue it, having neither heart nor hope in the labour. . . . It is, with most of them, a helpless drudgery—the mere continuance of an ungrateful pursuit which they can now neither change nor abandon" (138–39). Simms's point is that life becomes unrewarding, unremitting toil for young men who choose careers for which they are neither disposed nor competent. Simms argues that students lead themselves into such traps by allowing superficial considerations to interfere with their own honest self-assessment of whether they have the necessary aptitude for a profession. For some recent graduates, it is the "the love of gain," the allure of high salaries (148). For others, the professions "are chosen . . . in the hope to escape from the severer labors of society" due to a mistaken belief that professional work requires less diligence than other occupations (148).

Simms also claims that "the strongest lure which the Professions hold out to the Incompetent, is in their appeal to the social vanity" of these aspirants (148). Coinciding with O'Brien's observations, Simms explains that professional careers "in a country like ours, which enjoys none of the privileges of an [sic] hereditary aristocracy, are necessarily the highest passports to Society. They constitute our principal aristocracies" (148). Professional men are a natural aristocracy because the requisite skills involved in these occupations "imply special gifts of intellect from God, and, a superior education at the hands of men, [which] naturally clothes them with dignity & authority" (148–49).

Despite this ostensibly divine appointment, Simms acknowledges that young men motivated by greed, incipient laziness, or prestige may be able to fake their way through "a superior education" and enter the fields of medicine, law, education, the clergy, science, or letters (149). The aforementioned drudgery awaits them, but even worse, Simms argues, is the opportunity cost born by humanity and society. "Choice" repeatedly uses the word "usurpation" to describe the undeserved authority that unqualified men wield in positions that their ambition encouraged them to assume. Simms evokes the moral and social authority associated with the professions, noting "every man in a false position,—in a place for which his endowment leaves him unfitted,—must be dishonest. What right has he to be there? He defrauds the proper man. He defrauds the country" (144). The poser is not just cheating the qualified candidate for the job, but also the nation of its rightful economic, cultural, and political stewards. Progress is stymied when the wrong person or people are in the positions of authority represented by the professions.

"Choice" explains to his audience that there is a natural distribution of aptitudes, "a chosen Priesthood" of talent (141–42). Reflecting on the occupation for which one is best suited, therefore, will lead one to make a decision congruent with one's talents and with the benefit of society at large. Simms demands that his listeners ask themselves, "Have I really a call to this pursuit? Am I specially fitted for it? Does it seem, from all that I can see & learn of myself—after devout self-examination, of my own nature & resources, that, I have been endowed for this one profession in greater degree than any other" (145–46). Motivation matters, but only to the degree that it corresponds with fulfilling the profession's service to man and society: ministers attending to the spiritual needs of their neighbors, lawyers preserving order, physicians healing the sick, professors educating future leaders. Only then is the cachet and authority associated with being a professional justified since the high-minded aspirant contributes to the occupation's ability to manage national well-being. Rather than money or fame, suitable ambition's "grand motive is its own development—which seeks nothing, but the free exercise of great & conscious powers;—looking fondly forward, whatever the pursuit, to carry, on & onward, to yet loftier heights of art & civilization, the professional banner which it bears" (153). Simms thus reiterates the reciprocal relationship between an individual's abilities and responsibilities to society and the appropriate freedom and rights that are accordingly conferred, this time, though, with an emergent class valence.

"Choice" concludes by advising listeners that choosing a career will likely involve challenging conventional wisdom. Recognizing that one might not be suited for a desired profession or may be better qualified for a less-appealing occupation involves disregarding what the community considers to be markers of success—often wealth or renown or lifestyles associated with these qualities. The present materialistically inclined society, rather than the more progressive one that Simms imagines that the professions can lead, mistakenly "honour[s] him, as the Gentleman, who has no toils" and "give[s] preference to <u>Inanity</u>, in fine society" (154). Again, not unlike earlier orations, especially "The Social Principle," Simms denounces superficial values and insincerity, which discourage what is necessary for achieving and sustaining social permanence. For example, Simms argues that society's "false standards of honor & excellence" mean that "certain professions [are] the almost necessary conditions, by which to enter its conventional precincts" (154). These empty measures of success and artificial entrées to society breed the unhealthy ambition and pretension that encourage unqualified students to join the professions. Or, once there, even if marginally qualified, to go through the motions rather than perform their jobs with the earnestness that the moral progress of society demands.

The "Inauguration of the Spartanburg Female College," Simms's other major 1855 speech addressing the uses of education, approaches this topic from a more explicitly gendered perspective. Not that "Choice" is not gendered masculine—Simms takes for granted that his audience assumes that young men should be educated for an occupational life in the public sphere. In contrast, "Inauguration" supposes the argument still needs to be made for the education of women as well as for the proper purpose of it. It is probable, though, that the defense of educating women may be a rhetorical convention. Well before 1855, says O'Brien, "matters had progressed to concede the reality, if not the universal necessity, of female higher education" (1:258). This was particularly true in the South, where over eighty percent of women's colleges were located in the 1850s (Harper 5). As such, orations at the openings or commencements of female colleges discussing the need for or the benefits of educating women may be exercises in performative ritual rather than persuasive rhetoric. Anne Firor Scott's survey of these orations suggest they may constitute their own genre of collegiate lectures (69–70). Or they may be the timeless tradition of men presuming to explain what is best for women.

Regardless, what these orations do not do is encourage women to consider how to use their education in the public sphere to best serve their communities, similar to the way "Choice" does with respect to men. Not that Simms's demand that young men follow their endowment rather than their inclination offered them that much occupational freedom, except that which would benefit society. But still, "Choice" offers some agency in the public sphere. In contrast, male orators universally prescribed domestic affairs as the vocation proper to women, arguing "that an educated woman could inhabit the sphere more gracefully and conduct her female responsibilities more effectively" with a degree (Scott 71). This is the theme of "Inauguration."

Unlike his other orations, there is neither existing correspondence indicating a timeline for when Simms received the invitation to speak at the new women's college in Spartanburg, which was dedicating its chapel and opening its doors to students when he spoke there on August 22, nor any record of when he wrote the address. He mentions in the address itself that "[i]t has been written almost along the roadside, in a few brief hours of interval" (166) while on a pleasure trip through the western part of South Carolina that began at the end of July. This may account for why it takes Simms so long to arrive at his point in the oration. After flattering the founders of the institution, Simms reminds the audience of "vital duty of education, in its highest sense, as the great agent for all moral purposes," namely preparing the individual to play their role in the great march of progress (162).[1] "Inauguration" assumes a homogenous plan for all white women, a future based on the characteristics associated with their gender, which, more than any latent skills or abilities, determines their position in life and how education should prepare them for it. Simms does not intend this as a negative reflection on the status of women in America or as criticism. (Simms says he is "speaking of the country as a whole," though his attitudes and claims echo that of other Southern orators speaking on the same topic, which probably informed his own [172].)

In fact, "Inauguration" argues American women are unique in history for their assumption of positions of intellectual and emotional equality with their spouses without sacrificing their femininity. In ancient times, women would "only acquire distinction as she became unsexed" (172). In contrast, says Simms, "[h]ere, only, does she take her proper place . . . here only does she enjoy her proper authority—regulating the manners of society—refining the intercourse between the sexes—restraining the encroachments of insolence—checking . . . the outbreaks of ferocity" (172). This "proper authority," represented as the ability to ameliorate conflict and promote harmony, leads to mutual affection and cooperation between the sexes. As a testimony to the authority associated with this aspect of women's character, "Inauguration" claims that "no country in the world is man a greater dependent upon the woman, than in ours" (173). This reliance suggests an equality based on a mutual reliance between men and women despite the privileges typically afforded to man. The distinctions between men's and women's privileges (as well as the concomitant duties and responsibilities) are a consequence of the sphere—public for men, private for women—associated with those different characteristics.

Simms patiently distinguishes how women are different and the implications of these distinctions in relationships. (Needless to say, there is an assumed heteronormativity in this and all of Simms's orations.) Women, says Simms, demonstrate "household virtues," including loyalty, gentleness, emotional control, deference, affection, patience, sensitivity, solicitude, and humility. They also provide unquestioning support for the spouse and are nurturing to him and others deserving of her care. Simms delineates masculinity in "Inauguration" in ways he felt unnecessary to in "Choices." Men possess a "stern, inflexible will, which accords with authority and makes it respected"; they are adventuresome, competitive, assertive, courageous, inventive, curious, and broad-minded (177). "Inauguration" says of these masculine traits, "[t]hese are the properties and qualities which *make* nations . . . make laws . . . provide resources for society . . ." (177). These activities may be more visible and may have more historical prestige, but Simms counters that the private sphere is just as critical to support these endeavors and to encourage the men responsible for them: "there *must* be a household, and *one* must maintain it, while the other goes abroad, in toil, labor, peril and conflict" (174). Consequently, though woman does not do—cannot do—all that her spouse may, "she is not less his ally" and thus is his figurative equal (174).

Simms was aware of the dissent that existed about the constraints on women's participation in public life. According to the writer of *The Carolina Spartan* who reviewed "Inauguration," Simms broached the "the vexed and vexatious question of 'Women's Rights'" (Meta 2). Simms acknowledges that "[o]f late days it has become a frequent complaint with certain of the sex, that their rights, as women, are withheld them; that, presuming on his physical, rather than his intellectual powers, man has usurped something more than his share of authority—has denied them that share of power in social, if not political affairs, to which they may properly lay claim" (174). Due to propriety or to avoid conferring credibility to the objection, Simms does not specify who is claiming that women are being "degraded . . . to a rank of moral inferiority" (174). Perhaps Simms had in mind the arguments of writers such as Margaret Fuller, the New England Transcendentalist who had argued for the dissolution of separate spheres in *Women in the Nineteenth Century* (1845). "Inauguration" acknowledges that women may be more capable than some mediocre men in certain professions, but the oration responds with two lengthy arguments that reemphasize the aforementioned innate differences between women and men on which "authority" and "power" are contingent.

Simms warns that if women venture into the public sphere, they can expect "no longer to be observed with love and admiration; no longer to receive attention from devoted worshippers" (176). If they become the rivals of men, it will disrupt the harmonious relationship between the genders based on the complementary differences of their allegedly innate characteristics—"woman ceases to be his ally" (176). Moreover, Simms claims women will be the ultimate loser since they will also forgo the customary "privileges of a peculiar power . . . having certain sacred and special functions" due to their sex. In chasing the alleged rights of man, she'll lose "[t]he rights of *woman*" that constituted her equality and demanded respect as the natural authority within the domestic sphere (176).

The other counterargument "Inauguration" offers is whether women are physically, mentally, and emotionally prepared for the aggressive competition of business and government. Simms asks, "[c]an they exercise this weary, working, business faculty?" (176). The requisite qualities that men are supposedly exclusively endowed with to manage such activities are allegedly gifts from God. In what should have been an obvious fallacy if weren't so often repeated by Southern commentators on gender arguing that "the sexes had their spheres . . . founded upon their physical natures," Simms points to the physical differences between men and women as analogous to their mental and emotional capacities, thus validating their separate capacities and usage (O'Brien 1:257). "If God has given to man the supremacy of strength, it would seem almost equally clear that He has not decreed that the sway should be with woman. . . . If, in addition to this, we discern such moral differences between the two sexes as fully confirm the physical . . . the inference seems inevitable" (176–77). Since scripture also deeds the difference, it is "immutable"—nothing "can materially change these relations" (178). Consequently, difference is equitable in the eyes of God and society. Women, "Inauguration" argues in its almost-final words on this topic, "now occupies her natural sphere, and fills her proper position in the circle of humanity" (177). If inequality of natural difference is still imagined as unjust, Simms concludes by offering analogies from the environment to demonstrate that difference is a part of natural harmony.

Simms eventually returns to addressing the earlier focus of "Inauguration," namely, to argue that women must educate themselves to "maintain" their proper "rank" in life (178). Given the qualities women innately possess and given the domestic duties that are required of her, Simms offers here a curricular version of his occupational advice that he advocated in "Choice": Study the skills most compatible with one's endowments and their highest societal use. First, if women begin their adult lives and begin to contribute to society as spouses supporting husbands, women need an education that will facilitate this role. The oration imagines the emotional labor women will offer their men, moderating "the excess and violence" of passions, encouraging virtue, fostering a spiritual life, and keeping spirits up (179). She inevitably will need to accomplish these things "by love, truth, fidelity, devotion, and the exercise of that sweet humility" (179). She will "train his affections by these . . . and by her feminine tastes and fancies, her arts and her accomplishments" (179). Simms says, "[f]or these performances, her education must contemplate her manners," for which he prescribes the fine arts (179). He suggests poetry, painting, music, or sculpture, the latter "not sufficiently honored with regards of the sex," to improve on a woman's ability to artfully and imaginatively "win and to subdue" the more aggressive instincts of men at home (179).

Second, Simms acknowledges the necessity that women be intellectual companions, albeit not necessarily equals, to their spouses. He was not unique in this. Explains Scott, "[i]t was desirable . . . that wives have something more on their minds than the best recipe for scuppernong wine or the most effective treatment for measles" (68). Thus, "Inauguration" counsels, if women have higher aspirations than just the fine arts, the proper and the "true ambition of the woman, in the development of her mind, is to raise it to the dignity of his; so that she may commune with him as an associate, whom he will delight always to encounter; counsel him as a friend in whom he finds it grateful to confide" (180). Simms is more liberal in his recommendations of subjects that might help a woman become an intellectual companion to her husband. "Inauguration" suggests "the vast and various fields of polite literature—nay, the sciences, such as botany, astronomy—as regions in which she may find grateful employment." Simms advises pursuing these disciplines "without any miserable rivalry" begotten by pride or ambition, which may cause dissension within the household (180).[2]

Finally, Simms recommends educating women for their eventual roles as mothers. "[H]er relations to man and to society do not end," as a spouse, says Simms: "she is to be the mother of his children" (181). This is the second means by which women ultimately but indirectly exercise authority in the public sphere: "Not a man herself, she is to be the mother of a race of men—of heroes, statesmen, philosophers, priests, and poets—the most glorious orders of nobility which the world can anywhere behold. As the mother of men, and such men, she holds in her hands all the destinies of humanity through all surrounding ages" (181). Shaping the future of the Nation through childrearing was typical of both the older paradigm of Republican Motherhood and the more contemporaneous expectations of True Womanhood. In contrast to the emphasis on training children in the spiritual dimensions of Nature seen later in "Sense of the Beautiful," "Inauguration" focuses on a more conventional moral stewardship. "She is their first teacher, and at that only period when their morals can receive the readiest impress in the formation of character," offers Simms (182). With the absence of educated mothers at home, individual virtue is jeopardized as is the civic integrity of the next generation of the Nation's citizens and leaders.

The responses to "Choice" and "Inauguration" that survive were tepidly flattering and warmly enthusiastic, respectively. The difference seemed to correspond to how well the orations' themes about gender, education, and its societal relevance coincided with prevalent public opinion. *The Charleston Daily Courier*'s February 24 review of "Choice" offered generic platitudes about Simms's reputation and accurately summarized the gist of the oration, but it lauded only the fitness of the topic for the undergraduate audience, which was notably small in number ("Mr. Simms' Oration" 2). The review mentions bad weather, but the snide allusion to the empty seats and the lukewarm review of the oration's merits could also have been a response to the address's pointed criticism of the values of the students' elders. The reception for "Inauguration" was more enthusiastic. A review from *The Carolina Spartan* of August 23, 1855, claimed that "Inauguration" was "an address of rare excellence." Despite the proliferation of orations on women's education, the review enthused that "[f]ew addresses have been more appropriate to their occasion—few more replete with sound poetical thought, and fewer still—hasty as the preparation in this case evidently was—have excelled this in the freshness, richness and beauty of its imagery, or the chasteness and gracefulness of its style" (Meta 2). In keeping with Simms's earlier patterns of publication, he concurred to the printing of "Inauguration" since the address was particular to the occasion. The trustees of the school published it that year. However, Simms demurred when the Cresthomathic Society requested "Choice."

Simms claimed the manuscript "is yet altogether too crude, as a work of art, for the inspection of the critical reader" (*Letters* 3:370). He later acknowledged that "Choice" was "a favorite with me," perhaps because of its evergreen topic, and he subsequently delivered it to audiences in North Carolina, South Carolina, Virginia, Maryland, and New York (*Letters* 6:167).

Donald M. Scott and Jonathan Daniel Wells note the coincidental timing of the emergence of the professions and the lyceum circuit in the antebellum era. The latter provided an opportunity for members of the former to demonstrate their ascension to an occupation relevant to the public by the sharing and application of knowledge. Scott explains that a "public lecture signaled the possession of wisdom [and] general learning" and "because it was an act in the public good, it displayed civic character." Thus as a performance, the public lecture not only rhetorically conveyed a theme, it was also "an act in the construction of a professional or intellectual career" (797). Simms's lectures, "Choice" and "Inauguration" included, were akin to these kinds of performances. Aside from his success publishing literature and poetry, public speaking established Simms's credibility as a professional man of letters and as a public intellectual. It was a visible confirmation of a calling Simms might have sensed during the modest start to his education, albeit one that seemed very distant. If not of birth, he at least had the benefit of gender to see it come to fruition.

NOTES

1. The Spartanburg Female College was chiefly underwritten and operated by the South Carolina Methodist Conference, though the prospectus in the printed pamphlet of *Inauguration* explains that the school "is not designed for any sectarian object" (3). The college received its charter in 1854, opened on the day of Simms's address with four brick buildings, and graduated its first student in 1857 (Knight 421, 480).

2. The "collegiate course" of the Spartanburg Female College was even more diverse than Simms's recommendations. The pamphlet with the printed version of Simms's oration shows students were required to take English grammar and composition, arithmetic, geography, history, rhetoric, logic, botany, algebra, Latin, geometry, chemistry, natural philosophy, moral philosophy, trigonometry, French, astronomy, mental philosophy, and religion (6).

"Choice of a Profession" (1855)

It is reported of Abernethy, the celebrated Surgeon, that, on one occasion, appearing before his class as usual, at the commencement of a session, he seemed suddenly to forget the very business for which he came. His eye wandered absently around the chamber, and, for awhile, he surveyed the circle in a profound silence. When, at length, he did speak, it was only to confound his auditory. Instead of discoursing to them of nerves & muscles, bones & arteries, he cried out, in sudden ejaculation—"Good Heavens! young Gentlemen,—what is to become of you all!"

And well might he so exclaim! Before him were arrayed a body of 500 or more students, all eagerly seeking to enter a profession which was everywhere crowded to excess. Even were it possible that he should send them all forth, equally armed & accomplished for the successful struggle with Disease & Death, he yet well knew that it was not possible that all of them should secure the opportunities which their hopes & necessities could equally demand. Some of them,—nay, many,—the more modest and perhaps capable among them—would linger long in the shades of obscurity, & probably never emerge from it: A few, by dint of diligence & good fortune, might secure employment, & realize the anticipated opportunities & all their pecuniary results; while the more confident, presumptuous & incapable, would rush audaciously into the conflict, for which they have made no adequate preparation—would commit a thousand fearful errors in their ignorance & audacity, & perhaps never achieve a progress of any sort, except such as is only dishonoring to a professional career. In brief, of the Host before him,—not fifty, perhaps, would ever attain a success commensurable with their expectations; and, of this fifty, the proportion would be even smaller, of those, who, by reason of natural endowment, & faithful study, would deserve to do so! And this, my friends, is true of <u>all</u> the Professions! Yet, in all, the Candidates are eager, hopeful, confident; never once doubtful of the future & their own prospects;—all impatient to begin the wrestle with fortune, in the departments they have severally chosen!

To the good man and the wise, who has attained that culminating period— <u>"rel mezzo del cammin di nostra vita"</u>—who has already reached, midway, the perilous path of Life—who has survived its trials—withstood its temptations—escaped its lures; grappled bravely with its necessities—and won, at length, the highest place of security and rank which belongs to a successful career,—there is nothing more touching & impressive than the spectacle of a host of ingenious youth—ardent, bold, hopeful,—eager for the opportunity, & impatient of all those wholesome restraints which would keep them back from the struggle, until the gristle of youth has fairly hardened into manhood. They resent—and revolt—against the very training for success, as an offence to self-esteem, and as only delaying them, unnecessarily, in their march to triumph. They see the goal only—the ideal of hope and pride, or vanity and love of gain! They never once conceive how severe must be the conflict, in the gratification of either of these objects. They never once conjecture the exhausting length of the struggle. They feel only the eager enthusiasm of youth;—they only behold, at distance, the smiling Fortune, waving her fair white hands, with purple streamers, and beckoning them onward, to glorious heights, crowned with flowers, hallowed by the sunlight, over which hangs a bow of the brightest colours, and the most brilliant promise!

The Philosopher well knows that to one only, of the many, is this beautiful ideal, a real & attainable goal. To the greater number it is all delusion. He knows that the flowers will wither at the touch—the rainbow dissolve into vapor even while you gaze—that the bloom will disappear from the sunny slopes as you approach—the heights grow more & more inaccessible with the upward toiling footsteps; and that the becoming Fortune will elude the ardent embrace of the very worshipper she woos, and disappear, in darkness, from the enamored eyes which she has blinded with her witching glamour. He, himself, that Philosopher, walks amid the wrecks of bloom and promise; &, whatever his own acquisitions, he is, at least, no longer the victim of any delusion! But he feels, even as he surveys the Host of eager aspirants in his sight, that they can only be undeceived, in their roseate fancies, by the sad & trying discipline of an individual career—that no warning counsels of age will be heard by those who are still happy in the delusions of youth. They must work out their own problems—achieve their own deliverance as they may—and pass in turn, through the same fiery ordeals which have tried & purified himself!

Let us enter, if possible, into the moods of Abernethy, & look, with him, at the prospect which severally awaits his pupils. Their case is that of all students, in all the Professions. What is the degree of success which they may attain, and what the means which shall render it attainable? The inquiry is of a sort to justify all his doubts & apprehensions. He knows, for example, that he himself, is a remarkable exception to the common progress;—that, of all <u>his</u> associates, but few have ever attained either professional rank or fortune. Many have abandoned the profession in disgust. Many more but indifferently pursue it, having neither heart nor hope in the labour. They make no progress, report no discovery, do not even task themselves to keep pace with the current progress of their mystery. It is, with most of them, a helpless drudgery—the mere continuance of an ungrateful pursuit which they can now neither change nor abandon. They have reached that period in life when they can no longer engage in new occupations—when the mind instinctively recoils from unusual effort. They have exhausted their youthful energies in the disappointment of their youthful dream; and, with mental aims & physical strength equally unimpulsive, they are now capable only of the habitual toil, equally cheerless & profitless, of drawing water in a sieve! Defeat and Disappointment have encountered all the efforts of their manhood, and baffled them; and age, now, asks nothing more from Life, than to be permitted to pass out gently from its cheerless habitation. They see nothing before them, to encourage; and the backward glance reveals nothing but delusive mockeries. He beholds these unfortunates, as one by one, they sink out of sight along the wayside, leaving not a single trophy of well directed effort, or well conceived performance. They were simply the victims of their own dreams—dreams engendered by vanity, in the day of their strength, which became power, equal to their destruction in the day of their decline. And these victims are so many beacons, which might profitably warn other dreamers, were it not for that impetuous blood of youth—that eager passion—which suffers it to behold nothing, at the opening of its career, but that beautiful goal which blinds even as it beguiles.— The pathway of our philosophic Teacher has, even thus, been strewn with the wrecks of youthful enthusiasm—and, as he looks about him, over the host of hungering aspirants,—each eager to begin the same delusive in pursuit of a phantom,—without a single calculation of the dangers and disasters of the progress, he may well exclaim, as I do to those, in the same category, who may happen to hear my voice,—"Good Heavens, young Gentlemen, what is to become of you all!"

His sympathies declare themselves in this exclamation. He would discourage none. He will cheerfully teach, honestly counsel, and generously assist. He is no churl, but a good, thoughtful, & benevolent man. What he can do, to prepare the way, & direct the progress of the young beginner, will faithfully be done. He is not insensible to their claims, or to the claims of society. He sees in them, the representations of society, having a thousand interesting relations, with humanity and its safe progress, which, as yet, they do not conceive for themselves. He beholds the future in their hands, even as he sees <u>them</u> in the hands of the Future! They constitute the germs of posterity to him. He feels, that, in some degree, the destinies of the race, no less than their own, must be confided to their keeping. Shall it be for good or for evil? Shall they maintain, for the great family of man, his present <u>status</u>, and possessions, and add glorious increase, through their own individual performances, to the common capital of Humanity? These are the special concerns of the Professions. This is their mission. It is for this reason, beyond all others, that they called, <u>par excellence</u>, the Liberal! They are supposed to be especially the guardians of the wisdom of Past ages—the special priesthood, having most sacred functions—on whom, Humanity, with all her glorious trains of Art and Science, Literature & Philosophy, Life & Justice, Knowledge & Religion, must absolutely defend. How natural that he should look with trembling & anxiety, to the character, the talents, the industry, the aims of those, who aspire to be the guardians of such Holy Trusts! The results, of their lives and labours, to themselves, though not to be disregarded; are really of insignificant consideration, when we look to their social impossibilities. What, to the race, or to the generation, if they do fail to realize the individual advantages which were naturally the first objects of their aim? If they acquire no fortunes—attain no eminence, no rank? If they toil on to the close of a long career, and, to the last, still feel the necessity of toil as a means of simple existence. This, even where they may be well endowed for the vocation, and ably working in it—however cruel the fortune to themselves,—is yet, so far as Humanity is concerned, a subject of small consideration. They may toil laboriously and die poor, yet still establish the noblest claims to the honours & gratitude of society and man. One does not necessarily labor in vain, though he may achieve but little for himself!

All these considerations occur naturally to the thought of the philosophic teacher as he surveys his classes. But it is not likely that this remoter view of the subject was in the mind of Abernethey when he uttered his ejaculation. His thought did not probably extend beyond the mere pecuniary prospects of his pupils. He regards them, simply, as so many young persons choosing a career, which, he well knew must defraud the expectations of most of them. He felt that none of them fully estimated his own objects, the obstacles to his progress, the self training and sleepless diligence which are essential to success, & the thousand baffling caprices of Fortune, which are apt to set at nought the best industry, and the most persevering talents. He knew that, to many of these young men, pecuniary success was necessary to existence—that, to most of them, it was the real & only object of desire. Necessity, quite as much as vanity, or ambition, was urging their studies, and goading them to that zealous endeavour which yet lacked the higher stimulus of Genius. Many of them were in training with reference to the wants & succour of large dependent families. There are invalided fathers who look to some of these young men to take their places in the professional harness. There are widowed mothers, who have pinched their domestic comforts that they may provide the means of a higher education for an only son. In his mind's eye, the teacher beholds one of these widowed mothers. Even now, pursuing her midnight toils, with the needle, by a dim light, in some lonely forest cabin. Her tears drop silently upon the garment which she shapes or embroiders. A young sister's fingers are busy, at the same time, with painful labours, seeking to eke out the slender pittance, which shall sustain the young man in the distant & expensive city where he pursues his studies. His professional success is to recompense them for these midnight toils & pains, by present devotion to his studies, by future Cares and Comforts, by reverence & protection. In silence, as they work, mother and sister brood together, with tearful hopes, over these natural expectations. Hope lightens their labors, sweetens their cares, elevates their thoughts, makes gladsome the promise in the prospect. They dare not otherwise than hope. Were they to doubt, they would die! They do not doubt, but that the Good God, who loves to behold the spectacle of struggling & unrepining virtue, will finally crown their toils & hopes, equally, with fruition!—All these thoughts naturally occur to the Philosophic teacher as he looks over his classes. A thousand such histories are in daily progress in every portion of the Earth. He has known a thousand such himself. He doubts not, that of the thoughtless, eager, hopeful and impatient groups around him, there are many who depend, on just this sort of resource, for the means of present study. The bread they eat, is salted by a mother's tears! The clothes they wear, are wrought by her midnight toils, in anxiety and self-denial. The very sleep they take, upon luxurious couches, robs her eyes of those slumbers which are so essential to the health & happiness of age! Ah! Should these sacrifices of maternal & sisterly love be made in vain! Should the young student fail! Should the only son prove worthless!—insensible, in appreciation of these toils & pains—heedless of his own duties—his honour—and ungrateful to their love! Should he be a vain, weak, heartless & capricious boy—base of spirit— selfish in the search after his own pleasures—without any generous sentiment of gratitude—without any elevating ambition, urging him perpetually, to the use of the midnight lamp, as patiently & persevering as that poor mother & sister pursue <u>their</u> toils in <u>his</u> behalf;—then come, to them, the bitterness of mortified hopes & wasted cares—the desponding spirit—the salt, salt tears—the sister's anguish—the mother's broken heart!—We will suppose better things, though this melancholy history is one of too common experience! We will take for granted that the young man for whom Love thus labors in poverty & solitude, only cheered by Hope, is not ungrateful; not insensible—feels all that is done for him;—that he strives honestly, earnestly, and with all his soul set upon his tasks, in the pursuit of professional knowledge;—that he, too, keeps <u>his</u> midnight vigil, with study; & that he strives faithfully to compensate the Love which provides, with a kindred passion that longs anxiously for the opportunity to requite it!— "But" says our sage Professor, "is even this altogether sufficient for success?" And the question leads him to yet more searching considerations of what the Professions demand. Even honest toils, & patient industry, & persevering study, will not wholly suffice for those more exacting pursuits, which seem to imply an original destination. Diplomas may be obtained, but the Professions are never acquirable by the inferior intellect. They are secrets of the temple. They imply a chosen Priesthood. The God must call for them, first, and only. They are the superior agents through which he works on the higher necessities of man. They are not to be chosen, at pleasure, by those who aim only at pecuniary results. No one has the right to degrade them to the rank of mere trades, to be acquired as one acquires the use of common tools. No one should assume that they can be duly represented by the exercise of mere will & simple industry. The very phrase—so common in our ears—choosing a Profession—what an impertinence! As if the boy were equally endowed for all. He has universal genius—has only to decide, and be a Lawyer; to put on black garments and a white cravat, and a lugubrious image, and become God's representative to perishing souls; a preacher, a prophet, a divinely inspired man!—to emulate the emphatic nod of my Lord Burleigh, and become at once a master in the art of Healing. All these several vocations demand several endowments. If the individual be not chosen by the Profession, he will as vainly as impudently choose the profession for himself!—There is no doubt that, in all the professions, there are certain inferior labours which common faculties may execute: These might, perhaps, be profitably separated from the superior, & assigned to an order of serving brothers, such as formed a class among the Knights Hospitaller of old; and were known in the Catholic abbeys in the same character; persons, who, modestly, forbore all vain aspirations; who asked of God permission only to do those things which were fairly within their powers; content to fetch wood and water, to perform servile offices—any labour, the meanest, in the cause of humanity: Who, in the Priesthood ministered only in parochial duties; watched the sick, nursed them; buried the dead, wived the living: Who, among Lawyers, as in Great Britain at the present day, were scribes simply, and attorneys; did office work; made records; drew up arbitrary writings, & so forth; among Physicians, were assistants, compounding drugs; bandaging wounds; perhaps bleeding, & doing subordinate offices which required mechanical dexterity rather than thought.—These, however subordinate, are necessary duties of the several professions, demanding ordinary agencies; and under a proper division of labour, easily disposed of in inferior hands; leaving to the superior those only which can employ them most profitably & might be undertaken by no other. These distinctions of duty, indicate a wise policy, if in reference to economy of time merely, and without regard to higher requisitions. The Serving Brothers, in neither profession were ever suffered to undertake those severer trusts, which implied the noblest offices of intellect or inspiration. And were it that the vanity of the young would be content to humble itself to these subordinate agencies, there might be some plea for that reckless audacity with which so many thousand incompetents rush into the professions! These, in their full & proper exercise, demand special & very superior endowments. They imply gifts of a divine distinction, the lack of which, no mere industry, however urgent;—no mere will, however determined, will enable us to supply. Saint Paul ought to be a sufficient authority on the subject, even if our own daily observation should fail to lead us to similar convictions. "There are," he tells us—"diversities of gifts. To one, is given the word of wisdom; to another, that of knowledge; to another, faith; to another, the gift of healing; to another, the working of miracles, to another, the gift of tongues; to another, their interpretation; the Deity thus, as he says, "dividing to every man severally, as <u>He will</u>." It is not then as <u>we</u> will! But as He wills! And what a terrible arrogance it is, when we substitute our will for his! Here, in the language used by Paul, each of the Professions is clearly indicated;— Education, Law, Literature, Science, Medicine & Religion. Here is just such a distribution of faculties, under the head of endowments, as, under God's direction, rather than that of vanity or Mammon, would keep the Professions from being crowded any where! Were each of us but to follow the toils indicated by his endowment, there would not be one person too many in any of the professions;—and there would be no mischievous & fatal practice; no quackery, no charlatanism; no fraud of any sort of either. And surely, it is obvious that such a division of labour among men, so arbitrarily indicated, is a most essential necessity for preventing that conflict of opinion among Professions, which has grown into a proverbial conviction that they must always disagree. It is evident that God has never so profligately bestowed his gifts, as that they shall operate to the utter defeat of their own uses, and to the hurt of the very races for whom they were meant to bring healing & protection. The Professions are crowded, not because of the excessive endowments of Humanity; but because Vanity, Presumption, Ignorance, Cupidity—false notions of self & society, on every hand, prompt fools to rush in to provinces where the very angels fear to tread. It is thus, my friends, that the Blind are said to lead the Blind. Hence the false Prophets that swarm the land at all seasons. Hence all the mischiefs done by licensed Ignorance—hence the abuses, the usurpations & the downfall of Governments— hence most of the corruption, growing, and festering as they grow—which precipitates the fate of Empires & the destruction of a race. Reading the histories of men, as we should read them quite as much in search of beacons as of guides,—examining in what states & communities have fatally erred,—you will come to but the one conclusion—that the most direct & destructive agency of Evil, has been invariably the incompetence of men in power; this incompetence being equally mischievous in reducing the people to its own level of comprehension, and in precipitating the Fate which it needed the highest wisdom to avert. We have had recently before ourselves a marvellous example, of the most imposing character, and of still impending danger, to one of the greatest of nations, in the miserable policy of the British ministry in rushing without due preparation into the war with Russia. Here, you have been permitted to see how destructive of the securities of a nation is the rule of presumption & imbecility. The military chiefs are inefficient, and inert. The civil administration makes no preparation;

takes no precautions. The army is inadequately provided with the necessaries of war, no less than of life. The agents employed are improvident & worthless; and while the French are well employed & well provided; the British, starving & freezing in camp or bivouack, are hurled recklessly upon ruin, under a Generalship, that seems equally blind, deaf & heartless. But the worse exposure lies in that gratuitous exhibition to the world's eye, of the terrible decline of resource— of that lack in vigilant wisdom—that lack of method, order, forethought and sagacious plan, which constitutes statesmanship. There is not only loss of power, and capital, strength, men & money, but of <u>prestige</u>; which, in the case of such a power as Great Britain, is the most dangerous as the most humiliating. Instead of laying bare the weakness of Russian power, it makes the most lamentable exposure of its own. What follows; but new combinations of hostile forces against a Kingdom which has made itself odious to all in turn? The probabilities are that this Russian war forms but a first act, in a terrible drama of nations, in which Britain, stript of her Indian colonies, shrinks, by rapid contraction, to a second or third rate power.—Now, as politics & Government properly constitute a Profession, they represent, in considerable degree, the Evils which defeat the virtues of all the professions. These are all to be found in the imbecility & presumption of those who usurp their powers;—and this imbecility is the more dangerous as it usually possesses, for a time, at least, a most wonderful faculty of inspiring trust. Fully conscious of its own deficiencies, in the real essentials of its place, it arms itself with audacity. In the lack of wisdom, and the necessary endowment, it farther justifies with the wisdom of the serpent, which is Cunning! It pieces out the lion's skin with the Fox's tail. It employs arts which subsidize the cunning of others—it engages in traffic of mutual service,—which, in politics, we call logrolling—and does not scruple, in the maintenance of place, at the sale and sacrifice of all the precious trusts yielded to its keeping. For, my friends, every man in a false position,—in a place for which his endowment leaves him unfitted,— must be dishonest. What right has he to be there? He defrauds the proper man. He defrauds the country. He can only maintain himself in his position by the practice of habitual fraud. Hence, in politics, he is demagogical. By bluster he will stun the ears; and, by his own, and the helping cunning of others, blind the eyes, of that society whose powers he abuses, to the exclusion and denial of all those who possess the appropriate gifts for station. In the professions, he will band with other mediocrities against the meritorious, or he will fasten upon the more ignorant classes of the community, and maintain himself, so long as he can, to the gross wrong, and sometimes grievous hurt, of humanity. It is scarcely a matter of consolation to know that such pretenders are exposed at sometime or other. They are unhappily succeeded by a new set of the same school, who travel over the same grounds, with equally mischievous footsteps, and if you will be at the pains to follow them, and trace the thousand ramifications of evil on every hand, which they diffuse, you will perhaps arrive with me at the conviction that they are the true sources of most of the worst mischiefs of society;—those which degrade and demoralize society, and finally destroy its most enduring characteristics. It is thus that men come to despair of medicine as an ass;—learn to despise religion as the mere fraud of a cunning priesthood; and regard Law as licensed iniquity. So, in literature, banding as a <u>cliqueism</u>, which is only one of the thousand forms of the mutual admiration society, they become false mediums, interposing their dicta between the truly meritorious & the people. Our Philosophic Professor readily conceives all these dangers; as he well understands that the Professions exercise—and this is a matter of vast importance—an authority over society, apart from, and even superior to, their mere professional duties. They are social, as well as scientific authorities. If incompetent to their professional responsibilities, they must lack also in moral; and, lacking in moral, how much greater must be their mischievous influence upon society, in all those relations which do not involve professional wisdom? Next then, my friends, to the expression of his fears, with respect to the individual fortunes of his pupils, he will be very apt to exclaim—"Good Heavens! young Gentlemen, in such hands as yours, what is to become of the Human Family."

Thus feeling, thinking and fearing, he would probably begin his course of tuition with some such exordium as this:

"Young Gentlemen, you are here to acquire my profession. But, young Gentlemen, your first duty is to be honest! You must not undertake this profession, if you fancy that you can succeed in any other. The Professions do not recognize universal Geniuses. The Universal Genius, my young friends, is one that can never accord to any one Profession, that concentration of will, thought, and soul, which it requires. You cannot serve God & Mammon. Before you undertake this, or any profession, you must first honestly assure yourself that you are especially fitted for it. Your mind must habitually run upon it, & with such a will, such an inevitable direction, that you find it impossible, with any effort, to turn your thoughts to any other. You must really be sure that you feel an interest & a pleasure in <u>this</u> study, which is afforded you by no other subject of pursuit or inquiry. Be sure that you are governed by no motive, short of a love for knowledge, for its <u>own</u> sake, & for the efficient development of your own peculiar powers. You are not to choose this profession or that, because, in the existing condition of society, it promises to be especially distinguished or profitable. You are in no degree, to regard the profit or the loss to yourself; since this is a matter which involves your truth, your honor, your obligations to your race. You are not to impose a fraud upon your people. Your only question, and it is a vital one, is simply this—"Have I really a call to this pursuit? Am I specially fitted for it? Does it seem, from all that I can see & learn of myself—after devout self-examination, of my own nature & resources, that, I have been endowed for this one profession in greater degree than any other. If not thus endowed, my young friends, you are scarcely fitted for any profession. But you are unquestionably fitted for something. It is for you to find out what that something is." Suppose he adds—"And, Gentlemen, the best proofs of the fitness & endowment, are—that you do address yourselves, <u>lovingly</u>, to your studies—with a hearty zeal, that suffers no temptations to turn you aside from your appointed tasks. You are to remember, that, having emerged from the schoolhouse, it is expected that you will rise, of your own thoughts, to a full appreciation of what is required at your hands. You are boys no longer, to be watched and sentinelled, catechized & punished. You are now to feel, as well as to understand, your own responsibilities, for the virtues that are in you, at once to yourselves, to society & God. Your discretion has begun: you are about to put your mind & nature to their best uses—& the great question of each,—solemnly urged, in the secrecy of his own heart—without suffering vanity, cupidity, or any base desire to conflict with the answer—a question to be urged unremittingly until you do receive an answer; is one as brief as it is direct:—"What am I appointed to be & to do? What can I do best? What am I good for?" Ask honestly, earnestly, & under the prescribed conditions, & the answer is inevitable, in the case of him who is good for any thing. Having found your answer, you are then to do your duty; with all your heart, all your soul, all your strength—regardless, equally of the Profit & the Loss. Decide then, at your peril, what profession you will choose! Your whole future, honor or shame, glory or disgrace, rests upon this first choice which you make in life!"

It is not denied, my friends, as society is at present constituted, that ordinary common sense, patient industry and honest application, may enable us to maintain a decent rank in the profession—may enable us, in short, to escape rebuke for presumption, & to acquire a tolerable share of the business of the community; reaping a certain amount of pecuniary reward. To acquire enough of a profession, to deceive those who know nothing, is the simple secret of the Quack, in all the professions. To obtain mere formula, demands not only very little endowment, but even less of industrious exertions, on the part of the student. In our country, especially, a most unwise facility of access, is accorded to the urgency of the young beginner. The standards are graduated to the impatient appetites, & the inferiority of the general education. To lisp the common formula, parrot fashion, constitutes very much the sufficient "open sesame" to all the professions; & a moderate accumulation of dicta, will enable a bold and dashing graduate to assert himself, unquestioned, in a community where most studies are too superficially pursued to render society very critical in any. Is not this very much the amount of <u>ultimate</u> acquisition, with a very large proportion? Do we not see thousands who never take one step in advance, beyond the slight elevation which they have reached, in order to gain the diploma? This done, what of labour follows, on the part of the student, as student still, is the mere accumulation of examples, and the classing of his cases under arbitrary alphabetted heads. The practitioner thus works by authorities wholly, who should be a growing authority himself; and there will be thousands, quite satisfied with this slender degree of acquisition, who never pass beyond it—constituting a mere mob of mediocrities; not one of whom can teach what he yet professes to know—all of whom feel their way tremblingly at every step, uncertain of results, ignorant of cause & doubtful of effect—relying upon simple dicta which they know not how to apply, and upon laws which they have been able to memorize, but never to digest! And it is upon such poor drivellers as these, that the health & life of a people,—the rights and liberties of a people—the elemental welfare of a people—must in millions of instances depend. What an awful reflection for the young man, having any conscientiousness at all, to feel that Life & Death are in <u>his</u> hands—that Liberty and Law depend upon his knowledge & wisdom—that the soul's eternal safety, is entrusted to his spiritual guidance!

We may take for granted that our Philosopher, whether Abernethy or Arnold, Mittenmaier or Comte, or any of the great teachers, in any of the departments, looking around among his classes, is frequently oppressed with the self-reproachful reflection, that he is unwisely contributing to a great public grievance. He beholds but too large a proportion of those whom he undertakes to prepare for the professions, who can never succeed in any—who have no just right to success—who evidently regard the profession, not with any view to the development of their individual gifts, for they posses none within <u>his</u> province; who seek the diploma, rather than the knowledge;—whose sole object is <u>gain with ease</u>; sinking the profession to a mere trade; & having no sort of notion of those superior objects, of Wisdom & Humanity, which the Profession should always contemplate. There is not one of these great teachers, who does not feel many compunctious visitings, as he reflects upon his own agency, in thus contributing to the most serious of all the evils which afflict society. They excuse themselves, <u>to</u> themselves, by a tacit reference to society itself. Society demands, society tolerates, society sanctions this self-degradation. They argue—"If we withhold the service, it will be performed by others, perhaps less competent," and, as they cannot wholly prevent the evil, they naturally persuade themselves that they may somewhat lessen its amount by the better education which they can bestow, & the superior fidelity with which they will perform their duties.—I need scarcely say that the argument is a deceptive one. The true duty which we owe to society is every where to discourage, & not delude the incompetent. This we rarely attempt. We recoil, at the outset, not only from what seems a rudeness & a cruelty, but from a task which we hold to be hopeless of profitable result; and they directly contribute, not only to sanction, but to stimulate a mischief, the agency of which, upon Society, we all secretly deplore.—But the Philosopher naturally asks "Why should these young men enter a Profession at all? Why embark in studies which require such especial gifts, such a rare combination of gifts—such strict and trying discipline? Why attempt pursuits, in which they cannot only reach no distinctions, but in which, exposing their absolute deficiencies, they are so much more likely to incur disgrace?" There are a thousand manly employments, in which such broad backs, stout limbs, and vigorous muscles, might admirably exercise themselves to profitable ends, without exposing, and putting to discredit, the poor head, by urging it to assertions which only discredit itself, & lead to the disuse of its proper faculties. These questions, my friends, open to us the whole mystery. There must surely be some pressing motives which persuade Incompetence to such audacity; to a folly which is so likely to be followed by so many heavy penalties. Now, what are these motives? They are, unhappily, such as seldom declare themselves frankly to the student, and, like all self-delusions, they show themselves in the disguise of virtue. It is but a friendly act which shall lay them bare to detection, & enables the young beginner to see justly, and, for himself, how he is commonly deluded. They may be summed up in a brief catalogue. The Professions are supposed to appeal especially to the love of ease, to the dislike of physical labour; to cupidity; and to the vanity of the individual. They appeal to the love of ease, as they seem to require no such severe drilling, nor so protracted a term of ordeal & preparation, as mechanics & the trades. A course of two years probation, studies carelessly pursued, will suffice, in most cases, to secure a diploma in either; while mechanics and the trades, will demand an average apprenticeship of five or seven years. Where the social position is so humble, & the primary education of so limited a kind, as to seem not to justify any approach to the professions, then the same motives, in part, the love of gain, the escape from heavy labor, prompt another, and still larger class, to enter occupations, which, in the more civilized states of Europe, are confided mostly to young women. Labour, we are told, was the terrible penalty for a mortal sin; but we learn but half of this moral, unless we are taught also, that, by the Christian dispensation, the desire to escape the penalty, is not less a sin than the original offence which incurred it. Nevertheless, it is unquestionably the great struggle with a large portion of mankind, to shift its burdens upon any other shoulders than their own; and the Professions are chosen by too many, in the hope to escape from the severer labors of society. A vain hope, my friends, since there is no more laborious life in the world, than that of the Professions, when honestly pursued—They appeal to the ignorant cupidity of another class, inasmuch as they promise large compensative results for a moderate outlay of capital. Such, at least, is the notion among the thoughtless. But the strongest lure which the Professions hold out to the Incompetent, is in their appeal to the social vanity. The Professions, in a country like ours, which enjoys none of the privileges of an hereditary aristocracy, are necessarily the highest passports to Society. They constitute our principal aristocracies. They take rank by prescription, & confer rank. The very fact, that the Professions imply special gifts of intellect from God, and, a superior education at the hands of men, naturally clothes them with dignity & authority. For these, and other similar reasons, they are always of intense desire with all those who regard social position as a paramount concern. Unless, therefore, the conscientiousness of the student be very strong & active, and associated, besides, with that noblest wisdom, which teaches the knowledge of oneself, his vanity, cupidity, or distaste for labour, will prevail;—will get the better of his good sense & his honesty; and he will struggle, however idly, and with no matter what miserable means, for a distinction, which will not only prove worthless in his hands, but prove his own worthlessness in the eyes of others! He will turn from the very employment, in which, being useful, he would be honorable; to become a mockery & a fraud in that which he undertakes. He will thus inflict a twofold wrong, at once upon his own nature & upon society—the one, by a neglect or perversion of his own true gift—for every human being has his gifts;—the other by an imprudent usurpation of the place & trust which belong to a different endowment. And the evil will not rest here. No mischief ever ends with the single error in which it begins. It is the fruitful mother of an endless progeny, & entails a thousand evils upon society. Worst of all, it tends to habituate society to this sort of usurpation;—till, grade by grade, step by step,—insensibly, except to a very few—the guardian & conservative securities of a race are withdrawn—the God-chartered intellects, in all the departments disappear, & are totally superceded by the Incompetent. Then, it is, that all motive to honourable ambition is taken away, and the true aspirant no longer strives for a position which is coupled with no distinction. As Shakespeare hath it—

> "<u>Degree</u> being vizarded
> Th' unworthiest shows as fairly in the mask."

Merit pines in obscurity. Conceit & arrogance reign rampant in the land. Then it is that the armies of the republic are sacrificed by worthless Generalship—the Government of the Country abased by wretched Politicians—its foreign diplomacy disgraced by demagogues at once dirty & dishonest—the Professions & Arts degraded by a Quackery, which would only move our ridicule, were it not of such terrible consequences to Humanity. You may judge of the mischiefs done to Society in the Professions by the Pretender, by what you see of the vices & danger from the same sort of person in political affairs. And such, already, is the degradation we have reached, in this province, that, in many places, you cannot persuade the really able & honest man to become a candidate. The conditions of the canvas would work for him a forfeiture of self-respect. He cannot enter the field with bribery & corruption. He cannot fling filth from hands & mouth <u>ad libitum</u>. Besides the distinction of politics are no longer enviable. Thus it is that society becomes the victim to its own moral weakness—is sacrificed by its own imbecilities; whether in arts or arms, in Government or Law; in medicine or Divinity. The more loose & tolerant we show ourselves of presumption & cupidity in high places, the more surely do we destroy our own securities. There is no measuring the disastrous consequences to a people from this most fruitful of all sources of abuse and error. They enure to the remotest periods in their deteriorating effects; & end, finally, in their destruction of society, unless there shall happen suddenly to arise, at the moment of greatest dearth & danger, some God-appointed intellect—some prophet mind—capable, by great performances, to repair the faults of great usurpations! It is indeed, fortunate for mankind, that Imbecility, however audacious in smooth waters, has such an unerring instinct in the moment of exigency, & usually skulks & sneaks out of sight when the Danger becomes pressing. Your fair-weather seamen are always ready enough, when the storm rages, to yield up the helm to any body who is then bold enough to take it.

Once establish the fact, of the meanness of motive, in the choice of a Profession, and you establish, conclusively, the gross inadequacy and incompetence of the party. There is, my friends, a moral necessity in <u>mere aim</u>, which determines the character of the individual. What is really the object of his ambitions—wealth, show, vanity; or the desire to achieve famously, grandly, nobly, virtuously, wisely, usefully? It is <u>the aim</u> which the individual takes in life—the real object of his ambition or desire; and not the adventitious, or contingent advantages,—which must determine his rightful claim to his position. This must be sustained by the steady regard with which he pursues it; neither turning to the right side nor the left—the <u>will</u> with which he works;—the fact that he <u>can</u>, and <u>does</u> work, <u>con amore</u>;—with equal discretion & zeal—with equal ardor & results; these constitute the best credentials of fitness & endowment. The brave, truly honest, capable mind, shrinks intuitively, from any false position. He aims to <u>do</u>; not to <u>pretend</u> to do;—to <u>Be</u>, not to seem! It gives <u>him</u> no satisfaction to <u>appear</u> the thing which he is <u>not</u>; but to achieve the object which is within his power. To him, it is no source of pride or gratification, that Society arms him with a weapon which he knows not how to wield; crowns him with a sceptre which confers no authority! He is <u>coerced</u> by the exigencies of his own nature, to achievement; to positive performances, which imply wrestle & strength; trial & obligation; and take equal intellect & effort. He must work—must seek out real work—he cannot help but work! The very ambition which constitutes a necessary element in every mind of talents, or Genius, is coupled with an enthusiasm which takes no excuse—which leaves him no choice of occupation, but keeps him unhappy until he can grapple with his decreed duties with all the sinews of his soul! He, as naturally, turns to the <u>one</u> employment, over all others, in which he can work to most advantage. He falls inevitably into his proper place. He has but a single aim, and it determines him finally, & before it is too late, in the direction of his proper labours. It may be—no doubt has been,—that, in thousands of cases—moved by seeming, or absolute necessities—by social influences—by the wishes of parents,—the examples and arguments & young associates; he has, at the outset, made a mistake in his vocation. But, thus endowed, and honest, he will recover himself in due season, & with a celerity corresponding, in degree as his faculty is demonstrative, will take the right course which his endowment requires. That his gifts are peculiar, implies the necessity of aim. All great have thus been distinguished; even where Poverty & Convention have reared a thousand appalling barriers between themselves & their object. You harness them in vain to the drudgeries of life. They break away from plough and anvil. They are taught in no mortal schools. They have divine teachers, who sing for them, in the choiring stars, and fill their souls with a deep religious thirst, which compels them to aspire. Voices speak to them in the winds, telling of far lands & seas, which rouse their curiosity to that ardency which brings Adventure & Enterprise in their train. The rock by the wayside, the flower & the leaf, the running water, and the successive seasons, are all so many moral teachers, which do more than teach;—which inspire and persuade! For all such persons are remarkably endowed with the keenest senses and sensibilities; a most necessary feature in mental endowment; since, by these alone, are they ennobled to find the clue to other hearts, and this clue to hearts, is an essential one in every professional career. Briefly, they have gifts, and these are coercive. He who is born with bow & arrow in his grasp, must need become an archer. He who feels the wings growing at his shoulders, will soar, however much society may seek to restrain his flight. The impulse, strongly and genuinely felt, is irresistible, & a sure sign of the endowment. Those who lack this singleness of aim, who never feel this strenuous impulse, to one profession more than to another, you may be sure were destined to no such elevated duties. If they seek the higher places of art, in society, they are governed wholly by the baser motives, one or all, which I have indicated. Nature has decreed them to humbler toils; happy, if they can so control the vanities of their own hearts, as to grapple cheerfully with their appointed labours, & compel the respect of society, by the virtues of diligence, industry and the modest pursuit of Fortune in comparative obscurity!

To the ingenious & thoughtful mind, the question occurs, indeed, as a surprise—why any one should be so besotted as to propose to himself a profession to which he can do no honour. None other, will the profession honour, though Society may honour the Profession. <u>He</u> gains nothing from social or professional distinction, who cannot wield his art, or his office, with equal skill & power, even as the accomplished Cavalier flourishes his rapier! Why should a man, for example, seek political position, unless with some conviction that he is capable of effecting some great social or governmental reform or progress—some noble scheme for human improvement,—the ideas of which crowd his thoughts by day, and haunt his dreams by night? Why ask social aids and agencies, the object of which is some great utility, when one has nothing to develop?—When there is no voice, crying from, and to, his secret soul,—like that which roused the boy Samuel, from his midnight slumber, compelling sleep from his eyelids, and goading him to the altars with a prophetic necessity!—It will not do, my friends, to excuse the Pretender by any plea of ambition. Can you conceive of such a monstrosity in Nature as an ambitious blockhead? You may conceive of a vain, but never of an ambitious one. It is a ridiculous impertinence to speak of ambition in any such connection. It is <u>not</u> ambition, by which such a creature is moved—and if not cupidity, it is a poor, sneaking, silly, miserable vanity; just that sort of vanity which prompts a person having no talents for a military career, to don sword & epaulette, and sport the gay plumage of the soldier! When war breaks out, you hear no more of these Holiday soldiers. And of just this petty order, are most of the motives that prompt to the Professions, on the part of those who lack the honorable impulses of a true endowment. It is the child passion for drum & feather;—vanity, not ambition! Is it ambition, think you, which has persuaded the Dullard to the Bar, where he blunders away the rights of his clients, while the widow & the orphan cry aloud to his conscience, "You have made us Beggars!" Ambition, which prompts the Quack to Medicine, where he experiments upon precious lives; Manhood, Youth & Beauty, with no knowledge of what they need, or what might save; no happy instincts, which conduct to the mysterious remedies, which God has every where planted around us, remedial of all disease;—ambition which elevates the Drone into the Pulpit, where drowsing all the while himself, he purrs a silly undersong of sleep, like a fat tabby on the hearth rug, while Immortal Souls, on all sides, slipping over the eternal precipice, cry out to him, as they perish—"We are lost, lost forever, through your blind guidance." Ah! my friends, when the Professions are thus incompetent, there is just as little ambition, in the case, or Conscience! Now, ambition is always conscientious. If it errs, it is from the excess of its zeal, never from selfishness. It drives a fiery team, and the steeds, sometimes, run away with it!—A great deal too much is said about ambition, absurdly, and in its disparagement, by those who deal in cheap commonplace moralities. They know nothing of the matter. They confound the Monkey with the Lion—inspiration with presumption! Ambition is truly, in one sense, the last infirmity of noblest minds; but an infirmity only as regards the saving policy of the individual himself, irrespective of society. It is a policy of self-sacrifice, & considering the mere successes of the actor, not to be commended to himself. He must lose, do what he will, who works for renown! But it is an infirmity, the very nobleness of whose aim redeems all its errors. At least, society has no reason to complain, and still less to sneer, at the toils which unselfishly contemplate only the great progresses of the race! The Passion by which the Angels are said to have fallen, it is yet an angelic passion. It implies almost angelic powers. It is the passion for <u>real</u> power; & not for its pageantries. I could wish that this passion were more commonly felt among our young men. So far from being a common one, as is erroneously thought, it is a very rare & infrequent passion; so rare,—so powerless, as a <u>motor</u>, that there is scarcely a drivelling, dirty passion in Society that does not take the start of it; run ahead of it; get the better of it; and crush it out in human bosoms. The love of money, the lusts of the flesh, the vanities of society, all these triumph over it; & exile it to the cell of the silent student; the sad enthusiast in seclusion; whom the vulgar world looks down upon in scorn. Ambition is never entertained by the selfish, the infirm, the weak, the base, the purposeless & unperforming. It is always a quality of high aim, intense earnestness, unflagging zeal, and sleepless industry. It is a quality of <u>work</u>, especially, and loves the wrestle of Life, not merely with Toil, but with Trial! It shrinks from neither. You cannot well task it beyond its courage, if you may beyond its strength. It craves occasion, and opportunity, only, as its only object is performance! It asks no favor, no indulgence, no reward; would rather work without either, than not be permitted to engage in that labor which is craved by its Endowment. Its prayer is only that it may be suffered <u>to do</u>! Yield it the occasion,—give it the opportunity—let it fairly grapple with its appointed duties, and it gives no rest to its hands, no slumber to its eyelids. It would scorn the power, were it not for the performance. It is not content to wear the crown,—it must also wield the sceptre. The pageant does not blind its eyes;—it is the glorious opportunity that woos them! Merely to hold rank & place, offers no temptation to that endowment whose only, & grand motive is its own development—which seeks nothing, but the free exercise of great & conscious powers;—looking fondly forward, whatever the pursuit, to carry, on & onward, to yet loftier heights of art & civilization, the professional banner which it bears. This is the only true ambition! All others, having no such aim & purpose, are simulacra—miserable mockeries—frauds upon society—the fruit of a shameful self-deception, if a self-deception at all,—or of a shameless impudence, which confounds place with dignity, & assumes that once upon the pedestal, the mere ape may become the Apollo! The very fact that the throne implies the Sovereign, makes us only revolt the more when we behold its desecration by the subject. He who thus usurps the false position—rising to the station which he cannot honor by corresponding nobleness of performance,—only exposes himself to our contempt & scorn, the higher he ascends before our eyes. In his proper place, at the foot of the altar, or on some of its lower platforms, he might not have won our applauses, but he would have escaped our loathing. In his false position, the throne becomes his pillory; and he looks out from it, not to fields of honour, but to a grinning infamy, which is not the less certainly felt, as it is so commonly left unexpressed by society. Society, itself, strange to say, governed by its own narrow impulses of self, or by its reckless caprices, not unfrequently despises the very creature whom it arms with an authority, which must degrade, and may probably destroy itself!

Regarding all these considerations, and their perilous consequences, our Professor may well ask, why this insane pursuit of professions in which Incompetence can acquire no distinctions? Why Law, Medicine, Politics, Literature, Divinity—each of which demands great natural gifts, & the most laborious training—when, not only nothing can be won from their pursuit, but when a thousand other fields of employment lie open on every hand;—in all of which Society has an earnest need—all of which implore enterprise & groan for performing Industry.

The answer lies in the error of Society itself, and this brings us to another evil, the fruit of mere vanity, the mischievous results of which are endless. Society has established false standards of honor & excellence, which tend to discredit arts & occupations, which are quite as honorable as the Professions; and has made certain professions the almost necessary conditions, by which to enter its conventional precincts. In the staple states, for example, we distinguish between the Planter & the Farmer, & to the disparagement of the latter—the distinction implying really superior merit in superior wealth only. We ignore the mechanic arts, as implying physical labour; the Law for which, at the same time, constitutes the very foundation, & the final article, of the Religion we profess. We honour him, as the Gentleman, who has no toils—no necessities or cares of Fortune; thus making Idleness a virtue; while we exclude Industry, one of the elementary virtues, from our respect; and too frequently treat it with a contempt & exclusion which should be due only to demerit. We give preference to <u>Inanity</u>, in fine society, while, in the same circles, we hold <u>Performance</u> in scorn & contumely. Nay, so tenacious are we of these absurd distinctions, that, even the Fine Arts, which, in theory, we are compelled to recognize as Honorable, are yet discredited through the Individual Professor; unless their pursuit happens to be crowned with Fortune; and you will find but few of our Gentry, even where possessed of their gifts, who is willing to work in them manfully as a Professor. He is willing that you should recognize him as an Amateur, condescending to an art; but not as one who strips to it, whether from the coercion of his own genius or the necessities of his own life. The more wealthy classes too rarely address themselves to their individual duties; and thus contribute to the social disparagement of the useful. It is one of the terrible evils of wealth, in our country, that the Planter too infrequently takes charge of his own estates. Yet, what loss to themselves, as well as to the country, follows their absenteeism. We devolve the trust of great estates, too commonly, upon ignorant, inferior, & irresponsible classes; when we should bring to bear, upon their working, all of our better knowledge—the benefits of a scientific education; and of tastes, which, properly exercised upon the inferior, would be lifted into the rank of virtues.—And yet, dear friends, what a wilderness of work lies before us, in the South, imploring our energies, ennobling the worker, & rewarding, in a thousand ways, the Zeal & Industry, which shall grapple bravely with the necessity. Are there no new lessons to be learned in Agriculture itself? We are scarcely thoroughly masters of the mystery of growth & nurture; of soil & affinities, of any one of the plants upon which we yet mostly rely for food & commerce. Can we get these new lessons from slaves & overseers? Does it not need the concentration, upon them, of all of our thoughts, our best energies, & our most curious analysis? Are there no new wildernesses of waste to be developed by cultivation, into glorious garden spots of fertility & beauty? No mountain barriers to be pierced by our Engineers, & subdued to pleasant avenues leading to regions of retreat, salubrity & beauty? No vast swamps to be rescued from the wave—reclaimed, converted to Empires of wealth & grandeur, such as reward & illustrate the indefatigable genius of the Hollander? All of these performances demand genius, and art & science, as well as Industry, and would crown the conqueror with imperishable honours. Have our mechanic arts attained perfection? The world, even now, with all its mighty boast of progress, has not yet recovered the lost arts of the Phoenician, Assyrian & Egyptian; and cannot well conceive, by what wondrous mechanical agencies, they were enabled to heave the very mountains into symmetrical relation, in their stupendous masonry & their gigantic pyramids. The grand conceptions of [the] Greek & Etruscan still mock & defy our ambition & invention. The provinces of mechanics & manufactures—nay, even those of agriculture—the fields, forests, swamps & mountains—still stretch interminably around us, affording ample fields, at once for enterprise & Genius; in either of which every Conquest is glory no less than gain. What we do lack for the Conquest is Ambition!—The ambition to do great things—and not petty ones!—Sloth, Vanity, Conceit, Presumption—these achieve no conquests, any where, or only over Cap, and bell & feathers!—As our Professor thinks of these appropriate fields, lying in naked fallow around us, and thinks how much more honorably and appropriately his classes might engage in them without fear of rivalry, and in the pursuit of a really laudable ambition,— his note probably changes. He claps hands & cheers; no longer cries out, in equal commiseration & reproach, "Good Heavens, what is to become of you all!"—but "Heavens, Young Gentlemen, what glorious fields for Ambition invite your enterprise, equal to all your endowments, & capable of rewarding all your industry. Here you shall never come in conflict with each other; here you can, by no possibility, do mischief; here you will dishonor no office; wrong no confidence; discredit no profession; and here you may find Eminence from all! Here, the very hammer, in a brave hand, may become a sceptre; the plough encloses a principality; the augur, makes you a triumphal arch of granite, through the hitherto incorrigible mountains. Only, he cries, only, young men, show yourselves ambitious! It is ambition that we want;—Ambition, which is born of Endowment, & which always carries Enthusiasm in its train. Discard, I pray you, the poor conditions of a decrepit society. Assert your individual manhood against Convention. Better reject all society than suffer it to debase you; for society debases all those whom it keeps from the exercise of a proper manhood. Treat with scorn its poor inanities—its wretched traditions & superstitions—its pretty commonplaces of conversation—the small penny worth of wit of small, smart people about town,—and its drivelling herd of licensed blockheads;—leave all these;—and go forth to the real conflicts of life; and to its permanent & original conquests, with all the vigour of a perfect manhood! I, for my poor part, would rather build my native town of Charleston, into a great city, than wear the proudest crown of Christendom! I would rather enjoy the reputation of draining my native swamps of the Cooper & the Ashley, covering them by impassable barriers from the Sea, and clothing their fields with Rice, than be fifty Polk, & Pierce & Harrison, Presidents of this Confederacy! Nay, I should regard it as a far nobler exercise of life; a far higher achievement of pride and power; to be able to convert ten thousand acres of our ordinary poor pineland levels, such as you may find every where, into a glorious garden spot, than possess all the public & private honours, of all the States of Europe! Here are fields, open at once to profit and ambition. Here are labours, of every variety, for mind & body, which are a thousand times more honourable than any professional career, pursued without distinction. All labors which are honest, are honorable; since all imply an ideal; all exercise the intellect—will tax the highest—and are susceptible of indefinite improvement. The Ideal, let me remark, used vaguely every day in speech, & too frequently supposed to be in antagonism with the <u>Real</u>, is, in fact, only the <u>Possible Real</u>;—the most perfect notion of the Real, to which the highly endowed ambition constantly aspires. There is not, accordingly, any occupation, however seemingly humble, which has not its ideal. The merchant sees it in the discovery and development of new fields for commerce—new marts and objects of exchange & trade. The mechanic, in new inventions, which convert common ores & minerals into winged steeds of flight & fire. The agriculturist, in creating new forms of Use & Beauty upon this Earth; Art & Science, thus, embracing Labour, and from the simplest agencies, evoking the perfect ideals, of mind, and majesty! Thus it is, that, to the Scientific Thought, thus exercising in its natural province, the simple Tea kettle prefaces the miracle of the Steam Engine. And it is not possible, for any mind, engaging in appropriate labors, & pursuing them with a loving ardour, not secrets and discoveries, equally brilliant and useful, which shall crown itself with honour, and bless the races of men with new possessions, which gradually tend to their perfect civilization. In all vocations, there are motives to ambition, incentives to enterprise, materials for Genius, rewards for Industry, infinitely Superior to any, which can possibly result to Incompetence, struggling like an Elephant in a Quagmire, in the depths and mazes of an inextricable Profession. Thorough tillage, or Farming, Staple Culture, Engineering, the Mechanic and the Fine Arts,—all reveal to us fields of enterprise, the working of which, at this very time, constitutes the paramount necessity of our Southern States. We lack our proper share of labour—we lack Home Industry, & Home Thought upon it,—which alone make Home sacred;—we lack in enterprise, curiosity and art—we lack in useful ambition! We are daily importing the agencies which are essential to the maintenance, no less than the progress & improvement, of our condition in town & country. We should need to import none! The necessities of life, in the higher exactions of Civilization, are pressing heavily upon us, demanding the development of our individual gifts. No mind need be unoccupied—no field need be as naked fallow. Let us only ignore the unwholesome standards of a frivolous convention, and clothe ourselves in the noblest sort of ambition,—to be useful, according to the several qualities and virtues that are in us;—working, watching, achieving; aiming grandly, & wisely; & conquering bravely; and not waste gifts, genius, Life; showing ourselves in petty, puerile, conceited attitudes, of vanity and Indolence, cursed & crushed by a poor, slavish, ridiculous convention. Let us be <u>something</u>,—not the shadows of something!—Men, not monkeys; and Honor is ours, and Profit is ours; and the sweeter, prouder, consciousness, so necessary to self-respect, that we are the Beings, that we appear, and have done our best towards the just development of our real endowments. I have shown you, apart from the Professions, ample provinces for the exercise of all your talents & energies, in the cultivation of which you will best contribute to perpetuate the objects contemplated by a noble & conquering ancestry.

"They,—our fathers—made the nation!
      We must save it! We must say
Such shall be its sovereign station,
      Glorious in the eyes of Day!
What shall make a nation glorious?
      What but Toil and Art? The toil,
Which, alone, is all victorious
      Springing from the soul, and soil!
Rising o'er the nation's ruin,
      When its Laws are in the dust:
Saved by arts, that still recurring
      Keep the Precious in their trust!
Toils of Art—the generous duty
      of the Genius, worker, man!—
That make things of worth & Beauty,
      Things of worship—as they can!
They build temples for the spirit,
      Where, like Gods, the virtues shine,

And bestow, as they inherit,
      Models, glorious as Divine:
Clothe the giant tree with pinions,
      Send it forth on ocean wide,
Till they win, from all dominions,
      Homage for their works of pride:
Hew the forest, bare the prospect,
      Span the chasm, drain the swamp;
Rear the Dome, whose swelling aspect,
      Soars to Heaven, & wears its stamp:
Rend the marble from the quarry,
      And with Labour, Art and Prayer,
To its shapeless masses marry
      Glorious form, and godlike air:
Raise the shrine that tells the glory
      Of the Sires who saved the land;
Every shaft a Patriot story,
      Of great soul, & conquering hand:
How they toil'd in deserts sterile,
      For the bitter bread they ate:
How they fought, in fields of peril,
      'Till they rear'd the sovran state!
They shall Ask, with voice incessant,
      Laws of Life to man convey;
Warn the Future, teach the Present,
      Point to Fame, and lead the way.
Thus should we, old virtues heightening,
      Follow in the sun's great eye,
'Till, with utmost glories brightening,
      High we stand, among the High!
'Till, a music, faint and failing,
      Grecian Art & Song shall be [become]
And Italia's voice of wailing,
      Hails our shrines, beyond the Sea. [her own grown dumb]
Whilst far seeking admiration,
      In remotest lands shall turn,
Fill'd with loving veneration,
      Where our Prouder planets burn.

"Inauguration of the Spartanburg Female College" (1855)

We are assembled, my friends, on one of those occasions which all good men approve, and upon which they assume that God himself smiles with favour and encouragement. We are this day assembled, to plant the seedling of a tree whose fruits are to be gathered by posterity. Our children are to rejoice in its shadow; its odours shall refresh their senses; its fruitage is to bring solace to their souls. They will gladden in its growth; grow happy as it spreads in foliage; grow wise in virtue as they gather in its golden harvests. These are decreed to nourish their souls with thought and contemplation; to enrich their lives with goodness; to strengthen and endow their minds with the most precious of all mortal knowledge. The hands which shall plant this tree; the benevolence which hath conceived it, the bounty which shall water it, the loving care which shall foster and protect it; are all of a sort to claim kindred with that Divine Benevolence which hath graciously planted a whole world for the blessing and the benefit of man, and is, we believe, never better satisfied with its work, than when he is eager to reap and gather all that is good and grateful in its productions, during the progress of the successive seasons.

All labours of unselfish affection, and of unforced benevolence, my friends, carry with them a Divine sanction. They are all so many demonstrations of our fond, though inferior efforts, after a Divine example. He who plants a tree beneath whose boughs he himself can never expect to obtain shelter—of whose fruits he himself can not hope to partake—hath done a work over which the good angels clap their hands in approbation. By such performance, he hath shown himself superior to the obtrusive tendencies of self—he hath shown himself worthily superior to the vulgar necessities and appetites of earth. Nor shall he fail of *his* fruits also, though he may gather none directly from the little seedling which his benevolence hath hidden away in the ground for the benefit of other generations. He who plants *for* the future, plants for himself in the future, and shall live by the very fruits with which he fills the mouths of others. It is decreed that the good which lies in our performances, shall, in some way, enure to our own health, stature and happiness—shall, in some way, receive compensative blessings from the great benefactor of mankind. If our lips taste nothing of their mortal fruits, from the bounties which we set to grow in earth, our souls shall be fed, on a superior inheritance of fruits, in a world where the soul alone is decreed to seek for food. There shall be golden apples of eternal sweetness, for the hungering appetites of those who have shown themselves with souls full of a loving sympathy for posterity. There shall be fountains of immortality gushing forth always, in the cool shades and valleys of eternity, to cheer and succour, and sustain and nourish, the thirsting affections of him who hath shown love and good will to man on earth. And man himself will bless; and, long seasons after, when the mortal benefactor shall have disappeared from mortal eyes—when his presence shall no longer challenge mortal regard or gratitude—the voluntary tributes of a grateful future shall do homage to his memory. His name shall be a spell to waken loving senses to attention. His noble charities shall be followed by glowing eulogies from genial lips. His grave shall be crowned with the tribute of perpetual flowers from duteous hands. The aged will bring their young to the place where he sleeps, and shall tutor their infant souls with the sweet and saving lessons of a loving veneration. The widowed mother shall gently lead the only hope of her lonely years, to the spot, and train its young knees to bend in prayer and blessing beside the grave of her unknown benefactor. He, with an eye ranging far beyond the provinces of mortal time, has considered, long before its birth, the great wants, of soul, mind and affections, of that infant nurseling. A holy foresight hath possessed his thought, before the cloud veil of eternity had passed between his senses and the earth. He hath blessed the child with his bounty, even in the womb of its mother—in the womb of unborn generations.

He hath said, in his secret heart—"These children are so many heirs of God—are so many seedlings of immortality; and God, in crowning me with wealth, hath made me his almoner. Shall I not care for *his* children; for these seedlings of immortality?" They must be trained, duly and heedfully, for the eternal destiny which awaits them. They must be rendered worthy of that high communion with divine aspects, and blessing and beautiful intelligences, which throng to welcome them to the green pastures of the good shepherd.

Yet, ere they can hope for this, they are destined for perilous trials, and terrible temptations, and an ordeal under which the feeble, unsuccoured nature must always sink. They must be strengthened for the trial, for this fiery ordeal, that may consume where its purpose is to purify. There will throng about the footsteps of these dear children, day and night, a thousand hostile and cruel spirits, the sworn subjects of the Prince and Powers of the Air! They will fasten upon the young heart of the child, like so many wolves, raging, ravening, forever seeking to devour. They will insidiously awaken and pamper into authority all the instinct lusts and appetites in the bosom, until these, too, shall become ravening wolves, that demand forever the sacrifice of innocent victims to the passions. These hostile spirits will crowd about the soul, in the guise of innocent affections, tastes and sympathies, and lure it on, through a glozing pathway, seemingly all sweets and flowers, until they beguile it to the sudden brink of the horrid precipice, and hurl it down forever.

This is a terrible history. One of the few histories that we know to be true. You are all so many living witnesses of its truth. Your eyes have seen the actors in this fearful drama, moving on to this catastrophe, under this glozing and insidious guidance, as certainly as if chained to the car of fate, and borne to ruin without will or power of their own. Your ears have all heard the cry of some despairing soul, plunging down into the rayless abysses of gloom and terror—a single cry of a mortal agony from its quivering lips, as it goes from sight—a howl, rather than shriek or cry—giving forth but the one awful syllable of despair—"Lost! Lost! Lost!"—as it plunges down into that horrid abode of immortal agony—over the portals of which, Dante, in his fearful vision, read the inscription, in characters of living fire—"*Lasciate ob ni speranza, voich' entrate!*"—"*Leave hope behind, all ye who enter here!*"

The benevolent man—he who would be the true benefactor of his species—broods over this terrible danger with the perpetual question, "How shall we save all these young souls from this fate—from these fearful and subtle spirits—these forever-haunting emissaries of the enemy of man—this awful power of evil—which is yet the necessary foil of good; in the triumphant wrestle with which alone can virtue realize her better destinies?"

There is but one answer:

We must furnish better spirits for their communion. We must pre-occupy the young soul with good tenants, who shall man and guard all its avenues, and keep out all assailants, with the shield of virtue and the spear of wisdom. The angels of love, and faith, and truth, virtue and intelligence, must be made to garrison the youthful heart, until its own wisdom shall become equal to its own defence. They must be made to seize upon the infant instincts, and regulate all their earliest impulses and cravings—to leash in the fiery passions, even as we halter the wild horse—until they shall learn to submit patiently to the curbs of discipline, and work only in obedience to the gospel law of righteousness.

These agents are to do yet more. They are not only to train and tutor the instincts, and to subdue the passions to docility—they are to train thought itself in the right direction, the only goal of which is truth. They are to give light and air and exercise to the infant germ of reason, so that it shall gradually develop, through the agency of fancy, curiosity, enthusiasm and a generous ambition, that seeks development only, into the glorious flower of a pure and powerful mind! And this duty involves the necessity of employing gratefully, and exercising duly, something more than that naked and cheerless faculty, which we improperly describe as reason. The taste, the fancies, the imagination, the sympathies and affections, these are the essential properties of a noble intellect, demanding much more care in cultivation than the one bald faculty to which they are the absolute wings and soul and spirit, without which the reason would be marrowless and purposeless, and a mere fraud upon humanity. They are especially to study and discover what is peculiar in the endowments of the individual—by which, indeed, he is an individual—his secret *motor* and use—so that they may address to each the particular influence, argument and practice which are best calculated fully to develop this individuality.

And this is the vital duty of education, in its highest sense, as the great agent for all moral purposes. For it is one of the most beautiful and wonderful of all the designs of God, in the creation of man, that he has invariably individualized his subject creatures, each with a nature peculiar to himself, which markedly separates him from his fellow. The infinite variety of nature, shown every where, in all her works and attributes—"which nothing seems to stale"—is no where more surprisingly displayed than in the infinite diversity of traits, in mind and body, which are exhibited among men. As there are no two trees alike in the same forest—no two leaves alike on the same tree—so no two children are wholly alike, whatever their general resemblance, though sprung from the same parents, and trained up under the same paternal authority. It is accordingly, in the training of these thousand exquisite diversities of temperament, character, susceptibility and force, that education becomes so equally difficult and essential—that we require so many good angels, each having different offices, to take possession of the hearts of our young, and assist us in protecting and strengthening them against those forces of evil which find young passions and appetites such ready auxiliaries in the overthrow of the very citadel they are appointed to sustain.

It is happy for us, my friends, that the simple *need* of this succour, once felt and urged with honest prayer and faith, is always sure to receive it; so that the benevolent man, when he endows the institution which is dedicated to the just training and development of infant humanity, does not simply bestow his wealth—does not simply erect a temple and decorate a shrine! He calls down, by the simple act of endowment, legions of bright angels from Heaven, to take possession of, and to protect it. Is this mere fancy and figure? Not so, if you believe that God takes the same interest in the affairs of earth that he did five thousand years ago—not if you believe that the well being and virtue, the blessing and the just performances of men, are as precious in the sight of the Creator as our scriptures teach us. To the cold and callous nature, feeding on clay, sworn to sensual delights only, all this seems mere dream and delusion. *We* see no angels thus busied in our ministry. *We* recognize no angelic harpings—hear no oracular voices. All of our associations are of the earth and earthy, and we regard the vulgar reason which devotes herself to our daily necessities—the mere scullion of the household—as the simple, sole authority, to whose counsels we should defer, and whose ministry alone we must acknowledge. And, with the eye of reason only, we behold none of these gracious and saving intelligences. But neither do we see the Prince and Powers of the Air, Lucifer and his subtle satellites, though they, too, are here, as every where, busy in sapping the foundations and scaling the battlements of our eternal Hope!

I have a more grateful, though you may call it a transcendental faith. I believe that even as these hostile spirits are busy in the subversion of all human structures, which contemplate the gradual elevation of the man to the heights of hope and promise which constitute our moral, social and intellectual ideals; from the very moment of the erection of the sacred fabric, even at that very moment, do the celestial champions of Heaven descend for its protection! More gather the angelic hosts of virtue, no less eager, ready, vigilant and powerful, than those malignant spirits that labor in the cause of evil. Michael stands in panoply of perfect mail at the portal, and confronts the bitter enemy with the spear of Ithuriel. He clothes the passions in the golden armour of Discipline, and times their march to action by the musical cadences of order and obedience. Gabriel arrays the host by means of veteran aids who have fought a thousand battles with the same ancient enemy—Virtue, Prudence, Zeal, Innocence, Truth and Reason—glorious cadets, whom no enemy has yet had the skill to circumvent; while Raphael, the soul succourer, sounding his golden trumpet, wings the glad spirit onward, with a divine enthusiasm, in its march upwards, to those glorious heights of equal sovereignty and security, where the man himself, his full powers all developed, becomes in turn an angel; and hosts, besides, each having different duties, all of which contemplate different natures and necessities in man, follow in the train of these, for the strength, the succour, the elevation and the blessing of that favorite race, for which the Deity has declared a destiny, the happy realization of which is the true aim of all human education.

These minister in turn to our tastes, our fancies, our sympathies, our passions, as needfully as to our sovereign reason. Some pass into and possess themselves of the heart, that lake of fire in which the passions and affections find their life and glow. Others make their way to the brain, which is the seat and throne of the intellect; while others again, to whom these are equally tributary, glide into the soul, which is the winged and ethereal element in our humanity. These are all tributaries, loving counsellors and assistants, in every work which contemplates the good of man. They are bound, by inevitable conditions of their office, to obey, in co-operation with the more lowly agents, whom man assigns to the same service; and we no sooner build the altar to Truth, Virtue, Education, or Religion, than hosts of pure and powerful spirits descend to bless and cherish it. They come to the succour of Priests and Teachers. Insensibly, perhaps, they help to render the young mind susceptible to its lessons. They unite with us in the consecration of the Temple. Their voices advocate our prayers. Their harpings help onward the feeble music of our chaunt to celestial senses; and on their lips, no less than ours, the name of such a man as Wofford becomes synonymous with Benefactor.

Do not suppose me extravagant in these fancies. Ordinarily, we take but a mean view of the necessities, objects and essentials of education. We do not, in the first place, contemplate properly its aim. Our highest uses regard only the mind's exercise and activity. But, education properly considered, is the source of all religion. It is false and fraudulent if it does not contemplate the final destiny, the whole career, and the due exercise of all the faculties of man. It should have heed equally to his passions and affections, his sympathies and tastes, his moral and physical virtues, as well as to his brain and intellect. These, for the due exercise of either, require to be developed together. Nor must we lose sight of, or treat with indifference, a single faculty of the subject. It is not for us to bold slightly any of the powers or qualities in the individual man, though society may not recognize their proper uses. We are to take these for granted. The talents, few or many, high or humble, must be put to proper interest. We can ignore none of them with safety. When the scriptures report to you the parable of "the talents," they really speak of the faculties. These constitute the peculiar moral capital with which each man enters the world.—These we are required to cultivate to the utmost stretch of our capacity; and we are not to ask in what degree they are estimated by society. Society may suppose that it has no use for Priest, Poet, Orator, or Statesman. We know that society too frequently treats their several missions with indifference, if not contempt. But God has use for them, and *his* endowment of each, with his peculiar faculty, implies a trust for proper exercise; and without this exercise of the individual faculty, the soul never finds development. Education, accordingly, is the thorough tillage of the soul, as well as the affections and the intellect. If we believe this, shall we wonder or doubt that God, whose ministers are made

> "To speed
> And post o'er land and ocean without rest,"

should vouchsafe us myriads of bright angels that lend their succor in aid of priest and professor, counsellor and teacher? If we keep in mind his supposed objects in our creation—the high destiny which he contemplates for us—the high rank among animals which we already hold—his own wisdom and benevolence—it will be easy to conceive the presence and continued succor of a host of glorious allies, guarding all the avenues of the heart, solicitous of all the powers of the mind, bringing wings to the soul, and watchful of every faculty, however insignificant in our eyes, with which the Deity has thought proper to endow the man.

It is of vast importance to the education of society at large, that this doctrine should be recognized in all its extent. We are but too much in the habit of treating with scorn those qualities of the mind which are exercised especially in behalf of the soul; to regard only those as necessary and useful which contemplate our mere social prosperity—which lead to affluence, social power, or merely individual ambition. And these standards we reconcile, after a strange fashion, with an avowal of religion—of the religion of Christ, who specially teaches that these very things are to be held in scorn! Honoring them, in his spite, we reject with scorn the more sacred endowments. How shall we insolently presume upon God's favour, whatever our prayers, purifications, lustrations or ovations—our grand rites, or common daily services—if we yet neglect to put to use a single faculty, however humble, however little it may promise for profit or aggrandizement, which he has confided to us for exercise and just development? How say to him, "This faculty is surplusage. We better know our true wants than Him who made us!" Yet these faculties, thus ignored, had probably been the very ones which might have saved the great nation from overthrow and ruin.

And how vast and various are these faculties, many of which society leaves unused, or totally unvalued. How little does the farmer, after a thousand years of labor in the field, know of the art which he professes. How merely mechanical is the routine drudgery of his life. Even as a farmer, with all his experience, the higher faculties of thought, essential to his occupation, remain undeveloped; hence he makes no progress. And, consider—to indicate the higher social standpoint from which you are to survey the subject of education—consider for a moment, what comprehensive and general powers must unite in the formation of a great poet, philosopher, orator, statesman, or discoverer of any description.— Think of the training and exercise necessary for the development of the grand total of the endowments, in either of these great teachers of mankind. Imagination, reason, the *habit* of thought, the suggestive fancy, the curious and restless tendency to search, the free command of language, the faculty of keenest observation, the nice discriminating judgment, the large experience, the perpetual aim or purpose, fixed and definite; the knowledge of the universal humanity; every pulse, every passion of the human heart; every secret and motive of society. To teach these their due play and exercise—to train the tastes, to guide the study, coerce the industry to the desire for these acquisitions; to warm and stimulate the energies; to make them urgent and steady, and so regulate them as that thought shall become the habitual, not the eccentric exercise of the mind. These are all essential requisites of the great master in any of the departments—these make, of the great teacher, a philosopher—perhaps, the most grand and noble, as the most really useful, of all the benefactors in the world.

Let us linger for a few moments in the survey of that province over which such a philosopher should have control, and for whose succour, in the proper government of which, as I contend, God vouchsafes heavenly auxiliaries, benign spirits, angelic visitants, that strive forever against the agencies of evil, for the full possession of that much beleagured empire, the heart, the brain, the soul of man, leaving none without divine support, in the great conflict of humanity for life! Could we lay these bare to examination, even as the anatomist lays bare the nerves, the bones, the arteries—could we see, in its secret recesses, the tangled thought, the wandering affections, the restless eagerness and discontent of this eager and longing soul—could we trace the purposes of the one, the weaknesses of the other, the yearnings of the last; hear their secret moans as well as their open merriment—their sighs as well as songs—their agonies of doubt, as well as the shouts of their impulsive rapture; watch the progress of that pioneer Imagination which guides them all—going before Thought and Purpose, even as the fiery column, alternating with pitchy darkness, led the way for the wandering Israelites through the wilderness; note the capricious play of that Fancy, which cheers the pathway, even as a bird that flits along beside us from thicket to thicket, singing as she goes; watch the first flights of that soul, which, through all passions and impediments, under this guidance, still longs to strive upwards ever and win the empyrean; could we behold all this progress, of what lives and struggles in the nature of living man, then, and then only, might we fully comprehend and appreciate the wide, the various uses, the singular difficulties, and the grand ennobling necessities of education. But thought fails in the pursuit, study falters in the search, and language limps in the vain effort to describe the curious and complex processes. We may only hope to conceive the fullness and variety of the subject through the means of metaphor and figure. Let us try to do so.

I have, my friends, just returned from a visit to your own glorious mountain region of the Apalachian; and this journey, by the way, must furnish my apology for the short comings of this oration—must plead to you for its imperfections—as it must certainly fail equally to meet your expectations and my own standards. It has been written almost along the roadside, in a few brief hours of interval snatched from a painful labor, and under constant interruption.

I have made the pilgrimage to the waters of the beautiful Keowee, whose grateful murmur, like a voice of love calling in the wilderness, has come to my ears with a sweet melancholy, reminding me touchingly of Martha Calhoun, that noble young creature, the model of womanly strength and grace, cut off in the middle of her day, under whose grateful auspices, in whose sweet companionship, I had once hoped to make this pilgrimage!—I have penetrated the beautiful valley of Jocassee—a spot worthy of its musical Indian name—a nestling place among the mountains for brooding hearts and warm romantic sympathies— scooped exquisitely out of the bosom of a rugged empire, as if to prepare for the reception of some gushing human fountain. I toiled up the kindred mountains over difficult pathways, obscurely traced out along the brink of great abysses. I lingered beside and beneath the rolling and rushing torrent of the White Water, and grew thoughtful as I watched the glorious play of the living sun-bow, arching its awful chasms with light and beauty. Through tangled thickets, massed valleys of laurel, we plunged forward till we passed into the delicious valley of the Cashiers, and toiled up the steep battlements of the mighty Whiteside mountain.

Thence I beheld billowy ranges of tower and cliff and crag, ridge over ridge, vale succeeding vale, green forests crowning their blue summits, far, far away, in the infinite distance—a realm spread out like the sea, vast as its circumference, irregular as its billows—a wonderful illusion of the ocean, without bound or limit save in the faculty of vision itself—all finally wrapped at last, in the grey mists and fleecy robes of the ethereal distance. And the wild gusts shook the lofty forest tops in the deep gorges: and rolled up in storm to the steadfast summits; and the storm cloud hurled its bolts of fire across the hollows; and the thunder roared against the heights, and a nameless Terror brooded along the impending cliffs, as if meditating the awful plunge below.

And, as I gazed, a mighty image arose before my soul's vision—and I beheld the mysterious mother, Nature herself, throned in her tangled sovereignty of waste; wild torrents roaring around her; great winds swaying her solemn forests into music, the tumults of which, while they raised the choir of storm into sublimity, did not impair its awful symphonies. These were her voices—voices of moaning and complaint—for in all her grandeur there was gloom; and the desolation of her state rendered valueless all her profligate wilderness of wealth. Her voices of cataract and storm were calling upon *art* for succour and deliverance. She was imploring man—he to whom all her empire was decreed—to come to her assistance. He alone could open the pathways to her Empire and make it fruitful. She needed his pioneer to trace out the avenues to her grand abodes—to grade her summits; to span the gulfs with his arches; to render safe the march along the stupendous precipices. She needed his industry to lay bare the tangled wastes of valley beneath her heights, and to clothe their bosoms in yellow harvests, ripening in a generous sun for the scythe of autumn. She demanded of him the art which should strew her highway with flowers; which should make her crags blossom with the rose—which should crown her ledges with noble architecture—which should raise her statues of living marble out of the massed stolidity of her now cold and silent rocks. Melancholy in her glorious solitude; gloomy in all her grandeur; Nature was thus crying out everywhere for the succour and the help of man—for that culture of art, which should soothe, with the sweets of Beauty, her dark, and terrible, and sterile aspects.

And thus, in the same sterile, irregular, tangled condition—a wild sovereignty of gloom and thicket—the great soul of Humanity cries aloud to Education for her rescue. Education bears the same relation to Humanity that culture does to nature. Education is culture. In both cases the necessity is to remove the undergrowth, to clear the way for progress, to level obstructions; to crown with fruitfulness the great valleys which now lie waste; to open up the beauty, the nobleness, the symmetry and the grandeur of the prospect; so that all that is good and worthy, pure and sweet, elevated and symmetrical, shall have due development; so that all that is susceptible of growth and improvement, whether in the wild domain of nature, or in the tangled ignorance and profligate excess of humanity, shall be duly brought forth, and a full opportunity afforded, in either case, for making the subject, the pure and perfect creature, which it was decreed to be by Heaven.

In the nature of man, even as in the realm of nature, the pathways are to be laid open to otherwise inaccessible heights, through mazy and interminable wastes of thicket. The heart is to be weeded of all dangerous and poisonous growths of foliage; and plants of healing, and flowers of beauty, are to be set to grow in their places. Fields of production must succeed to the profitless undergrowth of weed and fungus; and thought, without impediment, must be taught to rise to the heights of vision, from whence the soul shall be able to behold all the glories and beauties of its world, the world around it, and the world above. In these progresses, Education unfolds to the individual his own pioneer faculties; his own secret resources, which conduct through discovery to art. He finds with what wondrous talents the Deity has endowed him, for the conquest of the universal nature; what wondrous faculties of conversion, as well as of conquest, are confided to his hands; how easy is it to subdue the wild, to cultivate the barren, to make the empire of beauty second to that of terror.

And, even as the wild beast lurks in the mazy realms of swamp and thicket; as the wolf howls beside the close of the squatter; as the panther screams from his mountain-top; and the rattlesnake and adder crawl and crouch, ready with deadly fang, beneath the bush, or the slivered boulder; so lurk the wolves of passion and hate, the fanged vipers of cunning, and falsehood, and suspicion, and fraud, in the secret places of the human heart. These too, their expulsion, their destruction, constitute the great duties of education, even as cultivation is needed in the domain of nature for opening her treasures to humanity, and shaping for utility and art the resources of her abundant empire.

The world has always, to a certain degree, been conscious of the primary necessity of education. Man, by nature, is a self-educating animal; his self-development being determined in its rapidity, by the circumstances, the pressure and the necessities of his situation. That he can rise to these necessities, and from his own resources of thought, provide for the encounter with external pressure, is in proof of his superior destiny. Education is, indeed, the first necessity of human society. Its convictions, on this head, is coeval with the first step of society to improvement. The moment that man felt the necessity for building himself a shelter, finding clothing against cold, shelter from heat, building walls for protection against a foe, he began to take lessons in art, which were all so many lessons for his own education. Education was coeval with the first advances of man to association. Without it there was no society. There could be none. Education implied law as well as art. Until these were secured, man was but a brute individual—a mere animal; and so he continued, until he began to exhibit his own cravings after knowledge, and to develop the secret forces of his own nature, by which he was to control, to subdue and to cultivate, the resources of the natural world. In progress as this was achieved, did his own mental and moral world develop also. It is, accordingly, a merely brutal condition of humanity, which finds a people wholly unexercised in the elevated and inspiring duties; which, exercising the race in the appointed tasks of conquest, and conversion, in respect to other races, and to the material world in which it lives, as naturally effects its own self-elevation, and the gradual conversion of humanity into a thing of soul and immortality. Where society fails in these duties, a natural deficiency of resource must be implied; where this deficiency of faculty exhibits itself for any length of time, it is in proof that the race is of simply pioneer character, like our redmen, having only a certain limited career of performance assigned them, and destined, in process of time, to disappear, and give place to superior races; or where, as in the case of the African, the intellect is too low and inert for self-performance and expansion, and is decreed to receive all its impulse to development, in that degree of which it is susceptible, from the coercive rule of a conqueror and master. With people destined for any progress whatsoever, education is the only and the grand agency, including schools which contemplate the equal necessities of the soul, the affections and the intellect.

But the plastic and highly susceptible nature of man, stimulated by curiosity, eager with impulse, with a thousand pathways opening before his footsteps on every hand, a thousand avenues leading to pleasures of taste and appetite, reminds us that education may develop mischievously one class of his faculties to the total subversion of another—may lift his inferior nature into authority, and overthrow the nobler endowments which have been accorded him. Perhaps, if we could rightly examine the curious minutiae of such a history, we should really discover that this was the very error lying at the bottom of all the mischiefs of the world.

The instincts of the world, as declared by its various efforts, discover the right direction in the matter, have shown that such was its misgiving. Accordingly, all the great nations of the earth, in degree as they have advanced in knowledge and power, have exhibited an earnest solicitude in behalf of the proper sort of education—the problem of most importance and difficulty, where the phases of simple truth are so mysterious and contradictory. With all our acquisitions of art, science, wisdom, learning and power, we may still give a wrong direction to the human heart and intellect, which shall impair the powers and diminish the resources of the individual, and possibly inflict the worst evils on society at large, wherever he may happen to attain authority among his people. We read this result of ill-education in all the histories of all the nations; but education is itself, a self-repairer, and they are all working onward to the true; and as evil is necessarily of temporary action and effect, so have we a sure guaranty for the gradual correction of error, and the steady, clear progress of man towards the truth. We are not to be discouraged if the progress is slow, and if defeat is frequent. Our instincts lead to perseverance. Education itself implies it. The world still strives, in spite of all its disappointments, resulting from, and in changed conditions, and the transfer of power from one region to another. The something gained by each generation, is usually retained for the benefit of a more fortunate posterity. The remarkable examples of Greece and Rome, in ancient periods; of France, Germany and Great Britain in modern, will suffice for reference. In all these, there has been a wonderful coincidence of method in the matter of education—without any concert of design, especially in the promotion of the grand essentials, for procuring discipline—always the first necessity; for tasking and exercising memory; for compelling the exercise of reflection; for grounding the mind in laws; for instilling the assured experiences of time; and for making thought, with all its tributary energies of curiosity, observation and memory, aided by its natural endowments of imagination, fancy, causality, comparison—a perpetual seeker after truth, wisdom, virtue and justice—the grand ends contemplated by education. In these labours we are familiar with the results which have been attained by these several nations. We behold them in their gradual rise to eminent power and majesty—in their spread of empire; in their acquisition of treasure; in the development of their glorious arts. We read them in the biographies of their remarkable men—the great shining lights of time, the models, the examples of virtue, philosophy, heroism; in their arts and sciences, to which we address the eyes of our young, and by which we fondly endeavor to guide their uncertain footsteps.

Amidst all their diversities of plan, involving, no doubt, many and serious mistakes, we are encouraged, as we see what have been the fruits of their several systems; as we trace the several grand progresses of human civilization. We see the working, to one benignant result, in the great names and achievements of our own people—in the wise foresight of our own great statesmen, achieving a social and patriotic organization, for which more famous nations have striven in vain; in the vigorous growth of our infant art and literature; in the spread of a superior and beautiful Christian morality, which acts as the great regulating agency of the intellectual performer. All of these progresses, in our case, are briefly the results of the accumulated experiences of humanity, in mental and moral training, of six thousand years of aggregated society. We have simply brought to bear, upon our peculiar exigencies, the wisdom of the past; and have, happily, adapted the lessons of older nations—lessons of defeat as well as triumph—to the conditions of a new empire. And we have done so, somewhat because of the fact that our empire *was* a new one, in which we were enabled to strip law and education of the conventional trappings and artifices of an old and corrupting social organization.

This was much, but we have more to do; more to learn; and, in addition, have not only to correct our own mistakes, and purge our own excesses, but to rise to the appreciation of higher standards than we now possess; higher aims—such as are still lacking to place us in equal eminence with some of the ancient nations. We are quite too tolerant of our teachers. The necessities of a new condition, such as ours, are naturally apt to be slavish and inferior. We are required to watch closely and work rigorously, lest it become more so. We narrow our province of education, too much, down to its merely mechanical, or, at best, social exactions. We have yet to learn that society itself, is too much, everywhere, a creature of slavish conditions; and that one of the most important purposes of individual education is, through him, the elevation of society, in accordance with the standards of the individual. The education of the individual has lifted him into the wondrous creature of strength, and soul, and aim, and aspiration, that here and there, in all lands, we find him, and his uses are in the gradual training of society to the just appreciation of his morale. We must not suffer our vanities to mislead us with the absurd idea that society has, anywhere, ever attained the rank which belongs to its real condition; and this is one of the true causes of the frequent defeat and overthrow of society. Man is still wanting, in a thousand essentials, to render him the creature which he is yet destined to become. Education, however, though still imperfect in system, needing to be pruned of many excrescences, to be improved by numerous additions, to be changed and modified, according to climate, physical and social need and advance, and the new necessities of altered political and local conditions, must still be admitted to have achieved wonders, in the elevation of the animal man, from the period when he roved a naked, a reckless and improvident savage, to his present noble, grand and imposing stature—the conqueror over all the tribes and empires of the earth.

Thus, educating man for conquest, conversion and supremacy, over all the provinces of nature, it is an improvement and advance of modern upon former times, which exhibits a similar concern for the education of woman. Regarding her as solely tributary to the more powerful sex, it has been too much the case to pass carelessly over the claims of her intellect to proper cultivation and education. Even in Greece, famous for the exquisite and beautiful symmetry of her educational philosophy, woman never rose into her proper rank, as a social ministrant; as a human counsellor; as a judicious friend; as a consoling and strengthening sympathiser. Her position was that rather of an attendant—a drudge—or the creature of mere sensual contemplation. Even her Aspasia, famous as the companion of so great a states-man as Pericles, famous for her intellectual vivacity, her arts and her accomplishments, was permitted to arrive at this distinction only by the forfeiture of some of her most ennobling and endearing qualities as a woman.

The case was still worse in Rome, though she boasts of the patriotic virtues of her Virginias and Cornelias. When we hear of her recognized woman—when she rises into rank in the pages of recorded history, it is rarely because of her merits as matron or virgin. She could only acquire distinction as she became unsexed and unfeminine—as she put on the hard nature, the bolder manners, with the more intense cravings and ambition of the man. It is a very great error to suppose, as is but too commonly the case, that the feudal period of modern history was more favorable to the culture and position of the sex. That period which we call the age of chivalry, threw an artificial halo about the sex in courtly places, such as the great centres of France, Provence, and, possibly, in portions of Great Britain; but even in these courtly centres, woman was, at best, the mere creature in a pageant—a tributary only to a false system which sought its meretricious aids in all quarters, and subsidized even religion, with as little scruple as it did the gentler sex. In brief, as Sismondi tells us, the age which we fondly designate as that of chivalry, and eulogize for its grace, purity and near approach to perfection, existed only in brilliant fictions. They were not real, not natural. It was illusion only! And how could it be otherwise? Periods which are essentially those of war—nations which have lived wholly by their perpetual strifes with one another—are never favorable to the elevation, the culture, or even the safety of woman. It is only during the reign of peace that the feminine virtues and graces demand and obtain full acknowledgment among men, and rise into a rank which compels respect, and ensures elevation and honorable recognition. The last forty years of peace in the civilized world, dating from the close of the career of the first Napoleon, has done more towards the recognition of woman, as a being of mind and soul, purity and excellence—as the ally and counsellor, the companion and consoler of man—than was done by the three hundred years preceding; and it is no small boast which *our* country can utter, with honesty and in triumph, that in no part of the world has she yet risen to the *status* which she this day enjoys in ours! Here, only, does she take her proper place—speaking of the country as a whole—here only does she enjoy her proper authority—regulating the manners of society—refining the intercourse between the sexes—restraining the encroachments of insolence—checking, without fear of defiance, the outbreaks of ferocity—and every where compelling the deference and sympathy of all classes, in all conditions of society.

This is a great and noble triumph for our country, and it is one of those, of which we may boast without any rebuke for arrogance, or suspicion of hypocrisy. It is perhaps due to our gradual growth, as a people, from a condition of comparative isolation, into that of large and mixed communities of opulence and refinement. The sexes have grown equally together. In no country in the world is man a greater dependent upon the woman, than in ours. Here she fulfils conditions which, as they elevate her duties, raise her into authority and place. Here, perhaps, is she more certainly in the position which she should occupy, than in any other country. She is neither degraded by necessity to servility, nor raised by convention to an artificial rank, the pageantry of which is but too frequently inconsistent with her own claims and endowments, and calculated to make duty distasteful to her mind. We have scarcely yet reached, as a people, that artificial period, the result of very unequal distribution of wealth, false ordering of society, and inequality in the numbers of persons disposed to marry—when marriage, a natural law, becomes a hopeless quest to thousands of the dependent sex. With us, accordingly, marriage is not a consideration of so much doubt and uncertainty, as to render the woman the sacrifice of society. Such a fraud upon affection, no less than faith, as is but too commonly known in Europe, as the *mariage de convenance*—in other words, of cupidity—is rarely known with us. The consideration of marriage is as potent here with the male as with the female sex. The wants of the man are as urgent as the necessities of the woman. With us, accordingly, the heart is permitted to breathe freely, to declare itself freely, and a just appreciation of the claims of individual charm and character, are allowed to weigh, irrespective of the fortunes of the party. The tastes and fancies and sympathies, are allowed to grow, and to exercise the liberty of selection. Our homage to the sex is made to personal virtues, graces, beauties; our choice depends upon true and earnest sentiment, and honest passions, and not to the exactions of cupidity. And there is so little want, so little poverty, in our country, that no slavish necessity need compel the woman to make sacrifice in marriage, of a single sympathy. No heart here, need be laid on the altar of Mammon, ere it can find devotion, or win Love into willing worship. Hearts, with us, need not famish for that unbought, unbuyable affection, which is the only food upon which hearts are destined to feed and to be happy.

This one condition, of the equal relation of the two sexes, in so vital a respect, lifts the woman into a position of independence, which is no where quite so high or perfect as with us. In the ranks of wealth, in the old States of Europe, you will no doubt find a class of women occupying a degree of liberty, perhaps, which is very far beyond anything of which ours know. We have small circles in our great cities which strive for and emulate their privileges. But their liberty is but too apt to become license; and the license which is dangerous to the man, becomes death, nay, something worse than death, to the woman. These small circles do not really mingle with society; claim to be above it, do not in any way affect it, except with revulsion; and are, accordingly, indifferent to the opinions which might otherwise subdue their license under law. But I need not consider these anomalous and exceptional cases. Enough that I have truly described to you, in my portrait, the conditions and relations of the sexes, as they exist together in the rural districts of the South.

Raised here to the elevated rank in which I have shown the sex—regarded with this just and proper veneration—it naturally becomes the policy of society that woman should maintain herself in it, and justify her maintenance of it by her own developments. The only process for effecting this object is to make her education worthy of that of the man; to bring about the full development of her mind, so that it shall yield him that adequate companionship, without which there can be no permanent sympathies between the parties. She is decreed to succour and strengthen his affections—to cheer his despondency—to invigorate his energies—to console him in defeat,—to counsel him with that wisdom, the purest and perhaps the profoundest of all, which is born of a true heart, and the devotedness of a perfect love. As *his* education contemplates energy and execution, so hers must contemplate watch and ministry. Her faculties are necessarily peculiar to herself, as they regard his necessities rather than his powers. In the things which he needs to execute, which lie within the purpose of his endowments, he perhaps does not require her succour. But she is not less his ally, though she does not take the field in armour beside him—though she serves neither as pioneer nor conqueror. She is to exhibit the household virtues; there *must* be a household, and *one* must maintain it, while the other goes abroad, in toil, labor, peril and conflict. She must exercise the timely economy, the guardian watch, the regular method, the sobriety of love, which never can be diverted from its post; the gentleness which restrains excess; the affections whose mournfullest reproach is conveyed in a tearful and placid submission. And how profound must be the wisdom which shall teach all this; and how much more profound the wisdom, born of virtue, which is to learn all this; the patient, receiving wisdom, which is always the profoundest. She is to encourage the adventures of the man, watch lovingly his toils, and with sweet offices of affection, requite all his exertions. And this leads us to what is peculiar in the nature and constitution of woman, a subject, the examination of which, should necessarily precede any plan which contemplates her education.

Of late days it has become a frequent complaint with certain of the sex, that their rights, as women, are withheld them; that, presuming on his physical, rather than his intellectual powers, man has usurped something more than his share of authority—has denied them that share of power in social, if not political affairs, to which they may properly lay claim; and has thus degraded them to a rank of moral inferiority, inconsistent with the original decrees of nature.

The complaint is made in rather vague and general terms, and is urged with much more passion than argument. The complaining parties are not quite agreed among themselves as to the specific rights of which they have been robbed, and do not suggest the processes by which justice should be done them. I am afraid that, even were the charges admitted, the claims conceded, they would still find it a somewhat difficult thing to appropriate, or even to determine, what are the rights which they would exercise. Would they have the right of suffrage—enter the market place and scramble at the polls with brute violence, for the privilege of putting in their votes? Their husbands, brothers, sons, are their representatives, doing this very duty. Do they distrust the ability, the honesty of these, to do the duty wisely and faithfully? But they would themselves, perhaps, be the incumbents of office? It is not that they hold society to be ill-governed by man—not that they suppose themselves altogether capable of ruling something more wisely; but they have an ambition to figure also in the ranks of politicians, statesmen, governors. Now, the right, here, depends wholly upon the capacity. We have no rights inconsistent with our endowments. Even among men, there is not more than one in fifty of those who enter office, who have any just right to be there; and unless the woman really supposes that she can improve the government of man in human affairs, by her superior capacity for it, she can offer no sort of argument in behalf of the claim to supersede him. It is true, no doubt, that there are thousands of women superior to numbers of men whom we find in legislative assemblies; but this class of men are not legislators; they are the mere dead weights of power—used as the balance wheels and fixtures, the ropes, wires and pullies—a part of the machinery of government, but with no share in the motive-power. Would she rank with such as these, by simply taking her seat in the eyes of the people, and possibly helping to fill their ears with harangues of terrible commonplace, such as hourly afflicts us, *ad nauseum,* in all such assemblies now? This is the desire of a vulgar vanity, ridiculous enough where men are the actors, and doubly ridiculous should woman occupy the stage. Now, nature accords no rights to vanity! *The capacity to be useful in one's proper sphere* is that alone which affords the only real right which we possess in this province. And, unless the sex can assert a superior faculty over the man, for the government of states and nations, there can be no good reason for altering the relations of the parties in political affairs.

But they claim to be endowed for the professions? Are they? If so, what prevents them from entering the professions? Law, no doubt, is a very inviting profession to those who possess metaphysical powers—argument, logic, eloquence; and law, in all countries, and especially in ours, is the great secret and mean for the acquisition of political power. There is no law excluding women from the professions. Let those who complain, try them, if they will. If they can succeed in law, they will probably succeed in procuring office. But they will require to go through a like probation with the man. There is an apprenticeship of years, not only in making acquisition of the rudiments of the profession, but in establishing such a reputation in the community, for knowledge and business talents, as will secure patronage. Are they prepared for this probation? Can they exercise this weary, working, business faculty? In the meantime, they must forego the present interesting relations which exist between the sexes. All these must be changed! The moment they become politicians and professors in the science and arts, they rise into attitude, in society, as the *rivals* of men—keen competitors for power and its profits; no longer to be observed with love and admiration; no longer to receive attention from devoted worshippers; to turn only to meet with homage, and smiling, only to diffuse joy and radiance throughout the assembly. Their sex had privileges of a peculiar power, but only because of their recognition as a peculiar sex, having certain sacred and special functions, as a class; all of which were of so tender, so delicate, and so attractive a character, as tacitly to compel forbearance, and secure for them prompt and favoring acknowledgment from all classes of society. In setting up as the rival of man, she loses what is special in the rights of woman. The rights of *woman* she, in fact, possesses now; it is, in truth, the rights of *man* which some of these inconsiderate champions of the sex contend for. They hunger for double power and double privileges. They would unite in themselves the privileges of both sexes; and, possibly, with a very imperfect capacity for either. In becoming the rival of man, woman ceases to be his ally. What then? There is a contest between them for power—not for a *share* of power, mark ye, but for the whole. Woman in conflict with man—man with woman! What becomes of the world under these circumstances? What will posterity say? Will there be any posterity to say anything? Is this fulfilling the conditions on which both parties were created? Is not the whole pretension simply and mournfully farcical?

Without discussing farther these uncertain claims made by a singularly unfortunate few among the sex, it will, perhaps, be quite sufficient to regard, passingly, the vital differences between the two sexes—differences which really contribute the absolute sources of union between them, and the most grateful equality; and to indicate these differences as fully justifying the very *status* which the woman now enjoys in relation to the other sex.

It is needless to urge that, physically, at least, the power is with the man; as needless to insist that, where God has confided the power, He designs that its exercise should rest. For, as Milton happily puts the case—

> "What is strength without a double share
> Of wisdom? Vast, unwieldy, burdensome,
> Proudly secure, yet liable to fall
> By weakest subtleties—not made to rule,
> But to subserve where wisdom bears command."

If God has given to man the supremacy of strength, it would seem almost equally clear that He has not decreed that the sway should be with woman; and

Holy Writ is sufficiently decided in affirming this position. If, in addition to this, we discern such moral differences between the two sexes as fully confirm the physical; if we find the man to be in possession of the stern, inflexible will, which accords with authority and makes it respected; the earnest, eager impulse, which forever prompts inquiry, adventure, and discovery; the intense and craving spirit which demands struggle and trial as the agencies for development; the determined execution; the bold energy; the sleepless thirst equally for sway and knowledge; the more daring purpose; the greater design; the more inventive faculties; and the more wide and comprehensive general capacity;—the inference seems inevitable. These are the properties and qualities which *make* nations and preserve them; which make laws and compel obedience to them; which provide resources for society; which open new provinces for the progress of society; which foster society by arts, and protect its possessions from assault by arms. These qualities and endowments, which declare themselves in the man, while he is yet a boy—independently of training and education—and for the due regulation and maturing of which, alone, do we employ education—seem fully to determine the rank which man should hold in relation to all other living creatures; the duties which he owes to them, to himself, and to the Creator; and indicate, with sufficient distinctness, the sort of education which is proper for the development of *his* faculties, and the proper conduct of his performances.

If, on the other hand, we find the faculties of woman to be, ordinarily, wholly different from these; if we find her nature to be more sensitive and timid; more dependent than determined; more anxious and solicitous than reckless and confident; less adventurous, less eager, bold and daring; less concentrative, intense and energetic; less inflexible of will; more fond of repose than of action; of grace and beauty, than of strength and power; preferring peace to strife; the sweets of home to the wild waters of adventure; if we find her better able to watch than to fight; better able to nurse and heal, than to hurt and wound; shrinking rather than audacious; trembling rather than brave; delicate rather than vigorous; easily diverted, rather than tenacious of purpose; loving rather than proud; with stronger inhibitiveness than man, and so less adventurous; with far superior philoprogenitiveness, and so, intuitively, fonder of children and better prepared to take care of them; more cautious; more reverent, more benevolent, and so, more capable of just, and fine, sweet and graceful, rather than powerful and passionate impulses; if we find all these differences between the two sexes, obvious from the first steps of childhood, independently of all human training; and if the characteristics of the woman be such, almost universally, in all nations, as I have described them to be; then what follows? Do we not see that she now occupies her natural sphere, and fills her proper position in the circle of humanity, even as it was assigned her at creation? And no struggle, no effort, however daring; no art, however subtle; no expectation, however high; no toils of the one sex, or concessions of the other; can materially change these relations. They follow original types, that are as immutable as any of the laws of God; they are among the first laws of God, and contemplate the essential harmonies of society, which, for preservation and perpetuation, demand these very inequalities. They render the tie between the sexes coercive—it is the great human and social necessity. The harmonies of love are born of these very differences, even as we owe the beauty of the landscape to its inequalities; the beauty of the stars to their differences of size, color, splendour; the delight of music to those transitions, modulating the extreme, in the tones which art is required to wed together, by happy conciliations, for the birth of harmony. Woman is a lesser light, perhaps, in the firmament of humanity, but not less beautiful, or necessary to the music of the moral spheres. Shall we deem it a wrong to her, that she should be denied to enter the chariot of the sun! Hers is not a borrowed light, like that of moon and stars, but one growing out of the affluence of her own nature, and commissioned with lustres suited to her own province. From the first choral song of creation, when the stars first sang together, her sphere was appointed, and the first voices of revelation, declared her rank among the other orbs. Can we doubt of this, when we know, that, in all nations, she has held the same relative position to man from the earliest periods of time. Can such coincidence be the result of a coincident injustice, ranging throughout the human world? And how shall we suppose that God, designing her for a superior destiny, has yet suffered this grievous wrong—this perversion of justice—of her powers and His purposes—to be perpetrated, perpetuated, for so many thousand years, and in nations, the special rule and government of which he had, for so many centuries, reserved to Himself exclusively, his own anointed priests, his own inspired prophets? To prove the wrong of which she is supposed to complain, the usurpation of her rights which has been asserted for her, we must accuse the Deity of blindness to his own purposes, and the violation of his own invariable laws.

The question need trouble us no further. Enough, that in our passing consideration of it, we have indicated the peculiar characteristics of the sex. Its peculiarities afford us clues and guides which are essential to our present objects and proper question. How shall we so educate her, as that full justice shall be done to her peculiar endowments; so that she may rightly serve in the general purposes of creation: so that she may wisely reign in that province, in which man gladly hails her as the sovereign?

We shall find the answer to this question, when we shall have answered another. What is her especial allotment? She is decreed to be the wife and mother. These are her rights. On this subject there can be no question. No usurpation can wrest these from her; no ambition contend with her in these relations. Here she is alone, without a rival. If, having these provinces to herself, she claims to share, also, in all those which man has reserved to himself, *she* is the usurper! And will not these provinces suffice any ambition? To those who will examine their wealth, value and authority, there can be none richer, none which more religiously involve the idea of power. They constitute noble relations with society, among the very noblest that man acknowledges. As a wife, she is his ally, the nearest to his heart, the keeper of his affections. She is to keep them young and healthy—to guard and freshen them with her own—closely to clip and cling around them, even as the fruitful vine twines about the sustaining oak; making beautiful to other eyes, with her flower and her foliage, the roughness of those lineaments in him, born of his very strength and majesty, which might otherwise too greatly awe and repel. She is to *teach* his affections, through her own, so that his power shall be subdued to meekness; so that his passions, even while they work to their mutual security and good, shall be shorn of their excess and violence. She is to *lift* his affections by refining them, so that they shall become virtues—noble and generous, like his strength and stature—so that he shall always feel the magnanimous joy of a great heart in the privilege of protecting and sheltering the feeble and confiding, and of loving the gentle and the good; and as, by these means, she compels his heart to assimilate with hers, so does it become a partaker in her grace and innocence. So does she borrow of his strength, and rise into a due sympathy with, and full appreciation of, the grandeur and greatness of his mission. All this can she achieve by ministries, little short of the angelic—by love, truth, fidelity, devotion, and the exercise of that sweet humility which has a more subduing and elevating virtue still, as the true foundation, not only of all proper human success, but of all religion.

She is to train his affections by these, through these, and by her feminine tastes and fancies, her arts and her accomplishments. She is to win and to subdue him with sentiment and music, and thus make her appeal to those powerful motors in his mind, Imagination and Sensibility. For these performances, her education must contemplate her manners, her own susceptibilities, the nice appreciation of the delicate, the genial, the true. The Fine Arts are within her province; poetry and painting, as well as music; the exercise equally of voice or hand; or, where the musical faculty is not present, or active in her mental endowments, then other arts and exercises which shall repair the deficiency; and it will be found that, by the liberal gifts of Providence, he or she who is found wanting in one faculty, is usually provided with others which are equivalent in value, and which, duly exercised, shall realize equally useful results in a proper course of training. Elocution, for example, may properly be made a study with the sex. Few persons read well, with just emphasis, with due economy of voice, with due moderation, or with a proper sense always of the sentiment which is to be conveyed.

Sculpture, the working of clay and marble, is not sufficiently honored with the regards of the sex. It is not more beyond their province than painting and music. A girl may shape vases in clay quite as easily as flowers in needle-work or tapestry. And why not? Some of the most beautiful specimens of ancient and modern art come to us in this form and of these rude materials. The art is an exquisite one, and should commend itself especially to the women of our country; all those, in particular, who languish for provinces in which their genius may be developed. The notion that working in clay or marble is unfitted for a female hand or genius, is pure absurdity. The labor is not drudgery—it is art, rather than labor, that is needed for it, and it is one of those arts which may give exercise to many others. The Vase, beautifully wrought, into a noble and classic form, may be covered with exquisite landscapes, to which the baking process will almost ensure, while the vessel remains unbroken, eternal duration. To encourage the timid ambition, we may mention that one of the European princesses of the present day, has acquired high distinction among living sculptors for her achievements in marble.

There are a thousand like fields in which the genius of the woman may exercise itself profitably, and gratify all its cravings for fame. Wherever the art or employment calls for fancy, taste, delicacy, discrimination, it appeals to her peculiar endowments. We need scarcely refer to the vast and various fields of polite literature—nay, the sciences, such as botany, astronomy—as regions in which she may find grateful employment. These fields have already been penetrated by the sex, and they have established in them the highest claims to honor, as teachers and discoverers. In these regions, woman may seek and find a thousand opportunities for the exercise of genius, talent and industry, which shall place her honorably beside the being whom she is unwilling to recognize as a superior, but whom it is still her natural solicitude to please. If this be the object of her mind, as it is the instinct of her heart, there need be no change in the relations of the sexes. There are fields of exercise for both, in which, though pursuing parallel lines, they shall yet work harmoniously together, in the common cause of humanity. And it must not be supposed that we subject her to a law which necessarily humiliates, when we suggest that most of her efforts and arts should be designed for the conciliation and delight, the happiness and comfort of the sterner sex. The solicitude of man, in like manner, seen under whatever guises or aspects, is equally great to win her favour. We work for each other, and if we work lovingly, without any miserable rivalry, we work for mutual comfort, security and happiness. The true ambition of the woman, in the development of her mind, is to raise it to the dignity of his; so that she may commune with him as an associate, whom he will delight always to encounter; counsel him as a friend in whom he finds it grateful to confide. She is the mistress of his domestic hours—of the most sweet and peaceful hours of his life. She must make home the temple of domestic peace. Her song and smile must sweeten his sadness, cheer his weariness, and weave the rainbow of felicity out of his very tears. Setting aside the trifles and the toys of girlhood, the petty vanities, the small ambition which made her eager for the admiration of merely roving eyes, she must so rise in strength, through love and duty, as to enter into the necessities of *his* life, with the warm, knowing interest of one who would gladly share them all. This is to put on the true dignity of woman—to fulfil all its noble conditions; to give security to the hopes of the infant generations. Happy and secure will be that household where the wife can prove herself thoughtful over the cares of her husband; can strengthen him bravely to endure and wisely to encounter them. If, at length, he falls, in a too unequal contest with a peculiar fortune—like the great oak, stricken by the bolt that strikes only to destroy—she is then to twine herself about his ruins, like the loving tendrils of the vine, and hallow with her fond embrace the noble column of greatness which her love hath failed to save.

But her relations to man and to society do not end here. She is to be the mother of his children. Not a man herself, she is to be the mother of a race of men—of heroes, statesmen, philosophers, priests, and poets—the most glorious orders of nobility which the world can anywhere behold. As the mother of men, and such men, she holds in her hands all the destinies of humanity through all surrounding ages. Can any trust more ennoble her than this? Can any tie afford better security for the affections and respect of husband and father? Can any human employments require more intellect, or prove more exalting in the eyes of those who think and feel? Would she exchange these affairs for those of the small politician, the poor statesman, the driveller at the professions, the scuffler at the ballot-box, seeking the petty privilege of voting for Tom, Dick, or Harry, of whom, after a single term in Legislature or Congress, we hear nothing again, and of whom nobody cares to hear? How feeble must be that intellect, how contemptible that vanity, which would exchange, for these employments, the glorious privilege of being a nursing mother for a race of men! In this capacity she moulds the moral of a thousand coming generations. Her watch, love, prudence, judicious direction and sleepless ministry, constitute, after all, the only securities of the young. Teacher, preacher, counsellor, friend—all fail—and must fail—if the mother fails;—if the home education hath not been solicitous of duty—hath not risen into the guardian authority and wisdom which shall shape the infant nature rightly, and give the first direction to its childish thought and its animal impulse! Her tender cares—the life and joy which she imparts from her own breast—establish such a power over the child that she can win him, by merely opening her bosom, from the very brink of the precipice; and, so long as he remains feeble, and until the energies of his expanding thought and will supervene to make him impatient of the small empire of home, she continues to maintain this almost exclusive sway over his mind and his affections.

In this province she has no rival. What, through this medium, must be her power for good or evil? She thus helps to shape the future—helps to shape the *government* of the future; and wo to *her* if she cannot open her eyes to the grand, but awful responsibilities, involved in the duties of a mother! Wo to us, and to the child, if *her* education be not made to contemplate, over all, this most beautiful, most endearing, most precious and sacred of all human relations; if she be not rendered capable, by her training, of taking charge of these infant germs of the successive generations—their minds, their hearts, their souls—their hopes, their health, their security—so that they shall walk alone, work prosperously, with none to make afraid—with brows erect in the sight of heaven and man—honoring father and mother, and becoming, in turn, the objects of loving and dutiful affections from their own progeny. As a mother, she is especially responsible for the future of their lives. She is their first teacher, and at that only period when their morals can receive the readiest impress in the formation of character. She holds, almost exclusively, the strings which guide their first feeble, tottering footsteps; and it cannot be otherwise. This is her inevitable duty as the mother. The cares of the father, abroad—his province necessarily leading him abroad—devolve this duty entirely upon her; devolve upon her the immediate formation of the child's moral; and hence the vital importance of a nobly educated mother; not a vain, weak, pretending creature, aspiring after the denied and the impossible, but "a woman nobly planned," pure and strong—one who, in acquiring all that the mind needs for development, suffers herself to forfeit nothing of the exquisite sensibility which makes the basis of her power—the delicate refinement, the beautiful tenderness, which make and keep her feminine.

Madame Campan, in reply to a question of Napoleon touching the education of the young, seems to have felt all the importance of the woman in relation to society. "Sire," said she," let us have a school for the education of mothers." Napoleon's quick instincts readily conceived the vast volume of this answer, and said, characteristically—"Let it be so. That is exactly what we want!" Volumes could have said no more. Would you have the proof of the significance in this summary? Read history—read biography. You will everywhere see that most great men trace their own most noble developments, and all their successes, to nobly-nursing mothers. As little may we doubt that many a foolish mother has destroyed the dearest child of her affections—has perverted, in her doting ignorance, the true nature and the proper powers of the boy—has robbed him of his own natural virtues—has defrauded him of the use of his natural endowments—has made him a rebel to herself, to society, to God—made him the victim of constant mistake and constant defeat, and, in thousands of cases, as if she had been a Fate designed for his destruction, has conducted him, with her own hands, to the awful retributions of the justly offended laws.

That there should be women to despise this office, only proves their vanities to be superior equally to their sensibilities and wisdom. There can be none nobler—none half so noble—none which will more completely need and exercise the highest powers of male and female intellect. The wisdom to comprehend the child, the intellect to guide, the strength and art to govern; these will task every art which we may acquire, every faculty which we may possess from nature. And, if we train the faculties of the young to their full uses, we govern the world and society as directly, and as effectively, as if we ourselves sat in the high places of law and authority, and shaped, with our own words and deeds the decrees of the nations. Who but a blockhead—vain, weak, presumptuous and ridiculous—can conceive of anything humiliating from such an employment? Is it a wife and mother who indulges in such a notion? Let her go with me to yonder stony summit of Apalachia, and there meditate the examples which we shall there behold. Go with me to that mighty pile of rock, six thousand feet above the sea, mass beetling over mass, black, wild, savage; great cliffs hanging loose in air; great caverns yawning between them; the sheer precipice, prominent above the chasm, which blackly stretches a thousand feet below—without stay, or step, or ledge, in the interval, upon which the mountain deer might stand with safety, or without terror and trembling! A stern, dark, awful peak, around which the storm raves unfelt, and the lightning strikes only to pare and sliver the edges of the defying granite. Here, in this crag—eyrie of the eagle—according to the traditions of the red man—

> "The Eagle nest,
> The Magic Mountain of the Blest,
> Where the Wahcondah's form, at first,
> In glory o'er the forests burst;
> And rent the giant rocks in twain,
> And spread below the sunny plain;
> And piled on high each mighty tier,
> Of hill and boulder, layer on layer,
> Until they rose to mortal eyes,
> Meet realm for sovereign of the skies;
> Torn by his thunders, by his ire,
> Scathed, till each summit blazed with fire,
> And made secure, in height and storm,
> From bold approach of mortal form."

But not without inhabitants. In the highest peak, on the side most precipitous, overhanging the dismal chasm of a thousand feet, the eagle has made his home, in a slippery cavern, a great crevice, opened by the bolts of heaven. There dwell a pair of these mighty birds, in whose grandeur, daring, solitary might and magnanimity, great men have always been pleased to find their noblest models. There they breed and train their young to their own bold and powerful employments. You see, even as the sun rushes up into the heavens, that the male bird darts out to bathe in his beams, and to drink vigor from his ascending fires.

His eye challenges that of the sun, and his great metallic wings grow golden as he rolls among the burning vapors. He sails free; hangs suspended on his own centre, and, at an incomputable distance he beholds his prey, the deer, the sheep, browsing upon the hillside, thousands of feet below. Swifter than any flight of arrow—a rush like that of the bolt—a hurtling tumult of wings, that rattle like plate armour as he goes—he descends upon his victim, which he bears up in his steely talons—each stroke of which is death—to the overhanging precipice where his mate and young ones keep. He is the purveyor, the warrior, the hunter—the conqueror! He performs the masculine office.

But his mate, is she degraded in hers? Is hers one to mortify her nature—to revolt her instincts—to humble her pride. She tears the food for her young—she watches their nest—she trains their little wings in flight. Hardly less powerful than the male, she can, in degree, execute his trusts, should the bolt of the hunter strike him down in flight. But she has her own. See her as she watches, calm, immovable as the rock itself, while the stealthy viper crawls upward from the gorges to her summits. In a moment, he is writhing in her beak! and, as the wolf and panther tread along the precipice, she dashes out upon them, with fierce bill, and bloody talon, every stroke of which is a terror, while her sharp, triumphant shrieks attest to her returning consort, the flight of the assailant. And, when no foes invade her home, see her as she trains her young to the edges of the precipice, and flings them off into the gulph and the abyss. Then, as they flutter—falling—she darts below them; bears them up—upon her back; flings them up again, into space, and beats the drowsy atmosphere beneath them, giving the buoyancy of the winds to their efforts, and showing them how to lift and fan their little winglets, in that exercise which shall enable them to use and sway, in future flight and conflict, the very winds which generate the storm!

Do we see no meet examples in this history of a mother's care and duties—the sources of her pride and satisfaction? Is there anything ignoble in these exercises? Do they degrade the female bird, in relation to her mate? would they degrade the human mother? She is thus to feed, and nurture and cherish *her* young; to teach their infant wings to fly; to sustain their infant efforts; to watch over and protect their slumbers from the enemy. She must watch that the vipers of cunning and treachery, and deceit and envy, do not crawl to their nest—to *her* bosom, or to theirs—commissioned to destroy; that the wild beasts of passion, hate, malice, lust and wrath, do not openly invade, even as the wolf, the tiger and the panther, where they slumber, upon the very verge of the moral precipice! Oh! surely, my friends, there are no virtues more honored among men than those which belong to the duties of wife and mother. Every instinct, every sentiment, every thought, every feeling, of the good and wise, unite to do them honor. Let them beware of the wretched and ill-grounded discontent, which makes them heedless of the powers which they do possess, in a vain struggle after those which would only enthrall and fetter, which would really degrade them could they attain; but which revelation and reason equally deny that they ever should attain! It would be the most fatal boon to the woman, which would convert her, from the ally, into the rival of the man! a boon which, forfeiting all her present distinctions and securities, would leave her wrecked and desolate, no longer an object of beauty and desire, but wasted, and a dishonored mockery, in society and life!

Endeared as she is to her mate, in spite of all his supposed tyrannies and usurpations—distinguished thus by her sweet relations of wife and mother—dear and precious because of her natural innocence, purity, beauty, and *dependence*—woman naturally claims the highest and most singular regards of man. And she receives them. He wisely decrees, day by day, as the world rises in civilization, that her intellect, not less perfect if less powerful than his own, should have select and appropriate teachers. All her capacities must be duly evolved for action in the serious drama of our mortal life. Her moral prudence, her exquisite tastes, her solicitous affections, her genius for art and for society—all these require that we should provide tutors worthy of her endowments, if we would have her the nobly-nursing wife and mother which constitute her great mission upon earth.

With this noble object are we now assembled—to consecrate by the offices of religion—by the sympathies of society—by the exhibition of a becoming zeal and interest, the collegiate endowment which shall this day begin its operations. Let your prayers unite with ours in behalf of this institution—so useful to woman—so necessary to mankind—so honorable to its liberal founders. Blest as we hold its purposes to be by Heaven, it only needs to be duly tended and cultivated by man, to crown with grace, virtue, beauty and knowledge, the future hopes and fortunes of society. And, long after *our* probation is over—when, one by one, *we* shall have passed from this busy scene of life—it may be that we shall rejoice to behold, from loftier spheres, the growth and the beauty, the shelter and the fruits, blessing other generations, of the little seedling which we this day plant for posterity. These hills shall bear evidence, in goodly edifices,—these valleys shout aloud in the joy of productive harvests—all giving proof of the fruitful virtues, springing, with its growth, into life and promise. There shall be songs from a thousand cottages, filled with youth and beauty, in honor of the grateful plant. Art shall cover your high places with appropriate temples—Genius shall triumph at their altars—Love and Innocence, Truth and Wisdom, shall decorate their shrines with flowers; and, in lifting woman into her position, of the loving wife and ally, the fondly nursing and the wisely guiding mother, we shall secure the dwellings of man in strength—his institutions in perpetuity and virtue; his heart, and its affections, in hope, in happiness and religion.

PART IV

Loud Voices, Empty Rooms

Introduction

Simms's new orations in 1856 and 1857 include several themes from earlier in his lecturing career. They speak to the social value of art in an age of rapid change, the usefulness of history as a guide to respond to present contingencies, and the distinguishing characteristics of regional identities. However, these motifs assumed new relevance and greater urgency in the late 1850s due to the events and sectional tensions associated with slavery's accompaniment of westward national expansion. These circumstances spurred Simms to adapt his standard topics to new purposes, chiefly to prepare listeners for Southern independence.

Despite Simms's established reputation as an orator and the salience of his themes, audiences in the late 1850s were less inclined to heed him. In fact, at the very point in his career when Simms aspired to professionalize his public speaking and expand the market for his orations, he was met not only with indifference but also with outright hostility. The volatile political environment was the likely culprit, including the consequences of his and his peers' earlier rhetoric on sectional character and rights. The assertion of Southern identity and prerogatives beginning in the 1840s had fostered an atmosphere wherein, by the late 1850s, these themes were either prosaic or inflammatory, depending on the audience. Thus, when Simms attempted in 1856 to reap the financial and ideological yields from two decades of public speaking, he instead suffered his most ignominious public failure and private mortification. His experience is representative of how Southern orators became susceptible to forces they had earlier set in motion but could no longer manage, and it was an inflection point that had dire consequences for his own individual critical legacy.

James Perrin Warren observes that Simms approached public speaking more intentionally in 1856, focusing on it more as a profit-making enterprise than he had earlier in his career (154). Contemplating the prospects of a speaking tour, the author wrote New York historian and illustrator Benson John Lossing on May 22 to ask whether he "can give me any hints in regard to this Lecturing business, which is new to me *as a business*" (*Letters* 3:434–35). In addition to advice on logistical considerations such as scheduling and fees, Simms was seeking guidance about new venues. For the first time in his career, Simms planned to speak in Northern cities.

The motivation for this more ambitious public-speaking tour evolved over the course of 1856. Initially, it was financial in nature. In April, Simms wrote Boston publisher James Thomas Fields to say, "I propose to gather up a few of my Lectures and undertake a rambling Lecturing campaign in the North the coming winter—i.e. if I see any reasonable prospect of their being desirable to others, & compensative to myself" (*Letters* 3:429). On May 20 he mentions the tour to *Southern Literary Messenger* editor John Reuben Thompson, writing, "I shall go, if the demand is sufficiently numerous. . . . My cares & children increase. I need to earn $3000 per ann. apart from the plantation, to live decently in broadcloth" (*Letters* 3:434). A growing family—six surviving children and his wife pregnant again—and the upkeep of Woodlands, their plantation home, were absorbing more and more of Simms's income from writing (Guilds 262). Speaking in larger, more prosperous boroughs rather than the small Southern communities that he usually addressed promised some financial relief.

The topics Simms initially considered using for his 1856 Northern tour suggest his awareness of the importance of discretion with unfamiliar audiences in partisan times to maximize ticket sales. He contemplated a new, unobjectionable two-part travelogue on the mountain scenery of western Carolina, and he offered organizers earlier, innocuous speeches such as "Poetry and the Practical" and "Choice of a Profession" (*Letters* 3:429, 436–37). However, by the end of the summer, at the same time his publisher Justus Starr Redfield was helping him negotiate "nightly employments for two months or more" in New York and New England, Simms's motivation, and consequently his topics, evolved (*Letters* 3:444). In a letter to SC Congressman James Lawrence Orr on August 30, he mentioned working on new speeches, noting that "long labours are before me of historical controversy" (*Letters* 3:442). Events far from Woodlands prompted Simms to see the forthcoming tour as not just as a source of much-needed income, but also as an opportunity to remedy what he believed were misrepresentations in an ongoing "historical controversy" over South Carolina's participation in the Revolutionary War.

Like many other topics in the antebellum period, American history had become weaponized in the conflict between North and South over the issue of enslavement. Regional historians and their readers wielded interpretations of the past "[i]n their frenzy to establish the legitimacy of their current positions" for and against enslavement, observes John Hope Franklin ("The North, the South" 18). The author of *The History of South Carolina, from its First European Discovery to its Erection into a Republic* (1840) as well as dozens of historical romances, Simms was especially sensitive to unflattering accounts of Southern history. Renewed allegations in 1856 that enslavement historically enfeebled the character of Southern society compelled him to start conceptualizing his tour as a series of rebuttals as much as a profit-making venture. Simms later recalled that "[i]t was especially important that the North should be disabused of the notion that the South <u>is imbecile</u>. Imbecile because of her slave institutions—imbecile in war—unproductive in letters—deficient in all the proper agencies of civilization . . ." (256).

These were allegations made by the Northern historian Lorenzo Sabine and amplified by Massachusetts Senator Charles Sumner. Sabine's *The American Loyalists* (1847) questioned the degree to which the "Whig leaven was diffused through the mass of her [South Carolina's] people" during the Revolution (30). He claimed that "it is hardly an exaggeration . . . that more Whigs of New England were sent to her aid, and now lie buried in her soil, than she sent from it" (32). He compared the number of enlistments from the thirteen colonies, pointedly observing that those from Southern colonies were proportionately less "compared with the States destitute of a 'peculiar institution'" (32). In other words, the practice of enslavement was responsible for diminishing South Carolina's ability to supply soldiers for its own defense or for that of other colonies. Enslavement thus made South Carolina "imbecile," weak and unable to sustain itself militarily or to contribute meaningfully to the patriot cause.

Simms had already challenged Sabine's interpretation prior to 1856. Simms's review of *American Loyalists* appeared in the July and October 1848 issues of the *Southern Quarterly Review*, and in 1853 he combined them and another review essay into *South-Carolina in the Revolutionary War: Being a Reply to Certain Misrepresentations and Mistakes of Recent Writers, in Relation to the Course and Conduct of this State*. Sumner was likely unaware of (or unpersuaded by) Simms's rebuttals, and the abolitionist elaborated on Sabine's allegations in two Senate speeches. The first, "Reply to Assailants: Oath to Support the Constitution; Weakness of the South from Slavery," was on June 28, 1854. In part a rejoinder to SC Senator Andrew Butler's assertion that the Revolution "was won by the arms and treasure of . . . *slaveholding* communities," Sumner cited primary documents to illustrate the feebleness of South Carolina's militia as well as the state's readiness to negotiate an independent peace with England (191). He then quoted notable Revolutionary-era Carolinians to demonstrate that fears of insurrections by enslaved people and runaways diminished the willingness of whites to enlist, concluding that the historical record is a "confession, not only of weakness, but that this weakness was caused by Slavery." Rebuking Butler, the Republican senator continued, "[n]ot by slavery, but in spite of Slavery, was Independence achieved" (212).

Sumner's second allegation of South Carolina's impotency was made in his May 21 and 22, 1856, "The Crime Against Kansas" speech. He renewed his argument with Butler, asking, "Has he read the history of 'the State' which he represents? He cannot surely have forgotten its shameful imbecility from Slavery, confessed throughout the Revolution, followed by its more shameful assumptions for Slavery since" (29). This time, though, Sumner extended his analysis of enslavement's enervating effect on South Carolina, postulating, "Were the whole history of South Carolina blotted out of existence, from its very beginning down to the day of the last election of the senator to his present seat on this floor, civilization might lose—I do not say how little; but surely less than it has already gained by the example of Kansas" (30).

Simms's extant correspondence following Sumner's first speech in 1854 does not include any references to it, a curious silence for such a vigilant guardian of the memory of South Carolina's Revolutionary experience. But the second speech in 1856, which precipitated Sumner's caning by South Carolina Congressman Preston Brooks, would engage his pen. The earliest existing reference in Simms's correspondence to "The Crime Against Kansas" and the subsequent imbroglio is late, September 7, when he writes James Henry Hammond that "Butler and [South Carolina Senator Josiah James] Evans are flooding me with the attacks of the Northern Press on South Carolina. . . . But [Butler's] blunderings have provoked them, & he is one of the victims in all the attacks. In brief he wants me to take up the cudgels and fight his battles" (*Letters* 3:446). Simms here grumbles to Hammond about Butler's presumptions, but as he would later admit, his exactness as an historian and his indignation as a Carolinian would not let Sumner's allegations go unanswered, even at the risk of alienating Northern audiences and thereby risking much-needed speaker fees. By September 20, Simms had completed the lecture that was his response to Sabine and Sumner, writing Marcus Claudius Marcellus Hammond that "I am drudging upon my Northern course . . . I have just finished one to be delivered in Boston, on 'South Carolina in the Revolution.'—If they will listen to me!" (*Letters* 3:449).

The orator uncannily anticipated the unreceptiveness of many of his Northern listeners following his delivery of "South Carolina in the Revolution" in Buffalo on November 11, in Rochester on November 13, and in New York City on November 18. The speech seems to begin inoffensively enough, with Simms condemning the politicization of history. He denounces any "outrage upon sacred histories," which in addition to slandering the reputation of the Revolutionary generation, also invalidates their legacy of virtue to which present-day Carolinians "refer their sons, when they would train them to honorable aims and a generous ambition" and by "which the future generations are to be taught becoming lessons & examples" (208).

Simms then corrects what he believed were the historical inaccuracies of Sabine and Sumner in lengthy detail. He claims they lacked the necessary context to understand the circumstances they cited to support their assertions about South Carolina's underwhelming support for independence, alleged to be the consequence of a slaveholding society's imbecility. In doing so, though, Simms was also challenging a more widely held Northern attitude about the South that transcended Revolutionary history. In denying the link between enslavement and indolence, Simms was attempting to combat the prevailing notion about the former's effect on the character of Southern whites, similar to his attempts in his 1840 "Barnwell Agricultural Society Oration." Eric Foner observes, for instance, that in Northern minds, "[i]nstead of progress, the South represented decadence, instead of enterprise, laziness" (51). Many antislavery advocates compared agricultural statistics or cited anecdotes from travelers' accounts of the South as evidence to support their case for the economic and social disadvantages caused by enslavement. Sabine and Sumner and their Southern counterpart, Simms, were instead looking to the past of the South to both make and to refute that charge.

"South Carolina in the Revolution" attempts to rebut these Northern allegations by offering alternative factors that limited the number of soldiers that South Carolina contributed to the Revolutionary cause, such as its heterogenous colonial-era immigrant population that possessed a spectrum of allegiances. Simms also includes examples of South Carolina's early enthusiasm for independence to counter the claims that enslavement weakened Carolinians' commitment to it, such as the state's call to create an independent Provincial Congress in 1774 and its drafting of a constitution in March 1776, prior to the Declaration of Independence. "[N]o imbecility here—no lack of will, resolution" was demonstrated by South Carolinians, claims Simms (214). He also references the state's defense of Charleston in June 1776 and the successful repelling of Cherokee and Loyalist attacks the same summer as confirmation of slaveholding Carolinians' military strength, sarcastically observing that "[t]hese were prodigious exertions for so feeble a State as South Carolina" (214). And though enslavement is never explicitly mentioned in the speech, Simms's detailed explanation of Carolinians' alleged willingness to surrender Charleston in 1779 as a misunderstood ruse and his lengthy tribute to the state's guerilla fighters are further attempts to persuade Northern listeners of the shrewdness and tenacity of South Carolina's patriots, the practice of enslavement notwithstanding.

Simms transitions to the conclusion of "South Carolina in the Revolution" by advising his Northern listeners that present-day Carolinians remain as vigilant of their rights and reputations as their Revolutionary forebearers. He returns to the sectional nature of the historical dispute, arguing that South Carolina is owed respect, both to its past and at the present moment as an equal peer in the Union. Simms argues that criticism by Sumner and others is a pointless attempt at intimidation: "Massachusetts gains nothing by showing that South Carolina is faithless as a friend, & worthless as a foe! Let her establish the fact in either case, & what follows? Is the argument meant to persuade the imbecile that she should yield without struggle?" (228). Simms bellicosely suggests that if, following all his historical evidence of slaveholders' confidence and valor, there still remains doubt as to the mettle of South Carolinians, there are less equivocal means to settle intersectional disputes than via historical interpretations: "Better, braver, nobler, the short process, of the mailed hand, & the biting weapon. Better for both parties—for the honor of the one, and the due conviction of the other" (228).

Simms ends "South Carolina in the Revolution" with disingenuous compunction for his pugnacity, pleading, "Forgive me, my friends, if I have spoken warmly; but you would not, surely, have me speak coldly in the assertion of a Mother's honour!" (229).[1] Unfortunately for the proud son of South Carolina, Northerners were disinclined to forgive or even hear his heated defense of her past and present character. The numbers of attendees at Simms's lectures progressively dwindled from 1,200 in Buffalo to 150 in New York City a week later as initial reviews of "South Carolina in the Revolution" circulated (*Letters* 3:456, 467).

The criticism ranged from reproaches of Simms's rhetorical improprieties to sectional protests to ad hominem attacks. The first category admonished Simms for violating the norms of popular lectures by delivering an oration with partisan overtones. The *Buffalo Commercial Advertiser* of November 12 noted "it was a literary production that they [The Young Men's Association] and their patrons expected—The lecture-room is the place to forget political and religious aspirations, and to cultivate our knowledge of science and appreciation of the amenities of polite letters" ("Home Matters" 3). Similarly, on November 12 the Buffalo *Evening Post* expressed "regret that [Simms] should have allowed himself to have so widely departed from his legitimate sphere as a Lecturer" in his discussion of regional antagonisms (qtd. in *Letters* 3:457n122). The second motif of criticism, an aversion to Simms's boasts about South Carolina, was likely inspired by the sectional distrust following the events of "Bleeding Kansas" and a presidential election decided earlier that month along regional lines. The November 13 Buffalo *Morning Express* observed that "[w]ith an impudence unsurpassed, [Simms] comes into our midst and makes an harangue abusive of a Northern State and running over with fulsome and false praise of the least deserving state of the Union" (qtd. in *Letters* 3:457n122). Likewise, on November 14 the Rochester *Daily Democrat* mocked Simms's and South Carolina's prickly honor, commenting the latter "is constantly fretting and fuming about the insolence of her neighbors, and threatening every morning before breakfast, to set up an independent kingdom" ("Quattlebum in Rochester" 2). The third vein of criticism was more personal in nature. The same Rochester review, for example, claimed that Simms had "a loud, imperious, crackling voice, and manners suited to an overseer of a plantation, where slaves have to be daily cursed and flogged" ("Quattlebum in Rochester" 2). The New York City *Tribune* was perhaps the unkindest, remarking on the ambivalence of South Carolina to its most devoted son of letters. On November 19, the Horace Greeley–edited Republican paper observed that "Mr. Simms, after spending a laborious life in efforts to write South Carolina into notice and admiration, is turned over, in his declining age, to the cold charity and empty seats of Northern lecture rooms" ("Review" 4).

Stung by the low turnout and the criticism, Simms cancelled his second and third speaking engagements in New York City (which were to have been the unoffensive series on southern Appalachia) on November 21, explaining to the organizers that "such is the antipathy felt to my topics—such the rancorous feeling which they have provoked,—that they (the committee [of arrangements]) could not only sell no tickets, but could not succeed in *giving* them away" (*Letters* 3:458–59). Nor did he wish to encumber the organizers of his other lectures with financial losses, as he explained in letters written to all of them on the 21st. However, these same letters are also characterized by terse assertions about the preservation of his honor. He explained to the Young Men's Association of Troy, New York, for example, that he was obliged to cancel his engagement with them "in consequence the singular odium which attends my progress as a South Carolinian, and the gross abuse which has already assailed myself, personally" (*Letters* 3:460).

To Southern friends that winter, Simms attributed Northern hostility to "the rancorous temper of Black republicanism; so completely does New England rule N.Y." and the "probable effect of the election" in which Democratic candidate James Buchanan defeated Republican John Fremont (*Letters* 3:466, 467). While plausible, Simms's claim that he was a victim of disaffected Northern Republicans is more likely reassurance about the relevance of his intellectual labor to the cause of his state. Historian Paul Quigley recognizes similar patterns of identification by Southern nationalists with a victimized South that they aspired to speak and write into independence. "[T]he imperatives of honor and masculinity moved back and forth between the realms of personal and southern identity," Quigley explains, especially among men like Simms, Edmund Ruffin, and William Lowndes Yancey, putative outsiders in their honor- and status-conscious culture (61). Cognizant of the fragility of their social positions, which ideological service to the South could solidify, they were inclined to interpret Northern criticism of the region that was the focus of their intellectual and rhetorical work as personal attacks. In a culture wherein masculinity demanded that any infringement on reputation be responded to publicly, Northern criticism thus tended to trigger virulent reactions. The political became personal, and their sensitivity and responses could be disproportionate, as the indignation in Simms's correspondence reflects.

Simms's accusation that support for Republicans was responsible for the hostility and indifference of his listeners also effaces a more probable explanation underlying the Northern reaction to "South Carolina in the Revolution." Simms misappraised the volatile rhetorical situation in the North not by underrating the influence of the emergent Republican Party, but by failing to account for the influence of earlier Southern antagonisms. First, Simms apparently underestimated how Brooks's caning of Sumner resonated with his Northern audience. Second, Simms seems to have overlooked the mutual regional distrust that he himself contributed to through his participation in a decade's worth of rhetorical attacks on Northern society.

While Buchanan's election may have disappointed New Yorkers like Greeley, not all residents of the Empire State were as committed to radical Republicanism as Simms would like to have imagined. Instead, Simms likely failed to give enough consideration to the galvanizing effect of the Sumner-Brooks Affair and its implications regarding free expression. To Northerners, Brooks's caning of Sumner epitomized Southern intolerance of dissenting ideas. Along with the raid on Lawrence, Kansas, by proslavery forces, Brooks's assault "stirred fierce and pervasive indignation by dramatizing the threat that proslavery Southerners posed to the lives and liberties of free Northerners," observes historian Michael E. Woods (150). Rather than the issue of emancipation, which remained divisive even among Republicans, the resentment of intimidation by "The Slave Power" united moderate and radical Northerners. Not just wielders of canes, but also bellicose orators whose speeches invoked images of "the mailed hand, & the biting weapon" were interpreted as threatening Northerners' ability to exercise safely their Constitutional rights.

New York newspapers, for instance, were quick to associate "South Carolina in the Revolution" with patterns of Southern bullying. For example, on November 12, the Buffalo *Evening Post* characterized Simms's speech as an "ill-digested, bitter and to at least nine-tenths of the audience, [an] offensive defence [sic] of South Carolina politicians of the Brooks school" (qtd. in *Letters* 3:457n122). Greeley's *Tribune* not only pointed out the parallels between the two South Carolinians on November 19, but also the egregiousness of Simms's miscalculation so soon after Sumner's assault. The article observed "it was not only a great lack of good taste, but a great lack of ordinary rhetorical prudence, to commence his discourse by a pointed attack upon Senator Sumner as a wicked and malicious maligner. Such an attack sounds too much like a covert apology for the brutality of Bully Brooks" ("Review" 4).

Even Simms's confidant James Henry Hammond perceived a relationship between canes and words, writing Simms on November 27 to say, "As I see it, you have gone North at a somewhat critical time for *you* & martyred yourself for So Ca . . . & for Brooks . . . who in his supreme vanity will think your sacrifice only a slight oblation. What Demon possessed you, mon ami, to do this?" (qtd. in *Letters* 3:465n136). Simms's response on December 8 is notable not only for its grudging, partial admission of the inappropriateness of "South Carolina in the Revolution" for the rhetorical situation, but also for acknowledging his apparent naivete regarding the climate that proved so hostile to it. He wrote, "I grant you that, if, at the outset, I had dreamed that I should have been denounced because of my local subjects, I would have taken others . . . who could have fancied that the rancour had become so universal & so universally blinding" (*Letters* 3:468).

Simms's rhetorical question at the end not only suggests his underestimation of the implications of the Sumner-Brooks Affair but also his apparent obliviousness to his own rhetorical contributions to the climate of mutual distrust that preceded it. Since around the time of "Sources of American Independence" (1844), Simms was among Southern writers and thinkers elaborating on the distinctions between Southern and Northern society. In the 1850s, he began to emphasize the degeneracy of the latter. For example, Simms observed in the *Southern Quarterly Review* in September 1850 that "[t]here is, in the Northern States, a growing and monstrous disregard of all the usually recognized securities of society. Mobs, riots, murders, mark the daily events in their progress. Wild philosophies, vague and vicious, penetrate the better informed circles. . . . Property is held by a doubtful tenure . . . Marriage is denounced, as hostile to the proper exercise of the legitimate passions [. . .]" ("The Southern Convention" 198). That Simms could not anticipate the animus that these and other similar diatribes by Southern nationalists would engender in the North taxes credulity were it not for his apparent conviction in what he had wrote. In other words, Simms may have been so persuaded of the truth of his own simulacra of Northern society that the incongruity of Northern listeners asserting their own regional sense of honor and propriety may have left him in disbelief.

Simms tried to make sense of his Northern experience in a three-lecture series he gave in Charleston on May 25 and 27 and June 1, 1857, that he titled Our Social Moral. The series title references the belief that regional populations possessed distinct cultural characters (the "social") as a consequence of their underlying values (their "moral").[2] Similar to most of his Southern peers, Simms believed the institution of slavery was the paramount source of the latter in the South, followed by other touchstones such as agriculture, faith, the home and family, and art. The "peculiar institution" transcended its material value as a system of labor, creating social relationships imagined to be "essentially moral rather than economic," explains Drew Gilpin Faust. "In the idealized system of human bondage [Southerners] portrayed, their particular values seemed fully realized. Duty and responsibility, not despised greed, tied master and slave together" (*Sacred Circle* 121). This supposed paternalism encouraged virtues of stewardship, discipline, and dignity that represented moral progress, which Simms and other writers differentiated from material progress as the true benchmark of improvement. The institution of slavery also allegedly encouraged social stability in an age of rapid economic change, an admittedly conservative security wherein rights, liberty preeminent, were accorded to one's ability to exercise them appropriately.

Southern intellectuals like Simms believed that free labor, absent the framework of paternalistic relationships and their associated values, "meant submission to laws of economic development that condemned the laboring classes to unprecedented exploitation, immiseration, and periodic starvation," explains Eugene Genovese. More problematic for the character of Northern society were the allegedly inevitable destabilizing consequences of this desperation: "Faced with unbearable privation, they [the Northern working class] would rise, were already rising, in insurrection. Worse, the intellectual freedom essential to all progress, including economic progress, was inexorably extruding every possible kind of utopian and demagogic scheme," similar to the ones Simms noted in his 1850 review (17). Despite its ostensible material progress stemming from economic growth and the expansion of freedom to working-class males, Northern society was characterized by the economic inequality, social instability, and the subversive ideologies that its system of free labor unleashed. This delineation of the character of the North, especially as an oppositional social identity to the South, was a popular motif of Southern intellectuals since at least the beginning of the decade, exemplified by Simms's denunciation of Northern mobs, murderers, and marriages (Quigley 12).

The South was ostensibly less susceptible to such anarchy thanks to the hierarchies and virtues generated by the practice of enslavement, but as Simms's earlier orations demonstrate, he was nonetheless wary that the priorities and values associated with materialism were taking root in a South that was becoming heedless of its moral character. By the 1850s, this anxiety was even a thematic motif in his regional fiction. David Moltke-Hansen observes that Simms's Revolutionary Romances of the decade were critical of how "[a]varice and the new, socially destructive methods of wealth's generation were undermining political resolve and corrupting arts'—and thoughts'—producers, productions, and consumers" ("The Revolutionary Romances" 304). Acquisitiveness, selfishness, and superficiality threatened the superstructure of alleged virtues emanating from the institution of slavery, which made the foundation itself vulnerable to Northern schemes, especially abolition. Like Simms's novels of the era, the 1857 Our Social Moral lectures are critical of these influences and Southerners' failure to thwart them. In particular, Simms reproaches Carolinians' indifference to the intellectual and cultural labor—such as his own—that he argues nurtures the virtues that constitute moral progress and that are proof of its resiliency. On the surface, his criticism of Carolinians' apathy echoes some of the symptoms Sumner alleged were indicative of the state's imbecility. However, rather than enslavement enervating the South, the Our Social Moral lectures posit that Carolinians' incipient weakness is ultimately a consequence of the influence of a materialistic mindset more typical of Northern culture.

The character of the South that Simms outlines for his fellow Carolinians in the three "Social Moral" speeches in May and June 1857 is vulnerable at that historical moment to threats from within and without. Internally, Southern materialism and the ensuing apathy toward local intellectual and artistic endeavors diminish the vitality of its society. Externally, Northern awareness of this susceptibility will continue to embolden their radical "schemes," which include assaults on Southern institutions. Simms alleges that the antagonism that precipitated and characterized the Northern response to his "South Carolina in the Revolution" was a warning sign of this. Consequently, Carolinians must resist their growing materialistic proclivities, become less complacent about the security of their social institutions, and support the artistic and scholarly class whose endeavors reinforce their regional character and its latent moral progress. With more stridency than 1844's "The Sources of American Independence," Simms claims that intellectual leaders, not political ones, can preserve South Carolina and the South.

"The Social Moral, Lecture 1" (hereafter referred to as "Lecture 1" to distinguish it from the second oration, titled "The Social Moral, Lecture 2") begins this admonition by arguing that Sabine's and Sumner's allegations of South Carolina's historical imbecility were more than mere rhetoric. Simms claims their interpretations of history are harbingers of future encroachments on the honor and the slaveholding prerogatives of Carolinians, positing that "all assaults upon the rights and possessions, the inheritance, on the institutions of a people, are always coupled with, or prefaced by, a defamation of their character" (231). Simms characterizes Sumner as "malignant" but also insists that the Northern politician felt confident enough to disparage Carolinians because of their alleged indifference to their historical reputation and because of Southerners' customary willingness to compromise their principles to preserve the Union (235). Simms scolds his listeners, explaining that Sumner's "courage comes from our submissions; his insolence from our forbearances; his judgment, upon our character, upon our own indifference to honorable fame!" (233).

Simms admits that this alleged apathy and deference does border on "imbecility." However, rather than enslavement accounting for it, as Sabine and Sumner alleged, Simms attributes it to Carolinians neglecting their own intellectual and artistic class. Any real or perceived weakness is "first due to our intellectual inactivity;—to the fact that we have lost curiosity, zeal, faith, enthusiasm, and that eager impulse to performance. . . . Energy and action are not original motors. They spring from deeper sources in the soul and mind . . ." (243). The stakes were existential rather than aesthetic. Indifference to ideas and art made a prosperous but complacent society vulnerable to one more ambitious: "When, therefore, you behold a people grown sluggards in the race, you may feel very sure that they are sluggish in intellect—that their virtues are feeble as their will—dead or dying out;—and that they must succumb before any stirring competitor in the great race for power!" (243). These grim counsels reflect Simms's belief that art was "the chief vehicle of civilization," says David Moltke-Hansen ("When History" 28). If the evolution of and especially the permanence of society was contingent on moral, not material, progress, then art and the first principles and the virtues it expressed were a social necessity. They demanded an audience. "Where the Imagination & Fancy remain without cultivation, the morals, as well as social progress of the people must be low & slow," Simms explained in a letter to a fellow South Carolinian starting a lyceum (*Letters* 4:422). For example, James Everett Kibler Jr. explains that Simms believed that "[t]he poet stood centrally in society as its best friend and guide . . . pointed to the central truths . . . [and] aided in the growing of the soul" ("Introduction" xii). Consciousness of and appreciation for these values demanded that people be vigilant that society progress in ways consistent with their core beliefs and priorities to preserve them. That direction could itself be guided with the influence of literature, which, prior to the specialization of disciplines, encompassed history (Busick 2). "[H]istory, when written as he [Simms] felt it should be, was a vast source of moral instruction and thus an engine of progress" by use of hindsight to provide guidance for the present day (Busick 9).

To illustrate the relationship between the public intellectual and the vigor of a community, Simms focuses on the social values of historians' labors. "Lecture I" explains that historians provide models of personal virtue for the present generation, claiming their interpretations of past events lead to "a just sense of what is really great and noble in the deeds of our ancestry;—and this right appreciation of their real virtues . . ." (239). The connections historians make to the past also foster the traditions and sensibilities that are cornerstones for group identity, pride in which deters antagonists who threaten its autonomy. However, the South, Simms warns, has been "perfectly satisfied that our Enemies should write our histories, and provide the teachers for our young;—that their infant minds should be trained and tutored by a people who were eagerly busied in the grateful labor of destroying our institutions, and casting a slur of perpetual infamy upon our name" (231).

Historians thus encourage the self-awareness, pride, and vigilance requisite to a community's solidarity and security. Any responsibility for the absence of historians, though, rests with Southerners themselves, according to Simms. "It is not the Histories that we lack, but the readers of them," he observes, also complaining that, generally speaking, "[a]s a people we read too little . . ." (244). The reasons for this neglect of the work of South Carolina's intellectual and artistic class are varied, though all have their origins in either the vanity or the acquisitiveness associated with materialism. Simms argues this in both "Lecture I" and

"Lecture 2." In the former, for instance, Simms' analyzes Carolinians' pejorative attitudes toward scholars. He decries the stigma that the fashionable, practical, and worldly associate with intellectual labor, which discourages its pursuit. "Here & there, only, do we see some single laborer, buried in his books, and pursuing his secret studies at great self sacrifice, in cell or studio, and we scorn him for his self sacrificing homage to wisdom . . ." Simms complains that "[t]he community <u>taboos</u> him [. . .] and his labors. He must be a blockhead to yield up present distinction, worldly gain, and sensual delights, in laborious searches into the abstract & the obscure" (244). Simms also denounces Carolinians' indifference to their own thinkers and artists, preferring instead what they imagine to be the superior ideas and work of outsiders, even when they may be antithetical to the character of Southern culture. "This miserable Provincialism is the source of some of our worst mishaps, as of some of our grossest absurdities," Simms explains. "It makes us reject and despise the native for the foreign; though the one strives in our battles, & the other openly toils for our destruction" (246).

"The Social Moral, Lecture 2" (hereafter referred to as "Lecture 2") of which only manuscript fragments remain, analyzes other contributing factors to South Carolina's sterile artistic and intellectual environment. One is the familiar complaint about the absence of forums for ideas in rural areas, whereas educated and creative minds can encourage each other in urban, cosmopolitan environments. "To be kept bright, minds must be brought into constant collision kept rubbing together. . . . This is the true secret of the activity of intellect among citizens. You rarely or never hear of great mental achievement emanating from the country." However, cities contain their own hazards. Despite Charleston's intellectual circles, the era's prosperity has encouraged acquisitiveness and frivolity among residents rather than an appetite for art and ideas. Simms observes with chagrin that "wealth & temptation . . . beguile from duty time & talent in a sort of life which was fatal to all proper living." Simms warns his audience that forgoing the support of artists and scholars to instead "yield up to society any large portion of our time is . . . to sap society itself of all stability & security."

Rather than "darting & driving through King Street, or the Battery . . ." in the pursuit of fashion and attention, Charlestonians must esteem art and ideas ("Lecture 2"). This will encourage the artists and intellectuals whose ideas and expression in turn inspire a society, strengthen its moral character, and ensure its posterity. "Lecture 1" ends with an elaborate image of ancient Athens, Simms's vision of this ideal. Simms visualizes a fervid interest on behalf of all Athenians in the work of the sculptor Phidias as he prepares and unveils "Zeus at Olympia." "It is a God that speaks to their senses. It is a God that suddenly fills all their souls," Simms imagines (252). Beyond offering an anecdote about how art redeems the sensual and spiritual capacities of Athenians, elevating their taste and consciousness, Simms is also trying to demonstrate that Phidias's achievement is representative of Athens's underlying social character, and, in turn, perpetuates it. The statue itself reflects the values of religious duty and aesthetic elegance, and its execution and its reception are an expression of Athens's core virtues, including refinement, confidence, and self-sufficiency. These are the same qualities that enable Athens to resist the assaults of antagonists and even time itself. "The great secret of Athens," explains Simms of its civilization's posterity, "lay in her mental independence! She made her own books—her own arts; had her own histories, and encouraged her own genius, in every department, esteeming the great poet, dramatist & painter, as fully as she did the great Politician, engineer or Banker. She did not, accordingly, have to wait upon opinion from abroad. She <u>made</u> opinion; not only for home, but for all the world!" (249).

The final speech in the Social Moral series, "The Antagonisms of the Social Moral, North and South" is a more dire admonition about the present state and inevitable future of Carolinians, and, as suggested by the oration's title, the South as a whole, if they become subject to "opinion from abroad." Simms's disastrous experience in the North the previous year provides the context for this warning. He explains that his tour is emblematic of the current state of crisis in sectional relationships, "ris[ing] into an importance which otherwise it would not possess" (253). He explains to his fellow Charlestonians that he went north to try and educate listeners there about not only the inaccuracies of Sumner, but also about the dangers of taking Southerners' indifference to their history as a license for further aggressions. Simms claims, "I held it vastly important to our future relations, that the truth should be made known, even to unwilling ears, if only to prevent those mistakes of policy, which, under false notions of our neighbors, so frequently lead to the most disastrous consequences" (256). Significant among these "false notions" is the assumption that enslavers are accountable to Northern courts of law and public opinion: "We are to understand, and to make them understand, that, socially & politically, we are their equals; and any effort which they may make us to appeal to <u>their</u> courts of judgment, are aggressions, usurpative & offensive, and a direct invasion of our independence" (258).

The South that is represented in "Antagonisms" is an aggrieved minority partner in the Union, its citizens subject to unjust arrogations by their Northern peers, who were motivated by the South's desultory social character. The speech is lengthened by a catalog of these injuries, epitomized by Simms's own experiences. He summarizes and responds to the Northern papers' criticisms of his defense of South Carolina's history, and he interprets a second-hand encounter with the Underground Railroad in Rochester as proof of the wanton indifference to Southern rights by a federal government controlled by Northern interests: "Here is an Institution [the Underground Railroad], openly avowed and existing, for carrying on a regular warfare against the sister states of the Confederacy. . . . Only think of the monstrous anomaly of an organization [the national government], asserting union and common necessities, which beholds, without rebuke or remedy, the perpetual warfare of one section upon the rights of another" (267).

Stepping back from the tour itself, Simms concludes that all spheres of Northern society—religious, political, educational, cultural—have become allied in a desire to end enslavement, which suggests there will be no internal brakes to abolitionism's momentum: "No circles escape the contagion—no place remains free of the usurpation—no class has the courage, or will, to resist the phrenzy, which, taking the guise of a Crusade, & armed with the coercive will of a vast majority, is inevitable in a community" (280–81). This marks a change in tone from the earlier sectional rhetoric of orations like "The Sources of American Independence" and the previous two speeches in the Social Moral series. Simms had previously suggested that either vigilance or the support of the region's intellectual class might be sufficient enough to safeguard or reinvigorate the character of the South and thus deter hostile influences. However, in "Antagonisms" he explicitly advocates preparedness for separation or for conflict for the sake of self-preservation. Simms concludes by counseling his listeners to take seriously the intentions of Northern radicals: "my advice is that you take them to mean the very things that they avow. They tell you, honestly enough, that they mean to abolish slavery in the South, that it is a war to the knife . . . until they succeed in their objects. And I believe them. Do you the same, by way of decent precaution . . ." (281).

Simms's characterization of the South's position and its fate was not unique in 1857, though his advocacy for the patronage of the region's artistic and intellectual class to try and better its standing was representative of the perspective of a much smaller group of Southerners. Simms's claims that Northern aspirations to end enslavement were a betrayal of republican principles and amity, for instance, reflected many radical Southerners' opinions. Robert T. Oliver describes it as a pattern of "reiterating that the States below the Mason-Dixon line were doomed to particular political inequality and inequity" (180). Other Southern historians also perceived this inevitability, including fellow Carolinian William Henry Trescott, who argued at the beginning of the decade that patterns in history demonstrated that "time has changed a compromise of interests into a conflict of sections, and the submission of one, or the separation of both is the only alternative" (11). Victimhood was also a staple sentiment in the orations of politicians such as Alexander Hamilton Stephens, Robert Augustus Toombs, Judah Benjamin, and William Lowndes Yancey (Oliver 182).

Vulnerability also provides the criteria for the affinity necessary for regional cohesion and independence. As Paul Quigley observes, Simms's and other radicals' emphasis on Northern aggressiveness toward enslavement "creat[ed] a potent sense of shared victimhood that provided a visceral stimulus for Southern nationalism" (53). By cataloging Northern antagonisms, from insults to the South's Revolutionary past to attempts to limit and abolish enslavement, Simms created a sense of susceptibility wherein a unified South and ultimately its independence were the only guarantees for maintaining Southerners' rights. Furthermore, by demonstrating that national comity was already ruptured by Northern disrespect and aggression, Simms offered the emotional prerequisites to independence that more moderate Southerners may have been reluctant to take. As Michael Woods notes, rather than claim that abolitionism "would destroy the emotional bonds of the Union," Simms and Southern radicals instead "maintained that those bonds had already been dissolved" by Northern aggressions (29). Secession was thus merely a legal recognition of an existing, irreconcilable break.

In assuming responsibility for marshaling public support for independence, the *Social Moral* lectures seeks to demonstrate how public intellectuals, rather than politicians, are the more authentic, reliable leaders of the South. "Antagonisms," in particular, is representative of Southern intellectuals' frustration with politicians' inability to remedy the South's ostensible victimhood at the hands of Northerners in the union. In particular, Simms's denouncement of "[t]he office seeker, and office holder, to whom fleshpots are precious things . . ." echoed criticism that Southern politicians were too beholden to the Democratic Party and their own political fortunes rather than the rights of the South, and thus could no longer be trusted to have the region's best interests in mind (281). Simms advises disregarding the counsel of Democratic politicians who choose to dismiss Republican policies as mere rhetoric rather than a genuine threat. Simms alleges that "[t]he Politician, anxious to save his party, swears there's nothing in it" (281). Rather than take that chance, the Social Moral series advocates instead for the intellectual class's warranted leadership. Faust summarizes how the members of the region's "Sacred Circle" believed intellectuals had a pair of responsibilities in public life: "to free the Southern mind from the domination of corrupt demagogues, both northern and southern, and to replace their leadership with that of the spiritually elect. This moral elite would release southerners from a reign of political corruption by subjecting them to the principles of truth in which alone man might find true freedom" (*Sacred Circle* 107). Simms's rhetoric of injustice may be a strategy to illustrate how public intellectuals inspire a citizenry to action to preserve their autonomy. By cultivating a collective sense of inequality and dishonor, Simms assumes the role he outlines in the Social Moral series, stimulating Southerners to a more robust vigilance of their rights and encouraging defiance of Northern attempts on them.

However, Simms's and the Sacred Circle's faith in their own leadership abilities encountered resistance amid the same complacency that Simms identified as the cause for the South's incipient vulnerability. Charleston's reaction to the Social Moral series is a conveniently representative example. In contrast to the dire warnings and urgent calls to action of the Social Moral series, the responses by Charleston newspapers were affably noncommittal. *The Charleston Mercury* of May 26 observed that in "Lecture 1" of the series Simms "dwelt, with great force, upon a leading idea, that the South had always left herself to be delineated, socially, politically, and morally, by her enemies." Yet though the *Mercury* ostensibly understood the oration's theme, it conspicuously avoided commenting on Simms's indictment of Carolinians' indifference to intellectuals and artists. "We attempt no analysis of his very interesting lecture, which we hope will be soon published," the writer added ("Mr. Simms's Lectures" 2). Likewise, *The Charleston Daily Courier* of May 26 flattered "Lecture 1" in generic terms, observing that the "discourse itself in matter and moral, was one richly stored lesson and utterance of wisdom and well-ripened sagacity." But it, too, averred responding, explaining that it "would only be unjust to the lecturer, and would fail in the thought quickening impulses and suggestive freshness which accompanied the lecturer. . ." Those whose thoughts may have been quickened the night before were few, for "the audience in numbers was not as we would have wished," observed the *Courier* ("Simms' Lectures" 1). Attendance on June 1 for "Antagonisms" was better, the "largest of his audiences," the *Courier* of June 3 reported, and they enjoyed the "*veritable*" words of Simms, "who enchained the attention" of his listeners ("Mr. Simms' Lecture on Monday Night" 2).

Simms's own assessment of the *Social Moral* series and his thoughts on Charlestonians' reception of them do not exist. He did not print the former, and extant correspondence contains no references to the critical reaction. Doubtless, following the vitriol of the Northern newspapers the previous year, he was at least cheered by the positive, albeit restrained, response in his hometown. But despite the praise, the apparent reluctance or lack of desire to engage seriously with his message, particularly any acknowledgement of the relevance of a native intellectual and artistic class to the autonomy of the region, may have reinforced his belief that his warnings were not being taken seriously. Of course, three years later, South Carolina did in fact assert its prerogatives and secede from the Union following the victory of a Republican president. Yet the Palmetto State never embraced its intellectual and artistic classes in ways Simms thought were appropriate, which epitomized his life-long conflicted relationship to the culture with which he most identified. Simms never stopped trying, though, probably because he took solace in seeming relevant to the political situation, even if his audiences ignored his appeal for the support of intellectuals. As Faust explains, Simms and other Southern intellectuals "defined themselves both as neglected prophets, speaking truth to an unheeding world, and as stewards, destined to provide practical guidance for the human race" (*Sacred Circle* x).

In contrast, Northern listeners proved to be especially and tenaciously attentive. The 1856 and 1857 speeches proved to be an inflection point in Simms's career and legacy as a national man of letters. Simms's comments in "Antagonisms" that the negative reviews of Northern newspapers proved "fatal to my mission" in

1856 were only partially true; the damage to his reputation lasted longer than he thought (272). Simms would resume speaking in familiar towns and small cities in the South prior to the Civil War, but he would never again attempt a sustained speaking tour, even after 1865. Moreover, as Miriam Shillingsburg has observed, memories of the 1856 insults may have contributed to the diminishment of his postwar stature among major publishers and critics ("Failed," 199). Simms experienced difficulties having his new work reviewed, fueling a gradual eclipse in his national reputation that lasted until the late twentieth century. Thus in an irony unforeseen by Simms, it may not have been that his words were heeded too little by his countrymen, but that his words were remembered too vividly.

NOTES

1. For the role of honor in Simms's address and the tour in general, see Todd Hagstette, "Private vs. Public Honor in Wartime South Carolina: William Gilmore Simms in Lecture, Letter, and History," especially pp. 51–58.

2. Citing Simms's 1843 review of the works of Washington Allston, Jim Kibler has noted that in terms of art, Simms defined the "moral" of a text to be the ability to "awaken thoughts, interests and inquiries in the mind, which hurry the spectator far beyond the scene" (qtd. in Kibler, *The Poetry of William Gilmore Simms* 10). However, given the orations' emphases on the relationship between regional character and moral progress, the conventional definition of moral, one connoting virtue, seems more plausible here.

"South Carolina in the Revolution" (1856)

For eighty years, my friends, the people of South Carolina have reposed securely in the faith that the fame of their ancestors was beyond reproach;—that they had no reason to dread the comparison of their deeds with those of any other people in this confederacy;—that their contributions to the national capital, of mind, moral and manhood, were of a sort to establish for them a perfect claim to the respect of all good men;—that they had given some, and not a few, of the greatest men in the country, to its several struggles for liberty & honorable renown;—that nothing, in brief, could take away, cloud or diminish, the glories of their Past, whatever might be thought of their performances in the Present. The Past, they were confident, was secure;—safe equally against the dull hoof of the ass, and the slimy trail of the reptile!

But the history, it would seem, must undergo revision. The old chronicles are to be ignored—the grateful traditions of three quarters of a century, are pronounced to be mere delusions; and there have been those to proclaim that the ancestors of whom we were so loud in boast, were in fact, false to their duties & their country;—recreant to their trusts—heedless of their honour,—faithless to their brethren,—traitors in the cabinet and cowards in the field!

These are substantially the allegations, made by a Senator in the Senate House; in sight and hearing of the assembled States;—while the Representatives from South Carolina, upon the same floor, assembled for grave deliberation upon the affairs of the whole country, are regaled with the cruel history, as it is poured forth with a malignant satisfaction, seemingly with no other purpose than to goad and mortify the natural pride and sensibility of a hated party! What other motive? South Carolina—her conduct in the Past, at least,—was in no respect the subject of present deliberation. Whether true or not, in substance, the assault was gratuitously wanton,—hostile to all the ends of council, and grossly subversive of all the parliamentary & social proprieties.

Was it true? If so, how happens it that South Carolina is identified with so many glorious passages in our history;—with so many of the brightest deeds;—with so many fields of battle;—with so many names of deathless men, which in the National records, are the recognized representatives of the noblest heroism—in fact, the received models of heroism whenever the song or story of the Revolution is the subject? How is it that she has acquired a spurious military and patriotic reputation, so distinguished in spite of the Chronicle? How is it that it has been left to the present day to make discoveries of her shortcomings in the past, of which the Past, itself, knew nothing? Is it, indeed, true, that Marion, and Sumter, and Moultrie and Pickens—the very greatest among the revolutionary partizans—were simulacra, myths—mere men of straw & vapor;—or did they stand alone, fighting & achieving victories single handed, and without any glorious array of followers? Is it true that Gadsden & Rutledge, Laurens and the Pinckneys,—to whom we owe some of the very first revolutionary mouvements, were common men;—worthless—mere makeweights in a struggle, to which they could accord neither soul nor intellect? Verily, if this be so, there was no Revolution;—the whole History is an invention.

But suppose these charges be untrue? Suppose the same malignity which made the assault upon South Carolina so wholly gratuitous, to have darkened the moral vision of the assailant;—obscured his perceptions;—made obtuse his faculty for discrimination between fact and falsehood;—making him ready to bear false witness in the case, and only too happy to do so? What then should be the atonement to that people from whose history he would tear away so many of their most brilliant records?—Do not mistake me, my friends: Do not suppose that I am about to engage in any review of the miserable politics of today. I know no subject so little calculated to provoke my consideration, as the small traffic of politics, in the hands of hireling partisans. It is an outrage upon sacred histories which I resent. It is the memories of a grand national epic, which I would protect from the assailant—the fame of great Sages and Statesmen—great Patriots and Warriors—that chronicle of Pride, upon which a whole people brood with satisfaction, & to which they refer their sons, when they would train them to honorable aims and a generous ambition. The blow is aimed, alike, at the Dead and the Living—the past, present & future;—robbing the one of laurels made sacred; consecrated forever by their tears and blood;—the other of all those monuments by which the future generations are to be taught becoming lessons & examples. The crime of the Incendiary who should penetrate your sanctuaries, and burn your archives, is nothing to this, since the memories of men may still cherish all the essential histories. But to tear away from the hearts of men their loving faith in the virtues of their sires—this is to slay the very hopes of a people, along with all their honest pride and most prolific impulses. This is to deprive them of all the most noble stimulants which goad a people to great performance. What must be the malice of a spirit which shall strive at such an object? What the desperate necessities of that party Hate which shall justify a policy so profane and Barbarous!

It will be permitted to a son of Carolina to assert her character;—to reassert her history;—and endeavour to maintain her argument; and every just and magnanimous nature, will not only accord to him this privilege, but will rejoice, with a becoming satisfaction, if he shall do so successfully. None but the base of soul can possibly feel pleasure in raking up, from foul & obscure sources, those proofs of lapse or shame, which shall go to detract from what is honorable in the history of any people. And such may somewhere be found in the progress of every people. There will be a momentary weakness of resolve;—a momentary sinking of the soul; among all nations; the wisest, the bravest, the best; in a long and trying conflict. Here and there, in all histories—even in yours—there shall be a failure among individual men, high in station. What nation is free from blot, cast upon its chronicles, by the feeble or the erring citizen? But, because of an Arnold, shall we decry a people? Because of an occasional lapse from virtue, or honorable courage, shall we insist upon the obscuration, or obliteration of annals otherwise glorious? What fool will insist upon such logic? Who but a malignant will shut his eyes against the noble performances of a race, while dilating with a base complacency, upon the occasional stain upon its scutcheon? In the case of States, such as ours, is it not the duty of the Philosophic Statesmen to take them in their entirety—the general course which they pursued—the virtues which preponderated—the great, and the good, & the valiant, whom they produced, & if need be to refer to a weakness, a fault, an error or a vice, to do so with sorrow, & not with exultation;—to do so, simply because of the requisitions of the truth, and not with the foul and malicious aim to make the failure tell against the unquestionable virtue. South Carolina asks only to be tried by the standards which are applied to other States. She asks no favour, but she demands justice. She requires, that, while you expose her faults, you do not suppress her virtues. Be sure of this, that if there be stains upon her shield, they are of virgin whiteness in comparison with those, which a diligent delver in the sewers of history, may discover, on many others, which now most loudly vaunt their purity!

It is alleged that the public services of South Carolina, during the Revolution were singularly disproportioned to her strength and ability. Let us look to this. In 1776 the population of South Carolina was estimated at 90,000, whites; an over-estimate, in my opinion; 80,000 would be much nearer the mark. The negroes were probably 120,000. The settlements were scattered over a forest country, covering more than thirty thousand square miles. South Carolina furnished 35,000 soldiers to the war. Massachusetts had a population of 352,000; and her contributions to the war were 88,000 men. Now the population of Massachusetts was all comprised within an area of 10,000 square miles, including the settled portions of Maine. They could be easily brought together. The people of South Carolina, rating but 3 white persons to the square mile, could be assembled only with great delay & difficulty. The people of Massachusetts were homogeneous; all form a single stock. Those of South Carolina were mixed up of all European nations; and almost one half of them were born British subjects; a large proportion of whom had been less than ten years in the country. They were, accordingly, so many foreign enemies in her very bosom. The settlements in Carolina, in 1776, lay chiefly along the great water courses of the country: the colonists have planted along the seaboard, and have only begun to approach the mountains. They have possessed themselves of fertile spots along the Peedee, the Santee, the Edisto and Savannah; have dotted little tracts, here & there, in the rich vallies of the Broad & Saluda. Some of these settlements are purely Irish; others purely Scotch; others German; others French Huguenots; others Quakers from Pennsylvania. A wild waste of swamp & forest spreads between these several settlements, which scarcely communicate with each other, and possess no public roads connecting them. The French and Irish settlements readily subscribed to the Revolution. But with the Scotch, since '45, the instincts were all loyal. Even Flora Macdonald, romantic rebel as she was, in Scotland, became, with all her family, and all the Highlanders in Georgia and the Carolinas, a dutiful subject of George the Third! The Germans were mostly with the crown; and when Drayton and others urged the argument of the colonies, they turned out their pocket sovereigns, and affectionately contemplating the Guelphic image, they said,—"But dere is King Tsherge on de geldt." In other words are we not to render tribute unto Caesar? The Quakers were not disposed to fight at all, & hostile to war, were, of course, unfriendly to the Revolutionists. These are the facts, and, for these, I offer no apology. Nor need we now apologize for the Loyalists. The day has gone by when these people can be made properly the subjects of reproach. They had their arguments for Loyalty, and these were founded equally in reason and in natural sympathies. They were faithful to their old traditions;—faithful to the laws and the authorities;—faithful to every sentiment in which their childhood had been trained; and were, accordingly, incapable of seeing, with the eyes of the natives, the same degree of provocation or wrong which they felt, or the propriety of that revolution which they held to be the proper remedy. Removed as we are from that period of passion and excitement, we have no quarrel now with the Loyalists. But with these facts before you, and a thousand such, which time does not suffer me to state, is it not a wonder that South Carolina should take part in the revolution at all; particularly as she had no such causes of complaint as drove the Eastern colonies into rebellion. Hardly one of the operating oppressions which prompted New England to resistance, affected her interests. She was purely agricultural. She did not employ machinery; was no competitor with British manufacture; sent no ships to sea in rivalry with British commerce. She lost no vessels by forfeiture. The King's arrow, on her forest trees, in the boundlessness of her wild domain, abridged no man's plenty. Great Britain furnished her a sufficient market; readily took & consumed all her raw productions, and yielded her manufactures at prices of which we had no reason to complain. When the Pirate infested our shores, he was driven off by British men of war. When assailed, on coast or frontier, by French, or Spaniard, or red men, the fleets and armies of Britain came to our succour. Carolina, in brief, was one of the pet provinces of Britain; and none of those selfish rivalries of trade, which, from a very early period, began to embitter the intercourse between old & New England, ever arose to disturb the pleasant intercourse which existed between the Province & the Mother Country. The Revolution found all the young men of wealth and family, pursuing their studies in British Universities. Would it have been wonderful,—or a matter of reproach, if South Carolina, under these circumstances had refused all part in the conflict?—wonderful, if there had been many who should see no good cause for the conflict; wonderful, if all of British birth, should ally themselves with the Royal, rather than the Republican cause? Let me tell you now who did so,—and who did not. The Scotch settlements every where: a large proportion of the Germans; for was not George the 3d. one of their own Princes? The great majority of merchants, most of whom were of British birth & opinion! What remained to the Republicans? The <u>native</u> agricultural population; the native mechanics; the native lawyers and professions, mostly; the people of Huguenot stock; and the Scots-Irish colonists, with few exceptions. These were the parties, which, in South Carolina, asserting abstract principles, rather than present necessities, raised the banner of Revolution in sympathy with Massachusetts—raised it among the first—nay, the very first, and sent their succours to Massachusetts, from the first moment when she was stricken by the Enemy. Yet the first shaft at South Carolina comes from the quiver of Massachusetts. We are among the first to adopt her quarrel, and to arm in her defence; we send her money, wines and provisions—rice and maize, arms and ammunition—Hundreds of thousands in value—and, in her gratitude—she sends us—but let me say nothing of this. Look to the History and you will see that no colony of this confederacy, ever showed itself more prompt—very few half so prompt,—in sharing the fortunes of Massachusetts, when that colony stood in danger, and when the sympathies of the most feeble, were precious to her as the breath of life! Yes, in that day, Massachusetts could send a Special Ambassador to Carolina, one of her chief men, imploring sympathy and succour. And he obtained it; yet even then there was one far seeing Carolinian who said to him—"I foresee that we shall only exchange one tyranny for another, New England's tyranny for that of Old England; & I confess, for one, I prefer to submit to the usurpations of the one rather than of the other!" How prophetic was this man's language, let the history of today declare.—Well, the South Carolinians joined with Massachusetts. In spite of all the odds against them—the Scotch, English, German & Redmen—all subsidized by the crown, and forming nearly one half of her population—the patriots of South Carolina threw themselves into the breach, among the first with Massachusetts! They knew the dangers! They did not stop to count the odds! It was in spite of the open and secret opposition of most of these hostile factions—in spite of that lack of homogeneity which is so essential to an insurrectionary movement; in spite of the lack of all that mean but potential impulse, from the <u>argumentum ad crumenam</u>, which is so all-effective with a mixed multitude,—that South Carolina engaged in the struggle. I contend that purer patriots were never found—that hands cleaner of self and of offence—freer from the reproach of base and selfish motive,—never grasped the weapons of war—never more bravely, or faithfully carried Life, property & sacred honour, as their pledges into the field, or for more generous & national purposes. I deny that you have any right to inquire into her mere numbers, when called upon to acknowledge her achievements; and when these achievements neutralize her deficiency of numbers, they enhance the glory of each several deed! I insist, that, as the aims and energies of her native population, gave direction to the politics and action of the State, & their courage and conduct finally fixed it in this direction, they are the only true representatives of the State;—which is not to be estimated by the conduct of those who opposed the revolution, and fought stubbornly against it, but by those who began it, clung to it through all odds of fortune, and maintained the conflict to its triumphant close! I contend that it is quite unnecessary, in claiming for South Carolina a position as eminent for patriotism & valour as any other State, to show a perfect unanimity among her citizens. It is enough to show that the native population, mostly, sustained by the French and Irish settlers, and opposed chiefly by the Scotch, German, English and Quaker settlements, did assert for her the noblest position from the beginning; did obtain ascendancy from the beginning; were among the first at the beginning, & persevered in it to the end; and this through a bloody civil war to which no other state was subjected; contending against odds the most unequal; fighting equally an enemy within & an enemy without; fighting for her Sister States, until exhausted; almost entirely deserted by her Sister States; never receiving any assistance, whatsoever, from her States North of the Hudson; but feebly and slowly succoured by the States South of it; and finally, with the most moderate help from their arms, coming out of the conflict triumphantly, though bleeding at every pore.

This is the true history, in the briefest possible summary. The records will prove it true in every syllable. The claims which Carolina asserts to a proper share in the work of the Revolution may be slurred over by ingenious misrepresentation, but she cannot be defrauded of them. They are to be estimated by the difficulties with which she had to contend; by the deficiency of her numbers; by the poverty of her resources; by the rancour and strength of her enemies; by the purity of her purposes; by the spirit & wisdom of the favorite sons who swayed her councils and fought her battles; & by the frequency and bloody severity of her fields of fight. Her claims are based upon the performances of those who strove in her behalf, and not upon the hostility of those who strove against her. It is not to be permitted that the former should be disparaged, by any count of the numbers of the latter. We cannot allow that her fame is to be smutched, because there were many, within her limits, with whom her champions were hourly doing battle. In fact, so far from disparaging her claims, this serves to make them brighter and more glorious. Her fame is the greater, in degree with the numbers who were thus, within her own bowels, laboring at her destruction. The more you increase the numbers of the foreign Loyalists in her domain, the more you heighten the merits of those who braved them from the first, nor shrunk beneath the conflict, when these were openly arrayed beneath the banner of Britain and sustained by British & Hessian Legionaires. I regard it, indeed, as the strangest sort of logic, fit only for a rascal reasoner, to be told,—as we have been told—by some of the blindly venomous maligners of Carolina, that, when, on the 21st of April 1775, Pinckney, Laurens, Lynch, Huger, Bull, Drayton, Gadsden & others, seized on the British forts & arsenals, and possessed themselves of all their arms and munitions, there were certain Scotch and English Loyalists in Charleston, who were ready to cut the throats of all these patriots! That there were hostile foreigners in the city, cannot be suffered to interpose between the State, as a whole, acting through the representatives of the native stock, and which perseveres, and succeeds, in spite of them. So, it is not to be permitted, when we show that these same Patriots captured an English cruiser, & sent off the gunpowder to Boston, which enables Washington to continue the leaguer of that city, that some mousing caviller should start up & cry aloud—"Yes, indeed; but, at that very time, you had certain foreigners in your city, dealing in flour & molasses, who would rather have seen that powder employed in blowing Washington sky high with all his rebels."—Yet such is the absurd logic by which her enemies would cancel the public debt to the patriotism of South Carolina.

It is quite enough for us to show, that, whatever the number of our Loyalists, there was a sufficient cohort of true republicans to decide the course, & determine the action of the State! And their merit is the greater, when this impulse is given to the Body Politic, so as to compel it in the right direction, by only a certain portion of its people; and in spite, as well of the active opposition, as of the passive resistance of mere masses among the rest. It is, in fact, the peculiar boast of Carolina, that, with her population almost equally divided, she was yet able to achieve so much;—to send into the field so large a proportion of the noblest and ablest Captains; & into the national councils so many of the boldest politicians & the wisest Statesmen. Her merit consists in being able, while contending with a formidable home faction, to make contributions of strength, wisdom, patriotism & valour, to the Common Cause, which no other State in the Union has ever exceeded, tho' placed under circumstances far more advantageous!

Let us now see what are the proofs of her imbecility?—which, if true, might well be excused, from the facts already stated in her condition. As far back as 1765 the first steps towards a continental union were taken in South Carolina, and before the measure had been agreed upon by any colony south of New England. She was the first of the Colonies to form an Independent Constitution, in March 1776, and prior to the recommendation of Congress to that effect. And she had thrown off the Royal Government from 6th. July 1774—and on that day had passed a unanimous vote to sustain Massachusetts in the vindication of <u>her</u> rights. No tardiness here—no waiting on braver & bigger colonies to take the lead! In January 1775, we find the first Revolutionary Provincial Congress in Session, preparing for the next republican act;—a constitution, which was passed, as I have said, in March of the following year. The same convention stamped money—established a court of admirality for the condemnation of British vessels; issued Letters of Marque & reprisal; &, in Sept. of the same year, seized the royal forts, turned their guns against the royal cruisers, & drove them from the Harbour of Charleston. Not slow, I think, these proceedings;—more—at Charleston the tea was seized; a second shipment, at Charleston & at Georgetown, was thrown into the sea; & by citizens who did not think proper to paint or disguise themselves for the occasion. Surely, there was no imbecility here—no lack of will, resolution, and utter fearlessness, confronting peril! South Carolina did not stop here. She raised four regular regiments, all her own. She put her militia in training. She armed & manned her own vessels for war; and, in three weeks after the battle of Lexington her little army was ready to take the field. And all this was done out of her own treasury. So far, no colony had shown more zeal, promptness and readiness; few half so much. Enough that her conduct provoked the especial hostility of the Crown. Her courage was shortly to be put to the final test. A powerful fleet and army appeared upon her coasts. Simultaneously with this, the Loyalist British leaders upon the frontier, themselves habited and painted like the Red men, brought down a multitude of the savage warriors along her borders, and began the work of massacre upon the exposed settlements. The assault, at the same moment, was made at both extremities of the State. The history, by this time, ought to be well known. The British fleet was beaten off from the harbour of Charleston, with terrible slaughter, by Moultrie, at the head of a force wholly of Carolinians. This was in June 1776; and the first battle after that of Bunker Hill. It was one of the best fought battles of the Revolution; and the first occasion which ever witnessed the defeat of a British fleet, and by a native militia, few of whom had ever before seen the smokes of an enemy's fire; with a fortress only half finished; with inferior metal, and not half the necessary supply of gunpowder. At the same moment, the Loyalists and their savage allies were chastised upon the frontiers; &, for the time, humbled into submission, & again by the native militia of the colony.—These were prodigious exertions for so feeble a State as South Carolina. They exhausted her resources. They loaded her with debt. Her spirit, always greater than her strength, led to one unfortunate result. It prompted friends & foes equally to overrate her ability to defend herself. To this it was due that, when her final peril came, she received too little succour from her Sister States of the South,—none, whatever, from those of the North; while her enemies, warned by previous experience, descended upon her, when they next appeared, with a force so overwhelming, as almost to render all resistance hopeless.

South Carolina was next required to succour Georgia, then the feeblest of all the Confederacy. She did so: she invaded Florida, in an ill advised and badly managed expedition; and her regiments were reduced, by want, exposure & starvation, to mere skeletons. Georgia had but one regular regiment, which, overcome in various combats, at length perished in the British Prison Ships. Hundreds of the Carolinians shared the same fate! Georgia was overrun; Savannah captured; &, in a vain effort to defend Savannah & Georgia, the regiments of Carolina suffered still farther diminution. She had to support both provinces, and keep off the invader with such forces as she, herself, almost single handed, could muster. Congress did nothing, or next to nothing! Arms, ammunitions, provisions; all were obtained from South Carolina.—This brings us to the close of 1778. But, up to this period, there was no abatement, either of heart or hope, among the Carolinians. A flag sent into the Port of Charleston by the British Commissioners, with threats and overtures, was answered with defiance; & the flag vessel driven from the harbour! Surely, no lack still, of a firm confidence, & a stern determination to bide the conflict! But in 1779 Georgia was overrun, Savannah in possession of the enemy, the British were encouraged to new enterprises. Savannah constituted a good base of operations, whence they could readily strike at South Carolina. The regular forces of the Carolinas, four thousand men, were under the command of Lincoln. He had marched with them into the interior of Georgia; on a most injudicious expedition, the objects of which were totally unworthy of the interests periled & the sacrifices made. He left 1200 militia men with Moultrie, to watch the enemy, on the banks of the Savannah. Prevost, the British General, a dashing Partisan officer, seized promptly the opportunity, thus afforded him, for attempting a <u>coup de main</u> on Charleston. His route, baiting the militia force under Moultrie, was through an almost uninhabited country of swamps & marshes. In all this region, there were not five hundred people. Beaufort, Jacksonborough, Dorchester, were mere villages of 20 or 30 families. The 1200 militia men of Moultrie, could offer no serious obstacle to the march of 4,000 British regulars, with an auxiliary force of Loyalists & red men, of nearly a 1000 more. Charleston, itself, contained only 1200 dwelling houses of all sizes, implying a white population of 7000 souls—a number, which, at the uttermost, could yield only 1500 fighting men. Of these there was, questionless, a large body of Loyalists; including, as I have said, the Scotch, English, German, Quaker, & trading population, generally. By these the British were supplied, at every period of assault, with secret intelligence. As one of the British officers said to Moultrie, after the final capture of the city—"You made a gallant defence, Sir, but had many traitors among you!" No doubt!—Our argument, claiming the highest credit for the defence, is founded somewhat upon this very fact, that there were so many hostile elements, in the very heart of State & city, against whom the Patriots had to strive, while fighting the foe without.—But Prevost is on his march. Moultrie with his Militia skirmishes with his advance; but must retreat before him if he would save the city. He sees the game of Prevost. He feels the danger of Charleston. The British General, meanwhile, lets loose all his terrors— his redmen & tories;—to ravage the country as he advances. With the torch & tomahawk, in either hand, you need not be told what sort of tragedies are en- acted or to be feared in this progress. There the Church of God flames; there the House of Man! You hear the crash of falling timbers; the shrieks of women, flying for shelter to swamp and forest. Old men are brained upon the ancestral hearth; babes are spitted upon the bayonet. The militia men know the danger, and scatter for their homes, maddened with their fears for the helpless and beloved ones; and when Moultrie reaches the city his force of 1200 is reduced to half the number. Meanwhile, the regulars of Prevost steadily march on. What of the city? When Prevost began his march, its fortifications did not exist. But, when he reaches the precinct, lines and an abbatis have been carried across the neck from the Cooper to the Ashley. The militia of the vicinity have come in to its defence. Moultrie arrives;—Rutledge with 600 militia from the interior; & Harris with 250 Conti- nentals. They have made forced marches to reach the place in season, & the next day the British appear. A sharp action follows with the Legion cavalry of Pulaski, and a body of Militiamen, in which our people are severely handled. That night the garrison lay upon their arms. The next day, a message was sent to the enemy asking upon what terms he would grant a capitulation. And here occurs one of those transactions which have been supposed to reflect upon the patriotism of Carolina, or her courage. It is one of those occasions, which, upon a partial state- ment of facts, without the proper weighing of the probabilities, or evidence, have been relied on to sanction the severest judgments. What are the facts? The Gov- ernor and his Privy Council open negotiations with the enemy, asking to know upon what terms the city may capitulate. For the details of this affair, there are really but two authorities, Ramsay & Moultrie, both Carolina historians. Both were present. Ramsay was even then the recognized Historian, busy in the accu- mulation of materials. He was experienced in affairs; circumspect, thoughtful, calm; a close observer; a correct thinker. Moultrie was brave & honest; in whom, as a man and soldier, the people had every confidence. It is his account which occasions the reproach. He describes the proposal to negotiate as seriously enter- tained, by a portion of the Council at all events; while Ramsay distinctly tells us that the object was simply to gain time, until Lincoln, with his regulars could reach the city, when he might fall upon the rear of the enemy. To prevent the assault, yet delay the British, so as to have them between two fires, was the object. Before the negotiations are opened, Rutledge sounds Moultrie, as the military man, upon the prospects of the defence. He describes the relative strength of the two forces. The British are reported to be 6 or 8000. Rutledge depicts the dangers from such a force, most of them Regulars, sustained by an auxiliary body of tories and red men; points to the weakness of the lines; the inferiority of numbers in the garrison, and makes out the worst case under the circumstances. Moultrie, in reply, thinks the place defensible; thinks the British numbers greatly exaggerated, & shows that ours have been underrated. Rutledge convenes the Council, and the result is the message to the British General. Prevost answers vaguely, that he will grant protection. Protection implies neutrality. To those who decline to take protection, he says, they shall be received as prisoners of war; their fate decided by that of the rest of the colonies. The reply to this rejects the proposal as dishonorable, & suggests a conference between a single military man on each side. At this conference, the American officer was counselled to propose neutrality on the part of the State for the rest of the war; her fate to be decided finally by the terms of peace between the United States & Great Britain. This, you perceive, was a far more liberal concession to the enemy, than he had himself prescribed, and which had been denounced, by the Council, but the day before, as dishonorable to the garrison. But Prevost rejects this offer, and requires that the garrison shall submit as prisoners of war. This requisition is at once rejected, and the Carolinians stand to their arms. But the British seek no farther to test their resolution. The conference is scarcely closed, before their army disappears under cover of the night. This is the substantial history, gleaned from the actual correspondence. Moultrie, however, after a lapse of 20 years, makes a narrative of his own, from memory, in which he undertakes to give the details of one or more dialogues, in which he reports one of the members of the Council as shedding tears at the idea of Surrendering, and all of them as looking grave. He speaks of certain things as having been said, but he does not recollect by whom, and, briefly, has indulged in the most dangerous experiment upon memory which a witness could ever undertake. He does not tell us that Rutledge was frightened, as some of the Northern writers, have told you. He describes him as grave & earnest, and as giving him an exaggerated estimate of the enemy's strength, and an inadequate representation of our own, according to reports which have reached the city, and which might be true or not. But all this amounts to little,—to no more than this: that the Governor & His Privy Council, were very grave and greatly troubled, as well they might be; that they naturally consulted the chief military man of the place, upon the resources which he could bring to bear in the defence; that, whether they felt this to be the fact or not, they, as naturally, presented to his contemplation the worst aspects of the case. This would be the very practice of the Lawyer & the Politician searching his own witnesses. This was the very practice of John

Rutledge. But Moultrie, a plain, rough, direct soldier, with no artifice, no strategies, can conceive of none but the single matter in hand. He was for fighting, as the shortest & best finish for a long argument, and if he reasoned upon the subject at all it was probably in such fashion as this. "Well, they are four or five thousand; we are three thousand. But we have the Lines. They will try to storm; but we shall drub them; we shall surely drub them! At all events, we shall try. Let them storm, and be ________ drubbed!" But John Rutledge wished to avert this very danger of a Storm. He too thought it possible that the British might be drubbed; but he preferred to convert the possible into the certain. He aimed at more. The capture of Prevost. We must negotiate. Hold out all sorts of lures to the enemy, so as to prevent the assault, until Lincoln comes in upon his back. He is near at hand. But Rutledge was not to allow this policy to be seen, either by the soldiery or the citizens; nay, the very members of his own Council, all of them, are not to know that these negotiations contemplate nothing but a <u>ruse de guerre</u>, to gain time. It will not do to spread <u>that</u> abroad. That will be to defeat the object, to precipitate the assault, and baffle the occult purpose of the negotiations. And, according to Moultrie's own showing, certain members of the Council came to him & whispered encouragement in his ears. They will stand by him to the last; and the militia said the same thing, and the people! They had got wind of these negotiations, perhaps ostentatiously made public; &, taking for granted what was on the face of them, had become angry; and, we are told, would have taken the Council by the throats, had time been allowed them. And all this, without dreaming that it was by this very policy of seeming to fear, and entreating negotiation, that the city was saved at last. For, how can you suppose that Prevost, at the head of 4000 regulars, and a large auxiliary force, would reject the gift of State and city, on the terms suggested, if he had not, at the last moment, become aware that he had been the victim of a delusion; that he would abandon the field, and the prey upon which he had only to close his fingers, the moment after the very conference, in which the surrender had been proffered to his arms. This has been the puzzle with critics & Historians—Lee & others— who never suffered themselves to look into the situation of Rutledge & his Council, and who have wondered, & blundered, over the wonderful blundering of Prevost, who could reject such a liberal offer. They do not note the meaning of the final refusal of the British General, to treat with the Council at all; and never seem to have conjectured that, having detected the <u>ruse de guerre</u>, in consequence of the receipt of an intercepted letter, Prevost had become satisfied that the offer was not made in good faith; was only a sham; and that, if it delayed him an hour longer, it would involve the safety of his whole army. He could now see the secret of this policy. To delay him where he was, was to enclose him between two fires, those of the garrison in front, and of Lincoln & his Continentals in the rear. The negotiation succeeded in its object. Time <u>was</u> gained. Prevost had dilly-dallied with fortune just one day too long. Would he have lingered a moment, forbearing the assault, had it not been for the negotiations; and would he have listened to any negotiations, if they had not held out some extraordinary temptations? What says General Lee on this subject. Lee has been referred to as one of the authorities in this matter; though, as regards the mere facts, he is no authority at all; not being within 700 miles of the scene of action, and not coming into the State for a long time after. He not only speaks of Rutledge "as an accomplished gentleman, a profound Statesman, a captivating orator, decisive in his measures, & inflexibly firm;" but he ascribes the safety of the city to these very negotiations. He says—"the whole day was spent, <u>intentionally</u> on the part of the besieged, & erroneously on the part of the Beseiger, in the adjustment of terms. Thus 12 more precious hours were gained." He mentions the proposal of neutrality, and forgetting what he has himself just said about the negotiating policy of Rutledge, wonders that Prevost should have refused it. And, in the very next chapter, he tells us, that, when in turn, Prevost was besieged by the French & Americans in Savannah, "he recollected the late transactions before Charleston, determined to imitate the example furnished by his Enemy on that occasion; and so answered as to protract negotiations, gaining time, by suggesting his own willingness to surrender, and getting so many hours for the necessary adjustment of terms." And this is all the secret, which could prove no puzzle, either for Philosophical Historian or the good military critic. Did Moultrie's force save the city? Not a bit of it. His army of 3000 raw militia men, could not have covered one fourth of the line of battery which he had to defend. What saved it then? The protracted negotiations, which gave time to Lincoln with his force of four thousand Continentals, made up of the Lines of the 2 Carolinas, and a body of Virginians, the rapid approach of whom, as ascertained by an intercepted letter of Lincoln, startled Prevost, in the midst of the conference, with apprehensions for his own safety; and, even as he read, he dispatched his Lieutenants to set the troops in marching order; and as soon as night had set in, he recrossed the Ashley, and made forced marches down to the coast, where he could be sure of cover from his shipping. Could he have gained the city, on any terms, at that very hour, would he have fled from it? Not so! He would have pressed in—taken any terms—manned the Lines against Lincoln, and achieved the very object for which he came. He was baffled by the Statesman Rutledge, who held out to his fancy the most promising of lures, and gradually drew it back from the eyes which it had sufficiently deluded. The military men were not suffered to know the secret object of the game. Nay, all the members of the Council, we have reason to believe, were not suffered to know. There are, in all councils, a certain number of fat and sleek and worthy men; who are honest without being sagacious; who love to talk, and will blab;—leaky vessels whom you do not condemn, but to whom you never entrust any liquid philosophies. To such as these, the occult virtue that lies at the basis of a mere fact, is never discoverable; and you charitably forbear vexing them with its burdens. But you are all sufficiently politicians to understand the great difference which exists between the puppet on the stage, & the wire puller behind the scenes. And you can readily conceive that our Council had certain among its members who could simply hold out their irons & wink. So, when Moultrie tells you, that one of the Parties wept, at the thought that the city must be surrendered, and that some other unknown Councilman said—"<u>Yes</u>"—to the question of surrender; there was no more profound meaning in it than in that Burleigh nod, which is so significant in the school of doubtful noddles. That Moultrie himself, a plain old soldier, should be for fighting right away; & that the fiery young Laurens should chafe at all negotiation, was simply a thing of course, in keeping with the character of both. But you find that there were certain of these Council men who whispered their secret encouragements in the ears of Moultrie; while the fierce old Patriot, Gadsden, one of the firmest, and the earliest of the champions of American liberty, would seize the stout old soldier by the wrist, and giving him a squeeze such as a blacksmith's vice fastens upon a nail head, would growl in his ears, "Hold on!—We are with you to the death, Bill Moultrie!"—With all the reserves and cautions of the Council, all their <u>open</u> deliberations <u>did</u> leak out.—What would have been the result, in a community full of loyalists, if the <u>secret</u> objects of the Council had been made known? Would not Prevost have been instantly taught the game which was played upon him? Would not the assault have followed the discovery. And what might have been the consequences? We know that Moultrie would have fought. He was well seconded. Marion was with him; and Laurens; and there were 3000 city & country militia who were in harness, and full of enthusiasm. But we also know that the lines were without strength; the citizens badly armed; too few for the extent of their fortifications; and the enemy, one third more numerous, and a well-drilled body, well armed, of British regulars!

We are not, my friends, to deal with historical reputations in the loose & reckless manner of the newspaper press: not to adopt, on partial statements, of an imperfect memory, every suggestion which may be construed into an import which will tell against the reputation of great men. The vulgar world is always eager to adopt a faith which will bring down greatness to a vulgar level. We are especially to regard the <u>probabilities</u>, which belong to <u>character</u>, whether of an individual or of a people, when called upon to decide upon isolated facts, which seem to tell against either. In the case of John Rutledge, the antecedents, & the subsequents, are equally adverse to the supposition that he behaved on this occasion with any lack of nerve or patriotism. He had been among the most impassioned advocates of the Revolution. When the battle of Fort Moultrie was to be fought, and Lee, the Continental General, proposed to abandon it, Rutledge said to Moultrie, "I will sooner cut off my right hand, than write such an order."

When, afterwards, Charleston fell into the hands of the Enemy, and the State was overrun; the people so well knew him,—so perfectly confided in him, that they made him their Dictator, requiring him, in the language of the ancient Roman, to see that the Republic should sustain no harm. And all the testimonies, concur in reporting him, throughout the war, as one of the most faithful of patriots; one of the most steadfast of men. And what shall we say of the contradiction, involved in the fact, that it was but a few hours before, that leading 600 men from Orangeburg, Rutledge, by forced marches had thrown himself into the city. Did he bring them to the city, only to surrender it & them to the enemy? He knew of Prevost's march upon Charleston—& had reason to believe from the reports, that his forces were far more numerous than they were proved to be after he reached the city. Why then should he so suddenly resolve to abandon the very object for which he came—to bring his 600 militia to the garrison, only that they might be lost to the country. The whole notion is an absurdity, to be misconceived only by those who were unable to follow out the subtle policy which governed the Statesman. It is very certain that his contemporaries never beheld the transaction which I have just discussed, in the same light with the people of today. Moultrie, himself, though no doubt greatly puzzled by the affair; never fancied that he was giving countenance to the notion that Rutledge was an imbecile. The very correspondence, by the way, which he publishes in this very connection, shows that he must greatly have misconceived the true purposes of Rutledge. There, but a little month before, we find Rutledge writing to himself, in this language—"Lt. Col. Prevost's proposition of a temporary neutrality, for a part of Georgia, is really too absurd and ridiculous to require a moment's consideration. It scarce merits any answer."—And yet, we are told, in a month after, that he seriously meditated this very absurd arrangement for South Carolina. The fact is almost patent, that, aware of this, as Prevost's own favorite proposition, Rutledge seized upon it, as the one lure, over all others, best calculated to beguile & to blind the British General, and secure the desirable respite for the city, of 24 hours from assault. All attempts now, to disturb a reputation, which, in his own time, was beyond reproach, are only discreditable to the assailant. In some of your newspapers, there have been recent labours of this sort, in which sundry authorities have been quoted, who are no authorities at all. Col. Harry Lee, for example, who, I have already told you, was not in S. C. till long after, gathers his details from Moultrie, and himself testifies to the wonderful vigour, firmness, power & patriotism of Rutledge, whom he knew during all the closing scenes of the war. Judge Johnson has also been summoned to the stand as a witness, but he was hardly born at the time, and he too relies upon Moultrie. Dr. Ramsay, I find, quoted partially, in a garbled extract, by one of our assailants, in support of Moultrie; but, curiously enough, he suppresses the significant words of Ramsay, who is the best authority, and who distinctly tells us that the sole object of the negotiations was to gain time. Ramsay was present during the affair, was intimate with the chief actors, conferred with them all upon the subject of his history, and had its secret clues, as well as obvious details, in his hands, in most of the cases which came under his own observation. Why should his positive evidence be garbled or ignored? Of Professor Bowen, and Mr. Flanders, who have written upon the subject, it is enough to say that they are commentators, not witnesses. As authorities, they are wholly valueless; and their very enumeration proves only an inveterate desire to establish a point, at all hazards, which, even if true, could serve no other purposes than those of an unpatriotic malignity. To study this case thoroughly, you are to have in regard a variety of relevant topics, which are essential to that grouping of fragmentary facts, into perfect truth, which is the great duty of the Historian. It is essential, for example, that you should know that the civil & military powers, were rarely in harmony in South Carolina, until Rutledge assumed the Dictatorship. They were rarely in harmony in any of the States. Moultrie had, long before this time, come into collision with the civilian; there had been almost an open rupture upon the question of separate jurisdiction. Some of his letters are extant, asserting his dignity against what he deemed the usurpations of Council. I have seen their replies, penned, like his, with some asperity. Nay, more there was a <u>quasi</u> quarrel between the parties on this very score, at the very moment when Prevost was thundering at the gates. I feel very sure that, while greatly honoured, as a soldier and a man, Moultrie was not often referred to as a councillor, save on military affairs. On this occasion, I have no doubt that all his misconceptions arose from the fact that he was only in part admitted to a knowledge of the proceedings in Council. The civilians sought him only for his military opinion, and took special care, perhaps, to let him understand, all the while, that the sword must always yield precedence modestly to the gown. Though something of a phlegmatic, he was the person to resent such treatment. He undervalued civilians in war; they did not seek him in Council. Here you have a solution of some of those difficulties which have puzzled the historians; very few of whom, in our country, know any thing of military affairs. We are not in possession of a single history, of any one of the States, in which a philosophic mind has weighed the import of mere facts in the narrative. None of them has done more than narrate the facts as they appear upon the surface. The clues to action, the motives to plan & purpose, have been unconsidered by any. What we especially need now, is such an Historian as will be able to enter into the analysis of character, & general probability, and to trace the action up to its original motive. Let me add that there are probably not more than half a dozen persons, at this time, in all the States, who, from a knowledge of details, or from the capacity to analyse them, are capable of an adequate judgment on this subject of our Revolution. Were they permitted to speak out fully—were not the day gone by for the reopening of the case,—their revelations would be absolutely terrible in certain quarters. If my view of the case, in the present instance, be correct, what a crime are we committing against character; against the simple truths of history; when we arraign the political philosopher, who actually achieves the success, upon the evidence of the soldier, honest though he be, who is yet suffered to behold nothing but the surface. It is my opinion, drawn from what I hold to be the best evidence—and from what is probable from the consistent performances of the man—that, so far from Rutledge failing of courage or conduct, we owe it to his subtle policy, that Charleston was saved from storm & sack. The strength of the city itself could scarce have saved it; Lincoln could not have appeared in season to do so. But for the negotiations which baffled the enemy for a day and night, we should have had the attack. We may calculate on the probabilities as we will. The assailants might have been baffled. But what are the probabilities? Four thousand British regulars, with an auxiliary force of a 1000 more, loyalists & Indians, against an untrained, badly armed militia of 3000, required to defend more than a mile front of field lines. I can only say that, in no part of America did the encounter of any forces, similarly disproportioned, result in any thing but defeat to the weaker party! It is enough to add, here, that, subsequently, when Lincoln faced the same enemy at Stono, the hardest fighting was done, and to the defeat of the British, by native Carolinians. But, even if Rutledge failed on this occasion, and thus forfeited his reputation in the past, which I do not admit—how does this affect the reputation of South Carolina? One of her Counsellors faltered you will say; but the rest were firm. The people were firm—the soldiers firm. If Moultrie & his followers saved the city, they were all native Carolinians. The Gadsdens & Laurenses, who bade him stand firm, & they would breast the shock with him;—the merchant, Edwards, who wept bitter tears at the bare idea of surrender—the enraged soldiery & people who swore fierce vengeance equally against the enemy without, & the Council within— these were all native Carolinians. What can be made of these facts against the fame & honour of the State?

Well,—we next find these same Charleston Militia led against the British Lines at Savannah, under the joint lead of Lincoln & d'Estaign. The combined armies were defeated with great slaughter, and the only show of success which they could exhibit was at the hands of Carolinians, they alone having won the enemy's ramparts, and planting their flag upon the walls. But, says one of our assailants, "Less than a year after Prevost's attempt—the people of Charleston were very ready to surrender to a British army." Another writes—"South Carolina with a Northern army to assist her, could not or would not even arm for the defence of her own capital." Let me say, <u>in limine</u>, to correct a very common error of these purblind politicians, that no troops, from New England, ever came to the succour of South Carolina. A regiment of Pennsylvanians came at the close of the war, when the fighting was all over. The Southern armies were wholly made up from the States of Virginia & Maryland, the two Carolinas & Georgia, with a small contingent from Delaware. The South sent a hundred men East of the Hudson, during the revolution, for every one that ever came South of it, except at the single siege of York. Even South Carolina, after the fall of Charleston, sent one thousand of her sons, to the Northern army, which they joined at Philadelphia, where they were reviewed by Arnold. And the Regiments of Virginia, Maryland & North Carolina, were among the constituents of the army under Washington, which was almost wholly employed at the North. Enough on this head. Let us now see what is meant when it is said that the Carolinians would not defend their chief city, and were quite ready to yield it to the enemy! It so happens that Charleston is the only city, which, in the Revolution, was defended by the Americans at all! Boston, New York, Philadelphia, all more populous & powerful, were yielded quietly to the enemy, without striking a blow; while Charleston was defended for six weeks, by five thousand men, against 12000 British regulars, supported by a powerful fleet; nor was she conquered at last by arms! She succumbed, to famine, only; though her batteries, and one half of her houses were in ruins! And this defence was made wholly by the troops of the two Carolinas & Virginia, behind mere field works which the French engineers pronounced untenable from the beginning! What would people have? If Charleston was badly defended, or not defended, what shall we say of those bigger, braver cities, who never stood siege a moment; never went into battery; never scaled a gun; never dedicated themselves, for a day even, to the patriotic diet, upon rats, frogs, and horse flesh, and found them luxuries! I do not reproach these cities. It was a wise policy of Washington, not to defend them, but to economize his army in the open field. This should have been the policy of South Carolina. They did defend their chief city & lost it, with all their garrison. Of the 5000 prisoners who fell into the hands of the enemy on this occasion, more than 3000 were South Carolinians. Now, count for yourselves. How many thousands more will this little State, of less than 3 persons to the square mile, be prepared, after all these contests & losses, to send into new fields of combat? Her own coast and border defence,—the defence of Georgia,—the invasion of Florida, and the Cherokees, have cost her thousands, and she is covered with debt as with a garment! Thousands, as we have said, of her population, are foreigners; British subjects; Loyalists, born & bred; and less than ten years in the country; and against all of these she has to contend! She is without arms and ammunition; without money; her regular troops are all prisoners of war; her one Brigadier, Moultrie, is a prisoner; her militia force,—what remains of it,—is scattered over a vast forest country, and without a leader! And Congress, it is now reported, has abandoned her; about to make peace, sacrificing her & Georgia, to the enemy, under the rule of <u>uti possidetis</u>. She has various small bodies of militia in the field; but they act without concert; and simply maintain watch over isolated settlements, to protect them from the local loyalists; from the red men of the borders; from the refugees of other States! Meanwhile, the conquering enemy, has sent his columns into the interior, overawing all the settlements; while his light detachments sweep the country dispersing the small squadrons which would still keep themselves embodied. And there is no help from abroad. No help from Congress—neither men, nor money,—not even the weapons of war! The Virginians & North Carolinians, when, hitherto they have been sent to help us, have come mostly without arms, without clothing, and have been furnished with both from our resources: —and these are now lost—exhausted. Is it wonderful that the people should be paralyzed for a season? That there should be an interval when Patriotism knows not where to turn, or how to resolve, or in what way to effect its impatient purposes of struggle. There would be nothing to surprise, if this should be the case. But there is a hope. These fierce New Englanders, for whom they first went into battle, they will surely help us! We shall have succours from that quarter! They number on the roll 118,000 fighting men. They go into battle with a rush. They rather love it! They are surely on the march even now! But no! No! These New Englanders cannot drive the enemy out of Rhode Island, though there the British only number a paltry 3000 men! Ah! my friends, why do they expect such wonderful things from South Carolina? But, sorely stricken, feeble, crushed, impoverished, without means or money; without a leader, South Carolina does not succumb to Fortune! She is <u>not</u> conquered! She does not suffer herself to admit a conqueror, though many of her people may despair. In the very moment when the British proclaim their conquest to be complete, she recovers her strength and courage! Marion, a cripple, limping with a broken leg, has sounded his bugle in the swamps, for the rally of the fugitives. Sumter takes the field, & his trumpet echoes along the Apalachian summits, rousing up the brave pioneers; calling back to the rescue of the State, the native sons of the South, who have wandered away from the settlements, in the pursuit of newer homes. These people are all sons of the Carolinas & Virginia, and it is easy to win them back to the succour of their maternal homes. Pickens, Williams, Adair, Lacy, Bratton, Roebuck, and fifty other Chiefs, are as actively at work along the Broad & Pacolet; the Peedee, the Tyger, & the Santee rivers; and, even in the moment of greatest prostration, there arose that brilliant race of Partisan warriors, all from the South—all to the <u>manor</u> born, who have never been surpassed, & rarely equalled, in any quarter of the globe! In three months after the British General had declared South Carolina to be a conquered province, he was forced to declare her to be every where in a state of revolt! What forces won the battles of King's Mountain, Musgrove's, Hanging Rock, Blackstocks, and a hundred other fields, where Marion, Sumter, Pickens, Williams, Bratton and Cleveland commanded? The forces of the Carolinas, & mostly of South Carolina. In the battle of King's Mountain, for example, Williams who was slain upon the heights, within 10 feet of the British Col.

Ferguson, led 400 South Carolinians into the field, a larger force than represented any other State on the occasion. So far from the people of South Carolina not taking the field they were never out of it;—winter & summer found them busy in perpetual sieges; skirmishes & battles! It was the Partisans who conquered all the small garrisons and outposts of the British;—Forts Motte, Watson, Granby, Georgetown, Augusta, Silver Bluff, Dorchester. The Continentals failed of success in nearly every battle;—before Camden, 96, Hobkirks, Orangeburg, Eutaw; and they alone were allowed a respite from service during the heats of summer; the Partisans being all the while employed; foraying & fighting; cutting off the British supplies, and providing our own! And these were all Southern militiamen; mostly of South Carolina—You have been told that South Carolina possessed during the Revolution a population more tainted with disaffection than any other colony. This is <u>not</u> true! Her tory population was brought into more active exhibition in consequence of the frontier position which she occupied; the facility of access to her interior; and the greater degree of virulence with which the civil war was waged within her borders; leaving no portion of her people a safe refuge from strife. This was due in some degree to the fact that she was almost the only field of conflict during the three last years of the war. Active operations had almost ceased every where else; the closing events made naturally the greatest impression; and the war carried its sting in its tail! The malignity of the strife was increased, in due degree with the increasing efforts of the British, growing desperate with the growing hopelessness of their cause. They strove equally for the failing credit of their arms, and in pursuit of those spoils which would help their fortunes. Hence their venom in conflict; hence the terrible extent of their marauding. South Carolina was a rich field which they gleaned to the uttermost. In so small a province, so thinly peopled, with the population, almost to a man in the field; on one side or the other; private feuds added keener rancour to the natural ferocity of war; and the conflict was invariably urged to the extremest issues. Greene says, "the people here pursue each other like wild beasts"; yet the critic of today, would tell you that they never fought at all—that South Carolina was lukewarm! Lukewarm! Such a people are never lukewarm! They work with intensity under every passion! And there were good reasons why, so far from being lukewarm, here, they should engage in the struggle with the bitterest intensity. There were popular elements in conflict, in our interior settlements, which we can scarcely find any where else. South Carolina was compelled to bear the blasting influence of a people unrestrained by the discipline of arms, and free from all responsibility, whom she did not know or own. To her fields, from 1778 to 1782, inclusive, came all the swarms of refugees, who had been driven out, in 1776, from all the colonies south of the Hudson! These had first fled to Florida, as the tories, north of the Hudson, mostly found refuge in Canada. So soon as the British armies penetrated Georgia and Carolina, all these refugees, a locust pestilence, following in the wake of the British, scattered them-selves over our plains. They were destitute, desperate of fortune, malignant as Hell! They ravaged, burned & plundered when they came. They had to revenge the past, and to provide for the future. They were sleepless in the pursuit of both objects; and these, alone, scattered in roving bands over the whole country, gave sufficient employment to the Partisans, who were compelled to break up into little squads, the better to protect each isolated settlement. The actual population was thus the prey of the intruder. These loyalists were not ours. To the people of the country, they were as strange of aspect, hirsute, wild, savage monstrous, as were the Scandinavians, when they first flung them- selves, with shrieks & songs of terror, upon the peaceful cities of Italy. Backed, as they were, by the British garrisons, at every commanding station, the wonder is how our Partisans should be able to maintain themselves at all. Their succours of Continentals, from with-out the State never exceeded 3000 bayonets. They got no money, no supplies, scarce any ammunition, and, for half the time, were half clad in moss, rather as a protection against the friction of belt and cartridge box and musket, than as a defence against the weather. The resources of South Carolina supported both armies, mainly, in three States, for nearly three years. Her advances accordingly, made her, at the close of the war, the largest creditor State of the Union. Yet, people will have it that she did not do enough! With her small resources she did as much as any other State in the Confederacy. But it is not allowed me, to pro-tract the subject, in consideration of the score of minor charges, which have been made against her. These come chiefly from persons even more ignorant than malignant. Either they know nothing of the History, or their moral lacks in its review. Enough that I repeat, in the briefest summary the true history which the Chronicles must every where sustain. The closing struggles of the war were in South Carolina mostly; the bloody frequency of her fields of fight, declare the superior earnestness of the contending parties; the final events made the most fearful impression; the venom & virulence of the war were reserved, as usual, for the last acts of this fierce tragedy, and South Carolina, where the last blood of the Revolution, and almost the first, was shed, was compelled to endure them all. Those who read the History, as they should, with no malignant determination to rake up the evil and suppress the good; to expose the base, and deny the noble; will soon be forced to admit that the exertions of South Carolina were unexam-pled in the case of so feeble a state; that she was one of the most self-sacrificing of the whole Confederacy; that her spirit was always greater than her strength; and so prompted friend and foe equally to overrate her ability! A few more words, my friends, and I have done. South Carolina was the first colony to second Massa-chusetts. She had no such interests at stake—no such causes of complaint, and plunged headlong into the conflict. Her battles followed close upon those of Lexington & Bunker. She defeated the first British fleet—is the only power that ever did defeat a British fleet. In those days it was no part of the policy of Massachusetts to deny or decry her services. It does not become her that she should do so now. The Past of both regions ought to be secure. Let the strifes of the Present be what they may, neither party gains by the brutal defamation of the other. If there is to be strife between our respective countries—if the future is to witness a conflict among ourselves—and this great empire be doomed to the convulsions of Civil War,—let the issues be unmixed; simple, single, unconfounded! If South Carolina, imbecile in the Past—be <u>now</u> imbecile—no matter from what cause—there need be no effort to prove the fact by argument. It will prove itself, in action! If imbecile, past and present, how absurd for the brave to go into the discussion! We scorn the imbecile; we do not contend with them! We crush them under foot, and feel that, while we do so, we do nothing. We argue with those only who can coerce our respect. Massachusetts gains nothing by showing that South Carolina is faithless as a friend, & worthless as a foe! Let her establish the fact in either case, & what follows? Is the argument meant to persuade the imbecile that she should yield without struggle?—submit,—that she may escape from blows & bondage? Ah! my friends, what <u>real</u> power, confident in itself, and noble in its courage, ever descends to such an artifice? Better, braver, nobler, the short process, of the mailed hand, & the biting weapon. Better for both parties—for the honor of the one, and the due conviction of the other. Standing, here, before you, on a purely Literary Mission,—with all my tastes, feelings, sentiments, habits, opposed to brutality & violence,—I yet deprecate no wrath—no censure; appeal to no sympathies; ask no forbearance. I demand, of a just and conscientious people; in a moment of comparative calm; in a hall sacred to peace, letters and the arts; I demand justice for my Mother Country. She has been more faithful to you,—more submissive—than she ever was to Britain; more true to <u>your</u> cause than she has ever been to her own! If she is now to perish,—if she is to be isolated by odium, that she may be more easily offered up at the altar, without sympathy or succour—be it so! Let the Future declare itself in its grimmest aspect, I shall not fear for her deportment in the worst of seasons. As neither Massachusetts, nor any other State, will gain any thing of honour when they lend a too eager [unintelligible word] to the defamation of the Past of South Carolina, so, be sure, the profit will be quite as small from her contemplated destruction in the future. If her doom is written, be equally sure, that she will fall no easy victim. With her lithe and sinewy limbs & muscles, she will twine herself around the giant caryatids which sustain the anchor of the great Confederacy, and falling like the strong man of Israel, will bring down with her, in a common ruin, the vast and wondrous fabric, which her own prowess has so much helped to raise. Then, if there shall be one surviving sister, sitting solitary in the desolation, she will remain a monument, more significant of ruin than all the wreck which grows around her—the trophy of a moral desolation, which, by perversity and wrong, by a base selfishness which knew not how to be just, or how to be human, has with fratricidal hand, destroyed all its own securities and hopes—a moral suicide. —Forgive me, my friends, if I have spoken warmly; but you would not, surely, have me speak coldly in the assertion of a Mother's honour!

"The Social Moral, Lecture 1" (1857)

In the midst of a serene period, my friends, at home—one, at least, in which, whatever may be our consciousness of present insecurity—none of us ever entertained a single fear of the safety of our Past—none of us ever fancied that there could arise any doubts in any minds of the virtues of our ancestry, or the value and excellence of <u>their</u> performances—we are suddenly put to the question on this very score, and it is charged against us that we are living upon a spurious reputation—that the ancestors of whom it has been our pride to boast, were, in fact, false to their duties and their country—recreant to their trusts—heedless of their honor—faithless to their brethren—traitors in the cabinet and cowards in the field!

These are, substantially, the allegations made by a Senator in the Senate House; in one of the highest council chambers of the Confederacy;—on an occasion the most momentous;—in the sight and hearing of the whole people; and, with our own accredited representatives upon the floor, in the same presence; bound, as it were, to the rack; & forced to hearken to the shocking history, as it issues, from the lips of a malignant enemy, and is addressed to the senses of a too partial audience.

Well might we be confounded! Of the history so delivered, we had never heard a syllable! We had been living on in a delightful condition of self-complacency—had been making perpetual boast of our ancestry—had flattered ourselves that their names and deeds could take rank—nay, <u>had</u> taken rank—with the most glorious and proud of all the nation:—That they had become the burden of song and story, and were among the most firmly engraven upon the brass and marble of authentic monuments.

So secure were we of all this that we had preserved none of our histories—scarcely cared to read them—never did read them—never gave them to our sons to read—never placed them in our libraries—never asked ourselves where such histories were to be found! So assured were we of certain fame and eminence of our great men, that we never made or procured their biographies;—never built them a single monument;—never sought out their graves in grateful veneration;—in many instances knew not, and know not, to this day, where those graves are to be sought! Nay, so magnanimous was our self-complacency, that we were perfectly satisfied that our Enemies should write our histories, and provide the teachers for our young;—that their infant minds should be trained and tutored by a people who were eagerly busied in the grateful labor of destroying our institutions, and casting a slur of perpetual infamy upon our name. Certainly in all these respects, our Christian patience, if not our self-complacency, has been wonderful indeed: Never, at all events, did any people, show themselves more admirably indifferent to their own memorials.

Well!—what should happen from all this virtuous indifference to Fame;—to the history of our race—to the education of our young—to all those moral safeguards and securities, of which most other nations are so jealous; which rest upon opinion—upon glorious traditions—upon memorials kept alive for the growing generations, by constant repetition, from truthful and from loving lips?

Just what has happened! Just what we might expect to happen.

In the midst of our serenest sky, the bolt has fallen among us! At the moment when we carried our proudest head, we find it suddenly covered in dirt and ashes! Our traditions are ignored as the delusions of vanity—the memory of our ancestors is fouled by the slanderer:—he has flung his filth upon the grave of that mother, whom we have neglected to protect with marble; he has violated and mutilated the sacred shines which we have failed to guard with an adequate and jealous patriotism. All our convictions of the Past, of which we have been so loud in boast, without caring to preserve the record, are mocked as absurd and ridiculous pretensions, entirely without foundation, and, for a brief period, at least, we were made to exhibit, in the eyes of the nation, the spectacle of the silly jackdaw stripped of all his borrowed feathers!

But, had we any reason to anticipate better treatment? Had not the experience of thirty years, brought us to the proper apprehension that some such exhibition was threatened? Were not the signs in our sky sufficiently ominous, during all this period of time? Did you not feel—have you not feared—for a long season, the open hostilities of the very people from whom you hear this slander? Did you not know that all assaults upon the rights and possessions, the inheritance, on the institutions of a people, are always coupled with, or prefaced by, a defamation of their character? Could we, as robbers and man-stealers—living in the daily exercise of a great wrong to humanity, be supposed to have any virtues? How should such a people be brave or patriotic, how pure or faithful—how wise, generous or just? How should a people, as little jealous of their reputation as of their securities, be supposed likely to spring up, in the panoply of armed men, to resent insult or resist aggression? Has not our Past always shown us submissive to the usurpations of this people? Did not the very conditions upon which we were content to enter the confederacy, betray our sense of its value to our very safety?

Our sense of innate weakness,—our fears of foreign aggression,—making us only too eager for the Union; and, to secure its blessings, did we not consent to an inadequate representation in the Congress—the negro of the North having full recognition, as an integral of society, while your negro, far more moral and quite as black, being held to be three-fifths of a man only? It was a monstrous mistake and feebleness of policy—even if not that prompted us to this concession?—to yield in so vital a matter a point of the most essential value as assuring us of a due representation in that Legislation, which could only be just to us, in proportion to our numerical weight?—to suffer rival states to pass into an examination of our social elements in order to their condemnation? Pride, policy, patriotism, all, equally requires that we should enter the Confederacy, on equal conditions with the proudest, or not enter it at all! By that one concession, we not only lost representation, but made a fatal moral admission, by which we ourselves have provided in some degree, the sanction for the warfare upon our institutions. Has our vigilance increased, since that period, proportionately with our growing knowledge of our dangers? Have we ever compelled the Confederacy to yield us equal rights—an equal share in the inheritance; adequate results from our acquisitions of territory, or proper securities for what we do possess? When we have fought the battles and won the victories, have we ever been favored with any fair division of the spoils? Never!—and the power which is false & partial in the distribution of its awards, must necessarily despise the weakness, the baseness, the grievances of a section which submits so placidly to every usurpation. How absurd to suppose that a people who yield so readily, in respect to their material wealth and power, will make any proper struggle to maintain their fame, or assert their character, when these shall happen to be assaulted by the slanderer! And when the slanderer is bold enough to confront us with his inventions—when, face to face, he blackens us at once to ourselves and to the world, do you not see that his audacity argues something more than his hostility? Do you not see that, when Hate grows into open evidence, the enemy is prepared to gratify all his passions?—that, having so far presumed upon our imbecility as to spit his scorn and venom into our very faces, he feels sure of his power to destroy! That the time rapidly approaches when he will seek to carry out all his purposes into action; and that, having denounced our institutions, he has prepared to raze them to the ground with violence! He argues for the future from what you have suffered him to gain already in the past. He has gained the religious parties of the country. He has destroyed the ancient party organizations, which, selfishly constituted always, are necessarily conservative in character. He has obtained the mastery in Congress and exults with the sense of a power which can no longer be arrested by mere legislation. He repudiates the federal compact, the Constitution. What remains, but his own will, to put to the test <u>his</u> resources and <u>your</u> courage? There is no check now upon the dominant abolition Party in Congress or in the Northern States, save in its own will, & that will, is now maddened into an exulting confidence in its own strength, which the slanders and insults of Sumner have shown to you, has no sort of respect for yours. Do you flatter yourselves with the notion that Courts and Congresses can do anything for a minority when a majority controls the one and publicly scorns the other? When a person shall take you by the beard & void his saliva into your face, do you doubt that if his mood so prompts him, he will hurl you to the earth and set his foot upon your neck! Do you not see that he has reached the logical conclusion, in his thoughts, that he may do so with impunity!

There is no mystery in this audacity, as there is no doubt in this argument. His courage comes from our submissions; his insolence from our forbearances; his judgment, upon our character, upon our own indifference to honorable fame! Having ceased to write or to read our own histories—having yielded rights and reputations equally to the usurper—having surrendered to him the keeping of our records—delivered our young to his schooling—our archives substantially into his hands, as their best custodian—how ridiculous to dream of his justice and forbearance! What reason to hope that he will not betray his trusts—and destroy or falsify your records! He <u>has</u> done so: Has placed his manufactured chronicles in glaring contrast with ours, by which he has continued to build up an overshadowing reputation, at our expense, and solely in consequence of our supineness and indifference. By little and little—by regular degrees—he has sapped our history of all its cementing truths: and gaining audacity from impunity—confidence in his own inventions, from our failure to disprove & denounce them—fearless now of contradiction as of punishment—he pours out boldly the entire volume of his long accumulating slanders—the gatherings of more than thirty years and we are suddenly made dumb—struck with shame and wonder at the fabricated falsehoods which but few among us are properly prepared to refute!—

For thirty years have I been a witness of this insidious progress of our assailants—have seen the gradual growth of these spurious claims on the part of New England—especially of Massachusetts—in Congress, and out of it— exaggerative of her performances and in disparagement of ours;—claims not only unfounded in themselves, but admirably calculated, if not designed, to disparage and discredit the just rights & reputations of all other sections. The same grasping selfishness that strives to usurp, for the North, all the <u>material</u> benefits of the Union, has been equally busied in the appropriation of all its <u>moral</u> credits. Its pretensions, when not audaciously asserted, were adroitly insinuated, and, in the ignorance of the true history, in which we keep our people, and especially our young, there was hardly a person to be found, or but a few, even among our statesmen, in the whole South, to give them their proper refutation. Thus it was that Mr. Webster, in our own city, could tell us with fearless front, that <u>our</u> plains had been whitened with the bones of New Englanders perishing in battle, in defence of <u>our</u> liberties; and there was no patriot among us sufficiently familiar with the facts, to rise up and gently correct the amiable, but most preposterous assertion. This was alleged as a just motive for the general recognition of that affectionate sympathy, which South Carolina was required to feel for Massachusetts —that loving sister, who has been so moderate in all <u>her</u> claims, so generous in all <u>her</u> sacrifices, so genial in her assertions, so very liberal to all other parishes than her own!

Mr. Webster believed what he said—fully believed it. He had been taught in the same lying histories in which our children are taught. And we had taught him nothing better. He was an American politician; and, like most of his class, was compelled to take his local history at second hand. Would he had been as well informed in American, as in Greek and Roman Literature,—but, like most of his order, he undervalued it. Had he known better, he would have spoken otherwise: for the Head of a really great man, is always honest, however willful his passions, however weak his heart. And, on this subject of our American Politicians, I must be indulged in a few passing remarks. Our people seem to regard the politician as a sort of universal Genius. He is expected to know and to do every thing. He is employed for every thing, and all other classes of the community, are apt to be passed over, making way for him, even when the duties contemplated, & the offices filled, are such as belong especially to the Professions. This is not a matter to occasion surprise. It is the natural result of popular institutions in every country in which the people are untaught. But, the fact is, that our Politicians are rarely better educated than the great body of the people themselves. As a <u>whole</u>, regarding the entire Confederacy, they seldom rise into the rank of an educated class at all. Their acquisitions are wholly superficial. Audacity, which is the result of position in public affairs; the gift of gab, which is as much the fruit of flatulence, as thought;—the habit of dealing in eternal commonplaces—rant and fury signifying nothing;—these, but too commonly contribute the whole capital of the American politician. He is the Demigod of the stump, armed, instead of bolt and thunder, with sesquipedalianism and slang. In due degree as he acquires facility from exercise, and with his success in the popular field, will he abandon that of study. The popular orator is rarely a student in any department, not even in that of the law. His readings seldom extend beyond the columns of the party newspaper, and he gobbles up his law authorities solely from the last volume of Reports. He seldom fulfils the conditions prescribed by Bacon, as essential to the great man—reading for fullness, writing for accuracy, & speech for fluency. If he speaks to the people, he is apt to disparage learning & education all together. He fancies that such terms of disparagement, will be grateful to those to whom education has been denied. I have heard, for example, one of the Governors of a State, that he has denounced learning to the people, as one of the processes by which a people are Enslaved; spoken of Shakespeare as a fool; and assured his audience, that, for his own part, he never permitted such an absurdity as a Grammar or a Spelling book in his House. Yet this man has been spoken of as one of the obvious popular candidates for the Presidency, Vice Presidency, Speakership and Judgeship. Nay, look at Sumner himself, one of the best educated and most accomplished men in the Senate,—so far as a mere scholastic Education can accomplish, a vain & weak man; wanting in good sense in affairs, and at best, but a fluent rhetorician. What gross ignorance of propriety, to say nothing more, was his laboured & deliberate assault on South Carolina—how brutally demagogical, —in what bad taste, and with what total disregard, not merely of the parliamentary, but of the social proprieties! What absurdity to suppose that he could bring wisdom into, or impress his conviction of right and justice upon a circle, a large portion of which he should outrage on the very threshold, by malignant defamation. He should have known as a scholar if not as a Senator, that courtesy and forbearance were the first essentials to a hearing, in any field of council; and, whatever the faults, vices or shortcomings of South Carolina, past or present, she was there as an equal, having a right to respect, especially from those who aimed to address her ears in the language of exhortation & wisdom. And for these only objects, proper counsel, legislative wisdom, harmony, union, justice,—were these Senators assembled. What motive could prompt this wretched man to employ such language as should defeat these objects—prevent wisdom—baffle counsel—disturb harmony—destroy union? What but Demagoguism? His appeal was not to the wisdom of the Senate House—it was to the insane faction—brutal and malignant, by whom he was sustained in political power. He argued thus: "—What I say shall goad the people whom my people hate. I will sting; I will wound; I will fill the wound with venom. I will prove that I can deal in Philippics, like Demosthenes, even though I have to appropriate from Demosthenes. Thus I shall win the admiration of my people, for I shall only represent that malignity which is their very life. Nay, shall I not, where we are now strong enough to destroy, spit our scorn upon the victims, whom we have bound and made ready for the sacrifice!" Here, you have the whole secret of Mr. Sumner's moral & policy on this occasion; and it declares for that vulgar sort of political education which is the only great essential for political life. And thus it is, that the demagogue trifles with the life of a nation, as ignorantly and recklessly as the child who fires the match above the magazine, never once dreaming of the explosion. And this poor, weak, vain creature, with just enough of smartness and learning to be vain, & just enough of human passion to be malignant, madly goads the passions of a whole people into phrenzy, without cause, without provocation, & fancies that there will be no victim demanded for expiation. How little, with all his reading in Greek and Roman lore, had he learned to estimate that powerful spirit which he audaciously invoked with taunts, and scorn, & falsehood!—Yes, had he studied well, in the history of that fierce democracy—

> "Which shook the arsenal, & fulmined over Greece,
> From Macedon to Artaxerxes throne,"—

He would have trembled at the thought of provoking to rage & wrath, a power more terrible than that of the lion, in his jungle, goaded by the shouts & stones of the Arab from the rocks! And a more fearful democracy than any that Greece ever knew, is here!—wild with the sense of a hitherto inexperienced liberty;—exulting in the conviction of a power totally unrestrainable by argument;—growing in prosperity beyond all law; and heeding the serenest wisdom,—the most perfect justice,—the most loving sympathy, for its becoming coercion. South Carolina as a State, or people;—as a subject, moral or historical—was in no way involved in the issue before the Senate. She was dragged into it by the head and shoulders;—brought in, like the blind Samson, to make sport for the howling Philistines; and like him, she was to bring down the house about their ears! Is any body simple enough to suppose that the violent scene which followed, was merely a strife between two individuals?—a brawl of persons, simply, involving no other issues & considerations than their single hates and & passions? If such, surely, how is it that it has roused the whole country, North and South, into such a fever of excitement as absolutely forbids thought and mocks all judgment? The individuals concerned are nothing here, to the deep moral issues which they represent. They declare only the gradual progress, from words to blows—from speech to action—of that terrible & unhappy strife of sections, which has now been breeding bad blood among us for more than a quarter of a century. We are only reaching a natural result, from the operation of well known causes. It is the beginning of the war. It is a revolution which is already in progress from the terrible throes of which we are destined to see arise a monstrous phantom, clothed with hissing serpents, breathing the pollution of blood, and speeding on fiery winds and wings, on its mission of Carnage and Havoc. Can you doubt that, had the chastisement of Sumner taken place in the House, rather than the Senate, the fight would have become pell-mell; and a scene of butchery must have followed, in which the Capital, and the Confederacy, would have gone down, in a storm of violence, that would have torn the whole Country with convulsions? Do you not see that opinion, in House and Senate, on this affair, and I may add, throughout the Confederacy, is wholly determined by the sections which each party represents? Suppose, then, these sections, or any great body of their respective peoples, to have been brought together, and confronting each other, and do you doubt, that the language which made Brooks fall upon Sumner, would, in like manner, have brought their congregated storms—and to blows? What less could we expect? Here, but a little while ago, we were all in a lively state of apprehension, lest the contemptuous dismissal of Mr. Crompton would move Great Britain to a declaration of War. And shall such slight show of disrespect, prompt a great nation to War—to a war which would injure all her commerce, millions in money, the lives of thousands, and perhaps her own continued existence as a living Power;—and shall we delude ourselves with the idea that such a war of bitter words and malignant passions, as now divides North and South, can be carried on for 30 years, nor realize its bitter fruits in blows? Shall a whole people be fed, for near half a century upon tiger's meat, seasoned with vipers' venom, nor raven like the one, nor sting fatally, like the other! And this is the daily food which Demagoguism serves up to the whole nation; and this Demagoguism is now our only Commissary! It supercedes the calm judgment, the independent mind. It crawls, or leaps, into all the departments. No place is secure. It has the agility of the cat, the impudence of the monkey, and, never scrupling at a somerset, it passes over the heads of the true men, into all the high places of the country. As all places may be made to contribute its agencies for attaining political power, so it eagerly grasps at all in turn. None is too high, none too sacred, or exacting, for its presumption. It will condescend to prescribe for Letters and the arts. It will take charge of morals and education;—will head the charitable society; become a leader in the church; a regent of the University; and the power which it will thus acquire, in these several and widely dissimilar fields, it will readily employ, in political barter, for its own further elevation! Of its training and education for either, you have all a sufficient idea. If Mr. Webster's knowledge of domestic history was so slight as to lead him to commit the most serious mistakes, in matters which really need but little investigation;—if Mr. Sumner, whose education, in school and college, was even superior to that of Mr. Webster;—should show himself equally prone to follow the same blind guidance;—what must be the deficiency of the ordinary politician! His knowledge, or rather his want of knowledge, it would be difficult to describe. His training generally—ignoring books, and patient study—has been mostly among men; and, unhappily, chiefly among those classes of men, who are apt rather to resent education as an impertinence, reflecting on their own deficiencies, than to welcome it as a power demanded for their protection. At best, he associates with but very few whose standards of education lie sufficiently high, to compel, or to counsel him, in turn, to become a student. He is the last person in the world, to rise to that serene moral prudence which men call wisdom—which is the great necessity of society in times of exigency like the present; and he is just as little capable, in ordinary times, to meet the exigencies of any agreement which not only demands research, but requires, that the Debater shall use, by a natural motion of his mind, from the mere details of the Fact, to the Secret, life-giving principle, or idea, by which all human events must be informed. Shall you wonder where the training is so unexacting, and the education so vulgar, that the public men of the times so generally fail to know even the mere facts in our condition, and show themselves so miserably unequal to all the philosophies which grow out of them! Shall we reproach Webster or Sumner with grievance? Have we any right to do so? Have we, ourselves, ever insisted upon proper standards of wisdom & knowledge among our public men? Do we not elect them through the newest caprices. Are we any wiser ourselves? Would the slanders of Sumner be uttered in 1856, had they been silenced by prompt and able refutation in 1830—for just so long have they been accumulating! No! We may reproach this man for malignity, but not ignorance! We have suffered the slanders which he only repeats at secondhand, to run the circle with the sun—to find their way into a thousand circles, and ten thousand volumes. Nay, we have put these very volumes into the hands of our children, and have summoned from abroad, as their teachers, those persons who have studied in no other books, and who cannot now be taught to yield their faith in them, to our, & to better authorities.

This is <u>our</u> history, my friends. The slanders of Sumner do not touch our Past at all. The shame and discredit are not with our ancestry. They are with us! Had we not been careless of our trusts, heedless of our duties and securities, there had been no reproach upon our Past. The reptile had never dared to crawl upon our altars; to smutch or to befoul them, but that we had abandoned them to the free invasion of any reptile! It is a great mistake, let me tell you, to say or to suppose, that our histories—such as would amply suffice for our defence— have been unwritten. This is a serious wrong done to our historians—the fruit of that gross ignorance of what <u>has</u> been done among us, which is perpetually showing itself in presumptuous assertion: The histories of South Carolina, are as full and satisfactory, comprehensive & complete, as those of any State in the Union. They are more so than most. With Lining, Milligan, and Chalmers, Oldmixon & Glen; Archdale, Lawson, Adair and Bartram; Hewatt and others, as contained in the useful collection of Carroll, Drayton, Moultrie, Ramsay and Mills; Johnson & sundry more, we have an almost perfect library, adequate to all our purposes, whether to teach our own people, or to confound our enemies. It is not the Histories that we lack, but the readers of them. I do not say that these Histories are perfect—are such as we <u>ought</u> to have, and <u>might</u> have. The rarely rise above the rank of chroniclers—are, simply, so many storehouses of fact—raw materials—which more elaborate Historians may shape to symmetry, and resolve into a philosophical narrative at some future day. But such is the character of nearly all of our state and colonial Histories. In fact, though we may boast some few picturesque historians who have written with taste, spirit, and considerable art, we have none, any where, who have ever risen to a full, just, philosophical analysis of the chronicles in which the fact and its proper commentary have been brought together in harmonious relation; all this remains to be done, & can only be done, when a proper sense of the necessity of such works shall become as apparent to communities as to individuals. South Carolina has been rather fortunate in her Historians, speaking of them with regard to the rather low standards of Historical writing, which prevailed in the country until a very recent period. Hewatt's History is well written; tolerably full, and, barring certain biases of sect and birth, tolerably just and accurate. His mistakes are mostly sectarian & political, and do not rise into perversions. The same merit may be accorded to Ramsay, who was a good writer and full of his subject. The other works are all copious as chronicles, though we need much of our colonial history, which must be drawn from foreign archives. If these books are out of print, they are all, fortunately, extant; may be supplied to any extent, and would be supplied whenever the public desire should demand them;—but, for thirty years, to my knowledge, there has been neither desire nor demand!

And yet, my friends, we, of Carolina, are reputed to be very fond lovers of our country. Hearken to our own assertions, and no people ever cherished a more devout reverence for the homes in which their lot has been cast—the soil which gave them birth, or the virtues by which it has been distinguished. Is this boast true? What are the tests of the true Patriotism?—that sentiment, of the soul, rather than the mind—which Schlegel has so happily styled "the glorious fault" of a people! We must first be sure that it is a legitimate sentiment;   that it is born, not of our own feeble, individual vanity, but of a true veneration—a just sense of what is really great and noble in the deeds of our ancestry;—and this right appreciation of their real virtues—not their mere names, or wealth, or social position—implies, in the first place, that we should know perfectly what they have done! We must preserve the record of their deeds as religiously as we preserve the titles to their estates in character—they constitute <u>our</u> estates in character. We must show ourselves capable of a just valuation of their principles and exhibit a laudable determination to emulate their performances—on all occasions, & in every field, whenever an honorable opportunity shall offer. The same law prevails with the community as with the Individual. What a mockery is that man who boasts of the deeds of a sire, yet does nothing of himself. We naturally doubt his legitimacy. We see, and feel, in the very virtues of the father, a terrible sarcasm upon the incompetence of the son. So with communities. They are required, if they would escape shame, not only to maintain, but to add to the capital of character which they inherit from the Past!

Tried by these Severe, but just & inevitable standards, how, my friends, will our Patriotism endure the test? I fear! I fear!—For, briefly to recapitulate, how very few among us are really familiar with the full histories of our State & people; how few know, or exhibit any desire to know, what are the real facts in their career. How many, even among our statesmen & Politicians,—who ought to know every thing according to their own & the vulgar estimate,—show themselves grossly ignorant of their deeds. We live on,—gluttonously, as it were—in the full enjoyment of the wonderful blessings of civil & religious Liberty which they won for us, through blood & trial, yet we not only know nothing of their fortunes, but are rapidly forgetting their very names. If we hear of them at all, it is in the false & fraudulent narratives of those who are hostile to <u>our</u> Institutions, and vainglorious of their own. Anything besides comes to us only in the mouthing declamatory harangues, at certain periods of self glorification, in which the orator escapes contempt and censure, only because of the deeper cloud that darkens the minds & memories of his audience. I have said that our records, even, in most of the Southern States, are to be sought for in the archives of foreign nations. There are some honorable exceptions. Georgia and Louisiana have both appropriated largely to this object; and these two states are largely in possession of great collections of manuscripts illustrating their colonial periods. It is in resources of this sort that our State remains deficient. Now, my friends, our debt, State and city together, is about ten millions of dollars—to be soon increased. This vast amount has been mostly spent in mere material projects—in rail roads, public buildings and munitions of war. Ten or fifteen thousand dollars would suffice to complete our records and give us an ample history of our State & people;—yet such an appropriation, which would put us in possession of a sufficient chronicle of all our sectional past,—which might enable us forever to silence the cavils of our enemies on this score—would be thought a great waste of money! What, to the mere utilitarian, is fame, and character, & the honorable record of ancestral deeds & glory? Our knowledge of the personal histories of the great and brave men who fought our battles in field & cabinet, even when of our immediate precinct, are mostly traditional. We speak of them only in vague & general phrases which, in process of time, because of our ignorance of details, must lose all their significance. Boasting of our warriors and statesmen, as second to none—and proud as we profess ourselves to be of their deeds and powers, we yet suffer them to pass off from the stage of action, with few or no plaudits and never a trophy! It is a mournful retrospect, that of our losses, during the last twenty years. Calhoun, Harper, McDuffie, Legare, Hayne—but why enumerate? The laborious struggle to raise a monument to Calhoun—a labour now devolved upon our women—having failed in all other hands—is conclusive against the hope of paying tribute to any other names! And the early, as well as the modern period is equally without its memorials. Gadsden, Rutledge, Pinckney, Marion, Moultrie Sumter,—and how many more to whom we owe unextinguishable debts of love and gratitude, all sleep in unhonored & almost unknown graves. Statesmen succeed to statesmen, heroes to heroes, and one set of names soon obliterates all the impressions of the preceding. It is the policy of demagoguism that it should be so. If we duly remember the past, and what great men have been among us—how should we tolerate the present? We can scarcely in the whole South, point to a single monument—<u>to a native</u>—reared by our hands, in proof of our veneration! I know of but two or three any where and they are all dedicated to foreigners—a fact which would seem to argue a singular jealousy of all native eminence or a deficiency of all native worth!

I confess to you, my friends, I have very little faith in the patriotism which exhibits such profound indifference. The omission would seem to show that, when we boast of our fathers, we do so, not because we honour them, but because we thus derive honour for ourselves. It is not to yield them homage, but to assert our own possessions. It is not the tribute of reverence, but the cunning of self-esteem. It is our egotism, not our gratitude that makes us eloquent. They have made for us a noble capital of character, among the nations, upon which we are not unwilling to speculate. It is precisely as if the son should brag of the inheritance left him by the Sire, while he forgets to raise the simplest headstone over the old man's grave!

Our patriotic boasting, lacking as it does, in an essential knowledge of the subject—lacking in the desire to know,—failing in all the proofs of a real veneration, is liable to the same suspicion.

Had Charles Sumner, my friends, been a wise man—assuming the possibility that wisdom should even be coupled with malignity—he would have addressed his attack to our <u>present</u>, rather than our <u>past</u>! He would have struck at our <u>living</u>, rather than our <u>dead</u>. The one might have been found vulnerable enough; the others are unassailable. They shine apart, superior to the storm, above the cloud, in the serene atmosphere of a calm bright sky, the guiding lights of men and nations! They sit, shrined each, in the atmosphere of a true fame, among the great prophet minds of all humanity, in all the periods of time! Their work was done, we have sufficient proof, well and adequately, according to the necessities of their periods and to the full use of all the materials which had been confided to their keeping. They ranked, while they lived, with the very noblest of European virtues! Intellectually they were unashamed by any comparison with the very ablest of European minds. Confining our survey to South Carolina only, I affirm, without fear of contradiction, that, whether in camp or council, in field or leaguer, in deliberate resolve, or in the fervid storms of action, her contributions to the national capital of greatness, were not only equal to those of any of her sister colonies, & superior to most, but equal to the possessions of a like kind in any of the States of Europe! England had no wiser councilors, nor firmer patriots, no persons better practiced in affairs than the Rutledges, the Gadsdens, the Pinckneys, the Middletons and the Laurenses of that day in Carolina; nor braver, nor more skilful soldiers, than her Moultries, Marions, Sumters, Pickenses and others, whom I need not catalogue. Their deeds are ineradicably on record, secure equally against the dull hoof of the ass, and the slimy trail of the reptile!

Would that our Present were quite as certain as our Past; that we could look around us and be sure of great spirits close at hand, calmly harnessing themselves for those conflicts which shall try men's souls:—sworn only to their country, and superior to the sleek service of party and selfish obligations: sworn only to the South—knowing no party, but that of their native soil, and having but one article of faith—"I know but the South & the South in danger!" Let us hope & pray that the occasion will find the souls which shall be adequate to the exigencies!—That the Hour will bring the man;—that God has not denied, to our living races, the soul & the strength, the courage & the Genius, which are necessary to our safety and duration. But has not our lachesse given us good reason for apprehension? How is it that we are now conscious, for the first time, of the foul shame and reproach cast upon our altars? The attack of Charles Sumner was an old story, repeated at second hand, from the pages of Lorenzo Sabine, and repeated by a thousand other assailants! Why does it awaken an indignation now? For ten years this book of Sabine has been on record; a book well written, with force, spirit, cunning; with an ingenious and plausible array of partial facts;—the argument, in short, of a subtle advocate, having a selfish & sectional object—a performance very far superior, in every essential of strength, subtlety and eloquence, to the labored & flatulent speech of Sumner. Shall it be said that we knew nothing of this book? Ah! my friends, we should have known! The world requires of every people that degree of curiosity: jealousy, study, and an eager sense of what is due to its safety, that it shall keep pace with events & duly inform itself of all the purposes of human intelligence. This is the condition of civilization, & so of safety. Civilization itself means this, and nothing less than this! Shall the sapper work against our defenses for years, and shall we sing on gaily, even when the towers are toppling about our heads? Shall we dance and drink, like Belshazzar, while Fate writes the doom of fire upon our walls?—That we lack in this quickening curiosity of thought; that we lack in this jealous vigilance of watch; that we drowse & dream, when the imminent danger demands the spur of a zealous energy; is the very search by which the assailant is moved to attempt our destruction! This is the true Secret, which lies at the bottom of all national overthrow! A people first sinks into imbecility, lulled perhaps by a Syren music, while the Serpent turns himself about their throats! If we can only be beguiled to drowse, the rest is easy! You will say, can these dangers be feared, simply as we show ourselves ignorant of a book. No! But because of certain supineness, no matter what the cause, which keeps us heedless & ignorant equally of books and men. Ignorance of books, after the world became possessed by [word illegible] was akin to death. Books now contain all the world's wisdom of six thousand years. They are the levers which shake empires; which overturn dynasties, & make and unmake republics. Shall we use them for our defense, or leave them solely to our enemies, a people that shows itself heedless of books, and supposes that there are any powers superior, is a people preparing to lay their own right arms upon the block; to lose arms and head,—strength, courage, everything, which is necessary to a nation's safety. You hear men complain that we lack energy and enterprise. This is our own daily complaint. We say the grass grows about our footsteps and we then complain only with reference to failing arts, and mere material objects. But this lack of enterprise is first due to our intellectual inactivity;—to the fact that we have lost curiosity, zeal, faith, enthusiasm, and that eager impulse to performance, which are needed to set all human wheels in motion. Energy and action are not original motors. They spring from deeper sources in the soul and mind; in the will, the faith, the courage, the intelligence;—from the sympathies, and affections, from the hopes, and aims, and imaginations;—and they are active only in degree, as the mental and moral qualities are in wholesome exercise. Where these are wanting, there is no performance, and but little virtue of any value. All the characteristics perish from their non application to daily necessities; & every idler among us is a public enemy. No matter how justly a people may think or feel; if they lack her penance, faith & feeling are but dry sticks which can never bear bud or blossom. The virtues are so many frauds. The religion is a cheat. It is under like laws, then, no matter what the education, no matter what the amount of popular intelligence, they must fail of wisdom, unless these possessions are applied to the daily uses of the race. The human mind, like a fountain, is commanded to give out, even as it takes in; or, like the fountain, it fails from its own stagnation; so, briefly, energy and enterprise, work, industry, in all the departments, are the only proofs of intellect, patriotism & virtue, as they are the great essentials of continued life & security. When you see a lack of enterprise among a people it signifies first a lack of intelligence & moral. That quickening curiosity which conduct one class of people to Books, the Fine arts, the Sciences, is grounded in the same moral necessities which conduct another class to trade, commerce, and mechanical industry. The mind furnishes the <u>motor</u>, in all the cases, through each individual takes the direction which his peculiar endowment will suggest. When, therefore, you behold a people grown sluggards in the race, you may feel very sure that they are sluggish in intellect—that their virtues are feeble as their will—dead or dying out;—and that they must succumb before any stirring competitor in the great race for power! The world is so constituted as to need the cumulative energies of <u>all</u> its people, commencing together in action—mutually depending—mutually giving and receiving. We can spare none of their agencies—waste none—admit none to escape from duty; for the bounty of God justifies no profligacy of resources, and he gives us no faculties to be laid away in lavender. Where any considerable portion of the people, in any community, show themselves sluggish, indifferent, inactive, unperforming, that people is doomed! The decree is final! "Why cumbereth it the ground? Cut it down and cast it into the fire!"

Either we have men of learning and education among us, or we have not? If we have, why should we get our histories and teachers from strangers? And if our own men can, and do, write our histories, why do we not read them? That <u>they</u> should neither write, nor <u>we</u> read, argues some singular deficiency in our mental resources, or a worse deficiency in our morals! But we boast of the men! We have them! We point proudly to their names, if not to their monuments, and we say— 'they are ours!' Then, my friends, the failures must be in us—us only! Our select men <u>have</u> done their duty. Where, then, are we?

I have said that this attack of Sumner was an old story, thrice baked meats from the oven of Lorenzo Sabine. But the same style of assault has been a thousand times repeated, in a thousand ways, by the Northern Press. Why did Sabine's and all other publications fail to arrest our attention and provoke our anger. It will be said, that we knew nothing of Sabine & the rest. There, my friends, is the mischief. We should have known. As a people we read too little; and so as long as the fabricated chronicles were confined to books only, they may have continued in circulation for half a century more, without moving our indignation. It is only when the living voice of the accuser, rolls out from the dome of the Capital, like a midnight tocsin, and compels us to hear, and makes us feel that everybody else must hear, that we become suddenly conscious that our reputation is in danger. It is unhappily only through our bugles of demagoguism, that we hear any thing. That we do not read is due to the same wretched causes which have moved us to loathe work, and shrink from enterprise. This in false notions of society. Here & there, only, do we see some single laborer, buried in his books, and pursuing his secret studies at great self sacrifice, in cell or studio, and we scorn him for his self sacrificing homage to wisdom in the shade. The community <u>taboos</u> himself and his labors. He must be a blockhead to yield up present distinction, worldly gain, and sensual delights, in laborious searches into the abstract & the obscure. And he is generally odious—our very instincts make him so,—since his practice reproaches our own. Our social standards are quite too low to compel study among our governing minds. We lack books. There is hardly a good library in our State,—none adequate to the wants of the student. We do not keep pace with the working mind of Europe or America. We are behind our time. We do not feel that goad of mental necessity, which is the only true spring of noble and honorable enterprise. Had we this, not only should we have known of the steady progress of slanderous opinion against us, but we should have been prepared to set our foot upon it, with triumphant refutation. But secure in our invincible self esteem,—our Chinese Wall—which shuts us in, equally from the Barbarians,— and ourselves, we never troubled ourselves on the subject of our real reputation, or the duties which it entailed upon us.

Meanwhile the book of Sabine was working its way, insidiously, in all other regions in preoccupying the public mind against us, and encouraging the assailants of our institutions, according as they become impressed with our imbecility. At the North, everybody reads: the Carman on his cart; the Hackman on his box; the pavior along the highways, in every moment of interval snatched from labour. And this is one of the great secrets of their restless energies, of their indomitable enterprise, of their reckless progress, which sets all present possessions upon a high cast of the die, fearless of loss, in the terrible intensity of their thirst for new acquisitions. And hearing nothing of our claims from ourselves, they all drank in, as so much law and gospel, the fictions of our enemies; these were grateful, as they promised them an easy conquest over us in that conflict which now certainly impends. When Sumner assailed the honour and performance of Revolutionary Carolina, it was only with such supposed facts as had been already made familiar to all the peoples north of the Hudson. We taught them nothing truer, or better. We left their tuition wholly to our assailants, & they are now so thoroughly drilled in the lying chronicles, that they feel outraged by every attempt to lesson them in the true. Nobody there ever thinks to question the facts in these false histories. We had never tasked ourselves, as a people, for their proper refutation, and the verdict went against us by default; and but for the gross publicity which attends all the proceedings of Congress, we should have continued to stroke our beards, with the complacency of a people, satisfied that, in all the world, there was nobody to take us by the beard. For one, I tell you frankly, I rejoice in the attack of Sumner. It has helped to arouse us; to waken us to indignation; to goad our self esteem into exercise, while working on vanity; to make us feel that we are <u>not</u> secure;—that there is no security for sloth and indifference, while all the world is heaving with the unrighteousness, daily, of new volcanic births. Another source of my satisfaction, is in this: it will prompt such a general re-examination of our history, as will enable us to convict, and burn, the false & rascally volumes in which we too much teach our young; will enable us to sift & expose the fraudulent pretensions to performance, on the part of Sections of our country, the patriotism & achievement of which have been always & equally without foundation. Our own periodicals would have done this; our own writers. But these were allowed to perish. There was never an author in South Carolina, that ever received a dollar from any local publication—never a publication that did not ruin its publisher. We suffered the local intellect, in the fields of art and literature to be every where ignored; to toil without reward in money or recompense in fame. We encountered all its claims with denial; its performances with contempt & sneer: though in all such cases we must have known that a most unselfish patriotism lay at the bottom of every such enterprise. I, myself, have lost more than ten thousand dollars, in frequent efforts to establish and sustain our periodicals, as vehicles for the local intellect! And this intellect was equal to all our mental, & moral, & social necessities, in every department. We might have had as ripe a scholarship, as profound a wisdom, as large & generous a philosophy, and as ideal development in art, equal to any in the world, had we but cherished the gifts of genius and the generous impulses of patriotism, which have been in our possession from the first. Training, only, & time, were needed for the full development of these gifts. But there was no motive to be trained; for there was no appreciation; and the demand, by inevitable laws, must always regulate the supply. And so, failure has been the invariable fortune of all attempts at domestic art or authorship. We had no faith in our genius, an error which began even before the Revolution, making us rather prefer an eccentric adventurer like Lee, or a sluggish intellect like Lincoln, to lead our armies, than any one of the brilliant array of native Partisan warriors, such as were furnished by every Section of the State. This miserable Provincialism is the source of some of our worst mishaps, as of some of our grossest absurdities. It makes us reject and despise the native for the foreign; though the one strives in our battles, & the other openly toils for our destruction. Thus we run after this foreign lecturer, who is <u>passe</u> in his own province, fills his pockets with our money, pampers at our feasts & with our praises, and he goes away to laugh at or defame us. And in degree as we are sycophant to the foreigner, are we insolent to the native. One of our own distinguished citizens who had been himself too much dismayed by this provincialism, suffered himself some years ago to say sneeringly in one of our periodicals, that English literature was good enough for us. He never dreamed of the obvious retort. So, also, was English criticism: & the [Southern] Review itself was, accordingly, an impertinence. I tell you boldly that in this little city, we have had genius in every department, equal to any in this Confederacy, but we have lacked in the self respect to recognize and to assert it. Ours are, in fact, a greatly and variously endowed people, who, with a proper ambition might occupy triumphantly every department. But we lack the proper faith in ourselves. I have heard a Southern artist say that he never allowed himself to read an American book. My answer was—'You do not, then, expect us to look at an American picture?' The native merchant & mechanic, in the same manner, will be very likely to suppose, that the Genius of the Nation is deficient in those fields which appeal to the higher tastes of civilization. He will be apt to say that the Fine Arts and General Literature must necessarily be of a superior grade in Europe than America. But what if I were to say, in reply, that such must be the case, also, with commercial and mechanical capacity. That would be held a great impertinence. Yet would it be more so than the first assumption. By what right does either of us suppose, that in our own crafts we are perfect—just what we should be—while, in that of our neighbor, nothing can be done or hoped for. What says right Reason on this subject! The law is, simply this: God leaves his people with an adequate endowment in <u>every</u> department, which is essential to the growth, the development and the securities of the race; and that the same family which produces the mechanic, is equally gifted to produce the great philosopher, warrior and Statesman—the great master, in every province of performance. We must believe in the race,— believe in one another. This is the first and great necessity. And this Faith is one which will produce its own fruits. We endow the Genius when we implore his succor. We create the art, when we crave its benefits. All that we need for this, is the appreciative sympathies which shall always be on the alert to know what each is doing, of a public concern, and to feel laudably interested in his progress. It is only a few years ago, that one of our own painters, a man highly honoured, of exquisite tastes and talents, one indeed, to whom you have recently done much honours—said to me—"Ah. Sir, my friends do not even come to <u>see</u> my pictures. I do not ask them <u>to buy</u>; but they do not care <u>to look</u>. They care nothing whether I paint or not." And yet this curious anxiety, this appreciative sympathy, are especially necessary for all those who toil for the glorious rewards of Fame! And if society would not interfere to corrupt the genius, he would finally triumph over society. The individual mind, the peculiar endowment especially, must especially beware of the enslaving influences of society. And for the sake of the young who may hear me, I must report one of the most fortunate discoveries of my own life. I discovered, at an early period, that an able bodied white man of 21, six feet high, and of strong abstemiousness, could live & grow fat on 12 bushels & a half per annum. I do not know but that this is the greatest of the discoveries of my life. For what did it teach me. The facility with which life might be maintained, and the capacity for honorable exercise & enterprise he urged to its utmost, within the smallest concession to convention. If it be so easy and so cheap for us to live, why should I sacrifice or surrender, a single impulse of my soul, a single thought of my mind, a single feeling of my heart, to any of the requisitions of society. These are more precious to me than life. They are life. Why should I duck my beaver to pretension; why be a parasite to the great: why forego the direction of mood or mind, even as God seemed to decree that they should work. Individual and mental independence, will make us heedless of the awards of society. The loss is to society itself. If we deny these awards to the man of Genius how shall we possess its fruits? We turn away incredulous, with ill-conceived scorn from the modest worker in arts and letters, as if his successes, which would crown our state with triumphs, would be disparaging to our own individual stature. Ah! my friends, for otherwise was it with the moral of the Athenians. Let us look back some two thousand years. It is the time of Pericles. The Pantheon had been but lately built. It is already the glory of Athens. Art already triumphs, not merely in the fostering care of the State, but in the affections of its people. And Phidias is the great Sculptor of the time. It has been bruited every where that he is about to commence a new achievement. It is, at first, a winged whisper throughout the city, that echoes along the walls, and grows gradually into a deep murmur that makes its way, through porch and hall, into court and chamber. It is said that the great sculptor has been busied secretly, modelling on a new subject, in his little studio, in the narrow lane that runs down west from the Acropolis. It is known that he has just received a huge and beautiful block from the pure white marbles of Pentelicus. There is a report, also, that large supplies of gold and ivory have been sent him from the treasury of the State, and Pericles himself, has seen to the delivery of these costly materials, at the studio of the artist. Nay, that great statesman himself, has been secretly closeted, for hours with the Sculptor, and keen eyes have noted that on these visits, Aspasia did not accompany the statesman: but it was observed that she lingered waiting his return at the porch of her dwelling, and flew eagerly as he came, anxious for his tidings. This said, accordingly, that the work is not yet sufficiently advanced, —the model not sufficiently developed for the conception,—to be submitted to the Eyes of one, to whom the graces themselves defer as an authority. Nay, more;—there is, today, a rumour, that Sophocles, himself, and the young Euripides, have both been called into consultation with Pericles and the sculptor; and it is supposed that some nice aesthetical questions, which are also mythological, are under discussion. What are these questions? What daring thing is Phidias about to attempt. What grand subject hath he chance to idealize; and which of the powerful Gods of Hellas is he about to lift among the constellations of the Pantheon? Will nobody tell us? Such is the cry! The people are in a ferment. They run hither and thither. They forget all external cares. <u>This</u> concerns the state, the individual; the glory of Athens, the honour of their Gods & Greece! They will give worlds to know. Even Ceravucius [?], the millionaire and in some respects the miser, has attempted bribes. One has heard it from another, who has heard it from a third, who got it from fountainhead, that he has offered a thousand drachmas to Cyllenas, one of the favorite workmen of Phidias, who confessed that his integrity was not above the bribe, but added, with tears in his eyes, that he knew nothing; that Phidias alone had been working upon the new subject, which none of the apprentices had been permitted to behold. This swells the mystery. What is the subject which the sculptor will suffer no vulgar eye to see, no 'prentice hand to touch?—None to know, save Pericles, & the two Dramatic Poets. Some of the chief men of the city, sharing the curiosity of the people, go to Pericles. But he smiles pleasantly as he replies—"My friends, I can now tell you nothing. But it is for all of us to thank the Gods, that they suffer us to live at the same time with a Genius, who can teach us a just conception of the their own divine attributes!"

It is not the city only. The grove & the academy are alive with the inquiry. What is the question which requires Phidias & Pericles, Sophocles & Euripides, to discuss together, and in such privacy; "Can it be any question touching the attributes of the unknown Gods?"

Here the Priesthood take the alarm, and look dubiously towards the studio of the daring Sculptor. They know that he is daring,—for he has the audacity of

Genius,—but they also know that he is protected by Pericles, and that, tho' he may not exactly subscribe to the creed which they teach, yet has a profound veneration of his own—is of a devout religious nature, with all his audacity; and that the people have quite as sound a faith in <u>his</u> virtue as in theirs. For these reasons they dare not touch him. "Yet must he beware!"

Then the discussion turns upon the probable material out of which the <u>chef d'oeuvre</u> is to be wrought. Is it to be of marble? There is that new block from the masses of Pentelicus!—Or, is it to be Chryselephantine—the costly combination of gold & ivory, which it is well known that Phidias affects; though, even in that day, the style & material were subjects of question among the art legitimates as it is still in ours?

No matter what the subject or material, it has thrown all Athens into a delightful fever of curiosity and anticipation. The whole people, as with one heart, feel that they are about to achieve, through one of their own sons, a new triumph over all the nations of the Earth.

Do we, Carolinians, ever rise to such a feeling? Ah! my friends, that question involves the necessity of a close and searching analysis of our social moral, which, with a few clues, I must leave to your own thoughts rather than my solutions. Suffice it that the great secret of Athens, lay in her mental independence! She made her own books—her own arts; had her own histories, and encouraged her own genius, in every department, esteeming the great poet, dramatist & painter, as fully as she did the great Politician, engineer or Banker. She did not, accordingly, have to wait upon opinion from abroad. She <u>made</u> opinion; not only for home, but for all the world! Her people, the very humblest and meanest, were capable. Through her home education, of detecting the slightest trippings,—whether in phrase, grammar or pronunciation of the popular orator and actor: and the hisses of Demos were the fruits of a criterion which never took its cue from the mutual admiration society; a paltry clique, or a bigoted circle of dilettante. They were the masters in all the provinces, and simply because of that earnest, mental enthusiasm,—that loving curiosity of temperament,—which lost itself perpetually in the subject of its study, and found its own genuine nature, most justly developed, by its objective inquiries into the nature of all topics which could, in any way, appeal to the Intellectual Seeker. The foreigner came among the Athenians, not to lord it, but to receive the law;—to learn, not to leer! They were not simply a smart, clever, showy people, easily deviated by trifles, and living in trifles only. They aimed at great, not petty triumphs. They were, in brief, an emulous, performing people—full of vivacity; graceful in play; have a full faith in their own mission; who seldom suffered the egotism of the individual to find its exercise at the cost of the race. They regarded the achievements of their great man, as so many contributions to the capital stock of the community; and never supposed, for a moment, that, in doing him honor, they were to forfeit any of their own personal proportions. Loving the performance, and glorifying in its greatness, they acquired, through mere sympathy, a personal share in the achievement; even as he who bows fervently in prayer, while the Prophet invokes the Deity, must partake of the blessing which his prayer shall win down from heaven! Athens, in its prime, was a city of but ten thousand houses, hardly much larger than ours, and not twice as populous: the whole state contained but two hundred thousand freemen to four hundred thousand slaves—but how large in the space which she occupies in the history of Greek civilization; how large her power even now, over the civilization of the world! The <u>Eye</u> of Greece, she was a soul to the universe! It was her sympathy with greatness, that made her great. That sympathy was the fuel that strengthened Phidias for his work, creating an Olympus for her, in the very market place! And Athens is about to be repaid, a thousandfold, for this loving sympathy with Genius. The work of Phidias is done—the great masterpiece—about to be uncovered—about to be inaugurated in the eyes of the people. Academies and schools are deserted. Shops are shut. Toil is forbidden. The drudge has respite. One of the grand Sabbath days of Society is appointed, when all have holiday; and the rulers of the tribe assemble, the castes, the classes, the orders, the professions; and Pericles marches at the head of the nobles and chief men! There, in that group, you see the two great surviving dramatic Poets: Euripides, the younger, with corrugated brows, great round prominent eyes, massive beard, & flowing waving hair like that of Milton. Equally salient of feature, with greater breadth of brow, prominent, aquiline nose, dilating nostril, well curled & oily beard, somewhat grizzly—darker of complexion, and of more grave contemplative aspects—Sophocles, his senior and superior, stands beside him; and as they walk apart, the lively impulsive people cry aloud their admiration;—for are not these the Poets—inspired—the chosen interpreters of the Gods? Oh! To behold that grand assembly, with the great of Greece all present! Who shall describe it. Yonder, you see is Pericles, that miracle of statesmen! He moves among the priesthood, and is habited like one of them. And there is Aspasia—a noble creature whom the moderns have slandered without knowing—who seems, this day, to unite the charms of Venus with the dignity of Minerva. Look at Alcibiades, at her side, in flowing robes, half borrowed from the Persian, rich & worn so gracefully, whose eager eye, and brave glances, already declare for that versatile genius, which was only cursed in its being born at so late a period, when Demagoguism had begun the overthrow of all the best Gods of Humanity & Greece. And near him stands a boy. Do you note that boy. He is but nine years old, and holding the hand of his Preceptor, Isaeus. That boy is the young Demosthenes. Who, at this moment, dreams of the voluminous thunders which are growing & gathering under that fair open brow of childhood—of those mighty Philippics, which are yet to roll like angry billows, rocking the very throne upon which sits the Macedonian despot, and moulding themselves into assailing armies, in those parted, smiling lips? But no, my friends. I am mistaken. The boy is <u>not</u> Demosthenes. Demosthenes is not yet born. He is not needed for his country so long as Pericles sways the destinies of Athens. But now, if the boy we look upon—warmed by the occasion—shall also grow inspired for achievement—shall feel as he beholds, the wings of a powerful enthusiasm growing as on <u>his</u> shoulders?—the mighty impulse swelling as his heart, stimulating him, with a generous ambition—eager to win their appreciative admiration, which, he sees, follows so fondly the great achievement—and, with the unconscious murmurs on his lips—"<u>Anch 'io son pittore!</u>" from that moment dedicating himself, his life, mind, soul, to some glorious art—Sculpture, Poetry, the Drama, Eloquence, Statesmanship or War! Oh! my friends, when we deny the tribute of our admiration to the achievement of our contemporaries, we cut off, from our own sons, the most powerful motives to great deeds—we stifle the generous impulses which swell the heart with patriotism, and make ambition one of the noblest virtues of the soul!

But the scene passes. There is a solemn music—itself a discourse of art, that seems specially to appeal to Heaven. This, too, is the work of a master. It is that of the great Timotheus, the musician of Miletus; he who added new strings to the Grecian cithara, and perfected the Lyre of the nation. Hissed, when he first appeared before the Athenians, he has nobly persevered, until he has succeeded to a complete triumph, at once over his art, and over the severest standards of Athenian taste and criticism. Now, they honour him with reverence. He is the <u>protégé</u> of Euripides. It was the dramatic Poet who first perceived the secret resources of his genius; sustained him against hostility, encouraged him to persevere: and who, now, with a satisfaction which he does not seek to conceal, beaming from every feature of his noble face, listens, rapt & wondering, to the glorious harmony, as rising into mightiest diapason, it rolls upward, shaking roof & rafter, as if by swelling billows of the sea! Silence,—and the ears of the great multitude, seem to fancy that they still hear the glorious chorus, as it melts away, and is smothered in the embrace of loving echoes. The hush is broken by the voice of Pericles. Such an oration—chaste, classical, original, and grand.—It is an essay on the Social Religion, as contradistinguished from that of the soul, though warmed by all its living virtues. It is Thought, born of Power suckled at the hearts of Beauty, clothed and attended by the graces, and borne upward, in Eagle flight, on the wings of Poetry and Eloquence. And the souls of that hushed multitude, are borne upwards with the orator: and they are all fitly moved and lifted; fitly won & subdued by sympathy and exultation, for the crowning scene which is to follow! Phidias, now, pale and sad of aspect, but with a rich spiritual luster gleaming from his eyes, emerges from the background. His thin lips quiver with his emotions, which, however keep him dumb. There is a murmur—only a murmur—as he appears, and he utters but a single sentence.—"To the Gods of Greece!"—and his hand waves, and the pulleys work.—the concealing curtains are drawn upwards and outwards,—and Silence, with electric shock, at once paralyzes the multitude. For a moment only! Then, with one choral burst, as of a single voice—but such a voice—a voice of the mountains & the Sea—they hail the new wonder of Athenian art. It is a God that speaks to their senses. It is a God that suddenly fills all their souls. It is the great colossus, in gold & ivory, of the Olympian Jupiter which they behold. Zeus, himself, with all his divine attributes, sits in majesty before him, even as he appears, solemn in council, before the assembled Deities, on the summits of Olympus!—Suddenly, then, Aphasia advances, and while Pericles grasps one hand of the Sculptor, and points upward with the other, she places a massive wreath upon his brows,—saying "Athens, glorying in the triumphs of her sons, this day, by my hands, crowns one of the noblest among them, with the cedar and laurel of Immortality. May the Gods of Hellas confirm, with their decree, this act of commemoration."—and even as she closed, [word missing] is a danger as [words missing] golden shields, in the sacrum—the Holy of Holies—the chamber [words missing].

Thus, my friends, was the Social Moral of Athens trained to perfection, to a generous ambition; to an eager sense of the Beautiful, & through the Beautiful, to the Grand, the Pure and the Eternal! Thus did the loving sympathy of her people, create the Sculptor, the Poet, the orator and statesman—and these, in turn, have perpetuated the glories of the race, in all the secure trophies of her wondrous arts. There is but one process by which to achieve these results and secure the same trophies. It is the love of a people—which has learned to discriminate justly, and to honor magnanimously the deserving objects—which alone can bring to birth that Genius, which shall maintain their institutions and perpetuate their Fame.

"The Antagonisms of the Social Moral, North and South" (1857)

It has been specially requested, my friends, that I should account to you, why I abandoned, almost at the outset, my tour of Lectures in the Northern States. It would be egotism only to suppose that any such narration would interest you, did it concern myself alone: but as this progress and its failure, has become involved in the politico-social relations of the two great sections of the country, now in absolute and direct antagonism, the history rises into an importance which otherwise it would not possess. As straws may be made to show the direction of the wind, so the simple career of an individual, may be made at times, to indicate the courses of the political currents, and especially the ebbs, flows, and overflows, which affect human communities. Believing then, that my narrative may be made instructive, I readily comply with the request, and trust that while I give it, it will occasion neither offense nor weariness. You may find it tedious, but may also, probably, find it profitable. To my mind, it involves many serious monitions, of great value to the Physicians of the State, and as I regard our people as approximating one of those periods of mortal crisis which are inevitable from the progress of all states, at certain almost regularly recurring times, I should be untrue to you, unjust to my own convictions of the danger which awaits you, were I to remain silent. The world, my friends, rarely shows us the spectacle, in any age, of any people, who have been able to maintain their independence, or preserve their liberties, for more than half a century;—certainly never, without going through the fiery furnace of foreign or civil war. And, duly aware of the trials which thus await humanity, a truly noble people will calmly and resolutely prepare themselves for every issue, and will deliberately study all those signs in the sky which seem to be the harbingers of convulsion. You will weigh my testimony, as that of all others, no matter how humble, with the serious consideration which is demanded by the vast value of the interests which you have involved in the Future. You will look at the blessings you enjoy, ask yourselves in respect to the rights which you inherit, the wealth you have at stake, the character which is your pride, the sires from whom you came, and the children who are to inherit after you. And I implore you especially to rise to such an appreciation of these interests as to become heedless of the mere medium through which you now receive your evidence. It is not now a season to sport with Thought, or ask of Fancy, the charm of colouring for speech. I shall aim at nothing of this sort. I shall employ no flourishes of rhetoric, but deliver to you a simple plain, unvarnished tale of experience. I do not come before you to amuse, and if you come hither only to find amusement, we are ill met tonight. I propose to tickle no ears with wit or fancy, to deal in no gaudy declamation. At this moment, my friends, I should as soon think of fiddling for you from St. Michaels' tower, while your city is flaming all around us.

My progress at the North, my friends, may be likened to that of a certain valiant monarch of the French, who,

> "With 20,000 men,
> Marched up a hill & then marched down again."

Or, rather, to that of one of the later Roman Emperors who set forth, with a vast armament, for the conquest of Britain, and returned home, bringing with him, as a trophy of conquest, only a basket of shells, which we may suppose the natives to have charitably flung at his head. For my part, if I failed in the oyster, I at all events escaped the shells. I brought none with me. If I could not return as a royal cruiser, bringing home rich argosies, I was resolved that my little craft should not be disparaged in her sailing trim by clumsy stowage and a vulgar ballast. I came as I went, accordingly,—came back, my friends, to my thirteen bushels of corn per annum. Satisfied, nay, happy, if having no better foods, I should yet be sure of my own, and the continued independence of my people!

You are to know, my friends, that for several years past, I have had frequent invitations to take part in the Lecture Circles of the Northern States; where the Lecture has grown into an institution; is one of the most efficient agencies of popular education, & exercises a vast influence upon the popular mind. Here it is otherwise. But the scene was too remote, my hands were usually too full of other labours, and I felt no adequate motive to compliance, until last year, when an earnest desire to vindicate our State and Section from the grievous slanders to which they have recently been subjected, furnished an impulse which proved superior to all personal considerations. These slanders of our Past, worked upon my mind, as I fancy, they worked upon yours. I felt that, in a fair field, they were easy of refutation. I had already, thro' the press, done something towards their refutation; but the publications of the South, which hardly circulate at home, still more rarely reach the North, and the Lecturing System of that region seemed to promise a much more ample field. I resolved to avail myself of it—to re-open the old chronicles for the instruction of those who had no opportunity for undertaking the task for themselves. I said to myself "the people of the North are surely not all hostile. There are thousands who will gladly listen to the truth—nay, be glad of a case made out, for them, in the defence of a section with which they are closely connected by ties of blood, trade and habitual association. Those, at least, should be put in possession of <u>our</u> argument, that they may be enabled to maintain our cause in their own precincts. As all events, the case should not be suffered to go by default. There should be an advocate—issue should be joined, and it should be shown to the world that, even while we deny the jurisdiction of a foreign tribunal, we are yet perfectly prepared to challenge its judgments. Our <u>lachesse</u> had already lost us much, and we have reached a crisis which required that it should no longer cause us surfeit." I proposed to make the survey of the revolutionary career of South Carolina, seizing upon the essential truths and principles, and using the details only where they were needed properly to illustrate the truth. A full summary of our Revolutionary career was essential to our character; and a people's character is their best security. A thousand mistakes & misrepresentations were to be corrected. The latent truths, lying concealed under mere facts, were to be developed and clues to be furnished for the explanation of difficulties which must occur in all the rude chronicles of a people. All our State and Colonial histories—so called—are, in fact, little more than imperfect chronicles, which need wise sifting, narrow scrutiny and a philosophical judgment. These, it is true, belong to the common law of historical analysis; and I should not speak of them here, but for the gross mistakes of the popular mind, from the want of that nice criticism which we need in order to a just grasp of our revolutionary career. I proposed to show how & where South Carolina stood in the Revolution —what was her condition, her resources—what she did—and what is her relative claim to respect, in a fair review of her performances, according to her means, as tried by those of other colonies. This is the only just method. But it is one of great difficulty, when it is remembered that, in South Carolina, as in all the purely agricultural states, the public mind has seldom addressed itself to the preservation of the public records. In the North, in all commercial states, where the density of the population causes a more general and incessant intellectual attrition, the case is otherwise. There, they have been perpetually busy in the assertion of their local claims. Sedulously devoted to this object, they have as sedulously ignored the services of all other regions. They have studiously exaggerated all that they themselves have meritoriously done, and, just as studiously suppressed every thing which might tell against their pretensions. This labour of love has, at length, succeeding in impressing upon all their own people, at least, the conviction that they have done every thing; and, as a natural consequence of their own position of assured security & preeminence, it has now become a part of the practice to disparage all other sections. To correct this tendency was one of the objects—at least to interpose a seasonable <u>caveat</u>, against a too precipitate judgment. I prepared other lectures, illustrative of our partisan warfare—a subject which deserves a volume to itself—in which I proposed to make the career of Marion, in some degree typical of the whole history, and of the peculiar advantages of such a warfare in a country like ours. Still farther—as there exists at the North a very singular degree of ignorance, in respect to our rustic life, our social moral, and the geographical features of our country. I prepared one or more Lectures, the better to illustrate our resources, character and society, with descriptions of our peculiar scenery. I very well knew that much of the prejudice of sections against each other was the result of mere ignorance, and I held it vastly important to our future relations, that the truth should be made known, even to unwilling ears, if only to prevent those mistakes of policy, which, under false notions of our neighbors, so frequently lead to the most disastrous consequences. It was especially important that the North should be disabused of the notion that the South <u>is imbecile</u>—imbecile because of her slave institutions—imbecile in war— unproductive in letters—deficient in all the proper agencies of civilization,—and so, incapable of defense against assaults upon these notions our enemies very strenuously insist, & in every form of phrase, & through every popular medium—the press, the pulpit, the Poet and the Politician. A miserable paragraphist will prate of the intellectual, moral and military deficiencies of a region which has produced a Washington, Jefferson, Marshall, Rutledge, Calhoun; Randolph—Marion, Sumter, Jackson, Scott & Taylor; a catalogue including all the master minds in statesmanship & war of which the whole country rings from the earliest period to the present—not to speak of Scenes, besides,—where wisdom, virtue, valour, eloquence, have established the government; given it its form and pressure; fixing our laws & national policy:—mistreating our rights in field & council;—and, in spite of these recorded names, the babble about our imbecility, as a race, will be uttered every where, by the most miserable scribblers of a venal press, & fanatic pulpit—by flatulent orators & trading politicians,—creatures who themselves have done, and can do, nothing for the nation;—and there will be nobody to rise up to confront them, with a manly indignation—to cry aloud—"Fools! Get ye to Jericho: till your beards be grown!" This is the daily history. Shall we stop to ask, wherefore this malignant desire to prove base & worthless, the sister states to which we are bound in solemnly written contract? Enough that it argues a condition of hostility which must ultimately break all bonds. There is a Rubicon in every progress which, once passed, return becomes impossible. Return for all who deal, in this language, is even now impossible. Now, my friends, once persuade a jealous, grasping, arrogant race, always usurping,—that the section which they hate and denounce is at once rich in wealth and poor in spirit;—worthy of the spoiler, yet feeble of will; wanting in energy and courage; slow in action & timid of resolve;—and you hold forth to them every motive for aggression and assault; you stimulate their arrogance, & endow them with audacity if not with courage. Now, unless we prepare ourselves for the last issues, it is well perhaps, if we may disabuse these people of such notions. It was somewhat my purpose to do this in my lectures—not merely to vindicate our ancestors, but to show, as indirectly and inoffensively as possible, that we inherit their blood & spirit; their intellect & will—that we are not resourceless in any of the elements that enable a nation to maintain itself in the arena with all other nations,—not imbecile, but particularly powerful, whenever the necessity for conflict shall become sufficiently apparent to compel the exhibition of our strength. This is the case especially with all agricultural people, who, sparsely settled, are slow to action; unaccustomed to daily attrition with the multitude, have little variety of movement: and wait always, some extraordinary impulse:—but who are firm when roused, concentrative of will & purpose, from the very absence of capricious impulse; are more fearless in action; more tenacious of individuality; more jealous of their liberation when threatened than all other people;—and, strengthened by a self-esteem which has been nursed in comparative solitude, find in patriotism only the exercise of a personal pride which never slumbers under the invasion of its rights. These are the virtues of a rural population. Next then, to the vindication of our past history, it was an object to assert our present resources; to disabuse our neighbors of the notion that the South is to be crushed at a blow, or crushed at all;—to afford such clues to the thinking mind, as to satisfy any mind, that an agricultural people, however slow to excitement, are always better prepared than any other, for national emergencies; can better grapple in the fields of war: can better endure a protracted conflict:—are endowed with peculiar virtues of moral—are earnest & steadfast—such a soldiery, as in all exigencies, has always proved the best bulwark of states & nations.

I especially avoided the subject of slavery. I well know that the time had gone by for any national discussion of this topic—that the whole case was prejudiced—that madness ruled the hour—that the people of the North were precisely in the category of those who, in France, in the days of philanthropic insanity, decreed the doom of the fairest portion of the tropical world;—surrendering, at Hayti, the civilization of Christendom to the usurpations of the savage. I well knew that, to use this subject, in any description of the rustic life in the South, would be only to provoke abuse and hostility. Besides, I was, myself, sick of the discussion. I had already, more than twenty years ago, published an elaborate review of our argument upon it, taking the ground, from which most persons then recoiled, that slavery, as it exists among us, was a great moral institution, of incalculable benefits to the human races, whether white or black—perhaps the most extensively benevolent in the whole circle of human philanthropy—authorized by the special sanction of the Deity—justified by the whole world's experience of its benefits—and, under proper definitions, perfectly legitimate when tried by the severest notions of civilization among mankind. But, though thus prepared to defend the Institution, I was restrained by the conviction that the discussion would be vain, and not only vain but unbecoming. A great people, my friends—a people equal to their liberties—must not recognize the tribunals of other nations when these become aggressive. The moral judgments of the age, are only to be regarded, in the absence of partisanship, & when they deal abstractly with the case. The moment that they become usurping & insolent—the moment that they propose to follow up opinion by assault,—then, a people must throw themselves back upon their paramount equality—their reserved individuality & rights,—and, if need be, the sword must decide the legitimacy of the cause which has become one of quarrel & aggression! Governed by these considerations, I avoided the subject of slavery. I could not recognize the right of those who had first stolen the negro, then sold him to us and pocketed the money, to the question the tenure by which we held him. If our little be not good, they are bound to make it so. They must come into court with clean hands before they can hale us thither. If our own practice be criminal, they are the original parties to the crime: and whatever our share in it, our responsibility is to the great father of the world's destinies, and not to them. We are to understand, and to make them understand, that, socially & politically, we are their equals; and any effort which they may make us to appeal to their courts of judgment are aggressions, usurpative & offensive, and a direct invasion of our independence.

I have thus endeavoured to show you upon what plan & principles my Lectures were formed; with what object; why certain Subjects were chosen; why others were forborne. Yes my avoidance of the subject of slavery was a matter of misconception and reproach. It was assumed, by certain of the assailing presses, that I had avoided the subject only because it told against us—because it exposed our asserted imbecility—and I was referred to an effort on the part of certain South Carolinians in the Congress of 1779 to authorize the employment, in war, of regiments of slaves—a measure tantamount to a confession of physical weakness on the part of the white population. But the imputation was a mere absurdity. Nobody doubted or denied that, in the revolution, the States of North & South Carolina & Georgia were deficient in population. This indeed, was a part of our own argument, by which we undertook to show how unreasonable it was to expect very powerful performances from colonies so sparsely settled and by such heterogeneous elements. So far as these states were concerned, the revolution was premature. But, even with this admission of weakness, it was resolved, and by votes & voices of Carolina chiefly, that the slaves should not be employed. Of what value then, this charge, though the measure was proposed by certain Carolinians, at a moment of threatened invasion, and after three years of the war had already elapsed in which South Carolina & Georgia had exhausted a large proportion of their strength, when it was decided by the very people, whose weakness was yet supposed to render it necessary. They, at least, would not acknowledge such weakness: and were willing to maintain the struggle without seeking such doubtful alliance. Thus answered, our assailants next changed the manner of attack, and ascribed our refusal to bring the slaves into the field, to our own fears; as if it would not have been the wiser policy, regarding the negro as hostile, to place him in our own ranks & regiments, under the <u>surveillance</u> of our own race, rather than leave him, almost without control, in full possession of the plantations! No resolve could more decidedly have shown how small was our fear of this people, when we see them left to cultivate the homestead, while all the white military population had gone into the field—left to the care of old men, and boys & women. No doubt some apprehensions were entertained, and expressed at first, in reference to this people, for they were Africans, not natives, & thousands of them, just brought into the country were in a state of comparative savagism. And, no doubt, that these apprehensions were brought before Congress, the better to carry the object of the Committee to which the subject had been confided. And well might the fear be expressed when the State was about to be overrun by a powerful & reckless enemy, who, it was readily conceived, would exercise every art of seduction which could prevail with an ignorant & barbarous race. But there was a policy, superior to that which suggested their military service, which required that they should be kept at the tasks of agriculture. The British felt this policy, even when they had overrun the country, and never sought to disturb it, except on one or two occasions of great exigency, when their occupancy was endangered. They felt how much wiser it would be to keep the negro busy, raising the food which was to maintain their armies; and so it was that, during the last three years of the war, the troops, both of Great Britain & America, in the two Carolinas and Georgia, were almost wholly supported by the rice & corn fields of South Carolina; while the tobacco & indigo of the same state, furnished a large part of the trading currency. All fears of the negroes soon died out with the experience of single campaign. When incorporated in arms, and under their own captains, as they were in some few instances, they were found inefficient; a disorderly mob; timid in moments of danger, and easily dismissed; but insolent in person, brutal in excess, and quite as likely to hunt as to help their employers. It was only when incorporated with white troops, in a subordinate capacity, and led on by white officers, that they could answer any useful purposes. It was because he saw them thus employed in the New England regiments, that John Laurens conceived the idea of subsidizing some five thousand of them in South Carolina, to be called Janissaries,—to be led wholly by white officers. He it was, who first originated the idea which brought the proposition before Congress. He urged that the negroes of the North constituted a considerable portion of the best New England regiments—that, kept under subordination by white leaders, they were tolerably efficient—in other words would fight well enough under the eye & guidance of their masters; were, in fact, many of them times employed by our own partisans, and so employed, were faithful, diligent & fearless. In the New England regiments they were scattered freely, formed no inconsiderable item among their best, such as Glover's regiment of Marblehead—nay, they formed some of the earliest & best patriots of that region, which has never accorded them proper honours—the very mob of Boston, which drew the first fire of the British troops, being led on by the negro Attucks; who, by the way, might well be honoured as their first martyr to Independence, as he was the first to perish for his patriotism, in that affair. Young Laurens knew all these facts, and others, and, carefully insisting that the negroes were to be officered by the superior race, he urged their incorporation with our soldiery. He was opposed by his own father, who argued powerfully against the scheme, and it failed of recognition. And why did he urge it at the particular time when it was brought before Congress? 1779. South Carolina & Georgia, the two feeblest colonies, were then threatened by a fleet and land force of from 12 to 15000 men. These two colonies, feeble at first, the elder only 100 years old, the younger but 40; the former hardly able to bring 10,000 men into the field; the latter not 3,000; both formed of singularly heterogeneous stock; both exhausted by numerous strifes, toils and misfortunes; both wanting as much in the <u>material</u> as the <u>personnel</u> of war; were evidently doomed, unless by extraordinary exertions, and the employment of the most extraordinary agencies, and the peculiar favour of Providence. The Northern States, with more than 100,000 men on paper could not send men enough into the field for the one army of Washington, which was filled with regiments of Maryland & Virginia & battalions even from North Carolina, and the very Committee of Congress to which was confided this measure of arming the slaves of Carolina, reported solemnly in March 1779 that the "Circumstances of the Northern army will not admit of the detaching of any force for the defence of South Carolina & Georgia." Strange, indeed! With but the show of an enemy in New England, the Continental Army could not muster 20,000 men—the circumstances of the army would not justify the draught of 5000 bayonets to the succour of the two feeblest of the Southern states. You can judge of the resources of South Carolina & Georgia, against the approaching army & fleet of Britain, of at least 12000 men, in all the panoply of war, when you remember that, with just this force of 12000 men, the British were enabled to maintain possession of New York against the united force of all the colonies under Washington—and to retain Newport, with 3000 men against all the power of New England. Washington never could procure sufficient numbers to attempt any thing against New York, and Greene could not command from all the 110,000 troops of New England, on paper, a force of 5000 volunteers, to expel the British from Rhode Island. No wonder—knowing the physical weakness of Georgia & South Carolina —knowing the immense territory which they had to defend,—twice or thrice the territory of any New England state,—that Laurens thought of arming the negroes. The very idea shows the confidence which our ancestors entertained in the fidelity of this caste; and their services were rejected—not because they feared them—for they left them in the charge of their women & children,—but because they thought them much more efficient as <u>field hands</u>, raising rice and corn, tobacco & indigo, than as <u>field soldiers</u>, doing execution in war. I might, as you see, have introduced this very subject of slavery, profitably, for my revolutionary argument, but did not, as I wished to excite no prejudices which would interfere with my mission.

To return from this digression

Provided, as I have shown you, with sundry lectures, wholly Southern in character,—I made my first public appearance in the flourishing town of Buffalo. The committee of the Society by which I had been called, had been permitted a choice of subjects. They, themselves, chose, as I wished, my Lecture on South Carolina in the Revolution. The very title of this lecture, under the warm & racing excitements occasioned by Sumner's speech, and Brooks's punishment of him, necessarily indicated a controversial performance. That it should be chosen, argued favorably for the public mind to my own. The auspice seemed to be good. It seemed to say,—we are prepared to hear the truth on this subject—let us have it. We have heard one side—let us hear the other. The tacit adoption thus, of the rule <u>audi alteram partem</u>, was in proof of honesty & fair mindedness, and I asked nothing farther from my audience. This was large, estimated at more than 1200 persons. During the discourse, I was heard, with frequent applause. <u>I</u>, myself, heard not a syllable of discontent. But, the next day, I was told that I had been hissed on one or two occasions, though the hisses were drowned by the applause. Fortunately, being rather deaf, I heard none of these exhibitions of discontent. I had not the slightest reason to suppose that I had given offence. I had certainly designed none. I had resolved, fearlessly, to assert the truths of history, but not to assail or irritate. The press, however, even that portion which maintained towards me the language of decorum, yet objected to the comparisons—not always odious—which I had made between the conduct of South Carolina, and other states on sundry occasions. It was said that I should have foreborne <u>all</u> comparisons—should have confined myself simply to the action of South Carolina. But this, my friends, was not always possible. I had a mission, which, under the circumstances, was [word unintelligible]. South Carolina was under this ban. She was herself the subject of odious comparisons. It was necessary, not only to assert her history; but to show what was that of her assailants; not only to defend her against the assaults of those who had mutilated her history, but to show where they had falsified their own. It was quite legitimate that I would endeavour not only to protect our own rooftree, but tear away from others their stolen garlands. For all such appropriation of borrowed laurels is a direct wrong to other sections. But, though quite proper, I did just as little of this as I well could. I made no comparisons, save in regard to issues which had been made already by our assailants, & only with the view to the establishing of correct standards, by which the audience, seeing what other colonies had done, or failed to do, under like circumstances, should be able to judge what should be expected of South Carolina. Thus, for example, when in answer to the charge that our people had failed to defend their capital city, it was quite proper for me to show that, in this respect, they had done much more than Boston, New York or Philadelphia. All these cities were seized & held by the British, without standing siege at all; and this too, at the very opening of the Revolution: when, we might reasonably suppose that each was in its fullest vigour. Charleston, of all these, was the only city that did endure a siege, a leaguer and constant bombardment of near two months, and this, after repelling & defeating two formidable assaults, and at a period—1780—when her resources and her strength had been materially impaired by the previous campaign, which had tried her strength equally upon the frontiers & upon the seaboard, in the defence of Georgia and in an invasion of Florida. This was the only sort of comparison which I made, and a just criticism will not only admit that it was quite legitimate and proper to my argument, but, under the circumstances of provocation, especially called for. You will believe me when I assure you that I strove, as much as possible, to forbear all gratuitous offence. I might have indulged in frequent sarcasm, and, by sharp recrimination, have shown to our assailants how much more penetrable their armour was than ours. But I forbore—they know not how greatly I forebore.

It was also made matter of grievous offence that I should refer to Mr. Sumner; that I should denounce his attack on S.C. as equally false & malignant. But why should I forbear Mr. Sumner? Is he immaculate? Was he not himself a wanton assailant? Did not his cold blooded, venomous, deliberate assault upon our State, so entirely gratuitous, invite and justify retort? So. Caro. was not the subject before the Senate. He went out of his way to spoil her, and in a more deliberate expression of malignant hatred than was ever suffered to show itself in Senate House before. This was not done in the heat of passion—it was a work of time, of cool deliberate purpose & studied preparation. And he had even submitted his anathemas to his friends—Seward and others—all perhaps equally prepared to wound as himself, but more shrewd and politic; & they counseled him against it. His philippic was the work of months—a closet labour—giving him time for thought, for better councils—a more Christian spirit;—but, in vain! The good angels, if we may suppose any to have been in waiting, while the venomous cauldron was boiling up under his ministering hands—boiling up with equal froth & venom—were unheard. He rejected all his better counsellors! The two main characteristics of this Senator, the sophomoric vanity, and the political ambition,—were too powerful to suffer either prudence or policy—his better moods, or the counsel of wiser friends—to have a hearing; and, having sharpened his javelin, and anointed it with venom from his concoction, no human argument, no social scruples, no Christian virtue, could keep his vanity from launching his bolt at the bosom of his victim. He had studied Demosthenes in the preparation of his Philippic; and the thought that all his people looked on lovingly to hear his thunders, was the irresistible motive for his eloquence! Why should I forbear him? Because he had been cudgelled? His slanders were on record, and still demanding refutation. His offence was still scored on our chronicles, and would there remain, even when the cudgel marks had faded from his forehead. There was no reason why I should forebear him. Yet, in some measure I did. I dismissed him as briefly as I could, with but a passing allusion, and a single comment. It was said that even this might have been foreborne. Not so! My Lecture was avowedly controversial. It was in reply to the assaults upon South Carolina; and this man, if not the most able of her assailants, was among the most venomous & most conspicuous. It would have been a mere paltry evasion, to undertake her defence, yet forbear all allusion to the very party who had made this defence necessary. It would have been a feeble affectation, on my part, to have done so, as it would be mere feeling, on the part of any audience to make the requisition. But, in alluding to Sumner, as the assailant of my country, I forbore all allusion to current politics—said nothing of the slavery or Kansas Questions—nothing of the Presidential election—forbore to discuss the virtues of Fremont, though claiming a birthplace in ours, as in sundry other states; and, did not, in fact, care a straw about whether he should be successful or not. The safety of the South, my friends, is not to be found in any party, or in the _morale_ of any President. The President, now-a-days, is a mere nose of wax, in the hands of party, or he is powerless in all respects. We are to learn, from this time forth, the great lesson, that we are to live & maintain ourselves by our own virtues, by our own vigilance, & wisdom, or we must perish! These are the only conditions of safety & security for a people, as for individual man; and that people who look to this or that Cabinet, for guardianship, is already doomed—to degradation!

I have shown you what was the opinion of the more moderate of the Buffalo press upon my Lecture. In respect to its claims, merely, as a Literary production, I had no reason to complain of their criticism. This was laudatory. But there were other presses that used a different sort of language. It would be difficult to describe to you, accustomed to regard the press as a reflection of society, its manners no less than its morals, the brutal character of these attacks, nor will I attempt to do so. It was by this press that I was first described as a Southern pauper seeking Northern charities;—it was said that the people of the North, sometimes called in a Southern orator or Lecturer, as they would a foreign fiddler, with his dancing dogs & monkey,—to amuse them. And much more of the same stuff. But the Southron, on this occasion, made them angry, & did _not_ amuse them; and to make him odious, he was denounced as having employed a speech of the most insulting kind to the people of the North; such as should properly have caused him to be hooted from the stage. The same presses joined issue with me upon my facts, showing a most lamentable ignorance of the history. For example; when

I stated that New England had never furnished any troops for the defence of Carolina, the press impudently asked if I had forgotten that Greene led an army to our succour? I could not reproach them for this ignorance, my friends, when I remembered, that, misled by false histories, thousands of my own people had labored under the same idle notion, until a very recent period;—until, in fact, my own humble publications, had disabused them of the error. Greene brought with him but a single aide, and he a Southron, when he assumed command of the Southern army. He found the <u>debris</u> of Gates's Continentals, awaiting him in North Carolina—an army made up <u>wholly</u> from the Southern states, & to be renewed exclusively from the same sources; for, with an obvious propriety, Congress had arranged that the military organization of the Country, should contemplate a geographical division of the troops of the two great sections. Yet, from the first, in consequence perhaps of the war opening first in the Northern States, large divisions from Virginia, Maryland, & North Carolina constituted a very considerable proportion of the army of Washington, and distinguished themselves in all the great actions in which he fought. In the siege of Boston, the rifle volunteers from these Colonies crowded thither, more than fifteen hundred in number, while the New England troops could not be prevailed upon to stay— when they were marching away, in fact, 5000 in a drove. And these same Southern riflemen constituted the most efficient portion of the force which Arnold led in the invasion of Canada.

The Brutal attacks of the Buffalo press preceded me to Rochester. There, I found the Committee by which I had been invited, labouring under considerable uneasiness. They too had chosen the same Lecture on So. Carolina, but a portion of them were disposed to recoil from it in consequence of the excitement occasioned by the Buffalo reports. A discussion took place among the members of the Board, at which I was present. Some of the members would have changed the Lecture. After listening patiently for awhile, I became a little excited, & said— "Gentlemen, you yourselves have chosen this lecture out of several that I offered you; you have already announced it, and I am here, prepared to deliver it, tho' the skies fall! If <u>you insist</u>, I will substitute another for it, but now, I frankly tell you, I prefer to deliver this. I owe it to myself to express this preference, if for no other reason than this: that it has been so shamefully misrepresented. It <u>is</u> controversial. It denies much of the history to which your ears have been accustomed. It endeavours to set some matters right in our history which have been grossly perverted; it defends South Carolina from the malignant misrepresentations which have been made of her history; and no doubt, on all these subjects, I express myself with a natural warmth, & no less natural indignation: but it is <u>untrue</u>, that I use disrespectful or insulting language to the people of the North, unless the truth itself shall be construed to mean offence. I think it very likely that what I say will be unpleasant to all that class who utter to themselves and listen eagerly to assaults upon the character and performances of the South; offensive to all those who have sworn the ruin of the South. But you deny that you are in this category, and with such a disclaimer, honestly felt, I do not fear that I shall give offence. I speak in terms of censure of Mr. Sumner? I deny the claims set up for Massachusetts as more pure, or true, loyal & valiant than other colonies, in the great struggle of the Revolution. But what of that? Is Massachusetts to be held more sacred from assault in N.Y. than South Carolina? If so, there is no value in any of your disclaimers of hostility to us. Are you to be required to hearken daily to the attacks on the one section, at which nobody seems to take offence, and shall it be a scandalous thing for a South Carolinian to retort, in your hearing, upon the assailant? Is this justice, or fair play? You are New Yorkers, or you are nothing. Surely, New York, at least, should be an open arena, as between Massachusetts & South Carolina. You should be able to listen patiently to me, as you have listened a thousand times, through a thousand channels, to the wholesale diatribes against my people!"

My remarks, of which the preceding is the substance, and very nearly the language, were echoed warmly by one of the Editors of the place whose name I take shame to myself for having forgotten. He said promptly:

"Mr. Simms demands nothing but what is just. You have repeatedly listened to such orators as John P. Hale, when the abuse of the South was all the burden. I insist that we shall equally hear the other side. I tell you that, if the Lecture is changed, I for one shall withdraw from the society, and shall denounce the whole proceedings in my paper."

This seemed to decide it. It was resolved that the Lecture should be delivered, and it was delivered. There was a full and showy assemblage of probably a thousand people. Excited by the previous discussion, & by the attempts made to prevent the Lecture, and by the assaults made upon me, I addressed some extempore remarks to the audience before opening, in review of this treatment; and while I spoke respectfully, & good humouredly, I yet spoke warmly, of the false relations in which the social elements of the country stood to each other, in consequence of the interposition of selfish & malignant parties. I asserted the claims of the South, upon the Northern people—the value of the Union to themselves especially, and assured them that its perpetuation could only depend upon the truth & justice & magnanimity. That any other bond of union must be false and hollow; that merely political ties & obligations, could never make, or keep the Confederacy whole, if there were not also certain sacred social sympathies, founded upon faith, good feeling & real kindnesses, to make the connection one of cement, rather than of law! All this was received favorably and with general applause. In the delivery of the Lecture, itself, I indulged in an occasional aside, in commentary, or explanation, at those portions which had given offence elsewhere and there was no voice of dissent that reached my ears. The audience was indulgent. Their attention was unbroken, even in those portions of the discourse, where the interest was wholly local, and required a minute examination of detailed operations. The applause was repeated at frequent intervals, and warmly followed the closing sentences of the Lecture. From the Lecture room, I retired with the Board, & a number besides, to their private apartments, where we were hospitably entertained. The circle was large & intelligent, consisting mostly of clever, active, young men, who were no doubt desirous of the truth,—desirous of progress, proper performances, and free from the malignant impulses of fanaticism and party—as free as they can be under those controlling influences of party, which, in the North, have warped & tortured society, out of all symmetry and form. It is all wild, disordered, anarchical, ready for chaos and disruption. And, the Northern mind, where not fanatical, is marked by a frivolity, a levity, which makes it reluctant to grapple seriously, with serious things—makes it unwilling to believe in dangers which it does not know how to meet; & is perfectly content, if it possesses the hour, and can sport and play, & seek its amusements. All this class of persons, and they are very numerous in all communities which grow to great & sudden prosperity, are flexible tools & creatures in the hands of more earnest & intensely working people. They never lead, they never engage in conflict, they shrink from new issues, and dread minorities. In their age, they become what the world indulgently describes as conservatives. They stand still, at all events, and as they find themselves alone, in solitude, with the world passing beyond them, they gather up their knapsacks, and mournfully follow the great march. Any people, living so wholly for show & appearances, are easily swept along with the masses. They lack individuality. In the conversation which followed in the little circle, we spoke freely of our issues, North & South; and I dealt much more freely with them, as pleasant companions, then I had dealt with my audience. There was intelligence, good sense, and good feeling among them; and I could not but regret that such admirable elements, for a noble social organization, could have no chance for proper exercise, in the condition of their country. The great lack of veneration in Northern communities, the wretched habit of refusing to recognize any thing as sacred; the habit engendered by a morbid self esteem, of striving to bring down, & trampling upon all authority, necessarily expatriates all honest leadership; and he who would acquire power, must first debase himself to servility; to popular sycophancy; to the adoption, pro tempore, at all events, of all the popular rages. But I must not expatiate here. It is enough that I had the warmest assurances of all the parties present of respect, & the most grateful feeling. They expressed no complaint, and gave me no reason to suppose that I had given any offense. On the contrary, passing beyond the mere courtesies of Hosts & Entertainers, they treated me with a warm kindness that took pains to give me pleasure.

My next stage was Syracuse. But here the Buffalo denunciations had again anticipated my coming and made a deeper impression. The committee positively declined my South Carolina lecture, & another, wholly innocuous was substituted for it. Syracuse, in N. York, is understood to be the hotbed of abolition. Here appears to be the grand central agency for what is called the Underground Rail Road. Here is an Institution, openly avowed and existing, for carrying on a regular warfare against the sister states of the Confederacy, to which they are pledged by the most sacred bonds of law, by all the ties which should give oneness and Entirety to a National existence. Only think of the monstrous anomaly of an organization, asserting union and common necessities, which beholds, without rebuke or remedy, the perpetual warfare of one section upon the rights of another. While conversing with a Gentleman at the depot, and while he was giving me the assurance, that the people of the North, were really very friendly to the South, <u>loved</u> the South in fact, were delighted with its generosity, hospitality and other vulgar domestic virtues, another came up and remarked to him, with a smile,—"They brought in five fugitives from Maryland last night, by the Underground Rail Road." Here was a rich commentary upon all this loving sympathy. Now, my friends, these are our brethren—great friends of the Union, sworn to the Constitution; obedient to its law—the people who rise up and call the Union blessed. Yet, here, they daily commit, or sanction such violations of Law, Constitution, Union, as would be cause of War between nations living under independent dynasties. Persons will tell you—O! These are only our fanatics, a poor despicable faction, whom we loathe and detest quite as much as you do. This is all nonsense, if not hypocrisy and impudence. These despicable fanatics rule the country, and these virtuous lovers of the South have neither the courage nor the will to oppose them with the energy of a proper personal or political manhood. No doubt that, in one sense, they cherish the Union, but only as the agency by which they prosper in uncounted prosperity. It is to them, the very health of life; it has made them rich and powerful, & keeps them so. No doubt they love the South, but it is as the wolf loves the lamb; covering and devouring it. They do not love it as the fountain of good faith and national honour; as the guaranty of law & justice, truth and magnanimity, but as the secret of spoil & profit. What is the idea of nationality, in any sense, which excludes these ideas, in respect to the integrals of the Confederacy;—which makes one party lie in wait, perpetually to assail, to revile, to disparage the other;—which makes it grateful to defame those very achievements of one section, which, properly recognized, became a portion of the national capital of renown & character;—which, trampling down right & justice, seeks only to exact tribute; which insists upon the obligations of the minority, and scorns and contemns all laws that bind itself—making a law for itself —a higher law—through which it rejects all fraternal obligations?

But I must not digress, even to declare my indignation. My next engagements were in the city of New York; a city of near a million of inhabitants—from its circumstances, the metropolis of the Union—a city rolling in wealth, arrogant with power, possessed of the vastest material resources: in which congregate so many of the finest intellects of the country, even as they congregate, for example, in London & Paris;—a city which derives more than half of its sustenance from the trade & commerce with the South. Here, if any where, the South should have a hearing—should have fair play. The general intelligence, here, should insist upon it: the very wealth & prosperity, should make it magnanimous & just; superior to fanaticism; to jealousy; to mere sectional influences; to all base and narrow standards. If these be here, as they must be to some extent, in every large city; at least, they will be kept in subjection by superior intelligence; by the natural play of circle against circle; by the contrasting interests of society and at large, by the very vanity of magnanimity. A large city like this, should naturally afford a sufficient body of highminded people, solicitous of right & justice; calm and judicious; thoughtful and earnest; who will confer upon it tone and character, and interpose, to prevent fanaticism from any preoccupation of the ground. Here, too, there must be two hundred thousand people, allied indissolubly with the destinies & prosperity of the South. It is their policy to maintain kindly relations with us, and they must naturally seek to possess themselves of every argument by which to assert the rights and morals of our section when assailed in theirs. Their own self respect, no less than policy, would seem to require this. It may be that thousands shall assail, but there will be other thousands to sustain. They will see that the advocate of the South shall have fair play, and a patient hearing. They will not only rejoice to hear him, but rejoice if he shall provide them with a proper argument so that they, in him, may also assert his argument. It was natural that I should reason thus on their behalves—as natural that I should assume, that, in that city, if any where, the chances would be altogether in favour of my having an indulgent hearing & a large audience. I had been honoured with a public invitation from several of the most distinguished citizens. Among these were Bryant, Bancroft, Broadhead, Francis, Duyckinck, and others, not merely in social position, but men of national reputation. My personal relation with Bryant had been most intimate for 25 years. We had shared the mutual warmth of hospitable ties; and though his political course had raised a barrier between us, wide, high, & deep, on political subjects, these had never been suffered to affect our personal relations of a quarter of a century. I had no wish to disturb his opinions. I cared not what they were. In the South none of us care a straw what are the opinions, upon slavery, of the old or the New England man, who eats at our board. We do not wish to coerce any man's sentiments. We demand only that we shall be left alone, in the enjoyment of our individual rights, or, as a community: and, in the degree & kind of civilization which we have chosen & continue to prefer. And, in my personal intercourse with Bryant & other friends at the North, this was always conceded. In spite, then, of all the politico-social differences which were tacitly understood between us, Bryant was one of the first to invite my Lectures in New York. He knew <u>me</u>, and took for granted, that I would be warm in the defence of South Carolina, and he was prepared to make the proper allowances for a warmth, which he, no doubt, as well as myself, held to be perfectly justified under the provocation. And such was the language of his paper after the delivery of my Lecture.—Mr. Bancroft's hospitality I had enjoyed many years ago in Boston. He, too, joined in the invitation. So did Mr. Brodhead, one of the local historians of New York. Dr. Francis, an octogenarian, well known to all the literary circles of that city; Mr. Duyckinck, one of the old Knickerbocker stock, the young amicable & talented Editor of the Cyclopedia of American Literature. That such men should invite my Lectures seemed a sufficient guaranty for their favorable reception. I was approached by a committee, who made a contract with me for one or more courses. These Gentlemen were experienced in such matters. They did me the honour to assume that I possessed a sufficient capital of popularity, as an author, to render the contract a profitable speculation to themselves. And the auspices appeared favorable on all hands. But, meanwhile, the hostile matter of the Buffalo press had found circulation. Echoes, in the same tone & temper, had been heard from other journalists. Letter writers had taken their cue from these sources, and had heightened report of my offences. They sought artfully to appeal to social, as well as political & historical prejudices. It is a common method of assault upon the South, in the North, to describe our people as an indolent & haughty aristocracy, who show themselves especially scornful of all the <u>working</u> classes, by reason of the degrading influences of slave labour. You will perhaps have noted that an article in the Edinburgh Review—said to be written by one of your own sons—represents us as having, in familiar use, the epithet "<u>poor trash</u>"—as applied to the poor & labouring class of whites among us—a phrase which I never heard so employed, in all my life! We have all heard "Poor Buckrah," used by the slaves themselves, in regard to those whites, who, owning no slaves, are yet very tyrannical in their treatment of the negro. It is them that the indignation of the negro, denounces a petty tyranny; but among the planters, the owners of slaves themselves, I doubt if there be a person in this assembly, who has heard such a phrase from their lips. And I am personally familiar with most the states of the South, Seaboard and interior, from the Chesapeake to the Mississippi. This sort of report of us constitutes a favorite staple of misrepresentation, and it was not to be left unemployed in my case. It so happened that somewhere, in my Lecture, I had used the word 'vulgar'—in the sense of men, low, base, and narrow minded. This was seized upon, among a score of other points, and I was denounced as having absolutely applied this epithet to the very people I was addressing. Now, in the case of a people with whom <u>appearances</u> and <u>social position</u> are paramount objects;—who are jealous, in the last degree, of exclusiveness and aristocracy; there could be no mode employed better calculated to occasion a popular odium which would be fatal to the Lecturer. My friends in New York began to feel, and to fear, all these things, and several of them came to me, as soon as I got back from Buffalo, and adjured me to strip my Lecture of every thing that might possibly be offensive to Demos. I went with them over the performance, yielded in some instances to their suggestions; striking out something, here & there, which prejudice and suspicions might contrive into gratuitous sarcasm—and was only stubborn on resolving not to yield every thing. I could not consent to erasures, which might, in any degree, impair the integrity of the discourse. My friends expressed themselves satisfied. They augured favorably from what they read. The sharper portions which were suffered to remain, were, as they considered, but proper hits —neither acrimonious nor malignant—and but a natural & legitimate use of obvious material. Speaking deliberately now, I aver that there was nothing in the discourse which did not fall strictly within the province of a proper historical criticism. What if there was an occasional sharpness in the tone—what if the temper of the speech <u>was</u> warmly Southron. Surely, under the perpetual & goading provocation to which the South has been subjected—these had their justifications—and with any, the smallest amount of magnanimity on the part of any audience, these traits would have been regarded as not only natural enough, but absolutely laudable!—But to the Lecture.

When I appeared in the Pulpit, I found about 150 persons, of both sexes, in the church. This, in a magnificent hall, capable of holding 3000 persons! So small a result,—taken in connection with the large calculations of my committee, was absolutely ludicrous. I did not feel it mortifying. I readily conceived the secret. The newspapers had done their work; my friends had shown their fears; and, according to every report, the very name of South Carolina was everywhere a word of odium; so that I was already fully prepared to understand that, even in this great city—this Babylon of all races—distinguished by its levities and lack of character—it was easy for a vigorous, powerful, concentrated party, fanatical of mood, despotic of will—embodying in its ranks almost the entire mind of the community—certainly all the great leading intellectuals—to coerce the public temper, on all occasions, and, easily, in the case of an individual who lacked the <u>prestige</u> of party for his support. This was my lack. Had I gone thither as a Party Politician, speaking to partisan topics,—I should, no doubt, have been sustained by a large party demonstration. Thousands of Whigs, Democrats, or Native Americans, would probably have gathered to hear and cheer me, at the foot of the Exchange. But to neither of these had I appealed. My chief support was that of personal friends, and that portion of the literary guild, which had not been tainted by abolition. But, I do not believe that I suffered the smallness of my audience to affect my mind or deportment. I was as cool, composed & free from cloud, as I am at this moment—nay, much more so. Satisfied that my audience, though small, was select, I consoled myself, <u>sotto voce</u>, with the prayer of Milton, for "audience <u>fit</u>, though few"; and to these I delivered myself of <u>my</u> history of Carolina in the Revolution, as respectfully, as if ten thousand had been present. And, through various sources, I heard of commendations, from worthy lips. Mouths of wisest censure did me the honour to approve. My friends, after this Lecture, endeavoured, in various ways, to account for the smallness of the audience. They ascribed it, in part to the opening of a new fashionable theatre that night (Laura Keene's); to a great public banquet and illumination at Jamaica, L.I.; to the attraction, for all the temperance societies, of a famous Lecturer (Mr. Gough) and to the high prices at which my tickets were sold. I could readily understand how these rival attractions might have had some influence with the mere seekers after amusement. But the appeal was not to them; and it is, perhaps, the severest commentary upon the people of the North, that, in an issue like the present, involving the pride, dignity & character, of a sister state, with which the alliance of interest, if not of feeling, is so close, there should not be found thousands, eager to ascertain her argument, in a case which had already been distinguished by such impressive events! But the <u>motif</u> of the next day's newspapers furnished a better solution of the problem. The leading abolition papers had repeated, with unction, the brutal assaults of those of Buffalo. I was again spoken of as the Southern pauper, abandoned in his age, by his own people, to the cold charities of Northern Lecture rooms; and every epithet of odium, which could be cast upon our Section, was employed in the connection, that we both might be rendered more odious. But the matter which was likely to exercise the worst effect, was in the studied identification of myself and my objects, with the affair of Brooks and Sumner. It was represented that a Confederacy had been formed among the South Carolina members of Congress, to assault Sumner in such a manner, as to ensure themselves escape from injury! This idea—this invention— upon which it is not necessary that I should make the least comment—is, by the way, elaborated, even more effectually, in the last number of the North British Review—and I must read you this extract, in order that you should find some relief, in a smile, once at least, during this tedious narrative. Our British Reviewer says—"We are assured that this assault on Mr. Sumner was preceded by a consultation as to the safest mode of perpetrating it. The notion of encountering him on equal terms, in one of the public walks, was speedily dismissed, upon the ground that he, being a stout man of acknowledged spirit, his assailant might get worsted in the struggle. A proposition to make a rush at him, from the higher ground, as he was ascending the steps of the Senate House, was abandoned for similar reasons, and it was at length determined to strike him when he was off his guard, or in a defenceless position; and to strike in such a manner as to disable him at once." These nice details of our Representatives in Secret conclave, you will perceive, are only an expansion of the rough general history, as given by the abolition press. Without saying actually, that I was one of the parties to this consultation, the same person described me as seeking to do, in the historical field, what Brooks had done in the physical. I was only another sort of bully, dispatched to hector the Northern people in their own homes. This imputation, as you may well conceive, once put in circulation, & so well calculated to provoke the most the most unreasoning temper of the people—must be fatal to my mission; and I was by no means surprised, accordingly, when, that very afternoon, my committee appeared before me, & said—in so many words—"We are afraid that you will have to give up your Lectures. We can do nothing for them. We have canvassed the whole city, in all its leading centres, and can neither sell the tickets nor give them away. Such is the offence taken by your allusion to Sumner, —who is described as in a dying state from the assault of Brooks—such the odium of South Carolina—such the rancour of public feeling, just after the election—that the common answer to our applications—is one of imprecation!— The answer is, in brief—'D—n South Carolina, and every thing that hails from her. We want no more <u>blowing</u> about South Carolina."—After this report, my friends, but one course remained to me, as a gentleman, and I said to the committee—"I release you from your contract." I communicated this result to Mr. Bancroft, as the first on the list of those who had invited my Lectures. He, and others, expressed themselves greatly chagrined—were disposed to think my committee mistaken in their report—admitted that there <u>was</u> a bad feeling in the community, but did not think it so rancorous or blind in character. They proposed to take up this experiment themselves—did so, without any encouragement or wish of mine—and failed. The effort was abandoned, and several of the parties were compelled to admit that the public temper was far more bitter than they had believed it. In view of the brutal and malignant assaults of certain newspapers, and with a full knowledge of the power which they exercised over communities which form no opinions independently of the Press, they concluded that my decision was a correct one; that there was no remedy; the case was prejudged fatally. One matter, tho' small in itself, will serve to show the degree in which I might expect justice from the press. At the close of my lecture, it was announced that my second lecture would be given two nights after. But the very next day my engagement was rescinded. The advertisements were all suppressed. Neither placard nor advertisement appeared on that, or the ensuing day; and that night I never left my lodgings. Yet these presses, stating none of these facts, nor the additional fact that there was a cold rainstorm prevailing, and that the church was never opened, yet described the Lecturer & his Committee as waiting in vain for the audience, and the former, as finally refusing to lecture to a small gathering of ten or fifteen persons. Invention was thus coerced in aid of the fact, in order to form a climactic finish to the story; and there was quite a howl of triumph over the event! They had gained a victory! They had succeeded in depriving the advocate of an odious section, coming alone, and only asking to rectify error, of all chance of being heard. Thus, my friends, the dominant spirit of the North suffers no opposition to its will & purpose. You can only obtain a hearing through means of your own party, and <u>the South has no party in the North</u>! Our few friends are too few, too feeble, too timid, to exercise power or command respect. There are some presses that affect our Cause, but they have small circulation and no influence. Besides, they wholly misconceive our argument, are not possessed of our facts; and never, in any case, meet the true issues. They assail the abolitionists; but, in a petty fashion, and not because they would serve us, but that they would resist a party which is a terrible despotism over themselves, & which, enthroned in power, with earnest passions at work, and working with a terrible intensity, sweeps over them, in every encounter, as easily & fiercely as the hurricane sweeps over a tract of reeds or willows. The mercantile classes, who are perhaps the only classes at the North, who feel the danger to which they are driving headlong, rarely take part in the conflict of opinion; and never think to move until the election approaches, when they naturally ally themselves with their party—no matter which, that promises most conservatism;—to maintain the <u>status quo</u> of trade being the only motive to their actions at any time. The literary guild, however favorably inclined to one of their paternity, have no sort of power in the action of political parties; and, unfortunately, but too many of the most able of the men of letters in the North, looking to political position, & leagued with the press, are identified with all the purposes & policy of the Anti Slavery Party.

The result of my experimental Lecture in the city of New York, involved, almost necessarily, the abandonment of all my engagements. If the temper of a city, like New York, which may be assumed to be somewhat cosmopolitan, showed itself hostile or indifferent to my topics, what could I expect farther East? If my Committee lost money by me in that city, there was good reason to suppose that similar and even greater losses would follow the experiment in other places; for the press was still busy at its work of prejudicing public opinion in anticipation of my progress. The Societies which invite the Lecturer contemplate certain profits to themselves, after paying his demands. But how should I consent to draw loss upon them? How, drawing such loss upon them, should I consent to receive their money? I could not deceive myself with the vain hope that, after the course pursued by the abolition presses, I could make a profitable tour into regions wholly occupied by abolitionists. The country papers were already engaged— following those of the city, in denouncing me as a Southern bully, insulting the very people who come to hear him. Nay, Blanche & Sweetheart—all the little dogs—were in full cry; and, by this time, I, too, was beginning to lose my temper, under a treatment to which my experience had never taught me to submit and which I had no means to resent. I could not reply to the blackguardism, it would have been mere Quixotism to attempt to repel the principle falsehoods of the Press. You beat out the brains of one lie, and fifty others, stand up from the scattered members. Reflecting, with as much coolness & deliberation as possible, upon the prospect before me, I decided that self-respect required that I should close my Portfolio and retire quietly from the scene. And so I wrote to the several Societies which had invited me, respectfully but firmly, expressing, in a few brief words, which I felt sure that the language of the press would sufficiently illuminate my necessity and the propriety of the dissemination to which I had come. As I had more than fifty of these letters to write, I made them very brief. I could not enter into details; nor were these necessary. From many of these Societies, I received answers entreating me to reconsider, & giving me assurances of cordial welcome. But I knew that such assurances must be based upon mere conjectures, which presupposed too much on behalf of committees, and their influence upon the masses. There is a power at the North, striding in between the people and all their social influences, which leaves the latter at a woeful discount, in the moment of collision. Fanaticism and Politics, in alliance, and in possession of the press, is of so terrible a potency in all the North that society has ceased to speak, does not decide for itself and dare not ask. Irrespective of faction and fanaticism, it has not Independence enough for the formation of its own opinion, nor courage for its assertion. A popular rage, once begun, no one thinks to arrest it. The individual is merged wholly in the mass; and a majority is unquestioned in its march, in utter disregard of every principle. Here & there you find little circles who moan over this condition; but you find no manly opposition. The abler men of the community sink wholly out of sight, except when unscrupulous; and then they affect the popular rage which they do not feel—which they only fear—and seek to direct the outlawry, making it profitable to their own hands, which they dare not oppose. There is really, therefore, no party, sufficiently strong, in any of the Northern States, to offer, even a respectable barrier to the progress of fanaticism. The little societies which aim at popular tuition, through the Lecture room, can in no way determine for their audiences. These they are compelled to conciliate. The Lecturer, himself, is but too apt to seize upon some of the popularized topics, in the hope of making little capital for himself; and he takes care, in doing so, not to come in conflict with the will which the masses have already declared. If he forbears this, he seeks only to amuse; and popular Lectures, even on moral subjects, are, half the time, made up from old Jest Books, and the stale bon mots of the venerable Joseph Miller. I felt that the key note once sounded through the North against <u>my</u> topics, I should be met Everywhere by anticipative hostility. All the rancorous bitterness of feeling & speech against South Carolina & the South would have renewal with hourly increase of venom. The topics, having been made of familiar phrases, through the recent general election, were easy of utterance; stereotyped ravings; which it requires no thought to frame, and which it was grateful for Passion to deliver. The defeat of the abolitionists in this election—a temporary defeat only, which only served to teach them their overwhelming sectional strength,—had yet left them full of fury. My subjects, and my manner of treating them, served only to fan the political fires; to afford new ingredients for that hellbroth which they had been compounding of all elements for so long a season. As one of my personal friends said to me,—"You are a Godsend to them. You are a fresh stick of Southern pitch-pine to be flung into their furnaces, that the fires by which they keep the party warm, may not burn down!" I was not willing to be used for such a purpose; not willing that my presence should be provocative to the renewal of that cancerous rage with which the name, the fame, the institutions & the safety of my country, were to be pursued. And again—I was not in any position whether public or private, to make me eager after a hearing, at all odds, & at every sacrifice of pride or sensibility; and a resort to any acts of conciliation, after the unscrupulous language of the press, would have been simply base & slavish. I did not seek the smiles of Society: I was not ambitious of political position. Though wanting in riches, I had never in all my life, surrendered a single sentiment of my soul, a single conviction of my mind, a single feeling of my heart, in the pursuit of gain. I had jealously maintained my independence, through long years of self denial, poverty, isolation, and frequent reproach. And why should I now, at the mellow term of fifty, make sacrifice of any of those sensibilities which I had held & nursed so tenaciously, as the best securities for the equal vigour, purity and power, of mind & soul! I had been willing to lecture professionally, in the hope of teaching the truth, and correcting the false,—with a vain hope perhaps, of doing some good to my country. But not to submit to vulgar defamation & the grossest sort of abusive misrepresentation. And doomed to the encounter with such assailants, I was necessarily stripped of all power of effecting good. And to lecture,—speaking to the necessities of the country—I must do so with a clear conscience, untroubled with the doubt that I am bringing loss, and probably odium, upon the several societies which entreat my labours. Besides, after the attacks upon me, I could not consent to deliver any other than my Southern lectures. It was a point of honour with me to do this. I could not, with any patience, have consented to discourse on ordinary moral topics,—as well expect the soldier, in the heart of the battle, to fling aside the proper implements of war, and confront the enemy with a popgun. My assailants had driven me to this position. I had other lectures, moral, social, historical, which might have gratified an audience. But these no longer suited my necessities. They no longer sufficed for me at a moment when I was a mark for general assault. My assailants had made the mistake of compounding mine with a political mission. Had I sought political power, I would have accepted this assumption. And I should have continued my lecturing career. The Politician recognizes the assumed rights of the Press to play the blackguard at pleasure. The filth and the venom are so many conditions of place & power. But <u>he</u> has resources which the literary man has not. If one party assails, there is another that cheers. With the literary men, the case is otherwise. He must stand upon the dignity of <u>his</u> profession, for there is nothing, of place or party, to compensate to him, the forfeiture of his self-respect.—With all these considerations in mind, I was compelled to decline the renewed applications of certain of the Societies which had entreated me to change my resolution; and to the implied reproaches of some of them, which suggested the inconvenience to which they would be subjected by my refusal, I indicated my own superior sacrifices—in loss of time, labour, expense, and money. In the latter respect, my decision cost me more than $2500. All this was stated, in order to show that I had not wantonly, & without due respect and consideration for them, withdrawn from my engagements. Two or three of these letters, I have seen in print. Others may have appeared also, which have escaped my notice. These, you will please remember, were not published by me, or with my consent. They were none of them designed for publication. <u>I</u> have not put in print a single syllable on the subject, & should probably never say a word in respect to it, were it not for the frequent enquiries of friends, & because of the natural claim, which my own people have upon me, to be satisfied in regard to a mission which so much concerns themselves. I had no motive for publication. I had simply made a venture, in a new literary field—which proved a failure;—it did not much matter why—since I had no reason to suppose, that, out of my own little circle, the world would care a copper about the result. I accepted this result without comment or complaint—should so accept it still,—but that the event invokes social & political considerations which are much more important to you than any interests of mine. It was enough for me that the failure did not lie with me. But the Northern Press is not quite satisfied. It has shown itself somewhat uneasy. There is something so monstrous in the idea, that, in a Confederacy like this, one member, one section, may be denounced & reviled with impunity, as a public enemy, and no advocate in its behalf should be heard, that the inevitable conclusion becomes one of terrible import, as showing how wretched is the tenure of sympathy in our alliance. In this headlong impulse which marks all their social conduct, they made a political mistake. They should have maintained appearances. They should have heard me as a matter of policy— should have crowded to hear me, as really anxious for the defence of the South, as a part of their own country—and then, if displeased, they should have charged the failure to my incompetence, and not to my facts or topics! These should not have disquieted them. They blundered politically through their blind passion. It is fortunate for mankind that malignity is seldom cold enough to be politic. It strikes, as the rattlesnake is said to do in the Dog days, blinded by its own venomous secretions. After the thing was done, and they began to see the inevitable result of their headlong impulse, a portion of the press felt the necessity of soothing our hurts. They saw that the rejection of an advocate from the South—one, too, disclaiming politics, and aiming only to defend her character from assaults, must prove, irresistibly the viperous hostility which pervades their society toward us. I do not know that our people need any new proof to this effect. If they have not long since seen it, then, I fear, there is no mortal surgery which shall couch their sight. But, whether they see this or not, I fancy there are very few persons not prepared to believe that my treatment was due to my topics. Indeed, all their attacks declared it. But some of the newspapers, subsequently, beginning to see the evil results of their course, have endeavoured to convey the idea that my Lecture was merely encyclopedic, compiled from common histories, with which they were all sufficiently familiar. But, my friends, this will not do! This very pretence puts them on the horns of a dilemma. If my history was so familiar, the mere compilation from accepted histories, why should it make them angry? If mere commonplaces, why rage against it? The other difficulty is even more embarrassing. If so familiar, how does it differ from Mr. Sumner's? And if it differs from his, yet is the one most familiar to them, why did they not rage against that of Sumner?—How happens it, being so commonplace, that it should come in conflict with that which they have striven to teach us as the true history? They certainly never delivered the same history to <u>their</u> people; and just as certainly it afforded them such a version of the history as they were by no means willing to hear. The same papers, with unheard of impudence, add—"So far from being hostile or unfriendly to the South, we love the South!" Ay, as the tick, the cow;— as the leech the vein upon which it fastens, clinging till the fountain of life runs dry! Nay, God, in his mercy, whatever else the doom he has in store for us, save us from that <u>attachment</u> which subjects us equally to the venom and the slaver of the toad!—It is a frequent subject of self congratulation, with the people of the North, that their magnanimity suffers to the South, that freedom of argument on slavery and other topics, which they themselves, in the South, are denied a corresponding privilege. I have had this taunt thrown into my teeth a thousand times, in this very progress. But this whole claim is an impertinence. There is no parallelism in the cases. The South, at the North, is purely on the defensive. The North, in the South, is aggressive. The North assails Institutions which are wholly Southern;—we hurt none of their institutions when we attempt the defence of our own. Their demand to enter our precincts & assail existing conditions, which are peculiar to us, is insolent and usurpative,—to teach a subordinate race lessons of disaffection, leading to insurrection, an aggression, which, were they to try it in France or England—seeking to make any classes discontent with Government & Law, would be punished signally, as treason & sedition. But you point out these distinctions to them in vain. They are insolent by habit, and usurpative of necessity. As for their toleration toward those who claim to speak <u>for</u> us, there would be nothing meritorious in the fact, even were it so; since they can lose nothing, and suffer no hurt, by any expression of opinion on subjects in which they have no interest. Besides we are brethren, are we not, and hail each other when we meet in argument, with "Dearly Beloved!" But, in truth, they exhibit no toleration. They are the most intolerant people in the world, and have been so from the days of Cotton Mather. They have never shown any indulgence to any who oppose their vanities or will. The old malignant leaven of puritanism, which made them loathsome to England; made them the persecutors of old women & quakers; the Dutch of Manhatta, made them the slayers & enslavers of the red men, and now the assailants of the South; still pervades their society, and will suffer no speech of censure, even where it amounts to no assault, on the part of the stranger. The foreign singer who is reported to have spoken disrespectfully of their graces, virtues, & wisdom;—the foreign actor, who was supposed to be less deferential than became the pauper seeking their <u>cold</u> charities—were both pelted & driven from the stage and country. Jealous even of that foreign Labour to which they owe so much, they have actually deprived him of arms, even when a regularly admitted citizen. And even Religion fails—when it happens to prefer another creed to their own—to protect the young virgins, in their own dwellings, from the brutal, midnight violence of an incendiary mob. I did not, could not descend, to conciliate this nest of vanities. It is a fine absurdity to talk of Northern toleration, whenever opinion shall offend its self esteem!

It is asked if I did not know all this before? I did! Scores of friends have said or written to me, North & South, "we knew what would be your reception. How should you expect that they would listen to you with forbearance! What must be the result of any attempt to correct those false histories by which they have manufactured a spurious reputation at the expense of the rest of the country? You call upon them to resign their laurels & heroism, & expect them to keep their temper? You refuse to give them that aliment of praise, upon which they have fed so long, that is has now become their essential diet? They can digest no other." I felt all this. I had known these people for 25 years; knew their history; comprehended perfectly their society. There were premonitions, too, of a more direct motive, which were of recent experience. Only last summer, an able writer of the South, an accomplished citizen, well known to all of us, had written a fine masculine poem, comparing the condition of the Hireling in foreign parts with that of the slave in our section. This work was actually stereotyped, in the press of one of the greatest of Northern publishing houses, when the Publishers suddenly became apprehensive to themselves of its publication, and refused to issue it. They feared to trust the resentful temper of their people, towards all those who should assert the Southern argument. All this I knew! If you ask me whether I had not reason to apprehend the treatment I received, I answer in the affirmative: To a certain extent, at least. I expected coldness & indifference, and I did not hope to give satisfaction. But, as I forebore politics, I fancied that I should have tolera-tion. Still, there was a consideration, such as I have already intimated to you, which made these apprehensions matter of little concern. It was essential that we should join issue with the slanderers of our history upon their own ground. That we should not allow the case to go by default. That we should exhibit to the world a readiness for this issue; that we should challenge the argument; and not suffice it to be supposed, that, conscious of our weakness in the morals of the case, we were compelled to resort only to violence, and shrunk from every other mode of arbitrage. We know that the course of Brooks contemplated only the punishment of violence, offence, the slander; and contemplated nothing beyond. It was necessary that, while showing ourselves capable of manly resentment for insult, we should at the same time, show ourselves equally prepared to answer in the grand forum of Conscience & Justice. And whether I was heard patiently or not, did not affect the result. It was enough that the world should know that we were ready for the issue, in any field, in letters, in justice, in morals & society, as in the field of physical warfare. Even if denied a hearing, the result was in our fa-vour. It cannot now be said that we shrank from the issue. It is on record that we challenged it, and joined issue on the facts. It is for the future to decide the case; and Posterity will thus be made to pause in its judgment, explore, examine, weigh and revise, where otherwise the judgment must have been taken by default. You now understand my motive and the reasoning by which I was governed. Enough that I proposed to meet the slanders of my people, and was in turn encountered by the slanderer.

My mission thus ended, my friends, the question will occur to you,—What, indeed, are the relations, Social, Moral—political, between this people and our-selves? Is it peace between us? Does it promise peace? Do you persuade yourselves that all the hubbub & clamour of abolition amount to nothing more than that "windy suspiration of forced breath" which characterizes the ordinary progress of mere political parties? Do you really feel secure—satisfied that the confederacy is held together by ties of amity and sympathy as well as law, against which the strifes of fanaticism must beat in vain? If so, no more need be said. But, in truth, you have no such grateful conviction. Party Politicians have striven to persuade you to this,—and the politicians, nay, the parties themselves have perished under the strokes of this fanaticism, in the very moment when they declared it con-temptible! The moralists and preachers have told you, this is mere wind & vapor; yet the churches are broken up, and the Preachers themselves, have become prophets of destruction; breathing towards you anarchy & blood. The schools, the colleges, to which you send your own sons, now teach hostility to the South as duty to God. The provisions of Law under the General Government are de-feated by risings of the people, and by state enactments; and, on all sides, you can hear but the one cry—"Delende est Carthago!" The Institutions of the South must be destroyed! Is there any potency in this cry. Nobody can better judge than yourselves! You have the evidence before you of what these people themselves declare, and must decide for yourselves what they mean and what it is in their power to execute. You hear the voice of society, which declares you foul, enemies of man, living in open hostility to the primary laws of God. And, under this social voice, you see the old parties of the Country destroyed; you see the amenities of society perish and the decrees of law despised;—you hear a fanatic Priesthood, harking on the dogs of havoc against you, and you behold a dominant faction—every where in power—which has but one article of faith—which makes but one declaration of purpose—and that is your destruction, as an independent social organization—all involved in your peculiar institution! The very foundation of a purely sectional party, is a virtual sunderance of the Union; and the object of this organization is avowedly the overthrow of your individuality at all hazards. The argument used by newspapers in New York only a few days before the last election, addressed to the working classes especially, held forth to them the assurance, that, with the election of Fremont, free labour would supersede that of the slave in the South, thus opening, a new and boundless province for their enterprise, and this is addressed to a class, counting millions of desperate men, whom a grinding daily necessity, makes reckless of every consideration of law, justice and the constitution. I have shown you that all classes are united against you; that even the leading portion of the Literati are Hostile; the abstract notions of the Rights of Man, promising a new Utopia to the Imagination, & naturally appealing to the sympathies of a class whose ordinary pursuits render them heedless of more literal or practical considerations. So, for a like reason, are the clergy; the more especially as there is no portion of the Northern Communities, who seek with more eagerness after popularity, and abolition now is the most open & obvious pathway to its attainment. Schools & schoolbooks all appealing to the popular sentiment teach the same lesson; and shall we doubt our danger—doubt that force is designed & will be used, to carry this sentiment into political power, & for your ruin, when all society urges it—when the very altar places hitherto dedicated to Christ have been specially consecrated to Moloch—when rifles, sabres, Bowie knives & bullets, are held to be the most grateful votive offerings, placed upon the altars, by the hands of childhood, women & the Priesthood? It needs nothing but the occasion—any concurrence of circumstances, such as the state of Parties in Kansas, may bring about the sudden trial of the respective strength and courage of the antagonist sections, bring them into mortal collision. And you are to remember that the issues are really rather social than political. Society is corrupted against you to the destruction of Party. In private circles, every where, even among your old friends, you find this indicated in a thousand ways. You find the books of Mrs. Stowe & a thousand others of the same school—the Dreds & Uncle Toms—lying—ay, <u>lying</u>—on every parlour table. No circles escape the contagion—no place remains free of the usurpation—no class has the courage, or will, to resist the phrenzy, which, taking the guise of a Crusade, & armed with the coercive will of a vast majority, is inevitable in a community, which only needs to know where the majority lies, to surrender, at once, to all its exactions. You go no where but to meet with controversy, which takes the most offensive tone on the threshold—a tone of equal authority and insolence. The very sight of the Southron is the signal for assault; and the waiters at the Hotels are thus indirectly taught to exhibit neglect and positive insolence to the people of a section against which all classes fulminate hate, malice and savage denunciation. It is in vain that you try to escape the discussion. It is forced upon you, <u>hic et ubique</u>, until your passion rushes to the succour of your reason, and you hurl your defiance into the teeth of that Insolence which you will fail to quell in any other way.—But, I must cease. I have wearied out your Patience. But this whole subject presents itself very seriously to my mind, as a Paramount danger, however it may look to yours. It may be that there is nothing in it. The Politician, anxious to save his party, swears there's nothing in it. The office seeker, and office holder, to whom fleshpots are precious things—more precious than the holy oil streaming down the beard of Aaron,—these are all prepared to prove to you that so long as they can get or hold office, there's nothing in it. That it is only a peculiar mode among the Yankees of making themselves merry. That they mean fun only. That when they swear your destruction they mean only to give you a very bad scare. They know that we of the South are a very timid race, and they practice upon our fears, as a wicked urchin, behind the door, operates upon the nervous system of his palpitating playmate. It may be so! It may be that when they revile you to your face, as a thief, a manstealer, and monster & a coward, they mean only to exercise themselves in the strong eloquence of the ancient British school, by way of a fresh revival of letters; when they rob you of your slaves, they would only relieve you of a very unprofitable property; when they usurp your territories, they would save you from the corrupting influence of gold; and when they swear solemnly, before God, to root your institutions up, in your despite, they mean nothing more serious than to come to your assistance next season & help in breaking up your land.—We may admit, for a moment, that they mean nothing. But, would it not be well to suppose that they mean everything. My notion is that they mean what they say. There are Politicians who will try to teach you otherwise. I propose a compromise between us. While the matter seems doubtful to you, whether the abolitionists mean to be simply funny, or in downright earnest, my advice is that you take them to mean the very things that they avow. They tell you, honestly enough, that they mean to abolish slavery in the South, that it is a war to the knife, and through life with you, until they succeed in their objects. And I believe them. Do you the same, by way of decent precaution, in spite of the Politicians. If then,—having destroyed them, having saved yourselves,—you should discover that nothing but fun was meant—then, my friends, I entreat, I implore you, to make the most prompt apology, declare your regrets in the most moving language; I can suppose that a man may, in jest, take his neighbour by the nose or beard, and get himself knocked over for it. But should the violent man find that he who took him by the beard, really meant nothing more than a clever jest, a compliment, or a courtesy, then, I am clear, that the other should make him a very neat apology, in the best English—but, be sure, that you have first knocked him down!

Appendix

Known Orations of William Gilmore Simms

Dates are believed to be the first public readings.

"Occasional Address for the Opening of the Charleston Theatre" (1837)
"Barnwell District Agricultural Society Oration" (1840)
"The Epochs and Events of American History, as Suited to the Purposes of
     Art in Fiction" (1842)
"The Social Principle" (1842)
"The Sources of American Independence" (1844)
"Self-Development" (1847)
"Poetry and the Practical" (1851)
"The Battle of Fort Moultrie" (1853)
"The Moral Character of Hamlet" (1854)
"Choice of a Profession" (1855)
"Inauguration of the Spartanburg Female College" (1855)
"An Oration—King's Mountain" (1855)
Series on the History of South Carolina (ca. 1856)
        "On the Colonial History of S.C. Lecture 1"
        "On the Colonial and Ante-Colonial History of S.C. Lecture 1—
             The Ante-Colonial Period"
        "Lecture 3—British Colonial Establishments in America"
        "Lecture 4—South Carolina Under the Royal Government"
"Marion, the Carolina Partisan" (ca. 1856)
"The Idylls of the Apalachian [*sic*]" (1856)
"South Carolina in the Revolution" (1856)
"The Social Moral, Lecture 1" (1857)
"The Social Moral, Lecture 2" (1857)
"Antagonisms of the Social Moral, North and South" (1857)
"The Ideal and Real" (1857)
"The Sense of the Beautiful' (1870)
"Constitution" (fragment, n.d.)
"Masonry" (fragment, n.d.)

<h1 style="text-align:center">BIBLIOGRAPHY</h1>

Baskerville, Barnet. *The People's Voice: The Orator in American Society.* Lexington: University Press of Kentucky, 1979.

Bakker, Jan. "Simms on the Literary Frontier; or, So Long Miss Ravenel and Hello Captain Porgy: Woodcraft is the First 'Realistic' Novel in America." In *William Gilmore Simms and the American Frontier,* edited by John C. Guilds and Caroline Collins, 64–78. Athens: University of Georgia Press, 1997.

Braden, Waldo W., editor. *Oratory in the Old South, 1828–1860.* Baton Rouge: Louisiana State University Press, 1970.

Brennan, Matthew C. *The Poet's Holy Craft: William Gilmore Simms and Romantic Verse Tradition.* Columbia: University of South Carolina Press, 2010.

———. "Simms, Wordsworth, and 'The Mysterious Teachings of the Natural World.'" *Southern Quarterly* 41, no. 2 (Winter 2003): 37–47.

Brophy, Alfred L. "'The Law of the Descent of Thought': Law, History, and Civilization in Antebellum Literary Addresses." *Law and Literature* 20, no. 3 (2008): 343–402. https://doi.org/10.1525/lal.2008.20.3.343.

Busick, Sean R. *A Sober Desire for History: William Gilmore Simms as Historian.* Columbia: University of South Carolina Press, 2005.

Butterworth, Keen, and James E. Kibler Jr. *William Gilmore Simms: A Reference Guide.* Boston: G. K. Hall & Co., 1980.

Carman, Harry J. "Jesse Buel, Early Nineteenth-Century Agricultural Reformer." *Agricultural History* 17, no. 1 (Jan. 1943): 1–13. https://www.jstor.org/stable/3739546.

Carter, Dan T. "Fateful Legacy: White Southerners and the Dilemma of Emancipation." In *South Carolina in the Civil War and Reconstruction Eras: Essays from the Proceedings of the South Carolina Historical Association,* edited by Michael Brem Bonner and Fritz Hamer, 137–51. Columbia: University of South Carolina Press, 2016.

Charles Carroll Simms Collection. South Caroliniana Library, Columbia, SC.

Dekker, George. *The American Historical Romance.* Cambridge, UK: Cambridge University Press, 1987.

Demaree, Albert Lowther. *The American Agricultural Press, 1819–1860.* New York: Columbia University Press, 1941.

Edgar, Walter B. *South Carolina: A History.* Columbia: University of South Carolina Press, 1998.

"Editor's Table." *The Southern Literary Messenger* 23, no. 1 (July 1856): 79. Making of America.

Endres, Kathleen L., and Therese L. Lueck, editors. *Women's Periodicals in the United States: Consumer Magazines.* Historical Guides to the World's Periodicals and Newspapers. Westwood, CT: Greenwood Press, 1995.

Ensley, Eric William. "Farmer Simms and His Agricultural Critique of Nash Roach." *The Simms Review* 13, no. 1 (2005): 6–10. The Simms Initiatives.

Faust, Drew Gilpin. "The Rhetoric and Ritual of Agriculture in Antebellum South Carolina." In *Southern Stories: Slaveholders in Peace and War,* 29–53. Columbia: University of Missouri Press, 1992.

———. *A Sacred Circle: The Dilemma of the Intellectual in the Old South, 1840–1860.* Philadelphia: University of Pennsylvania Press, 1977.

"Floral Exhibition." *Charleston News,* May 4, 1870.

Foley, Ehren. "Ellet's Women of the Revolution." In *William Gilmore Simms's Selected Reviews on Literature and Civilization,* edited by James Everett Kibler Jr. and David Moltke-Hansen with Ehren Foley, 294–99. Columbia: University of South Carolina Press, 2014.

———. "Isaac Nimmons and the Burning of Woodlands: Power, Paternalism, and the Performance of Manhood in William Gilmore Simms's Civil War South." In *William Gilmore Simms's Unfinished Civil War: Consequences for a Southern Man of Letters,* edited by David Moltke-Hansen, 89–111. Columbia: University of South Carolina Press, 2013.

Foner, Eric. *Free Soil, Free Labor, Free Men: The Ideology of the Republican Party before the Civil War.* New York: Oxford University Press, 1995.

Fox-Genovese, Elizabeth. *Within the Plantation Household: Black and White Women of the Old South.* Chapel Hill: University of North Carolina Press, 1988.

Franklin, John Hope. "The North, the South, and the American Revolution." *Journal of American History* 62, no. 1 (June 1975): 5–23. https://doi.org/10.2307/1901306.

———. *A Southern Odyssey: Travelers in the Antebellum North.* Baton Rouge: Louisiana University Press, 1979.

"From the Carolina Planter." *Edgefield (SC) Advertiser,* March 6, 1840, p. 2. https://lccn.loc.gov/sn84026897.

Genovese, Eugene D. *The Slaveholders' Dilemma: Freedom and Progress in Southern Conservative Thought, 1820–1860.* Columbia: University of South Carolina Press, 1992.

Govan, Thomas P. "Agrarian and Agrarianism: A Study in the Use and Abuse of Words." *Journal of Southern History* 30, no. 1 (1964): 35–47. https://doi.org/10.2307/2205372.

Georgini, Sara. "The Angel and the Animal." In *William Gilmore Simms's Unfinished Civil War: Consequences for a Southern Man of Letters,* edited by David Moltke-Hansen, 212–23. Columbia: University of South Carolina Press, 2013.

Guilds, John Caldwell. *Simms: A Literary Life.* Fayetteville: University of Arkansas Press, 1992.

Guinn, Matthew. "Emerson's Southern Critics, 1838–1862." *Resources for American Literary Study* 25, no. 2 (1999): 174–91. https://doi.org/10.1353/rals.1999.0004.

Hagenstein, Edwin C., Sara M. Gregg, and Brian Donahue, editors. *American Georgics: Writings on Farming, Culture, and the Land.* New Haven, CT: Yale University Press, 2011.

Hagstette, Todd. "Private vs. Public Honor in Wartime South Carolina: William Gilmore Simms in Lecture, Letter, and History." In *William Gilmore Simms's Unfinished Civil*

War: Consequences for a Southern Man of Letters, edited by David Moltke-Hansen, 48–67. Columbia: University of South Carolina Press, 2013.

Harper, Elizabeth P. *Socially Conservative, Academically Progressive: Higher Education for Southern Ladies, 1830–1900.* PhD diss, University of Virginia, 2005.

Hayne, Paul Hamilton. "Ante-Bellum Charleston." *Southern Bivouac* 1 (Oct. 1885): 257–68.

Higham, John W. "The Changing Loyalties of William Gilmore Simms." *Journal of Southern History* 9, no. 2 (May 1943): 210–23. https://doi.org/10.2307/2191799.

Hochfield, George. "An Introduction to Transcendentalism." In *American Transcendentalism: An Anthology of Criticism,* edited by Brian M. Barbour, 35–51. Notre Dame, IN: University of Notre Dame Press, 1973.

"Home Matters." *Buffalo Commercial Advertiser,* Nov. 12, 1856.

Hoole, William Stanley. "William Gilmore Simms's Career as Editor." *Georgia Historical Quarterly* 19, no. 1 (1935): 47–54. https://www.jstor.org/stable/40576370.

Horner, Winifred Bryan. *Rhetoric in the Classical Tradition.* New York: St. Martin's Press, 1988.

Kibler, James Everett, Jr. "The First Simms Letters: 'Letters from the West' (1826)." *Southern Literary Journal* 19, no. 2 (Spring 1987): 81–91.

———. "Introduction." In *Poetry and the Practical, by William Gilmore Simms,* xi–xlvii. Fayetteville: University of Arkansas Press, 1996.

———. "Perceiver and Perceived: External Landscape as Mirror and Metaphor in Simms's Poetry." In *Long Years of Neglect: The Work and Reputation of William Gilmore Simms,* edited by John C. Guilds, 106–25. Fayetteville: University of Arkansas Press, 1988.

———. *The Poetry of William Gilmore Simms: An Introduction and Bibliography.* Columbia: University of South Carolina Southern Studies Program, 1979.

———. "Simms the Gardener: Reconstructing the Gardens at Woodlands." *The Simms Review* 1, no. 1 (1993): 17–26, The Simms Initiatives.

———. "Simms's 'Barnwell Agricultural Society Oration.'" *The Simms Review* 10, no. 1 (2002): 2–4. The Simms Initiatives.

———, and David Moltke-Hansen with Ehren Foley. "The Man of Letters as Critic." In *William Gilmore Simms's Selected Reviews on Literature and Civilization,* edited by James Everett Kibler Jr. and David Moltke-Hansen with Ehren Foley, 1–12. William Gilmore Simms Initiatives: Texts and Studies Series. Columbia: University of South Carolina Press, 2014.

Kerber, Linda. "The Republican Mother: Women and the Enlightenment—An American Perspective." *American Quarterly* 28, no. 2 (1976): 187–205. https://doi:org/10.2307/2712349.

Knight, Edgar W. *A Documentary History of Education in the South Before 1860, Volume 4: Private and Denominational Efforts.* Chapel Hill: University of North Carolina Press, 1953.

Levin, Harry. *The Myth of the Golden Age in the Renaissance.* Bloomington: Indiana University Press, 1969.

Martin, Howard Hastings. "Orations on the Anniversary of American Independence, 1777–1876." PhD diss., Northwestern University, 1955.

McCardell, John. *The Idea of a Southern Nation: Southern Nationalists and Southern Nationalism, 1830–1860.* New York: W. W. Norton, 1979

McHaney, Thomas L. "An Early 19th-Century Literary Agent: James Lawson of New York." *Publications of the Bibliographic Society of America* 64 (Spring 1970): 177–92.

Meta. "Correspondence." *The Weekly News* (Charleston, SC), Sept. 6, 1855.

Miller, James David. *South by Southwest: Planter Emigration and Identity in the Slave South.* The American South Series. Charlottesville: University of Virginia Press / William P. Clements Center for Southwest Studies, Southern Methodist U, 2002.

Miller, John D. "A Sense of Things to Come: Redefining Gender and Promoting the Lost Cause in *The Sense of the Beautiful.*" In *William Gilmore Simms's Unfinished Civil War: Consequences for a Southern Man of Letters,* edited by David Moltke-Hansen, 224–37. Columbia: University of South Carolina Press, 2013.

Moltke-Hansen, David. "The Critical Revolution and the Revolutionary Critic." In *William Gilmore Simms's Selected Reviews on Literature and Civilization,* edited by James Everett Kibler Jr. and David Moltke-Hansen with Ehren Foley, 197–214. Columbia: University of South Carolina Press, 2014.

———. "The Expansion of Intellectual Life: A Prospectus." In *Intellectual Life in Antebellum Charleston,* edited by Michael O'Brien and David Moltke-Hansen, 3–44. Knoxville: University of Tennessee Press, 1986.

———. "Ordered Progress: The Historical Philosophy of William Gilmore Simms." In *Long Years of Neglect: The Work and Reputation of William Gilmore Simms,* edited by John C. Guilds, 126–47. Fayetteville: University of Arkansas Press, 1988.

———. "The Revolutionary Romances: *The Partisan; Mellichampe; The Scout; Katharine Walton; Woodcraft; The Forayers; Eutaw; and Joscelyn.*" In *Reading William Gilmore Simms: Essays of Introduction to the Author's Canon,* edited by Todd Hagstette, 295–316. Columbia: University of South Carolina Press, 2017.

———. "Southern Literary Horizons in Young America: Imaginative Development of a Regional Geography." *Studies in the Literary Imagination* 42, no. 1 (Spring 2009): 1–31.

———. "When History Failed: William Gilmore Simms's Artistic Negotiation of the Civil War's Consequences." In *William Gilmore Simms's Unfinished Civil War: Consequences for a Southern Man of Letters,* edited by David Moltke-Hansen, 3–31. Columbia: University of South Carolina Press, 2013.

"Mr. Simms' Lecture on Monday Night." *Charleston (SC) Daily Courier,* June 3, 1857. https://www.newspapers.com/image/604528582.

"Mr. Simms' Lectures." *Charleston (SC) Daily Courier,* May 30, 1854. https://www.newspapers.com/image/604520289.

"Mr. Simms's Lectures." *Charleston (SC) Mercury,* May 26, 1857. https://www.newspapers.com/image/605460314.

"Mr. Simms' Oration." *Charleston (SC) Mercury,* Aug. 19, 1844.

"Mr. Simms' Oration." *Charleston (SC) Daily Courier,* Feb. 24, 1855.

Nakamura, Masahiro. *Visions of Order in William Gilmore Simms: Southern Conservatism and the Other American Romance.* Columbia: University of South Carolina Press, 2009.

Newton, David W. "Voices from the Enchanted Circle: Simms and the Poetics of the American Renaissance." *Southern Quarterly* 41, no. 2 (Winter 2003): 23–36.

O'Brien, Michael. *Conjectures of Order: Intellectual Life and the American South, 1810–1860.* Chapel Hill: University of North Carolina Press, 2004. 2 vols.

Oliver, Robert T. *History of Public Speaking in America.* Boston: Allyn & Bacon, 1965.

"Opening of the Female College." *The Carolina Spartan,* Aug. 23, 1855.

Parrington, Vernon L. *Main Currents in American Thought.* New York: Harcourt, Brace and Co., 1927–30. 3 vols.

"Quattlebum in Rochester—A Politico-Historico-Literary Lecture, of the Caudle Kind." *Daily Democrat* (Rochester, NY), Nov. 14, 1856, p. 2.

Quigley, Paul. *Shifting Grounds: Nationalism and the American South, 1848–1865.* New York: Oxford University Press, 2012.

Rable, George C. *Civil Wars: Women and the Crisis of Southern Nationalism.* Urbana: University of Illinois Press, 1991.

"Review of South Carolina in the Revolution." *New-York Daily Tribune,* Nov. 19, 1856.

Reynolds, Thomas Caute. "Review of The Social Principle." *Southern Quarterly Review* 4, no. 7 (July 1843): 242–47. http://quod.lib.umich.edu/m/moajrnl/acp1141.1–04.007/250.

Rogers, George C., Jr. *Charleston in the Age of the Pinckneys.* Norman: University of Oklahoma Press, 1969.

Rogers, Jeffery J., editor. *Writing War and Reunion: Selected Civil War and Reconstruction Newspaper Editorials by William Gilmore Simms.* Columbia: University of South Carolina Press, 2020.

Rosenthal, Caitlin. *Accounting for Slavery: Masters and Management.* Cambridge, MA: Harvard University Press, 2018.

Sabine, Lorenzo. *The American Loyalists; Or, Biographical Sketches of Adherents to the British Crown in the War of the Revolution.* Boston: C.C. Little and J. Brown, 1847.

Scott, Ann Firor. *The Southern Lady: From Pedestal to Politics, 1830–1930.* Charlottesville: University of Virginia Press, 1970.

Scott, Donald M. "The Popular Lecture and the Creation of a Public in Mid-Nineteenth-Century America." *Journal of American History* 66, no. 4 (1980): 791–809. https://doi.org/10.2307/1887637.

Sellers, James B. *History of the University of Alabama: Volume I 1818–1902.* Tuscaloosa: University of Alabama Press, 1953.

Shillingsburg, Miriam J. "The Cub of the Panther: A New Frontier." *William Gilmore Simms and the American Frontier,* edited by John C. Guilds and Caroline Collins, 221–36. Athens: University of Georgia Press, 1997.

———. "Literary Grist: Simms's Trips to Mississippi." *Southern Quarterly* 41, no. 2 (Winter 2003): 119–34.

———. "Simms's Failed Lecture Tour of 1856: The Mind of the North." *Long Years of Neglect: The Work and Reputation of William Gilmore Simms,* edited by John C. Guilds, 183–201. Fayetteville: University of Arkansas Press, 1988.

"Simms' Lectures." *Charleston Daily Courier,* May 26, 1857. https://www.newspapers.com/image/604526080.

Simms, William Gilmore. "The Ages of Gold and Iron: From an Agricultural Oration." *Ladies' Companion,* May 1841. https://www.proquest.com/magazines/ages-gold-iron-agricultural-oration/docview/137171422/se-2.

———. "Critical Notices." *Southern Quarterly Review* 6, no. 12 (Oct. 1852): 520–54. Making of America.

———. "The Good Farmer." *Ladies' Companion,* Aug. 1841. www.proquest.com/magazines/good-farmer/docview/137139601/se-2.

———. "Guizot's Democracy in France." *Southern Quarterly Review* 15, no. 29 (Apr. 1849): 114–65. Making of America.

———. "Editorial Bureau—Agriculture in South Carolina." *Magnolia* n.s., no. 2, March 1843.

———. "Ellet's 'Women of the Revolution.'" *Southern Quarterly Review* 1, no. 2 (July 1850): 314–54. Making of America.

———. *Inauguration of the Spartanburg Female College.* Spartanburg, SC: The Trustees of the Spartanburg Female College, 1855.

———. *The Letters of William Gilmore Simms.* Edited by Mary C. Simms Oliphant, Alfred Taylor Odell, and T. C. Duncan Eaves. Columbia: University of South Carolina Press, 1952–2012.

———. "Our Agricultural Tradition." *Southern and Western Monthly Magazine* 1 (1845): pp. 73–84.

———. *Poetry and the Practical.* Edited by James Everett Kibler Jr. Fayetteville: University of Arkansas Press, 1996.

———. "Popular Discourses and Orations." *Southern Quarterly Review* 4, no. 8 (Oct. 1851): 317–51, Making of America.

———. *Richard Hurdis, A Tale of Alabama.* 1838. Columbia: University of South Carolina Press, 2014.

———. *The Social Principle: The True Source of National Permanence.* Tuscaloosa: The Erosophic Society of the University of Alabama, 1843. The Simms Initiatives.

———. *The Sources of American Independence: An Oration, on the Sixty-Ninth Anniversary of American Independence.* Aiken: Town Council of Aiken, SC, 1844. The Simms Initiatives.

———. "Southern Agriculture." *Magnolia* 4, no. 3 (March 1842): 129–42.

———. "The Southern Convention." *Southern Quarterly Review* 2, no. 3 (Sept. 1850): 191–232. Making of America.

———. *The Sense of the Beautiful.* Charleston, SC: Walker, Evans and Cogswell / Charleston County Agricultural and Horticultural Association, 1870. The Simms Initiatives.

———. *Slavery in America, Being a Brief Review of Miss Martineau on that Subject.* Richmond: Thomas W. White, 1838. The Simms Initiatives.

———. *South-Carolina in the Revolutionary War; Being a Reply to Certain Misrepresentations and Mistakes of Recent Writers, in Relation to the Course and Conduct of this State.* Charleston, SC: Walker and James, 1853. The Simms Initiatives.

———. "The Spirit of Emigration." *Southern Literary Journal* 2 (June 1836): 259–69.

———. *Views and Reviews in American Literature, History and Fiction, First Series,* 1845. Edited by C. Hugh Holman. Cambridge, MA: Belknap Press, 1962.

———. "The Western Immigrants." *Southern Literary Journal* 2 (June 1836): 270–71.

Sparks, Summar C. "Editing Young America: William Gilmore Simms and the New York Literary Wars." *The Simms Review* 22, no. 1/2 (Summer/Winter 2014): 5–18.

Stoll, Steven. *Larding the Lean Earth: Soil and Society in Nineteenth-Century America*. New York: Hill and Wang, 2002.

Sumner, Charles. *The Crime Against Kansas, the Apologies for the Crime, the True Remedy: Speech of Hon. Charles Sumner in the Senate of the United States, 19th and 20th May, 1856*. Washington, DC: Buell & Blanchard, 1856, https://archive.org/details/crimeagainst kanoosumn/mode/2up.

———. "Reply to Assailants: Oath to Support the Constitution; Weakness of the South from Slavery." *Charles Sumner; His Complete Works* (vol. 4), edited by George Frisbie Hoar, 172–227. Boston: Lee & Shepard, 1900. Project Gutenberg.

Tate, Adam L. *Conservatism and Southern Intellectuals, 1789–1861: Liberty, Tradition, and the Good Society*. Columbia: University of Missouri Press, 2005.

Towns, W. Stuart. *Enduring Legacy: Rhetoric and Ritual of the Lost Cause*. Tuscaloosa: University of Alabama Press, 2012.

———. *Oratory and Rhetoric in the Nineteenth-Century South: A Rhetoric of Defense*. Westport, CT: Praeger, 1998.

Trent, William Peterfield. *William Gilmore Simms*. Boston: Houghton Mifflin, 1892.

Trescott, William Henry. *The Position and Course of the South*. Charleston, SC: Walker and James, 1850.

Wakelyn, Jon L. *The Politics of a Literary Man: William Gilmore Simms*. Contributions in American Studies. Westport, CT: Praeger, 1973.

Warren, James Perrin. *Culture of Eloquence: Oratory and Reform in Antebellum America*. State College: Pennsylvania State University Press, 1999.

Watson, Charles S. *From Nationalism to Secessionism: The Changing Fiction of William Gilmore Simms*. Westport, CT: Praeger, 1993.

Watson, Ritchie Devon, Jr. *Normans and Saxons: Southern Race Mythology and the Intellectual History of the American Civil War*. Baton Rouge: Louisiana State University Press, 2008.

Wells, Jonathan Daniel. *The Origins of the Southern Middle Class, 1800-1861*. Chapel Hill: University of North Carolina Press, 2004.

Welter, Barbara. "The Cult of True Womanhood: 1820–1860." *American Quarterly* 18, no. 2 (1966): 151–74. https://doi.org/10.2307/2711179.

White, William B., Jr. The Ross-Chesnut-Sutton Family of South Carolina. Privately printed, 2002.

Whites, LeeAnn. *The Civil War as a Crisis in Gender: Augusta, Georgia, 1860–1890*. Athens: University of Georgia Press, 1995.

Wimsatt, Mary Ann. "Realism and Romance in Simms's Midcentury Fiction." *Southern Literary Journal* 12, no. 2 (1980): 29–48.

Woods, Michael E. *Emotional and Sectional Conflict in the Antebellum United States*. Cambridge, UK: Cambridge University Press, 2014.

Zuczek, Richard. *State of Rebellion: Reconstruction in South Carolina*. Columbia: University of South Carolina Press, 1996.